UNIX® Systems for Modern Architectures

Addison-Wesley Professional Computing Series

Brian W. Kernighan, Consulting Editor

Ken Arnold/John Peyton, *A C User's Guide to ANSI C*

Matthew H. Austern, *Generic Programming and the STL: Using and Extending the C++ Standard Template Library*

David R. Butenhof, *Programming with POSIX® Threads*

Brent Callaghan, *NFS Illustrated*

Tom Cargill, *C++ Programming Style*

William R. Cheswick/Steven M. Bellovin, *Firewalls and Internet Security: Repelling the Wily Hacker*

David A. Curry, *UNIX® System Security: A Guide for Users and System Administrators*

Erich Gamma/Richard Helm/Ralph Johnson/John Vlissides, *Design Patterns: Elements of Reusable Object-Oriented Software*

Erich Gamma/Richard Helm/Ralph Johnson/John Vlissides, *Design Patterns CD: Elements of Reusable Object-Oriented Software*

Peter Haggar, *Practical Java™ Programming Language Guide*

David R. Hanson, *C Interfaces and Implementations: Techniques for Creating Reusable Software*

Mark Harrison/Michael McLennan, *Effective Tcl/Tk Programming: Writing Better Programs with Tcl and Tk*

Michi Henning/Steve Vinoski, *Advanced CORBA® Programming with C++*

Brian W. Kernighan/Rob Pike, *The Practice of Programming*

S. Keshav, *An Engineering Approach to Computer Networking: ATM Networks, the Internet, and the Telephone Network*

John Lakos, *Large-Scale C++ Software Design*

Scott Meyers, *Effective C++ CD: 85 Specific Ways to Improve Your Programs and Designs*

Scott Meyers, *Effective C++, Second Edition: 50 Specific Ways to Improve Your Programs and Designs*

Scott Meyers, *More Effective C++: 35 New Ways to Improve Your Programs and Designs*

Robert B. Murray, *C++ Strategies and Tactics*

David R. Musser/Gillmer J. Derge/Atul Saini, *STL Tutorial and Reference Guide, Second Edition: C++ Programming with the Standard Template Library*

John K. Ousterhout, *Tcl and the Tk Toolkit*

Craig Partridge, *Gigabit Networking*

J. Stephen Pendergrast Jr., *Desktop KornShell Graphical Programming*

Radia Perlman, *Interconnections, Second Edition: Bridges, Routers, Switches, and Internetworking Protocols*

David M. Piscitello/A. Lyman Chapin, *Open Systems Networking: TCP/IP and OSI*

Stephen A. Rago, *UNIX® System V Network Programming*

Curt Schimmel, *UNIX® Systems for Modern Architectures: Symmetric Multiprocessing and Caching for Kernel Programmers*

W. Richard Stevens, *Advanced Programming in the UNIX® Environment*

W. Richard Stevens, *TCP/IP Illustrated, Volume 1: The Protocols*

W. Richard Stevens, *TCP/IP Illustrated, Volume 3: TCP for Transactions, HTTP, NNTP, and the UNIX® Domain Protocols*

Gary R. Wright/W. Richard Stevens, *TCP/IP Illustrated, Volume 2: The Implementation*

Please see our web site (http://www.awl.com/cseng/series/professionalcomputing) for more information on these titles.

UNIX® Systems for Modern Architectures

Symmetric Multiprocessing and Caching
for Kernel Programmers

Curt Schimmel

ADDISON–WESLEY

Boston • San Francisco • New York • Toronto • Montreal
London • Munich • Paris • Madrid
Capetown • Sydney • Tokyo • Singapore • Mexico City

The publisher offers discounts on this book when ordered in quantity for special sales. For more information, please contact:

Pearson Education Corporate Sales Division
One Lake Street
Upper Saddle River, NJ 07458
(800) 382-3419
corpsales@pearsontechgroup.com

Visit AW on the Web: www.awl.com/cseng/

Library of Congress Cataloging-in-Publication Data

Schimmel, Curt.
    UNIX systems for modern architectures : symmetric multiprocessing
and caching for kernel programmers / Curt Schimmel.
        p. cm. -- (Addison-Wesley professional computing series)
    Includes bibliographical references and index.
    ISBN 0-201-63338-8
    1. UNIX (Computer file). 2. Computer architecture. I. Title.
    II. Series.
    QA76.76.063S3756 1994
    005.4'32--dc20   94-14555
                                                      CIP

ISBN 0201633388
Text printed on recycled and acid-free paper
4 5 6 7 8 9 10—CRW—03 02 01
4th printing, February 2001

To my parents,
Harry and Doris

"It's kind of fun to do the impossible."
Walt Disney

Contents

Preface.. xv

Notational Conventions xix
    Constants xix
    Word Size xx
    Byte Order xx
    Bit Order xx
    Bit Ranges.. xxi
    Memory Size Units xxi

Introduction.. xxiii

Chapter 1: Review of UNIX Kernel Internals 1

1.1   Introduction... 2
1.2   Processes, Programs, and Threads.. 3
1.3   The Process Address Space 5
    1.3.1   Address Space Mapping 7
1.4   Context Switch 8
1.5   Memory and Process Management System Calls 9
    1.5.1   The Fork System Call 9
    1.5.2   The Exec System Call 12
    1.5.3   The Exit System Call 13
    1.5.4   The Sbrk and Brk System Calls................................ 13
    1.5.5   Shared Memory 14
    1.5.6   I/O Operations 14
    1.5.7   Mapped Files 15
1.6   Summary 15
1.7   Exercises.. 15
1.8   Further Reading 17

Part I: Cache Memory Systems...21

Chapter 2: Introduction to Cache Memory Systems................23

2.1   Memory Hierarchies... 24
2.2   Cache Fundamentals 26
        2.2.1   How a Cache Is Accessed....................................... 26
        2.2.2   Virtual or Physical Addresses? 29
        2.2.3   Searching the Cache 29
        2.2.4   Replacement Policies 30
        2.2.5   Write Policies 30
2.3   Direct Mapped Caches 33
        2.3.1   Hashing Algorithms for Direct Mapped Caches......... 34
        2.3.2   Direct Mapped Cache Example 37
        2.3.3   Miss Processing and Replacement Policy for Direct Mapped
                Caches... 40
        2.3.4   Summary of Direct Mapped Caching...................... 42
2.4   Two-Way Set Associative Caches....................................... 42
        2.4.1   Summary of Two-Way Set Associative Caches 44
2.5 n-Way Set Associative Caches... 44
2.6   Fully Associative Caches.. 45
2.7   Summary of n-Way Set Associative Caches 45
2.8   Cache Flushing... 46
2.9   Uncached Operation.. 47
2.10   Separate Instruction and Data Caches................................ 48
2.11   Cache Performance... 49
2.12   How Cache Architectures Differ.. 51
2.13   Exercises 52
2.14   Further Reading... 55

Chapter 3: Virtual Caches 59

3.1   Virtual Cache Operation 60
3.2   Problems with Virtual Caches.. 62
        3.2.1   Ambiguities 62
        3.2.2   Aliases 64
3.3   Managing a Virtual Cache 67
        3.3.1   Context Switch.. 67
        3.3.2   Fork... 68
        3.3.3   Exec... 71
        3.3.4   Exit... 71
        3.3.5   Brk and Sbrk.. 72

3.3.6   Shared Memory and Mapped Files 72
3.3.7   I/O.. 73
3.3.8   User–Kernel Data Ambiguities 77
3.4   Summary 78
3.5   Exercises 78
3.6   Further Reading 81

Chapter 4: Virtual Caches with Keys 83

4.1   The Operation of a Virtual Cache with Keys 84
4.2   Managing a Virtual Cache with Keys.. 85
4.2.1   Context Switch.. 85
4.2.2   Fork 87
4.2.3   Exec 89
4.2.4   Exit 90
4.2.5   Brk and Sbrk... 90
4.2.6   Shared Memory and Mapped Files 90
4.2.7   I/O... 94
4.2.8   User–Kernel Data Ambiguities 94
4.3   Virtual Cache Usage in MMUs 94
4.4   Summary 95
4.5   Exercises 96
4.6   Further Reading 98

Chapter 5: Virtual Caches with Physical Address Tags 99

5.1   The Organization of a Virtual Cache with Physical Tags 100
5.2   Managing a Virtual Cache with Physical Tags 103
5.2.1   Context Switch.. 104
5.2.2   Fork 104
5.2.3   Exec 105
5.2.4   Exit 105
5.2.5   Brk and Sbrk... 106
5.2.6   Shared Memory and Mapped Files 106
5.2.7   I/O... 107
5.2.8   User–Kernel Data Ambiguities 107
5.3   Summary 107
5.4   Exercises 108
5.5   Further Reading 109

Chapter 6: Physical Caches **111**

6.1   The Organization of a Physical Cache 112
6.2   Managing a Physical Cache 114
        6.2.1   Context Switch 114
        6.2.2   Fork 114
        6.2.3   Exec, Exit, Brk, and Sbrk 114
        6.2.4   Shared Memory and Mapped Files 115
        6.2.5   User–Kernel Data Ambiguities 115
        6.2.6   I/O and Bus Watching 115
6.3   Multilevel Caches 121
        6.3.1   Primary Virtual Cache with Secondary Physical Cache 122
        6.3.2   Primary Virtual Cache with Physical Tags and a Secondary
                  Physical Cache 124
6.4   Summary 126
6.5   Exercises 127
6.6   Further Reading 128

Chapter 7: Efficient Cache Management Techniques **131**

7.1   Introduction 132
7.2   Address Space Layout 132
        7.2.1   Virtually Indexed Caches 132
        7.2.2   Dynamic Address Binding 136
        7.2.3   Physically Indexed Caches 137
7.3   Cache Size Bounded Flushing 139
7.4   Delayed Cache Invalidations 139
        7.4.1   Virtual Caches with Keys 141
        7.4.2   Physically Tagged Caches without Bus Watching 141
7.5   Cache-Aligning Data Structures 142
7.6   Summary 144
7.7   Exercises 145
7.8   Further Reading 146

Part II: Multiprocessor Systems **147**

Chapter 8: Introduction to Multiprocessor Systems **149**

8.1   Introduction 150
        8.1.1   MP Operating Systems 151

8.2 The Tightly Coupled, Shared Memory, Symmetric Multiprocessor 152
8.3 The MP Memory Model 154
    8.3.1 The Sequential Memory Model.. 155
    8.3.2 Atomic Reads and Writes.. 155
    8.3.3 Atomic Read-Modify-Write Operations 158
8.4 Mutual Exclusion 160
8.5 Review of Mutual Exclusion on Uniprocessor
    UNIX Systems 162
    8.5.1 Short-Term Mutual Exclusion 163
    8.5.2 Mutual Exclusion with Interrupt Handlers 163
    8.5.3 Long-Term Mutual Exclusion... 164
8.6 Problems Using UP Mutual Exclusion Policies on MPs 167
8.7 Summary 168
8.8 Exercises... 169
8.9 Further Reading 172

Chapter 9: Master–Slave Kernels... 175

9.1 Introduction.. 176
9.2 Spin Locks... 177
9.3 Deadlocks.. 179
9.4 Master–Slave Kernel Implementation 181
    9.4.1 Run Queue Implementation... 181
    9.4.2 Process Selection for Slaves... 184
    9.4.3 Process Selection for the Master.. 186
    9.4.4 Clock Interrupt Handling... 186
9.5 Performance Considerations... 187
    9.5.1 Master–Slave Improvements... 188
9.6 Summary 189
9.7 Exercises... 190
9.8 Further Reading 192

Chapter 10: Spin-Locked Kernels 195

10.1 Introduction.. 196
10.2 Giant Locking 196
10.3 Multithreading Cases Requiring No Locks 199
10.4 Coarse-Grained Locking 200
10.5 Fine-Grained Locking.. 203
    10.5.1 Short-Term Mutual Exclusion 203
    10.5.2 Long-Term Mutual Exclusion... 204
    10.5.3 Mutual Exclusion with Interrupt Handlers 206

10.5.4   Lock Granularity... 207
10.5.5   Performance 208
10.5.6   Kernel Preemption 209
10.6   Effects of Sleep and Wakeup on Multiprocessors 209
10.7   Summary 211
10.8   Exercises 212
10.9   Further Reading.. 215

Chapter 11: Semaphored Kernels 217

11.1   Introduction.. 218
11.1.1   Mutual Exclusion with Semaphores.................... 219
11.1.2   Synchronization with Semaphores 220
11.1.3   Resource Allocation with Semaphores 220
11.2   Deadlocks.. 221
11.3   Implementing Semaphores.. 223
11.4   Coarse-Grained Semaphore Implementations 226
11.5   Multithreading with Semaphores 227
11.5.1   Long-Term Mutual Exclusion 227
11.5.2   Short-Term Mutual Exclusion 228
11.5.3   Synchronization 228
11.6   Performance Considerations 230
11.6.1   Measuring Lock Contention 230
11.6.2   Convoys.. 231
11.6.3   Multireader Locks 234
11.7   Summary 237
11.8   Exercises 239
11.9   Further Reading.. 240

Chapter 12: Other MP Primitives 245

12.1   Introduction.. 246
12.2   Monitors.. 246
12.3   Eventcounts and Sequencers.. 248
12.4   The MP Primitives of SVR4.2 MP..................................... 251
12.4.1   Spin Locks 251
12.4.2   Sleep Locks 253
12.4.3   Synchronization Variables 255
12.4.4   Multireader Locks 258
12.5   Comparison of MP Synchronization Primitives.................... 258
12.6   Summary 261
12.7   Exercises 262

12.8   Further Reading 263

Chapter 13: Other Memory Models 267

13.1   Introduction 268
13.2   Dekker's Algorithm 268
13.3   Other Memory Models 271
13.4   Total Store Ordering 273
13.5   Partial Store Ordering 278
13.6   The Store Buffer as Part of the Memory Hierarchy 280
13.7   Summary 281
13.8   Exercises 281
13.9   Further Reading 282

Part III: Multiprocessor Systems with Caches 285

Chapter 14: Introduction to MP Cache Consistency 287

14.1   Introduction 288
14.2   The Cache Consistency Problem 290
14.3   Software Cache Consistency 293
        14.3.1 Uncached Shared Data 294
        14.3.2 Selective Cache Flushing 296
        14.3.3 Handling Other Memory Models 300
14.4   Summary 301
14.5   Exercises 302
14.6   Further Reading 303

Chapter 15: Hardware Cache Consistency 307

15.1   Introduction 308
15.2   Write-Invalidate Protocols 310
        15.2.1 The Write-Through Invalidate Protocol 310
        15.2.2 The Write-Once Protocol 311
        15.2.3 MESI Protocols 314
15.3   Write-Update Protocols 315
        15.3.1 The Firefly Protocol 315
        15.3.2 The MIPS R4000 Update Protocol 316
15.4   Consistency of Read-Modify-Write Operations 317
15.5   Hardware Consistency for Multilevel Caches 318

15.6 Other Main Memory Architectures 319

    15.6.1 The Cross-bar Interconnect 320

    15.6.2 Directory-based Hardware Cache Consistency 322

15.7 Effects on the Software 324

15.8 Hardware Consistency for Nonsequential
Memory Models 327

15.9 Performance Considerations for Software 327

    15.9.1 Cache-Aligning Data Structures 327

    15.9.2 Reducing Cache Line Contention When Acquiring a
Spin Lock 329

    15.9.3 Matching Consistency Protocols to Data Usage 330

15.10 Summary 332

15.11 Exercises 333

15.12 Further Reading 335

Appendix A: Architecture Summary **341**

Appendix B: Answers to Selected Exercises **349**

Index **387**

Preface

The goal of this book is to provide practical information on the issues operating systems must address in order to run on modern computer systems that employ cache memories and/or multiprocessors. At the time of this writing, a number of books describe UNIX system implementations, but none describes in detail how caches and multiprocessors should be managed. Many computer architecture books describe caches and multiprocessors from the hardware aspect, but none successfully deals with the operating system issues that these modern architectures present. This book is intended to fill these gaps by bridging computer architecture and operating systems.

Written with the operating system developer in mind, this book explains the operation of caches and multiprocessors from the system programmer's point of view. While targeted toward UNIX system programmers, the book has been written so that the information can be applied to any operating system, including all UNIX variations. This is accomplished by explaining the issues and solutions at a conceptual level and using the UNIX system services as examples of where the issues will be encountered. The solutions can then be applied to other operating systems in the corresponding situations.

This book is intended to assist the operating system developer in two ways. First, the reader will learn how existing operating systems must be adapted to run on modern architectures. This is accomplished by a detailed examination of the operation of these architectures from the operating system perspective and an explanation of what the operating system must do to manage them. Second, the reader will learn the trade-offs involved in the different approaches taken by modern architectures. This will give the operating system developer the background needed when involved in the design of new computer systems employing caches and multiprocessors.

The reader is assumed to be familiar with the UNIX system call interface and the high-level concepts of UNIX kernel internals. The reader should also be familiar with computer architecture and computer system organization as would be taught in an undergraduate-level computer science course.

This book is an extension of a course I developed for UNIX system professionals in the computer industry. The course has been taught during the past four years in the United States at USENIX conferences, and in Europe at the EurOpen and UKUUG conferences. The course is a one-day tutorial and as such is limited in the amount of material that can be covered. This book covers all the course material on cache memories and multiprocessors in greater detail and includes additional topics.

This book is suitable for use in an upper-division undergraduate-level course or at the graduate level. Each chapter concludes with a list of exercises. The questions were chosen so that they could be solved with the information provided in the chapter plus some additional thought, rather than simply parrot the material. In many cases, the exercises build upon the examples presented in the chapter. Answers are generally expected to take the form of a short paragraph (four to five sentences in most cases, sometimes longer). The reader is urged to try all the questions in order to reinforce the concepts learned. Answers to selected exercises are provided in the back of the book.

We begin with a review of the UNIX system internals that are relevant to the discussion in the remainder of the book. The purpose of the review is to reinforce the concepts of the UNIX operating system and to define terminology used later. The book is then divided into three main parts: cache memory systems, multiprocessor UNIX implementations, and multiprocessor cache consistency. The first part, cache memory systems, introduces cache architecture, terminology, and concepts. It then proceeds to take a detailed look at four common cache implementations: three variations of the virtual cache and then the physical cache. The second part, multiprocessor UNIX implementations, looks at the problems and design issues faced when adapting a uniprocessor kernel implementation to run on a tightly coupled, shared memory multiprocessor. Several different implementations are examined. The final part, multiprocessor cache consistency, combines the concepts of the first two parts by examining the operating system and cache architecture issues that occur when caches are added to a tightly coupled, shared memory multiprocessor system.

A selected set of modern microprocessor architectures is used to illustrate the concepts where appropriate. Representing the traditional CISC (complex instruction set computer) processors are the Motorola 68040 and the Intel 80X86 line (80386, 80486, and Pentium). The RISC (reduced instruction set computer) approach is represented by the MIPS line (R2000, R3000, and R4000), the Motorola 88000, and the SPARC version 8 compatible processors from Texas Instruments (the MicroSPARC and the SuperSPARC). Several other examples, including Sun and Apollo workstations and the Intel i860, are also presented. A summary of the characteristics of these processors can be found in Appendix A.

I owe my gratitude to the people who offered their time to review the manuscript before publication. In particular, I would like to thank Steve Albert, Paul Borman, Steve Buroff, Clement Cole, Peter Collinson, Geoff Collyer, Bruce Curtis, Mukesh Kacker, Brian Kernighan, Steve Rago, Mike Scheer, Brian Silverio, Rich Stevens, Manu Thapar, Chris Walquist, and Erez Zadok. I would also like to thank the Addison-Wesley staff for their help and advice on this project, particularly Kim Dawley, Kathleen Duff, Tiffany Moore, Simone Payment, Marty Rabinowitz, and John Wait. They have helped make this a better book than I could have done on my own. I would also like to thank the many people who took the time to provide thoughtful feedback by filling out the course evaluations during the tutorial sessions.

Comments, suggestions, and bug fixes regarding the contents of this book are welcome and can be sent by email to `schimmel@aw.com`.

Notational Conventions

This section illustrates the notational conventions used in the examples throughout this book.

Constants

Decimal, octal, and hexadecimal constants are represented in the standard notation of the C programming language. Decimal constants always begin with one of the digits from 1 to 9. Octal constants begin with a leading zero. Hex constants begin with the sequence "0x". Here are some examples:

12345	decimal constant
07654	octal constant
0x3af	hex constant

Word Size

A *word* of memory is a four-byte quantity. Each byte is 8 bits, making a word 32 bits.

Byte Order

Memory is most easily thought of as an array of words. To refer to the individual bytes within a word, a convention is needed to number them. All examples showing the arrangement of bytes in memory use *big-endian* byte order. This means that the most significant byte (MSB) of each word (the "big" end) has the lowest address, and the least significant byte (LSB) has the highest address. The bytes in the word are read from left to right, most significant byte first. For example, the following byte numbering would apply to a machine with four-byte words:

	MSB			LSB
Word 0	Byte 0	Byte 1	Byte 2	Byte 3
Word 1	Byte 4	Byte 5	Byte 6	Byte 7
Word 2	Byte 8	Byte 9	Byte 10	Byte 11

Motorola, Sun SPARC compatibles, and IBM processors (except for the IBM PC) use big-endian byte ordering. DEC and Intel processors use *little-endian* ordering, where the bytes within a word are numbered in reverse order. MIPS processors can be configured to operate in either mode, with all vendors of MIPS-based systems, except DEC, choosing big-endian order.

Bit Order

The order of the bits within a word or byte follows little-endian order, meaning that the least significant bit is numbered bit 0 and the most significant bit of a four-byte word is bit 31. The most significant bit is always on the left. When needed to clarify an example, bit numbers are shown above the representation of a byte or word. For example, the following word is shown with the most and least significant bits in each byte numbered according to the bit order within the word:

31 24	23 16	15 8	7 0
Byte 0	Byte 1	Byte 2	Byte 3

Bit Ranges

At times it is necessary to refer to a contiguous sequence of bits from a word or byte. This is referred to as a *bit range*. Angle brackets enclose the bit numbers of the range. For example, the sequence of bits that form byte 2 in the above representation of a word would be expressed as "bits <15..8>". The most significant bit number always appears on the left followed by the least significant bit number on the right. The range represented always includes these two bit positions.

Memory Size Units

A *kilobyte*, which is abbreviated as *K* or *Kb*, contains 1024 bytes. A *megabyte*, abbreviated as *M* or *Mb*, contains 1024Kb. A *gigabyte*, abbreviated as *G* or *Gb*, contains 1024Mb. For example, 4Kb is 4,096 bytes, and 8Mb is 8,388,608 bytes. Memory sizes are always listed in terms of bytes. The abbreviations K, Kb, M, Mb, G, and Gb are all used in this text.

Introduction

For much of the history of computer system development, the desire to build faster overall systems has focused on making the three main components of a system—the CPU, the memory subsystem, and the I/O subsystem—all faster. Faster CPUs are built by increasing the clock speed. Faster memory subsystems are built by reducing the access time. Faster I/O subsystems are built by increasing the data transfer rate. As clock speeds and transfer rates increase, however, it becomes increasingly more difficult, and therefore expensive, to design and build such systems. Propagation delays, signal rise time, clock synchronization and distribution, and so forth all become more critical as speeds increase. The increased cost of designing for such high speeds makes it more difficult to achieve an effective price–performance ratio.

Because of this and other factors, system designers have widened their focus to find other ways to increase overall system performance. One of the results was the concept of the *Reduced Instruction Set Computer* (*RISC*) systems where the CPU instruction set was simplified so that a low cost, fast hardware implementation could be achieved. Another result was the development of cache memory systems. Caches increase system performance by storing a program's most frequently referenced data and instructions in a small high-speed memory, thereby reducing the load on the main memory system. Faster overall memory access is achieved by adding a small, cost-effective, high-speed cache instead of a costly, large-scale, high-speed main memory subsystem. The faster overall memory access time possible with cache memories is particularly important for RISC systems, as the use of a simplified instruction set generally requires that the CPU fetch and execute more instructions than a classical CPU architecture would to accomplish the same task. RISC systems generally require more memory bandwidth to operate at peak performance.

Faster I/O transfer rates can be achieved by running more devices in parallel as opposed to increasing the speed of any one device. This has led to the development of such things as *Redundant Arrays of Inexpensive Disks* (*RAID*), where multiple disks are run in parallel to yield a higher overall transfer rate. Such a technique can also be applied to CPU speed by increasing the number of CPUs in a system to create *multiprocessors*. Multiprocessors increase overall system throughput by distributing the system load across multiple processors.

Multiprocessors and caches are closely interrelated. Tightly coupled multiprocessor systems, where there is a single, shared main memory subsystem, need more main memory bandwidth as the number of processors increases, because each processor must fetch and execute an independent instruction stream as well as access an independent set of data from memory. Coupling a cache with each processor reduces the load on main memory by satisfying a majority of a processor's memory requests from the cache instead of the shared main memory. This is a cost-effective way to increase system performance.

While a cache can increase the effective memory bandwidth in a multiprocessor, the cache architecture can have an enormous impact on the operating system overhead required to manage it. This in turn will affect the overall performance of the system.

In conclusion, building faster computer systems is not simply a matter of increasing the clock speed of the CPU, for example. While such techniques will indeed yield faster systems, they will not necessarily be cost-effective solutions. By focusing on how existing system components can be utilized to deliver higher system performance, caches and multiprocessors have been found to be cost-effective solutions. So it is here that we begin our examination of the architecture of caches and multiprocessors and operating system issues they present.

1

Review of UNIX Kernel Internals

This chapter provides a review of the relevant UNIX kernel internals that are referenced in later chapters. It is not a complete discussion of the topic but is meant instead as a refresher on the fundamental concepts and terminology for those who are already familiar with them. This chapter covers uniprocessor systems. Multiprocessor UNIX system implementations are the subject of Part II of this text. Readers unfamiliar with the UNIX operating system or UNIX kernel internals should start with some selections from the references at the end of this chapter.

1.1 Introduction

The UNIX system is a multiuser, multitasking operating system that provides a high degree
of program portability and a rich set of development tools. Part of the reason for the success of the UNIX system is the portable set of application interfaces that it provides. This
eases the problem of porting applications from one vendor's system to another's. Another
part of the success of UNIX is that the operating system, commands, and libraries are themselves written to be easily ported to different machines, fostering a diversity of UNIX hardware platforms in the market.

The UNIX system is logically layered and divided into two main portions: the kernel and
user programs. This is shown pictorially in Figure 1–1.

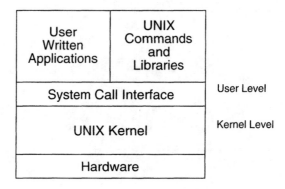

Figure 1–1: Logical layering of the UNIX system.

The purpose of the kernel is to interface with and control the hardware. The kernel also
provides user programs with a set of abstract system services, called *system calls*, that are
accessed using portable interfaces. The kernel runs at *kernel level*, where it can execute
privileged operations. This allows the kernel to have full control over the hardware and
user-level programs, as well as provide an environment where all programs share the un-
derlying hardware in a coordinated fashion.

The UNIX system call services have been defined largely so that they can be made to appear the same on all UNIX systems regardless of the peculiarities of the hardware. These
abstractions provide the high degree of portability of UNIX user-level programs. An example of one of the kernel's abstract services is *files*. UNIX files appear as an ordered byte
stream with no record or other type of boundaries within them. A user program can read
any number of bytes from any portion of a file without regard to any type of boundary

alignment. This frees the user program from having to concern itself with the physical sector, track, and cylinder boundaries of the disk when accessing a file. The details of how the file abstraction is mapped onto the available hardware are the responsibility of the kernel.

User applications, UNIX commands, and libraries (collections of commonly used subroutines) coexist at *user level*. User level refers to the unprivileged execution state of the hardware. User-level programs therefore execute in a restricted environment, controlled by the kernel, that prevents simultaneously executing programs from interfering with one another (either unintentionally or maliciously). When user programs request services by executing a system call, the system call will cause a transition into the kernel where it acts on behalf of the requesting user program to perform a service. Permission checks may be made to ensure that the program has permission to access the requested service.

Figure 1–1 depicts how the UNIX system, and most other operating systems, has traditionally been implemented: as a monolithic program. Over time, this implementation has been migrating toward a structured approach, where the kernel services are partitioned into independent modules. This increases the flexibility of the implementation and makes it easier to add, change, and port system services. It also makes it possible to migrate some services outside of the kernel and run them at user level in special server processes. This reduces the services the kernel itself must provide, allowing it to be reduced to a *micro-kernel*. Since the concepts and techniques presented in this book do not depend on the internal organization of the kernel, the organization need not be considered further. From this point on, the word "kernel" will be used to refer to that which provides the UNIX system services, whether it be a monolithic program or a collection of modules.

1.2 Processes, Programs, and Threads

A *program* is defined to be the set of instructions and data needed to perform some task. A *process* is a combination of a program plus the current state of its execution, which minimally includes the values of all variables, the hardware state (e.g., the program counter (PC), registers, condition code, etc.), and the contents of the address space. In short, a process is a program in execution.

When a user requests a program to be run, a new process is created to encompass its execution. The process exists within the system until it terminates, either by itself voluntarily, by the kernel, or by request of the user. The process itself is an abstraction the kernel provides to manage the program while it is executing. The process can be controlled to some degree through system calls that affect things such as the process's scheduling priority.

Through the process abstraction, the kernel gives the program the illusion that it is executing on the hardware by itself. User programs need not concern themselves with interactions with other programs on the system unless they explicitly wish to communicate with them in some way. (Several services are available for doing this.) Each process is given its own virtual address space and is time-sliced (on most implementations) so that many processes may share the hardware. The existence of other processes on the system is transparent to the user program. This makes new programs easier to develop and helps ensure portability.

Many modern UNIX systems provide a mechanism known as *threads*. A thread holds the state of a single flow of execution within a process. The state of a thread consists at a minimum of the hardware state and usually a stack. All UNIX processes have at least one thread of control within them, which represents the execution of the program. This is true for all UNIX systems, past and present. Systems that support threads allow multiple threads of control within a process at the same time. In this case, each has its own hardware state, but all execute within the same address space. On a uniprocessor, only one thread execute at a time. On a multiprocessor, different threads within one process may execute simultaneously on different processors. One of the advantages of threads is that thread creation involves less overhead than process creation, making it more efficient to implement a set of cooperating threads within one process than to implement a set of separate cooperating processes. In general, the number of threads executing within a process will have no effect on the topics covered in this book. Therefore, the sections that follow will refer only to processes, which will implicitly include all threads executing within the process.

With few exceptions (detailed ahead), *all* program execution, both user and kernel level, takes place within the context of some process. (This is true of most traditional UNIX kernel implementations but may be different for specialized implementations.) All user programs execute within the context of their own processes. When these user processes request kernel services through system calls, the execution of the kernel code that implements the system call continues within the requestor's process context. This conveniently gives the kernel access to all of the process's state and its address space. It also provides a way to record the current state of the kernel's execution on behalf of the user program. If execution of a system call needs to be suspended to await I/O completion, for example, the kernel's state regarding the processing of the system call is saved in the process.

The UNIX kernel schedules only processes for execution since all system activity, whether at user or kernel level, occurs within the context of some process. When using the traditional time-sharing scheduling policies, processes executing at user level may be time-sliced at any time in order to share the CPU fairly among all processes. Processes executing at kernel level are exempt from time-slicing. A switch to a different process while executing at kernel level is done only when the current kernel process explicitly allows it to occur.

One of the exceptions to the rule that all system activity occurs within processes is the execution of *interrupt handlers*. Interrupts are generated by I/O devices when they have status information to return to the operating system. The status information might include the completion of an I/O operation, for example. Interrupts are asynchronous to the execution of processes in that they can occur without warning at any time. When they occur, the UNIX kernel allows them to interrupt the execution of the current process. The system then executes the interrupt handler until it completes or until it is interrupted by a higher priority interrupt. Kernel-level processes have the privilege of blocking interrupts if they wish. This is done only to protect the integrity of data structures shared by the process level and interrupt handler code.

A second exception to this rule occurs with *streams* service procedures. The *streams* mechanism was introduced in the System V Release 3 UNIX implementation from AT&T, and it provides a framework for network protocol implementation.While a detailed discussion of *streams* is beyond the scope of this book, it is noted here that service procedures run outside of any process context, much like an interrupt handler, for performance reasons.

1.3 The Process Address Space

The kernel provides each process with its own virtual address space. Normally, a process cannot directly access another's address space; this provides a high degree of protection from interference from other processes executing in the system. Some implementations provide facilities to allow some portions of memory to be shared. Shared memory and mapped file facilities will be discussed later in this chapter. Other mechanisms, such as the vfork system call and threads, allow sharing of some or all of the address space between processes. For the purposes of this book, such mechanisms present the same issues as shared memory and will not be discussed further. Almost all UNIX system implementations use demand paging to manage the allocation of physical memory.

A process's address space consists of four main pieces: program instructions, initialized data, uninitialized data, and the stack. In UNIX jargon, the instructions are called the "text" segment, and the initialized data and stack are simply called the "data" and "stack" segments, respectively. The uninitialized data is called "bss," which takes its name from an old assembler mnemonic called "Block Started by Symbol," which was used to allocate uninitialized data space. The difference between initialized and uninitialized data is that the initialized data is the global and static program variables that were declared to have an initial value when the program was compiled. The uninitialized data is the program global and static variables that had no explicit initial value. For these, the UNIX system simply allocates memory in the address space that initially contains zeros in accordance with the semantics of the C programming language (the language in which the UNIX system is almost entirely written). The advantage of this approach is that the uninitialized data need not take up space in the program file.

Most systems that use 32-bit virtual addresses divide the full 4Gb address space between the user program and the kernel. While the actual start addresses of each segment are implementation-dependent, a typical layout is shown in Figure 1–2. Usually the lower 2Gb are available to the user and are commonly referred to as the *user address space*. The upper 2Gb are reserved for the kernel and are protected against both reads and writes from user-level code. This is the *kernel address space*. The kernel address space contains the kernel's

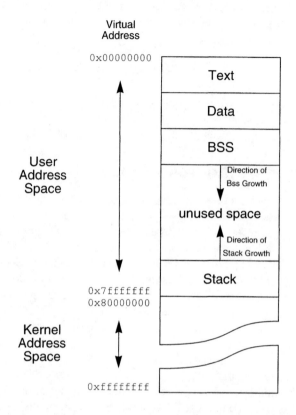

Figure 1–2: Typical process virtual address space layout.

text and data structures. When the kernel is executing, it can access the entire address space. This arrangement makes it easy for the kernel to run within the user process's address space while it is executing a system call on behalf of the user process.

The sizes of the user text and data segment are fixed when the program is compiled. They are simply copied from the file containing the program into the address space when the program is executed. The bss and stack segments can grow dynamically at run time. A section of unused virtual address space is left between them to accommodate growth. Stacks always grow toward lower memory addresses in this book. This is true for most computer systems.

The bss segment can be grown or shrunk via the `sbrk` system call. The bss segment can only be grown toward higher memory addresses. The stack is grown dynamically and transparently by the kernel as needed. When an access is attempted to the unused region below the currently allocated stack segment, a page fault is generated. The kernel checks the contents of the stack pointer register and if it contains an address that is less than the current top of the stack segment, the kernel then expands the stack segment to include the address in the stack pointer register and restarts the operation that caused the page fault.

Other types of segments, such as shared libraries and shared memory, may be included in the user address space. Shared libraries contain additional text, data, and bss for commonly used functions and services. Shared memory is described later in this chapter.

1.3.1 Address Space Mapping

The kernel is responsible for mapping a process's virtual address space onto the physical address space of the machine. Most machines allow any virtual page to be mapped to any physical page in memory. For example, the virtual address space of a process could be mapped as shown in Figure 1–3.

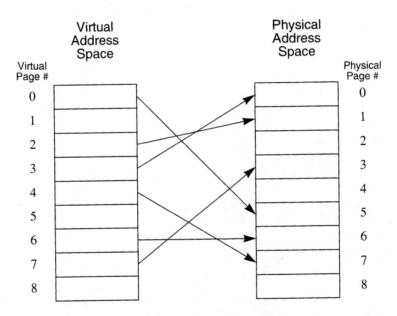

Figure 1–3: Address space mapping example.

The arrows in this figure show to which physical page a virtual page within the process is mapped. So if the process accesses virtual page 2, for example, the reference will be mapped to physical page 1. The mapping from the virtual to the physical address space is performed by the *Memory Management Unit* (*MMU*) for all addresses the process uses.

Each process has its own mapping associated with it and stored as part of the process's context.The kernel gives a description of the process's mapping to the MMU while the process is running.

Note that not all virtual pages need be mapped. For example, virtual pages 1, 5, and 8 in Figure 1–3 are not mapped to any physical page. These could represent unused pages in the process's address space, or they could be pages that are not presently memory-resident. If a process attempts to access a page in the latter class, the kernel pages the associated physical page into memory and maps the virtual page to the newly allocated physical page.

Likewise, not all physical pages in memory will be in use by a process. In the example in Figure 1–3, physical pages 2, 4, and 8 have no mappings to them from this process. These will be inaccessible to the currently executing process. These physical pages could belong to other processes in the system or could simply be unused. In either case, the currently executing process must not be allowed to access them.

The kernel can cause certain physical pages to be shared among multiple processes by mapping a virtual page in each process to the same physical page. (This will be discussed in more detail ahead.)

Most MMUs provide the ability to associate an *access permission* with each mapping. The two permissions most commonly used are *read* and *write*. This allows the kernel to map text pages as read-only while allowing read/write access on data pages.

1.4 Context Switch

The act of the kernel changing from executing one process to another is called a *context switch*. This involves saving the state of the current process so that it may be resumed later, selecting a new process for execution, and loading the saved state of the new process into the hardware. The minimal state of the process that must be saved and restored at context switch time is the contents of the CPU's registers, the PC, the stack pointer, the condition code, and the mapping of the virtual address space.

The acting of switching from one thread to another within the same process is called a *thread switch*. Since the process is not changed, there is no need to alter the address space mapping. Only the registers and other items listed in the previous paragraph need to be saved and restored. The reduced overhead of a thread switch compared to a process context switch is another advantage of using threads. In general, thread switches do not need to be considered for the topics presented in this book.

As stated, each process is given a separate virtual address space to give it the illusion of running on the machine by itself and to isolate it from interference from other processes. When a new process is selected for execution during a context switch, the old process's address space must be completely unmapped so that the new process will not be able to access it. The new process's address space is then mapped in so it can be accessed by the process.

Other types of state may have to be saved and restored based on the specific hardware being used. Caches, for example, may need management at context switch time depending on how they are implemented (this is the subject of the next several chapters). The kernel must ensure that all required pieces of a process's context are saved so that it may be resumed at a later time and its execution continued just as if the context switch never occurred. This is an important aspect of the kernel's duty to preserve the illusion that each process is executing on the system alone.

1.5 Memory and Process Management System Calls

The UNIX system provides several system calls for creating and destroying processes and for altering the process address space. This section presents a brief review of the internal operation and semantics of these system calls, since caches and multiprocessors have the most effect on the parts of the UNIX operating system that handle the address space of the process.

1.5.1 The Fork System Call

The fork system call creates a new process. The kernel does this by making an exact copy of the process invoking the fork system call. The process that invokes fork is called the *parent* and the newly created process is called the *child*. The child is given a complete copy of the parent's address space and process state that includes the values of the program variables, registers, PC, etc., and access to all the UNIX system services the parent had, such as the parent's open files. The child is created with a single thread of control that is identical to the thread within the parent that invoked the fork. Once created, the child process executes independently of the parent. At the completion of the fork, both processes are identical. The only difference between the contexts of the two processes is the return value of the fork system call itself. The parent is returned the process ID (the *pid*) of the child, while the child receives a value of zero. This allows each process to determine whether it is the parent or the child.

Since copying a large virtual address space could be time consuming, several optimizations are made. First, text segments are normally shared read-only between all processes that are executing the same program (and/or sharing the same libraries). This means that the text does not need to be physically copied to the child. The child simply shares the same copy the parent is using. Text sharing is possible because the UNIX kernel does not allow self-modifying code within the text segment. (When breakpoints need to be inserted into the text for debugging purposes, the kernel first creates a private copy of the text so that other processes executing the same program are unaffected.) A parent process about to `fork` with read-only text and read/write access to its other pages is shown in Figure 1–4.

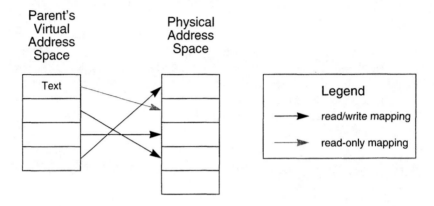

Figure 1–4: Before the fork: text is always read-only.

Next, nearly all implementations use a technique called *copy-on-write* to avoid having to copy the bulk of the remaining portions of the address space. Most UNIX processes `exec` (described in the following section) a new program soon after they `fork`. This operation discards the present address space, and so it would be wasteful to copy it during `fork` and then discard it shortly thereafter. Instead, the data, bss, and stack are not physically copied but temporarily shared read-only between the parent and the child. This is depicted in Figure 1–5.

Note that both processes still logically have write permission to the pages. Copies of individual pages are made when either the parent or the child attempts to write to a page. This way, only the pages that are written to are copied on demand, potentially saving a large amount of copy overhead if the child only needs to write to a portion of its address space before it `exec`s or `exit`s. Read-only, copy-on-write sharing is used as an efficient implementation technique only and is transparent to the processes involved.

Sharing continues as long as neither process attempts to modify any of the data. When one of the two processes writes to one of the read-only pages, a protection trap occurs which the kernel intercepts. The kernel makes a copy of the single page the process is trying to modify and uses it to replace the shared copy of the page in that process's address space. The process is also given read/write access to the new page. This is done only for the process performing the write; the other process's address space is unaffected. In this fashion, as much of the address space as possible is shared between the parent and child processes, with copies only being made on demand of the individual pages the processes modify. This

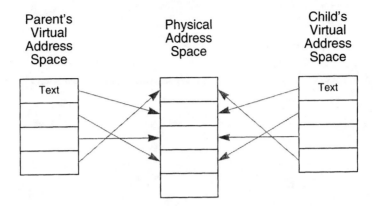

Figure 1–5: After the fork: all physical pages shared read-only.

is handled transparently to both processes, giving the illusion that a complete copy of the address space has been made. Figure 1–6 shows the state of the address spaces after the child in Figure 1–5 modifies its third virtual page. The kernel copies the contents of this page to a new physical page and remaps the child's address space to point to it.

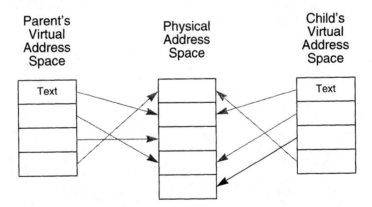

Figure 1–6: Address space mapping after child modifies a page.

To eliminate the need to copy pages for which there is only one mapping, the kernel keeps a count of the number of read-only, copy-on-write mappings to each physical page. So if the parent were now to write to its third virtual page, the kernel would recognize that there were no other mappings to the page and simply change the mapping to read/write without copying the page. The result is shown in Figure 1–7.

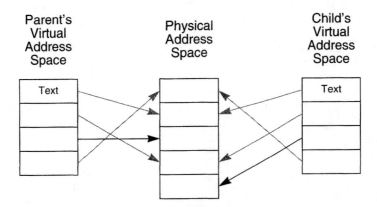

Figure 1–7: Address space mapping after parent modifies third virtual page.

The fork system call is a convenient mechanism to create a new process from the application viewpoint because it takes no parameters. Since the child inherits the entire state of the parent, there is no need to pass a complex set of parameters to the system call as is required to create a new process in some other operating systems. The child process determines what task it should perform based on the state it received from the parent. In most cases, the goal of the fork is to create a new process to execute a new program. To do this, the child prepares the state of the process by opening or closing files, possibly for I/O redirection, for example, and then executes the new program with the exec system call.

1.5.2 The Exec System Call

The exec system call changes the program a process is executing. Only the process invoking the exec system call is affected. The parameters to exec are the name of the file containing the new program to execute and a set of arguments and environment variables to be passed to the new program. A process that does an exec system call retains its state relating to most UNIX system services, such as its open files, its current and home directories, and so forth. The portion of its state related to the program itself, such as the contents of its registers, variables, PC, and address space, is replaced by those of the new program. More specifically, the text, data, bss, and stack of the old program, as well as additional memory objects such as shared memory, are discarded and a new virtual address space is created for the new program. The text and initialized data for the new program are loaded from the specified file, and the kernel allocates space within the address space for the bss and stack. The PC for a single thread within the process is set to the start address of the new program.When the system call is complete, the old program no longer exists within the process and the new program begins execution. The new program has access to the files the process had open before the `exec` system call since these are associated with the process and not the program.

As mentioned, `exec` system calls are frequently done after a `fork`. The most common case comes from the UNIX system command interpreters that create a new process to run each command. The command interpreter `forks` to create the new process, and then the child `execs` to run the command.

1.5.3 The Exit System Call

The `exit` system call causes the process calling it (and all its threads) to terminate. It is used when the program has finished its execution and wishes to terminate voluntarily. It is also possible for one process to terminate another with the `kill` system call (assuming it has appropriate permission). A process may also be terminated by the system if an unrecoverable error occurs. The steps the kernel takes to terminate and clean up after a process are the same in all cases.

To terminate a process, the kernel must discard the process's address space and disassociate the process from the kernel services it was using, closing any files the process has left open, for example. At this point, the process may temporarily exist as what is called a *zombie* in UNIX jargon. This provides a convenient means to maintain the parent–child relationship between processes until the parent has a chance to read the child's exit status with the `wait` system call. (Zombies are not relevant to the discussions in this book and will not be considered further.) Finally, the internal kernel data structures representing the process itself are freed. At this point, the process no longer exists and the kernel performs a context switch to select another process for execution.

1.5.4 The Sbrk and Brk System Calls

The `sbrk` and `brk` system calls are used by a process to allocate or deallocate space from its bss segment. The system calls take their names from the "BReaK address" of the bss segment. This is the highest legal address that can be accessed by the process within the bss segment. The region of virtual memory between the break address and the top of stack is not mapped to any physical memory and cannot be accessed by the process (ignoring shared memory and mapped files for now). The `sbrk` and `brk` system calls allow the process to change its break address either to grow or shrink the size of the bss segment. The `sbrk` system call takes a signed value that represents the incremental change in the break address, while the `brk` system call takes a virtual address that becomes the new break address.

If the process requests to grow the bss segment, then the kernel allocates the virtual memory just above the old break address, which allows the process to access that part of the address space. Newly allocated bss memory is defined to be zero filled. The bss segment can only be grown toward higher addresses, and its starting address is fixed. Physical memory to back the newly allocated virtual memory is allocated on demand, since it is referenced by the process. If the bss is shrunk, the virtual and physical memory in the range of addresses between the old and new break addresses is released. The access permissions are changed so that the process will no longer be able to access it.

1.5.5 Shared Memory

Some UNIX system implementations provide a system service that allows two or more processes to share a region of physical memory. This is commonly referred to as a *shared memory* segment. It is implemented by mapping the same physical page or pages into the virtual address space of two or more processes. The shared region of physical memory need not appear at the same virtual address in all processes; each one can *attach* it at a different virtual address if it so chooses. Shared memory is usually attached to the process in an unused region of virtual memory between the bss and stack segments.

Shared memory serves as a high-speed *interprocess communication* (*IPC*) mechanism, since processes can pass data through the shared memory without executing system calls and involving the kernel. When one process writes data into the shared memory, it is immediately accessible by the other processes sharing the same shared memory segment, since they are all sharing the same physical pages.

1.5.6 I/O Operations

The effects of I/O are important when considering memory operations. There are two system calls for requesting I/O from user processes: `read` and `write`. These system calls transfer data to a file or device from the process's address space (`write`), and vice versa (`read`). Some UNIX system implementations provide additional I/O system calls such as `readv`, `writev`, `getmsg`, and `putmsg`. (The effects of these on the topics presented in this book are identical to `read` and `write`, so only these two will be discussed.) Two different classes of I/O are available: *buffered* and *unbuffered*.

I/O to certain types of files is buffered in the kernel. The data is transferred between the kernel and the user process address space by a copy operation. The advantage of buffering is that it insulates the user program from knowledge of the characteristics of the physical I/O device. Programs need not be concerned with the block or record size, or by any alignment constraints. Disks, for example, are usually accessed by sector, meaning that the I/O must begin on a sector boundary and consist of some multiple of the sector size. When a user program reads from a buffered file, it simply specifies the byte offset it wishes the I/O to start at within the file and the number of bytes it wants to read. To maintain the file abstraction, the kernel translates the user's byte offset to the corresponding sector containing the data. One or more sectors are read from the disk into a kernel buffer, and the portion of the data the user wanted to read is copied into the user's buffer.

Unbuffered I/O bypasses this copy. This type of I/O is available to user processes and is called *raw I/O* in UNIX jargon. The term "raw I/O" comes from the fact that data copied through a buffer is considered to be processed, or "cooked." Data that is not copied is therefore considered to be "raw." With raw I/O, the I/O device directly transfers the data to the user buffer using *direct memory access* (*DMA*). Data that is buffered by the kernel during buffered I/O is ultimately transferred to or from the device using DMA as well. So it is possible to perform a DMA operation to either the user or kernel address space.

1.5.7 Mapped Files

Many UNIX system implementations provide the ability to map files into a process address space. Once mapped, the file is directly accessible as a region of sequential bytes in the address space. This allows the process to access the contents of the file using memory load and store operations instead of `read` and `write` system calls. Mapped files are logically similar to shared memory: multiple processes mapping the same file can choose to share the mapping so that changes made by one process appear in the address space of the others.

1.6 Summary

This chapter has reviewed the basic internals of the UNIX kernel. The UNIX system is a multiuser, multitasking operating system that provides a high degree of program portability between UNIX implementations by presenting the process with machine-independent abstract services. The execution of programs is contained within processes that maintain the current state of the program, including the virtual address space, the values of its variables, and the hardware state. The kernel provides each process with an environment that makes it appear as though it were the only process executing on the system. This is done primarily by giving each process its own virtual address space. User programs request services of the kernel by executing system calls. System calls exist to create new processes (`fork`), change the program a process is executing (`exec`), and terminate the process (`exit`). Many other system calls are also available, including ones to allocate uninitialized data dynamically (`brk`/`sbrk`), use shared memory, and perform I/O (`read` and `write`).

Readers interested in learning more about the UNIX system implementation are referred to the references at the end of the chapter.

1.7 Exercises

1.1   What would happen if a process tried to store data into its text segment?

1.2   The UNIX kernel will dynamically grow a process's stack as needed, but it will
        never try to shrink it. Consider the case where a program calls a C subroutine that
        allocates a local array on the stack that consumes 10Kb. The kernel will expand
        the stack segment to accommodate it. When the subroutine returns, this space
        could theoretically be released by the kernel, but it will not be. Explain why it
        would be possible to shrink the stack at this point and why UNIX kernels don't
        actually shrink it.

1.3   Construct a diagram showing how physical memory is shared between all three
        processes if a newly created child process (process C) immediately forks and
        creates a child of its own (in a manner similar to Figure 1–5). Assume copy-on-
        write is being used. How is the sharing affected if process C now exits?

1.4   If a process has two pages of text, one page of data, three pages of bss, and three
        pages of stack, how many physical pages will be allocated for the child during a
        fork if the kernel uses copy-on-write? How many if it doesn't use copy-on-
        write? Explain your answers.

1.5   If a parent and child process are sharing all pages of their stack segment with
        copy-on-write, and the child calls a subroutine that causes its stack to expand be-
        yond the allocated space, then the kernel will dynamically grow the child's stack.
        Explain the effect this will have on the parent's stack and address space, if any,
        and why.

1.6   What will happen if a child process that is sharing its data segment with the parent
        using copy-on-write does a buffered read system call where the buffer is located
        in the child's data area? What happens if it does a write system call instead?

1.7   Repeat Exercise 1.6 using unbuffered (raw) I/O instead.

1.8   Assume a process is using a shared library (i.e., has the text and data from a shared
        library mapped into its address space). If the process forks, how should the kernel
        treat the shared library regions? Assume the kernel supports copy-on-write.

1.9   If a process using shared memory executes a fork system call, how should the
        kernel treat the shared memory region? Assume the kernel supports copy-on-
        write.

1.10   If two processes are completely sharing their address spaces with copy-on-write,
        and the child releases part of its bss with the sbrk system call and then does an-
        other sbrk to set the break address back to its original value, what will the copy-
        on-write relationship be between the parent and the child?

1.11   Consider a process that does an `exec` system call of a program whose bss segment begins at address `0x10000` and ends at `0x20000`. The process stores the value `0x1234` into the word at location `0x15000`. Next it does a `brk` system call to set the break address to `0x12000`, followed by another `brk` to set the break address to `0x18000`. What value will the process see if it now does a load from location `0x15000`?

1.12   If two processes are sharing part of their address space with copy-on-write and one process exits, what happens to the read-only mappings of the other process?

1.13   Describe the differences between a single process with multiple threads and multiple processes using shared memory, each with a single thread.

1.8 Further Reading

[1]   Accetta, M.J., Baron, R.V., Bolosky, W., Goulub, D.B., Rashid, R.F., Tevanian, A., and Young, M.W., "Mach: A New Kernel Foundation for UNIX Development," *Proceedings of the Summer USENIX Conference*, July 1986, pp. 93–112.

[2]   Andleigh, P.K., *UNIX System Architecture*, Englewood Cliffs, NJ: Prentice Hall, 1990.

[3]   Bach, M.J., *The Design of the UNIX Operating System*, Englewood Cliffs, NJ: Prentice Hall, 1986.

[4]   Bic, L., and Shaw, A.C., *The Logical Design of Operating Systems*, Englewood Cliffs, NJ: Prentice Hall, 1982.

[5]   Bodenstab, D.E., Houghton, T.F., Kelleman, K.A., Ronkin, G., and Schan, E.P., "UNIX Operating System Porting Experiences," *AT&T Bell Laboratories Technical Journal*, Vol. 63, No. 8, October 1984, pp. 1769–90.

[6]   Bourne, S.R., *The UNIX System V Environment*, Reading, MA: Addison-Wesley, 1987.

[7]   Coffman, E.G., and Denning, P.J., *Operating Systems Theory*, Englewood Cliffs, NJ: Prentice Hall, 1973.

[8]   Crowley, C., "The Design and Implementation of a New UNIX Kernel," *Proceedings of AFIPS NCC*, Vol. 50, 1981, pp. 1079–86.

[9]   Deitel, H.M., *An Introduction to Operating Systems*, Reading, MA: Addison-Wesley, 1990.

[10]   Denning, P.J., "Virtual Memory," *ACM Computing Surverys*, Vol. 2, No. 3, September 1970, pp. 153–89.

[11]   Feng, L., ed., *UNIX SVR4.2 Operating System API Reference*, Englewood Cliffs, NJ: Prentice Hall, 1992.

[12]   Gingell, R.A., Moran, J.P., and Shannon, W.A., "Virtual Memory Architecture in SunOS," *Proceedings of the 1987 Summer USENIX Conference*, June 1987, pp. 81–94.

[13]   Kay, J., and Kummerfeld, B., *C Programming in a UNIX Environment*, Reading, MA: Addison-Wesley, 1989.

[14]   Kernighan, B.W., and Pike, R., *The UNIX Programming Environment*, Englewood Cliffs, NJ: Prentice Hall, 1984.

[15]   Kernighan, B.W., and Ritchie, D.M., *The C Programming Language, Second Edition*, Englewood Cliffs, NJ: Prentice Hall, 1988.

[16]   Krakowiak, S., *Principles of Operating Systems*, Cambridge, MA: M.I.T. Press, 1988.

[17]   Leffler, S.J., McKusick, M.K., Karels, M.J., and Quarterman, J.S., *The Design and Implementation of the 4.3BSD UNIX Operating System*, Reading, MA: Addison-Wesley, 1989.

[18]   Open Software Foundation, *Design of the OSF/1 Operating System*, Englewood Cliffs, NJ: Prentice Hall, 1993.

[19]   Plauger, P.J., *The Standard C Library*, Englewood Cliffs, NJ: Prentice Hall, 1992.

[20]   Ritchie, D.M., and Thompson, K., "The UNIX Time-Sharing System," *The Bell System Technical Journal*, Vol. 57, No. 6, July–August 1978, pp. 1905–30.

[21]   Ritchie, D.M., "The Evolution of the UNIX Time-sharing System," *AT&T Bell Laboratories Technical Journal*, Vol. 63, No. 8, October 1984, pp. 1577–94.

[22]   Rochkind, M.J., *Advanced UNIX Programming*, Englewood Cliffs, NJ: Prentice Hall, 1985.

[23]   Stevens, W.R., *Advanced Programming in the UNIX Environment*, Reading, MA: Addison-Wesley, 1992.

[24]   Tanenbaum, A.S., *Operating Systems: Design and Implementation*, Englewood Cliffs, NJ: Prentice Hall, 1987.

[25]   Thompson, K., "UNIX Implementation," *The Bell System Technical Journal*, Vol. 57, No. 6, July–August 1978, pp. 1931–46.

Part I

Cache Memory Systems

2

Introduction to Cache Memory Systems

Cache memory systems are high-speed memories that can increase system performance by exploiting locality of reference. This chapter explains the basic terminology, layout, and operation of caches. It explains how caches operate in conjunction with main memory and how data is located in the cache. It also covers hashing algorithms, miss processing, write policies, replacement policies, and set associativity. This chapter focuses on caches in uniprocessor systems. Multiprocessor caching is presented in Part III. By the end of this chapter, the reader will be sufficiently fluent in the operation of caches that the examination of operating system considerations can begin in the following chapters.

2.1 Memory Hierarchies

A cache is a high-speed memory system holding a small subset of main memory. It's physical location is between main memory and the CPU. Since it is faster than main memory, a cache offers the potential for an increase in system performance if frequently used instructions and data can be stored there for access by the CPU. Figure 2–1 shows a logical block diagram of a computer system containing a cache.

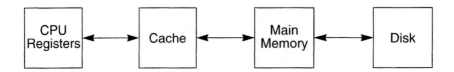

Figure 2–1: Cache location relative to other system components.

A cache improves system performance by exploiting *locality of reference*. Locality of reference is a property exhibited by most programs where a relatively small subset of the program's instructions and data is referenced repeatedly within a certain period of time. If the program's current locality of reference can be stored in the cache, the program will execute faster since the cache can supply the instructions and data faster than main memory.

A cache is only one component within a *memory hierarchy*. At one end of the spectrum is disk storage, which has very high density, low cost per bit, and (relatively) slow access time. At the other end are the registers within the CPU, which are few in number (low density) with high cost per bit but very fast access time. As we move from disk storage to registers, there is increasing cost, faster access time, and decreasing density.

Virtual memory paging systems have shown how a main memory system that is only a fraction of the size of the total virtual memory used by all processes in the system can yield good overall performance. Locality of reference makes this possible by requiring that only a process's current *working set*, those pages containing the process's current locality of reference, be memory-resident. The other portions of a process's address space can be saved on disk until needed.

Locality of reference extends to a finer grain than working sets. Within the pages of a process's working set, there will be certain sets of instructions and variables that a program will reference repeatedly within a short period of time. For example, consider the small C code fragment in Figure 2–2 that computes the product of matrices **a** and **b**. Assume that **a** is an **m** x **r** matrix, that **b** is **r** x **n**, and that all elements of **c** are initialized to zero.

```
for (i = 0; i < m; i++)
    for (j = 0; j < n; j++)
        for (k = 0; k < r; k++)
            c[i][j] = c[i][j] + a[i][k] * b[k][j];
```

Figure 2–2: Code fragment to perform matrix multiplication.

While this code fragment executes, it repeatedly references the instructions within the three loops, the elements of the matrices, and the loop counters. This will be the program's locality of reference while this code fragment is executing. Since the matrices contain more data than can be held in the registers, the CPU would have to reference main memory repeatedly if there were no cache, limiting execution of this portion of the program to the access time of main memory.

There are two types of locality exhibited in Figure 2–2: *temporal* and *spatial*. Temporal locality is the property that programs are likely to reuse recently referenced items. For example, the same element of the array **c** is referenced twice during execution of the innermost loop, as are the loop variables i, j, and k. Likewise, the instructions in all three loops are repeatedly referenced as well. All these references exhibit temporal locality. Spatial locality is the property that programs are likely to reference items that are near previously referenced items. Since arrays in C are stored in row order, the arrays **a** and **c** show spatial locality because the next adjacent element in the row is accessed on subsequent iterations. Likewise, sequential program execution exhibits a high degree of spatial locality.

The increase in speed and the reduction of cost of main memory systems have not kept pace with that of today's high-speed CPUs. If the speed of the CPU and main memory access time are too far out of *balance*, meaning that the memory is much slower than the CPU's ability to execute instructions and load and store data, then the CPU will be limited to the speed of the memory. Increasing the speed of the CPU in such a situation will do little to improve overall system performance since the memory system will still be the limiting factor. While one could build a large, very high speed main memory system that has an access time comparable to the CPU's ability to load and store data, the cost is generally prohibitive except for high-end mainframes and supercomputers. The alternative chosen by many of today's system designers is to use a cache.

By taking advantage of fine-grained locality of reference, a high-speed cache can fill the gap between a slower speed main memory system and a fast CPU. The locality of reference property applies at each stage of the memory hierarchy shown in Figure 2–1. Just as main memory holds a subset of the program (the working set), and the registers hold the operands of the current operation, the cache can hold the set of instructions and variables being worked on that form the fine-grained locality of reference. Because of locality of reference, the cache need only be a fraction of the size of main memory to be effective. Because of its relatively small size, it is practical to use higher speed memory devices than could be used for the main memory since not very many of them are needed. So the cache's high speed and exploitation of locality of reference work together to boost system performance economically.

2.2 Cache Fundamentals

Because locality of reference is exhibited by nearly all programs, caches are found on systems ranging from PCs to supercomputers. Caches can even be found integrated within most of today's microprocessor and memory management unit (MMU) chips. If not contained within the microprocessor or MMU chip, the cache will generally be located on the CPU board (called an *external* cache). Proximity to the CPU reduces the access time between the CPU and the cache. Latency could be greatly increased, with a corresponding loss of system performance, if the cache were located on a separate board that required a bus transaction to access it, for example. Some systems use both on-chip caches and external caches.

Caches can range in size from a few bytes to hundreds of kilobytes, or even a megabyte or more in large-scale systems. For example, on-chip caches today are typically in the 4K to 16K byte range. External caches are larger and can range from 128K to 4Mb. Cache sizes increase continually over time. For instance, the Intel 80386 has no on-chip cache, the 80486 has an 8Kb cache, and the Pentium has two 8Kb caches. External caches have grown from 64K as used by the MIPS R2000, up to 4M on the R4000.

Generally, the larger the cache, the greater the performance gain, since a larger subset of memory can be cached for high-speed access. As will be seen in later chapters, the size of the cache does not change the issues the operating system must deal with to manage the cache properly, only the specific algorithms that would be used. Cache performance is discussed further in Section 2.11.

A system may use separate instruction and data caches. This can further increase system performance, since the CPU can simultaneously fetch instructions from the instruction cache while loading or storing data from the data cache (see Section 2.10). As will be seen in Chapter 6, additional levels may be added to the memory hierarchy by using multiple levels of caches. (The next few chapters will concentrate on single-level caches.)

2.2.1 How a Cache Is Accessed

Caches are implemented such that their existence can be largely, or even completely, ignored by user programs. The goal of most implementations is to hide all details of cache management, either in hardware or in the operating system (as explained in the following chapters), so that user application portability can be achieved. This approach ensures that applications can be moved to different systems with different cache organizations, different cache sizes, or systems with no caches, without having to modify the program, an important benefit in today's marketplace. As such, programs simply continue to reference memory by addresses as they have in the past. No special coding techniques or addressing modes are needed to access the cache. The cache is accessed automatically by the hardware controlling the cache. One cache organization, the *physical cache*, can even be transparent to the operating system. This makes it possible to add caches to architectures that were not originally designed with a cache, such as the IBM 370 and the IBM PC, while still maintaining compatibility with existing system software. (Physical caches are covered in detail in Chapter 6.)

Since a cache only holds a subset of main memory, some way is needed to identify which portions of memory presently reside in the cache. Those portions of memory are said to be *cached*. This is accomplished by *tagging* the data in the cache with its main memory address. (The same is true for instructions in an instruction cache.) The hardware can then determine whether a particular memory location is cached by checking the tags of the data in the cache. So when the CPU issues a main memory address it wishes to fetch, for example, the address is sent to the cache and the hardware begins a search of the cache for the corresponding data (see Figure 2–3). If it is found in the cache, it is termed a *cache hit*. If the corresponding data is not found, it is called a *cache miss*. The frequency of cache hits to cache misses is referred to as the *hit ratio* and is expressed as a percentage of references that result in a hit or the probability of a hit occurring (a 90 percent hit ratio is equivalent to a 0.9 probability of a hit). The higher the hit ratio, the better the system performance.

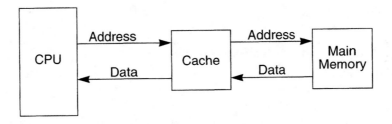

Figure 2–3: CPU fetching data via the cache.

If a hit occurs, the data is returned to the CPU just as if it had been read from main memory. If a miss occurs, the address is passed on to the main memory system where the addressed location is accessed. In this case, the data is returned to the cache and to the CPU. The data is stored in the cache after a miss to take advantage of temporal locality. The data surrounding the individual piece of data the CPU is fetching may also be loaded into the cache at this time to take advantage of spatial locality as well. (The amount of data loaded during a cache miss is implementation dependent as discussed ahead.) Because most programs display locality, hit ratios of 90 percent or more are not uncommon.

An important consideration in the design of a cache is how much data is identified with a single tag. It would be too costly, for example, to tag each byte in a cache separately. Therefore, one or more contiguous words from main memory are grouped together to form a cache *line* or *block*, and a single tag is associated with each line. A complete cache line is therefore composed of a tag and a data portion. The *line size* of a cache, however, refers to the number of bytes in the data portion. (The size of the tag is generally not included.) Typical line sizes for on-chip caches range from 16 to 32 bytes. Since the bytes in the data portion of the line are from contiguous memory locations, the tag only needs to contain the address of the first byte; the addresses of the other bytes can be inferred by their position within the line.

In addition to the address, the tag portion of a line also contains *control information*. One bit is always added to serve as a *valid bit* that tells whether or not the associated cache line is in use and contains valid data. The valid bit must be on and the tag must match for a hit to occur. When a cache is initialized during system reset or boot, all valid bits are cleared so that all instruction and data references initially go to main memory.

Another common flag stored in the tag is a *modified bit*. As discussed in Section 2.2.5, this is set when the CPU stores data into a cache that uses write-back caching. Other implementation-dependent information may also be present in the tags, such as a *key*, which is the subject of Chapter 4.

When a cache miss occurs, the number of bytes needed to fill an entire cache line is fetched from main memory and loaded into the cache. This is necessary since there is only a single valid bit that reflects the status of the entire line. It would not be possible, for example, to fetch only the single word that was referenced by the CPU on a cache miss if the cache line size was two words long. If both words were not fetched, then half the cache line would contain invalid data. The fetching of additional words from main memory is generally not a performance concern since the adjacent words may soon be referenced, due to spatial locality, and since most modern main memory systems are designed to read or write multiple words at a time.

Some implementations opt to use very long cache lines (128 to 256 bytes or more). The advantage of doing so is that it reduces the amount of memory needed for the tags, since one tag now covers a greater number of bytes in the data portion of the line. Fewer tags are therefore needed for a cache holding the same amount of data. The disadvantage of long cache lines is that the time needed to transfer a full cache line to and from main memory starts to become significant. To alleviate this, some implementations will partition a single cache line into multiple *sublines*, each with its own valid bit. Each subline can then be handled independently, almost as if it were a separate cache line, except that there is only a single address tag covering all the sublines in a line. This means that all the sublines contain data from contiguous main memory locations. The address of each subline is inferred from its position within the full cache line and cache line's tag. Fortunately, the use of sublines is transparent to the operating system and so it need not be a consideration in the discussions that follow.

2.2.2 Virtual or Physical Addresses?

Caches can be designed for access by either the virtual or physical address of the data or instructions. Likewise, the tags can be designed to contain either the virtual or physical address along with other information. The choice of virtual or physical address is fixed when the hardware is designed and has an enormous impact on the cache management techniques that must be used by the operating system to hide the existence of the cache from user programs. These complex issues will be the topics for subsequent chapters. For the remainder of this chapter, the type of address used to access the cache need not be considered. Either could be used with the same effects on the topics presented next. The following sections will simply refer to "the address."

2.2.3 Searching the Cache

Given the address of the data the CPU wants, the search of a cache for that data must be fast, since the whole purpose of a cache is to return the data faster than the main memory system could. The search technique must also be simple so that a high-speed hardware implementation will be both practical and economical. Techniques such as linear search, for example, are inappropriate for caches since they are too slow for all but the smallest caches. They are also difficult to implement in hardware since they would require a state machine or sequencer to store the current state of the search. Instead, most caches are searched using a simplified hash table technique.

To search a cache, the address from the CPU is hashed to produce an *index* to one or more locations in the cache where the corresponding data would be stored if cached. As with any hashing algorithm, different addresses will produce the same index. So the tags at these locations, which contain the addresses of the data that the locations are caching, must be compared with the address given by the CPU. If a tag matches the address from the CPU, a hit occurs; otherwise, it's a miss. Hashing is a useful technique for caches, since it limits the search to a small set of one or more locations (except in the case of a fully associative cache, described ahead, where hashing is not used). These locations can then be quickly searched in parallel by the hardware. These techniques are particularly important for large caches where there is only enough time to search a small portion of the cache. All of the foregoing activities are performed in hardware without software intervention.

2.2.4 Replacement Policies

Since the cache is smaller than main memory, some data must be discarded when new data is loaded during a cache miss operation. The data to be discarded is chosen according to the *replacement policy* of the cache (which is implementation dependent). Once selected, the discarded data is replaced in the cache by the new data. The tag associated with the data is also changed to the address of the new data so that it is correctly identified in the cache.

Replacement policies used by caches are usually quite simple. While the techniques of page aging and replacement found in memory management and virtual memory paging systems could theoretically be applied to caches, they would be too complex to implement in hardware. They frequently require large amounts of state or history information for which there would be insufficient space in the limited amount of expensive, high-speed memory used in caches. Typical cache replacement polices are LRU (least recently used), pseudo-LRU (an LRU approximation), and random replacement. These are presented along with the different cache organizations discussed later in this chapter. Fortunately, as is true for the previously discussed aspects of cache access, the replacement policy is transparent to the software as well.

2.2.5 Write Policies

When the CPU stores data, most implementations store it directly into the cache. Storing the data into the cache helps improve system performance for two reasons. First, stored data is frequently reread shortly after being written, due to temporal locality, so the hit ratio is improved. Second, the higher speed memory devices used in the cache can store the data faster than main memory. This frees the CPU to begin the next data load or store operation sooner than would otherwise be possible. Data written into the cache may also be simultaneously written into main memory as well. The cache's *write policy* (also known as the *update policy*) tells how data is stored in the cache and main memory.

To store data in the cache, the cache must be searched to see if it already contains data associated with the address being written. The same search technique used when reading data from the cache is used. The case where a hit occurs during a store will be considered first. Here, the data being written by the CPU replaces the old data in the cache line to take advantage of temporal locality.

While the cache is being updated with the new data from the CPU, the data may or may not be written to main memory, depending on the write policy that is used. The two possible write policies are *write-through* and *write-back* (also known as *copy-back*). If a cache is using the write-through policy, then the data from the CPU is written into both the cache and main memory. The write-through policy takes its name from the organization of the memory hierarchy (see Figure 2–1), where it is necessary to go "through" the cache to reach main memory. Write-through caching is used by the MIPS R2000/R3000 and the Intel 82495DX external cache controller for the 80486. The effect of the write-through policy is that memory is always "up to date," meaning that any data in the cache is identical to the copy of the data that exists in main memory (also referred to as being *consistent* with the cache). The disadvantage of this policy is that a main memory cycle is required for every write operation from the CPU, possibly slowing down the system.

The alternate policy is *write-back.* Here data is written from the CPU to the cache as before, but not written to main memory until forced out during line replacement or explicitly written back to memory by the operating system. This eliminates the overhead of extra main memory cycles that would occur with write-through caching if the same address were written to a number of times while the data at that address was cached. The disadvantage of the write-back policy is that the contents of main memory become "stale" or *inconsistent* in relation to the cache. Operating system intervention is usually required in order to regain consistency.

For example, consider what happens if a CPU with a write-back cache is executing the statement i=i+1 from a program (assume the value of the i is not previously cached). If the value of i in main memory is 1 before the statement executed, then when the CPU tries to fetch the current value of i, it will miss in the cache and will load the value of 1 into the cache and return it the CPU (Figure 2–4a). The CPU then increments i and writes the value of i back as 2. The write operation causes a hit in the cache, and the value of i in the cache is updated to 2. The write operation is complete at this point with the new value of i in the cache but main memory still holds the old value of i as 1 (Figure 2–4b). The new value of i in the cache is referred to as being *modified* relative to the value in main memory.

Cached Value	Main Memory
i: 1	i: 1

(a) State after i is read from memory.

Cached Value	Main Memory
i: 2	i: 1

(b) State after i is incremented.

Figure 2–4: Cache and memory values for i.

It must be ensured that the stale value of i in memory cannot be accessed by the program, since unpredictable results would occur. Likewise, it must be ensured that other processors on multiprocessor systems do not use the stale memory value either. (This is discussed in Part III.) The stale value of i will not be accessible to the program as long as the new value remains in the cache since the program will always hit in the cache before accessing main memory. The modified data will remain cached until the line is replaced.

Data written into a write-back cache could be replaced at any time during a subsequent miss operation. The modified data cannot be simply discarded since the program would end up accessing the old stale value in main memory on the next reference. Therefore, before re-placement, the modified data about to be replaced is written back to main memory auto-matically by the cache hardware. In order to differentiate between modified data in the cache that needs to be written back on replacement and unmodified data that does not, an extra bit, called the *modified bit*, is added to each tag. The modified bit is set in the tag for each line into which the CPU has written data. The modified bit is cleared whenever data is loaded during a read-miss operation, since the data is still in sync with main memory. By tracking the modified state of each line, the cache only needs to write-back lines when nec-essary, not on every store operation as write-through caching does. So the advantage of write-back caching is the potential for fewer main memory write operations, fewer bus op-erations, and better overall performance. The drawback is that there will be times when the operating system will need to explicitly force a write-back of modified lines to maintain data integrity (as explained in the following chapters). Write-back is also more costly to implement than write-through caching. The advantages of write-back generally outweigh the disadvantages, causing this technique to be widely used. For example, the on-chip caches of the Intel 486, Pentium, and i860 XR, the MIPS R4000, the Motorola 88200 and 68040, and the TI MicroSPARC and SuperSPARC (if no external cache is used) all use write-back caching.

 The preceding discussion has only considered the case of a cache hit during a data store from the CPU. If a miss occurs instead, then the actions taken depend on whether or not the cache supports *write-allocate*. When write-allocate is used, data stored by the CPU is always written into the cache on a miss (i.e., a cache line is allocated for the data) in order to take advantage of both temporal and spatial locality. To do this, the same type of pro-cessing that occurs during a read-miss is done. First, the replacement policy selects a line of data to be discarded to make room for the new data from the store. If write-back caching is used and the line chosen for replacement is modified, then the line must be written back to main memory. Next, the full cache line associated with the address that caused the miss is read from main memory. The full cache line (or subline) must be read since, as explained in Section 2.2.1, there is only one valid bit to cover the state of the line or subline. Once the line has been read, the data written by the CPU is then inserted into the line, and the cache tags for the line are set to reflect the address of the new data. The modified bit for the line is set if write-back caching is used. If the size of the data being written by the CPU is equal to the line size of the cache (e.g., storing a word into a cache with word-sized lines), then the main memory read operation can be skipped, since the line is about to be replaced by the CPU's data anyway. This is true for the MIPS R2000/R3000, which uses four-byte lines. Other processors that use write-allocate are the MIPS R4000, Motorola 68040 and 88200, TI SuperSPARC, and the external cache for the Intel 80486 (the 82495DX).

Some caches forgo the locality benefits of the write-allocate policy in favor of a simpler hardware implementation. When a store miss occurs in a cache that does not support write-allocate, the data is written to main memory alone, leaving the contents of the cache unchanged. This technique is used by the Intel 80486 and the TI MicroSPARC.

In most cases, write-back caches use write-allocate, and write-through caches do not. This is due to hardware cost: write-allocate would increase the cost of the otherwise low-cost write-through approach since a line must both be read and written to main memory on a store miss. Write-back caching works best with write-allocate; otherwise, lines that are written to that have not been previously read by the CPU would not be cached, causing all such stores to go to main memory. There are, however, exceptions to this. For example, the external cache controller for the Intel Pentium (82434LX) can be configured to use write-back without write-allocate, and the MIPS R2000/R3000 uses write-through with write-allocate. In the case of the MIPS chip, write-allocate is easy for the hardware to do since the line size is only four bytes, which eliminates the need to read a line from memory on a store miss.

Other variations are possible, too. For instance, the cache on the Motorola 88200 uses write-back caching yet updates memory whenever a store misses in the cache. This is called *write-once* and allows the line to stay in the unmodified state even though a store to it has just occurred, since main memory is up to date. Fortunately, variations such as these are transparent to the operating system.

The following sections will now explore several common cache organizations that will help reinforce the concepts just presented.

2.3 Direct Mapped Caches

The simplest cache organization is the *direct mapped* or *one-way set associative* cache. (The meaning of the phrase "one-way set associative" will become clear in the next section when two-way set associative caches are presented.) The on-chip data cache of the TI MicroSPARC uses this cache organization. It holds 2K of data, organized as 128 lines of 16 bytes each. In this type of cache, pictured in Figure 2–5, the address is hashed to produce an index to *one and only one* line (i.e., direct mapping) within the cache where the data could be stored. The cache can be thought of as a linear array of lines that are indexed with the result of the hashing algorithm. During a search, the tag at the indexed line is compared with the address to see if a hit has occurred. Indexing alone is insufficient since, as with any type of hashing, many different addresses will hash to produce the same index. When a hit occurs, the data is extracted from the cache line and sent to the CPU. If the tag doesn't match the address or the valid bit is off (remember that the valid bit is control information that is stored along with the address in the tag), then a miss has occurred since, in a direct mapped cache, this is the only location where the data could be stored. It is therefore unnecessary to search the cache further.

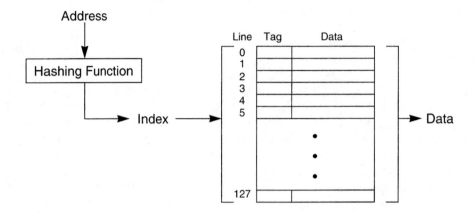

Figure 2–5: TI MicroSPARC direct mapped data cache.

Other processors using direct mapped caching are the Intel Pentium for its external cache, and all caches supported by the MIPS R2000/R3000/R4000.

2.3.1 Hashing Algorithms for Direct Mapped Caches

Cache hashing algorithms for direct mapped caches must convert a given address from the CPU into a line index in the cache. Since hashing is done in hardware, it must be both simple and fast. Simplicity is necessary to reduce cost and to allow for a fast implementation. Speed is important since the index is needed to begin the read cycle on the appropriate line of the cache. All of this must occur before the cache tags can be compared to see whether there is a hit. Because of these limiting factors, hashing algorithms used in caches rarely use arithmetic since these operations take too long.

The most common cache hashing algorithm is a *modulo* function that takes advantage of the fact that the number of lines in a direct mapped cache is usually a power of 2. This allows the hashing algorithm to simply select from the address a number of bits equal to the `log2` of the number of lines in the cache which are then used directly as the index. For example, consider the case of the data cache on the TI MicroSPARC which has 128 (2^7) lines and 16-byte lines. The hashing algorithm for such a configuration would be to select bits <10..4> from the address and use these 7 bits to select one of the 128 lines in the cache (see Figure 2–6). Since there are 16 bytes in each cache line, the low-order 4 bits of the address will select the byte(s) within the line that the CPU is addressing. Since the cache holds a total of 2K, we can see that this method of selecting the index causes all addresses of modulo 2K to index the same line in the cache (all addresses that match in bits <10..4> generate the same index). This will be referred to as the *modulo hashing algorithm*.

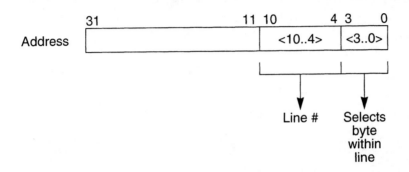

Figure 2–6: Cache hashing algorithm for the TI MicroSPARC.

Furthermore, addresses that generate the same index are said to be of the same *color*. A cache whose size is a multiple of the page size will be thought of as having as many colors as there are pages within the cache. The set of pages whose addresses hash to the same set of lines in the cache are said to have the same color. Cache color is a concept used to distinguish how pages index the cache. Its use is discussed further in Section 7.2.3. (See Figure 7–8 for a diagram showing cache color relative to pages in memory.)

Figure 2–7 depicts how the program's address space maps into the cache's memory. Since all addresses that have the same bit pattern in bits <10..4> will index the same line of the cache, addresses 0, 2048 (2K), 4096 (4K), 6144 (6K), etc. will all index or map to line 0 of the cache, while addresses 16, 2064 (2K + 16), 4112 (4K + 16), 6160 (6K + 16), etc. will map to line 1. As explained in Section 2.2.1, the tags will resolve the ambiguity, since they indicate the address of the cached data.

While the modulo hashing algorithm is the most commonly used approach, the bits used to select the line can come from any portion of the address. To see the advantages of modulo hashing, the following example will use the alternate hashing algorithm shown in Figure 2–8. The difference between these hashing algorithms lies in how addresses in the program index the cache. While in the first example (Figure 2–6) consecutive program addresses map to consecutive locations in the cache, the algorithm in Figure 2–8 causes whole ranges

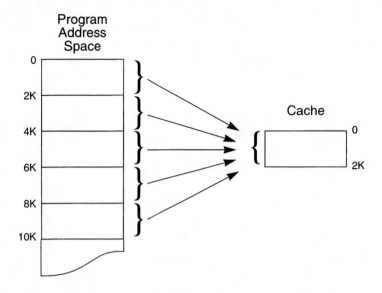

Figure 2–7: Address space mapping to cache using hashing algorithm from Figure 2–6.

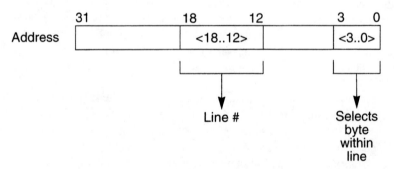

Figure 2–8: Example of alternate cache hashing algorithm.

of addresses (those that have the same value in bits <11..4>) to map to the same cache line. So all addresses from `0x0` to `0xfff` will index line `0` of the cache, all addresses from `0x1000` to `0x1fff` will be index line `1`, and so on. This effect is pictured in Figure 2–9.

While it is possible to implement such a mapping, it would not used because it leads to poor cache utilization (it is shown here for illustration only). For example, a small program that completely fits in the address range `0x0` to `0x1fff` would have all of its references map

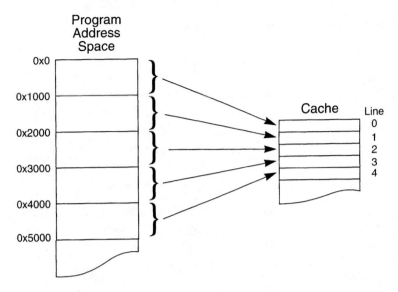

Figure 2–9: Address space mapping to cache using hashing algorithm from Figure 2–8.

onto the first two lines of the cache. Only 32 bytes of the 2K in the cache would be used while this program is running. In such a situation, one could expect a very low hit ratio and no measurable performance gain from the cache.

By contrast, one can now see that the hashing algorithm shown in Figure 2–6 provides a good mapping of addresses into the cache to maximize spatial locality. For this reason it is the algorithm of choice for all cache memory systems that use hashing.

2.3.2 Direct Mapped Cache Example

All of the concepts presented so far are now brought together to show a complete example of how look-up operations occur. For this example, we will assume we have a system that has 4-byte words and 12-bit addresses. The system contains a direct mapped cache that has 8-byte lines and a total of 8 lines. (Twelve-bit addresses and a small cache size have been chosen to simplify the example. Note that octal notation is used throughout.) Since there are 8 bytes in a line, that means bits <2..0> will select the byte within the line, and bit 2 by itself selects the word within the line since there are 8 bytes, or 2 words per line. The best hashing algorithm, based on the previous discussion, is to use bits <5..3> as the line index. Three bits are needed to index an 8-line cache, and choosing the bits directly above the bits that select the byte within the line makes the best use of the cache, based on locality of reference. The remainder of the bits in the address are used for the comparison with the cache tag (see Figure 2–10).

Address

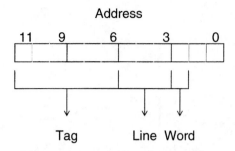

Figure 2–10: Example address bit usage.

For the example, we will assume the initial contents of the cache are as shown in Figure 2–11. In this figure, the symbol "---" in the Tag section indicates that the line is not valid. The two words in the Data portion of the line are separated by a vertical dashed line. The words in the line are in big-endian order, meaning that the word with the lowest address is on the left side of the line.

Line	Tag	Data	
0	---		
1	---		
2	---		
3	012	052	0777
4	---		
5	---		
6	---		
7	035	067	0

Figure 2–11: Initial cache contents.

For the first example, the CPU will issue a read of location 01234. The hashing algorithm selects bits <5..3> of the address, which give a line index of 3 for this address (see Figure 2–12).

Since this is a direct mapped cache, this is the index of the only line where the data for this address could be stored if it is in the cache at all. The cache control hardware takes the index and reads the contents of line 3. It finds a valid tag present and compares this tag with the tag portion of the address (bits <11..6>, which is 012). The tag portion of the address and the tag in the indexed cache line match, so a hit has occurred. Now the cache controller

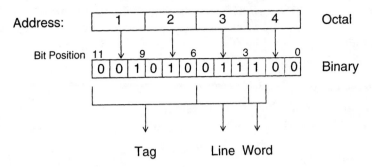

Figure 2–12: Breakdown of address 01234 for use by cache.

must select the correct word from the data portion of the line. Since bit 2 is set in the address, the CPU desires the high-order word stored on the right side of the cache line; the desired word is thus 0777.

An important thing to understand here is that it is not necessary for the cache tags to contain the entire address, as part of it can be inferred by its location within the cache. This is important because it reduces the total number of bits in a cache line and hence reduces the cost of the cache. In general, the tag contains only the address bits that are not used by the hashing algorithm. In the example, bits <5..3> select the only line where the data could be stored. The bits used to form the line index can then be omitted from the tag. Similarly, since the line holds 8 bytes, the low-order 3 bits of the address (<2..0>) need not be stored in the tags either. Therefore, it is only necessary to store bits <11..6> in the tags.

As a second example, consider what happens when the CPU tries to read from address 0130. The hashing algorithm selects bits <5..3> for the index, which is again 3, as shown in Figure 2–13.

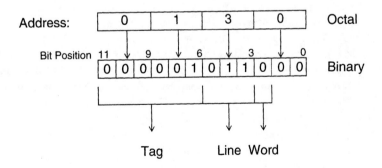

Figure 2–13: Breakdown of address 0130 for use by cache.

Line 3 is read and the tag from the address, 01, is compared to the tag in the cache, 012. They do not match, and so a miss has occurred. The address must now be sent to the main memory system to retrieve the data. The indexed cache line will then be loaded with the two words from main memory beginning at address 0130. Since bit 2 is 0, the low-order word of the pair is desired, and the word in the left portion of the cache line will be returned to the CPU.

As a final example, a read of address 06540 produces a miss since the indexed line (line 4) contains no valid tag, which automatically causes a miss.

The preceding examples along with several others are summarized in Figure 2–14.

Address	Line Indexed	Data Returned
01234	3	0777
01230	3	052
00130	3	miss
03574	7	0
06540	4	miss

Figure 2–14: Cache look-up examples using Figure 2–11.

2.3.3 Miss Processing and Replacement Policy for Direct Mapped Caches

When a cache miss occurs, the data must be read from main memory and returned to the CPU. The data is also loaded into the cache so that it will be immediately available should it be referenced again in the near future. If the cache line is larger than a word, additional words are read from memory so that a complete line can be loaded into the cache. This causes adjacent words to be *prefetched* at this point to take full advantage of locality of reference. Additional memory cycles may or may not be needed to read an entire cache line depending on the main memory system design. For best performance, the main memory system should transfer data in cache line-sized units, called a *burst mode* transfer. This allows an entire cache line to be transferred in a single memory operation. Without burst mode, the transfer must be done in smaller units, which increases overhead.

Once main memory supplies the needed data, a location in the cache must be found to store it. The location must be chosen so that the hashing algorithm will correctly locate the line during later look-up operations. In a direct mapped cache, this location is found by hashing the address of the first word in the line to produce the line index where the line will be stored in the cache. This is always the same line that was initially examined and resulted in the miss. The new line must be stored in this location since storing it in any other line in the cache would prevent it from being indexed during a later reference. This is the only replacement policy possible for direct mapped caches.

If the cache line being replaced during the miss operation was not previously valid, then the new data can be loaded into it and the tag set to indicate the address of the data. The line's valid bit is also turned on. If the line previously contained valid data for a different address, then this data will be discarded and replaced with the new line. If write-back caching is used and the old data was modified (see Section 2.2.5), then it must be written back to memory before being replaced so that the modified data is not lost.

As an example, consider again the example of Section 2.3.2 and the cache pictured in Figure 2–11. If the CPU tries to read the word at location 00130, a miss will occur since line 3 of the cache is caching data for the addresses 01230 through 01237 instead. If main memory contained the value 0222 at address 00130 and 0333 at address 00134, then after the miss was processed, the cache would be updated to that shown in Figure 2–11.

Line	Tag	Data	
0	---		
1	---		
2	---		
3	001	0222	0333
4	---		
5	---		
6	---		
7	035	067	0

Figure 2–15: Cache contents after miss processing.

The new tag and data have replaced the old ones. The rest of the lines in the cache are left undisturbed. The data the CPU originally requested, 0222, is returned to the CPU at the same time the new line is written into the cache.

2.3.4 Summary of Direct Mapped Caching

In a direct mapped cache there is a one-to-one correspondence between the address of the data in main memory and the location, or line, within the cache where it may be stored. Data is located within the cache by hashing the address, which produces an index to the one and only line in the cache where the data could be stored. A direct mapped cache can use either the write-through or the write-back policy.

A direct mapped cache is the simplest cache to implement because there is only one possible location to search for a hit during a read or write operation. This simplifies the control logic and leads to a lower cost implementation. Unfortunately, this is also the disadvantage of a direct mapped cache, as many different addresses will hash to the same line. A program with a pathological reference pattern, one in which the addresses of the data or instructions in its locality of reference produce the same index or a small set of indices, will not benefit from the cache since the hit ratio will be very low. Such a situation, where lines are constantly being replaced before they are hit again, is called *cache thrashing* (the name is taken from the same phenomenon in virtual memory paging systems). The following section presents an improvement to the direct mapped cache to reduce thrashing and increase the hit ratio.

2.4 Two-Way Set Associative Caches

A *two-way set associative cache* is similar to a direct mapped cache except that the hashing function produces an index to a *set* of two lines in the cache where the data may be stored. Each line within a set has its own tag, meaning that the cache can simultaneously store the data for two different addresses that hash to produce the same index. The Intel Pentium on-chip data cache is two-way set associative. It holds a total of 8K of data, with 32 bytes per line. This means there are 256 total lines in the cache (8192 bytes ÷ 32 bytes per line), organized into 128 sets (256 lines ÷ 2 lines per set). A representation of such a cache appears in Figure 2–16.

During a look-up operation, the hashing function produces an index to a set of two lines where the data could be stored. The tags of both lines in the indexed set are compared to the address simultaneously to see if either line generates a hit. (The tags of all lines within the set are compared in parallel so as not to slow down the cache access with a sequential comparison.) The goal of a two-way set associative cache is to reduce the cache thrashing that can occur in a direct mapped cache when two different addresses hash to the same index. In a two-way set associative cache, the two different addresses can both be stored in the cache. Examples of other processors using this type of cache are the Intel i860 XR and the external cache for the 80486.

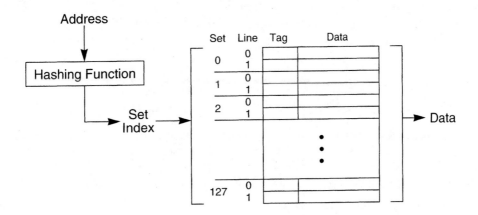

Figure 2–16: Intel Pentium two-way set associative data cache.

It now becomes apparent why a direct mapped cache is also called a one-way set associative cache. The terms "one-way" and "two-way" refer to the number of lines within each set (all sets in the cache have the same number of lines). The word "associative" refers to the fact that a set is a *content-addressable* or *associative* memory, as a hit is determined by examining the contents of the tags as opposed to the position (or address) of the line within the set. A direct mapped cache is a degenerate case of *n-way* associative caches, since each set only contains one line.

The hashing algorithms used with two-way set associative caches are identical to those used with direct mapped caches except that fewer bits are needed since, for the same amount of total cache memory, a two-way set associative cache will have half as many sets as a direct mapped cache. So the hashing algorithm for the cache shown in Figure 2–16 uses bits <11..5> to select the set. As before, bits <4..0> select the byte within the line (since there are 32 bytes in a line).

The replacement policy is slightly more complex. As with direct mapped caches, a line that is loaded during a miss operation must be placed where it will be indexed and found during future look-up operations. This will be within the set indexed by the hashing algorithm. But with a two-way set associative cache, there are now two possible lines within the set that may be chosen for replacement. Either line could be chosen, since both lines in the set are always searched during look-up operations. Ideally, one would like to replace the line that will not be referenced again for the longest period of time since this will improve the overall hit ratio in the cache. Unfortunately there is no way to know the future reference pattern of the program. Temporal locality suggests that LRU replacement within the set is appropriate, so most implementations, such as the Intel 80486 external cache, utilize it. It both is easy to implement and produces reasonably good results. It works by adding one extra bit per set (called the MRU bit for "most recently used"). Each time a hit occurs within a set, the MRU bit is updated to reflect which line within the set generated the hit. When a line within a set must be replaced, the cache first checks if either line is marked as invalid. If so, then that line is replaced. If both lines are valid, then the MRU bit indicates which one was used last, and so the other line is chosen for replacement. The MRU bit is then updated to indicate the replaced line.

2.4.1 Summary of Two-Way Set Associative Caches

The two-way set associative cache attempts to improve cache performance over a direct mapped cache by indexing a set of two lines where the data may be stored. A two-way set associative cache is slightly more complex and expensive to implement since the tags of both lines of a set must be compared in parallel and a more complex replacement policy is needed.

The advantage over direct mapped caches is that cache thrashing can be reduced. If multiple addresses in a process's locality of reference generate the same index, two of them can be cached simultaneously, while a direct mapped cache would always have to replace the line. Note that the performance of a two-way set associated cache will never be less than that of a direct mapped cache with the same number of lines. In the worst case, if the program generates addresses in an order such that each address indexes a unique line, then the performance of a two-way set associative cache will be the same. If, on the other hand, the locality of reference consists of different addresses that generate redundant indexes, then the two-way set associative cache will have a higher hit ratio, since it can simultaneously cache the data for two different addresses that generate the same index.

2.5 *n*-Way Set Associative Caches

There is no theoretical limit to the number of lines in a set; four-way and higher set associative caches are not uncommon in today's machines. For example, the on-chip caches of the Motorola 68040 and 88200, the Intel 80486 and i860 XP, and the TI SuperSPARC data cache are all four-way set associative. Since no indexing is done within a set, there is no requirement that the set size be a power of two. A case in point is the instruction cache on the TI SuperSPARC which is five-way set associative.

Hashing algorithms for these caches follow in the same line as those for two-way set associative caches: the modulo hashing function using the number of bits equal to the $\log_2$ of the number of sets is used.

Strict LRU replacement is generally not used for caches with more than two lines per set because it requires too much state information. Instead, pseudo-LRU algorithms with limited history are commonly used. All of the processors just mentioned, except the 68040, use this technique. The designers of the 68040 chose to omit the additional state information needed for pseudo-LRU and used a pseudorandom replacement policy instead.

2.6 Fully Associative Caches

The set size of a cache can be increased until the number of lines in a set equals the total number of lines in the cache. At this point, the cache is termed *fully associative*. In a fully associative cache, there is only one set, and it contains all the lines in the cache. No hashing or indexing is needed, since there is only one set in which to look. As with any *n*-way set associative cache, all lines within the set are searched in parallel. As implied by the name, a fully associative cache is searched in its entirety on every look-up.

The appeal of a fully associative cache is that it can minimize cache thrashing, since any piece of data may be stored at any location in the cache. Theoretically then, if a program's locality of reference is less than or equal to the size of the cache, it will achieve a 100 percent hit ratio and gain the highest possible performance boost from the cache.

Fully associative caches are more expensive to build than identically sized caches with fewer lines in each set because all lines in the cache must be searched in parallel. This is the main reason why fully associative caches are rarely used for instructions and data. When they are used, it is usually for small, special-purpose caches that have a high degree of temporal locality, such as *translation lookaside buffers* (*TLBs*). TLBs cache recently used virtual to physical address translations inside the MMU. Small, fully associative TLBs are practical since most programs exhibit locality of reference, meaning that the translations for the working set will be used many times. Also, since each translation maps a full page of data, few translations are needed to yield good performance. For example, the TI MicroSPARC uses a 32-entry fully associative TLB, while the SuperSPARC has 64 entries. The TLBs on the Motorola 88200 and all MIPS processors are fully associative as well.

2.7 Summary of *n*-Way Set Associative Caches

As can now be seen, all the cache organizations from direct mapped to fully associative follow the same organizational guidelines: each has an algorithm for choosing which lines to search, each has a replacement algorithm, each can use either write-through or write-back, but the main difference is the number of lines in each set. At one end of the spectrum is the direct mapped cache, which has only a single line in each set. For this type of cache, all addresses that hash to the same index must compete for a single location in the cache where they can be stored. The replacement policy for direct mapped caches is trivial since the only candidate for replacement is the single line that was indexed by the hashing algorithm.

At the other end of the spectrum is the fully associative cache. It has only one set, which includes all the lines in the cache. No hashing is needed for this type of cache since all lines are examined during each look-up. LRU replacement for caches with large set sizes is not practical, making random replacement common.

As the set size increases from the one-way set associative or direct mapped cache toward a fully associative cache, the goal is to reduce the cache thrashing that occurs when multiple addresses hash to the same set. Increasing the size of the set allows more data whose addresses produce the same index to be stored simultaneously in the cache. So increasing the set size can potentially increase the hit ratio and system performance. The disadvantage of large set sizes is the additional hardware cost and complexity since the tags for all lines within the indexed set must be compared in parallel. It is this fact that prevents caches with large set sizes from being used for all but the smallest caches.

2.8 Cache Flushing

All cache implementations provide the operating system with the ability to remove data from the cache, known in general as *cache flushing*. Depending on the cache organization, this may be necessary to prevent stale data from being accidentally referenced and to maintain *cache consistency*. (Cache consistency has a broader meaning in multiprocessor systems. This will be discussed in Part III.) Exactly when a cache needs to be flushed depends on its organization and is the subject of the next several chapters. Cache flushing takes two forms: *validating main memory* and *invalidating the cache*.

Validating main memory is the act of writing-back modified data in a write-back cache to main memory. As discussed in Section 2.2.5, this is done automatically by the cache during replacement of a modified line, but it may also be done under explicit control of the operating system. An explicit validation operation will cause the data in the line to be written to main memory, and then leave the data in the cache with the modified bit turned off (since it is no longer modified relative to the copy in main memory). Validating main memory allows the operating system to bring it up to date at any time. It is used to prevent the stale copy of the data in main memory from being referenced by other parts of the system that do not use the cache. If the operating system specifies a cache line to be written back to main memory that is either not in the cache or not presently modified, the validation operation does nothing to the cache. This type of flushing never needs to be done with write-through caches since memory is always in sync with the contents of the cache.

Invalidating the cache is the act of discarding data in the cache *without* first writing it back to main memory if it was modified. This capability can be used with either write-through or write-back caching. It is used by the operating system to discard stale data in the cache. This may happen if the main memory copy of the data is updated independently of the cache, which causes the cached copy to become stale. Invalidating it from the cache causes a miss to occur on the next reference to the data, which causes the correct copy of the data to be reread from main memory.

Write-back caches generally allow the separate operations of validating main memory and invalidating the cache to be combined into a single operation, since they are a commonly used sequence. In this case, the validation of main memory is done first if the line is present in the cache and modified, so that the data is not lost. This is then followed by an invalidation of the cache line.

Either type of cache flushing can usually be done on a per-line basis. Most implementations allow the operating system to specify the address of the data to be flushed. The address is then looked up in the cache and is flushed if a hit occurs. If a miss occurs, the cache is left unaffected. The MIPS processors work in this fashion. Some implementations may allow a group of addresses, e.g., a page or even the entire cache, to be flushed at once. The TI MicroSPARC and SuperSPARC allow the latter with what they term a "flash clear" capability. The Motorola 68040 and 88200 support flushing by the line, the page, or the whole cache at once.

2.9 Uncached Operation

Most implementations allow the CPU to access main memory directly and bypass the cache. This is referred to as *uncached* operation. If, for example, an uncached read is done, the data will be read from main memory even if the address would have caused a hit in the cache. In this case, the cached data is ignored and the value from memory is returned. All of the processors mentioned in this chapter support uncached access. It is usually selectable on a per-page basis via a flag in the page table entry.

Uncached operation is useful when accessing locations in memory whose values can change independently of writes from the CPU (referred to as *volatile locations* in the C programming language). For example, a memory mapped status register for an I/O device would contain a value that changes based on the status of the device. Uncached accesses are normally used to access such registers, since any cached value of the status register would be stale as soon as the device's status changes.

Uncached accesses can usually be used for any memory reference. They can also be useful in situations where frequent cache flushing would otherwise be required to maintain cache consistency, which can degrade system performance.

2.10 Separate Instruction and Data Caches

The use of separate instruction and data caches is now commonplace in computer systems. This effectively doubles the cache bandwidth since it allows the CPU to prefetch instructions from the instruction cache while simultaneously loading or storing data into the data cache. Such an organization is pictured in Figure 2–17. All processors mentioned in this chapter, except for the Intel 80486, have separate instruction and data caches for their on-chip caches.

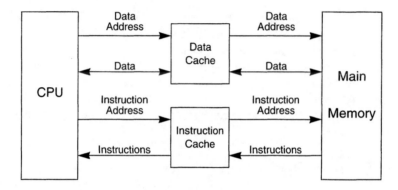

Figure 2–17: Separate instruction and data caches.

Since both caches may access main memory at the same time (for miss processing or write operations), cache access to main memory is arbitrated by the hardware and is transparent to the software. Note that there is no way to store directly into the instruction cache. The instruction cache is therefore a read-only cache.

The most important aspect of this organization is the lack of a direct interconnection between the data and instruction caches. The instruction cache will not check for instructions in the data cache if it misses in the instruction cache. It will always complete the miss by reading the instructions from main memory. Likewise, misses in the data cache are read from main memory as well. Stores into the data cache do not affect the contents of the instruction cache. While this is the simplest implementation, it generates possible cache inconsistencies, since the contents of main memory may be cached in more than one place. These inconsistencies can never occur if a single, combined instruction and data cache is used.

Consider the case of a program that uses self-modifying code. This includes programs such as LISP interpreters, as it is not uncommon for them to partially compile the program they are interpreting. (The compiled code is usually written into the process's data area.) Two possible inconsistencies arise if instructions are dynamically generated in the data area for execution. First, if write-back caching is used, a recently written instruction may not have been written to main memory yet. This means that the instruction cache will fetch stale instructions from memory if the program tries to execute these new instructions. Second, once the dynamically generated instructions are cached in the instruction cache, any writes the program does to replace those instructions with new ones will have no effect on the contents of the instruction cache. The new instructions will be written into the data cache and eventually into main memory, but the instruction cache will not know to fetch the new values. It will continue to execute the old, stale instructions until a line replacement removes them. In this case, the next reference to those instructions will cause a miss and the new instructions will be fetched from memory.

Unfortunately, the operating system can do nothing to hide the presence of the caches from such programs because it has no way of knowing when the program will attempt to execute portions of its data space. The only solution is to provide a special system call so that the program can inform the operating system when it has finished generating a set of instructions that it now wishes to execute. The operating system can then validate main memory, if write-back caching is used in the data cache, and invalidate the contents of the instruction cache. (On architectures that provide special instructions to flush the cache, a special system call may not be necessary if the application can execute the cache flush instructions directly.) Flushing of the instruction and data caches is usually implemented as separate operations by the hardware.

In general, whenever the operating system needs to invalidate cached data to maintain consistency, it must invalidate the instruction cache as well. The specific instances of each depend on the cache architecture and are discussed in the following chapters.

While it is possible to build a system where the hardware automatically keeps the instruction cache in sync with the data cache, this is rarely done. Such a system would require that the instruction cache be checked and possibly invalidated every time a write was done into the data cache. The extra instruction cache accesses needed to do this could interfere with instruction fetches and slow them down. Instances of self-modifying code are rare enough that it is not worth the added complexity in hardware.

2.11 Cache Performance

While a complete discussion of cache performance is beyond the scope of this book, the following observations can be made. The first is that cache performance depends not only on the design of the cache, but also on the application reference patterns. Therefore, trying to judge cache performance with benchmarks and generalizing the results must be done with care. While it is easy to write a benchmark that gets a 100 percent hit ratio, such results are meaningless when attempting to apply them to real applications. For example, the following program will get a near 100 percent hit ratio in the cache:

```
while (1)
    ;
```

After the first execution of the loop, all instruction references will hit in the cache. Conversely, the following code fragment, which multiplies each element of an array by the constant c, will experience a relatively low hit ratio (assume the array is larger than the cache):

```
for (j = 0; j < YMAX; j++)
    for (i = 0; i < XMAX; i++)
        matrix[i][j] *= c;
```

Since arrays are stored in row order in C, a cache miss will occur on each execution of the innermost statement when using a cache where the row size is greater than the cache line length (assuming the array is not initially cached). Such a situation is particularly bad since caches with long line sizes will fetch a large amount of data that will never be used. Interchanging the two for loops will increase performance due to spatial locality. Even though each element is only read once, the fact that the cache fetches an entire line at once means references to consecutive elements are likely to generate a hit. An exception to this is a cache with a small line size, like the MIPS R2000/R3000, whose line size is four bytes. If each element of the array matrix is also four bytes, then there will be no spatial locality benefits.

Even though cache performance is application dependent, the following generalizations can be made at an intuitive level (while they are not true for all applications, they are true for many, including typical UNIX commands). First, write-back is preferable to write-through as programs will typically modify variables multiple times due to temporal locality. Even if they don't, write-back caching generally doesn't add any performance overhead since writing through a line or writing it back later on line replacement both require one memory cycle. The increased complexity to maintain a modified bit for each line and handle write-backs is well worth the cost. In the worst case, where there is no temporal or spatial locality, a write-back cache with write-allocate will perform one extra read of the line. Cases that completely lack locality are rare enough that they will not noticeably affect performance.

Next, increasing the set size is generally helpful as well. This is particularly true for small caches (1K or less) as it allows more of the cache to be utilized even if multiple addresses generate the same index. Large sets are less important for very large caches (1M or more) since the probability of one piece of data replacing existing cached data decreases as the number of lines increases.

Increasing the line size generally helps cache performance due to spatial locality. The disadvantage of long lines is the overhead required to fetch the data during miss processing. Long lines are not found in small cache organizations since it would mean there are few individual lines. More frequent replacements would therefore occur.

Cache performance can also be influenced by the operating system. Different cache organizations require flushing under different circumstances. A number of techniques can be used to reduce the amount of flushing that must take place. This is important as frequent flushing is time consuming and reduces the amount of time that useful data will be cached. These techniques are discussed in Chapter 7.

2.12 How Cache Architectures Differ

The caches found in today's computer systems vary in many ways. The most significant differences are in the following areas:

- cache size

- line size

- set size

- use of write-allocate

- replacement policy

- look-up by virtual or physical address

- how the lines are tagged (by virtual or physical address or other information)

- write-through versus write-back

The first five items affect the performance of the cache and, with one exception (set size), are not a direct concern of the operating system from the point of view of maintaining cache consistency. Set size must occasionally be taken into consideration and is covered in Sections 3.2.2, 4.2.2, and 4.2.6. The last three items in the list affect performance as well, but they are also the items that affect the operating system. These items determine the amount of explicit cache flushing the operating system needs to perform to completely hide the existence of the cache from the programs running on the system.

The following chapters present four different cache organizations and describe the conditions under which the operating system must perform explicit flushing. The different cache organizations examined vary in whether the virtual or physical address is used to look up and tag the lines. The differences between write-through and write-back caching are considered in each case.

2.13 Exercises

2.1   Other than I/O controller device registers, what other things would uncached data be useful for?

2.2   Explain what would happen if the valid bits in a cache were not cleared during system reset when a system is powered on? (Memory devices used in caches generally power-up with random contents.)

2.3   Why does each line in the cache need its own tag?

2.4   Why would a hashing algorithm that used bits <9..2> of the address to index a 512-line direct mapped cache be a bad choice? What if the cache were two-way set associative instead?

2.5   Explain why it is or is not possible to have a cache whose line size is not a power of two when using the techniques described in this chapter.

2.6   Consider a direct mapped cache with 1024 lines indexed by bits <17..8> of the address. Each line contains 16 bytes. Is this a good hashing algorithm if programs typically only occupy the range of addresses from 0x1000 to 0x4fff? Explain why or why not. What if the cache is 16-way set associative instead?

2.7   Consider a write-back, two-way set associative cache with 4096 lines and 16-byte lines. What bits should be used for the hashing algorithm and why? How many bits are needed in the tag portion of the line to hold the address (assume 32-bit addresses and random replacement are used)? What is the percentage savings in the total number of bits needed for the cache when using the minimum number of bits needed in the tags for the address versus storing the entire 32-bit address?

2.8   What hashing algorithm should be used with a 7-way set associative cache with 256-byte lines and 512 sets?

2.9   Consider the following two alternatives for the organization of a direct mapped, write-through cache. Both alternatives will store 2048 (2K) bytes of data (not including tag and control bits). One organization will use 4-byte lines and the other will use 32-byte lines. What is the total number of bits that will be needed in the cache for each alternative including data, tag, and control bits? Discuss the trade-offs pertaining to hardware cost and performance that should be considered when choosing between the two alternatives. Assume the system uses 32-bit addresses.

2.10 Consider an environment where text processing programs are run often. These programs are characterized by the fact that they frequently copy strings from one location to another, and generate strings in buffers. Would it be better to use write-back or write-through caching in such an environment? Should write-allocate be used? Explain.

2.11 Describe the cache locality of the following code fragment. The system uses separate instruction and data caches, both of which are 8K, two-way set associative caches with 16 bytes per line. The data cache uses write-back with write-allocate. (Assume `ints` are 32 bits.) What happens if the line size is increased to 256 bytes?

```
struct {
        int     rec_id;
        char    rec_name[16];
        int     value;
        int     flags;
} array[1000];

...
int i, sum;

sum = 0;

for (i = 0; i < 1000; i++)
        sum += array[i].value;
```

2.12 A system uses a two-way set associative cache with 8 bytes per line and 16 total lines. The cache uses write-back with write-allocate as well as LRU replacement. Assume that all lines in the cache are initially invalid. Main memory contains the following data:

Address	Data
01230	33
01234	44
01270	7
01274	8
02270	67
02274	42
03270	43
03274	46
03650	100
03654	200
06730	120

06734			210
08670			10
08674			20
08600			64
08640			76
09830			333
09834			355

The following memory references then occur (each references one full word):

load		from	01234
store	5	to	03650
load		from	08670
load		from	08674
load		from	01274
load		from	08670
store	99	to	09834
store	12	to	02270
load		from	01230
load		from	06730
load		from	03654
store	37	to	03654

Draw a picture similar to Figure 2–11 showing the contents of the cache after the memory references listed above have completed. Include the state of the modified bit in each line. Also, show the final contents of main memory.

2.13   A program zeros memory by storing a word at a time into consecutive memory locations. Observe what happens on a system using a write-back cache with write-allocate when the memory block being zeroed is not initially cached. Assuming the line size is greater than a word, the first store to each line causes a miss and the line is read from main memory. The program then stores zeros into the line, causing the old data read from main memory to be replaced. It is therefore a waste of memory bandwidth to read the line since the data will never be read by the CPU. Assuming that the address of the start of the block of memory to be zeroed always corresponds to the beginning of a cache line, and that the amount of memory to be cleared is a multiple of the cache line size, then suggest a special-purpose cache operation, such as a new instruction, to make zero-filling memory more efficient.

2.14 Further Reading

[1]   Agarwal, A., Hennessy, J., and Horowitz, M., "Cache Performance of Operating System and Multiprogramming Workloads," *ACM Transactions on Computer Systems*, Vol. 6, No. 4, November 1988, pp. 393–431.

[2]   Agarwal, A., Horowitz, M., and Hennessy, J., "An Analytical Cache Model," *ACM Transactions on Computer Systems*, Vol. 7, No. 2, May 1989.

[3]   Alexander, C., Keshlear, W., Cooper, F., and Briggs, F., "Cache Memory Performance in a UNIX Environment," *SigArch News*, Vol. 14, No. 3, June 1986, pp. 41–70.

[4]   Alexandridis, N., *Design of Microprocessor Based Systems*, Englewood Cliffs, NJ: Prentice Hall, 1993.

[5]   Alpert, D., and Flynn, M., "Performance Tradeoffs for Microprocessor Cache Memories," *IEEE Micro*, Vol. 8, No. 4, August 1988, pp. 44–55.

[6]   Cohen, E.I., King, G.M., and Brady, J.T., "Storage Hierarchies," *IBM Systems Journal*, Vol. 28, No. 1, 1989, pp. 62–76.

[7]   Cole, C.B., "Advanced Cache Chips Make the 32-Bit Microprocessors Fly," *Electronics*, Vol. 60, No. 13, June 11, 1988, pp. 78–9.

[8]   Deville, Y., "A Low-Cost Usage-Based Replacement Algorithm for Cache Memories," *Computer Architecture News*, Vol. 18, No. 4, December 1990, pp. 52–8.

[9]   Duncombe, R.R., "The SPUR Instruction Unit: An On-Chip Instruction Cache Memory for a High Performance VLSI Multiprocessor," Technical Report UCB/CSD 87/307, Computer Science Division, University of California, Berkeley, August 1986.

[10]   Easton, M., and Fagin, R., "Cold Start vs. Warm Start Miss Ratios," *Communications of the ACM*, Vol. 21, No. 10, October 1978, pp. 866–72.

[11]   Gecsei, J. "Determining Hit Ratios for Multilevel Hierarchies," *IBM Journal of Research and Development*, Vol. 18, No. 4, July 1974, pp. 316–27.

[12]   Goodman, J.R., "Using Cache Memory to Reduce Processor-Memory Traffic," *Proceedings of the 10th Annual Symposium on Computer Architecture*, June 1983, pp. 124–31.

[13]   Haikala, I.J., and Kutvonen, P.H., "Split Cache Organizations," *Performance '84*, 1984, pp. 459–72.

[14]   Handy, J., *The Cache Memory Book*, Boston, MA: Academic Press, 1993.

[15]   Higbie, L., "Quick and Easy Cache Performance Analysis," *Computer Architecture News*, Vol. 18, No. 2, June 1990, pp. 33–44.

[16]   Hill, M.D., "The Case for Direct-Mapped Caches," *IEEE Computer*, Vol. 21, No. 12, December 1988, pp. 25–41.

[17]   Hill, M.D., and Smith, A.J., "Experimental Evaluation of On-Chip Microprocessor Cache Memories," *Proceedings of the 11th Annual International Symposium on Computer Architecture*, June 1984, pp. 158–66.

[18]   Hill, M.D., and Smith, A.J., "Evaluating Associativity in CPU Caches," *IEEE Transactions on Computers*, Vol. 38, No. 12, December 1989, pp. 1612–30.

[19]   Jouppi, N.P., "Cache Write Policies and Performance," *Proceedings of the 20th Annual International Symposium on Computer Architecture*, May 1993, pp. 191–201.

[20]   Laha, S., Patel, J.H., and Iyer, R.K., "Accurate Low-Cost Methods for Performance Evaluation of Cache Memory Systems," *IEEE Transactions on Computers*, Vol. 37, No. 11, November 1988, pp. 1325–36.

[21]   Lorin, H., *Introduction to Computer Architecture and Organization, Second Edition*, New York, NY: John Wiley & Sons, 1989.

[22]   Mano, M.M., *Computer System Architecture, Third Edition*, Englewood Cliffs, NJ: Prentice Hall, 1993.

[23]   Przybylski, S.A., *Cache and Memory Hierarchy Design: A Performance-Directed Approach*, San Mateo, CA: Morgan Kaufmann Publishers, 1990.

[24]   Rao, G.S., "Performance Analysis of Cache Memories," *Journal of the ACM*, Vol. 25, No. 3, July 1978, pp. 378–95.

[25]   Short, R.T., and Levy, H.M., "A Simulation Study of Two-Level Caches," *Proceedings of the 15th Annual International Symposium on Computer Architecture*, June 1988, pp. 81–9.

[26] Smith, A.J., "A Comparative Study of Set Associative Memory Mapping Algorithms and Their Use for Cache and Main Memory," *IEEE Transactions on Software Engineering*, Vol. 4, No. 2, March 1978, pp. 121–30.

[27] Smith, A.J., "Sequential Program Prefetching in Memory Hierarchies," *IEEE Computer*, Vol. 11, No. 12, December 1978, pp. 7–21.

[28] Smith, A.J., "Cache Memories," *ACM Computing Surveys*, Vol. 14, No. 3, September 1982, pp. 473–530.

[29] Smith, A.J., "Cache Evaluation and the Impact of Workload Choice," *Proceedings of the 12th Annual International Symposium on Computer Architecture*, June 1985, pp. 64–73.

[30] Smith, A.J., "Problems, Directions, and Issues in Memory Hierarchies," *Proceedings of the 18th Annual Hawaii Conference on System Sciences*, 1985, pp. 468–76.

[31] Smith, A.J., "Bibliography and Readings on CPU Cache Memories and Related Topics," *Computer Architecture News*, Vol. 14, No. 1, January 1986, pp. 22–42.

[32] Smith, A.J., "Design of CPU Cache Memories," *Proceedings of the IEEE TENCON*, August 1987, pp. 30.2.1–30.2.10.

[33] Smith, A.J., "Line (Block) Size Choice for CPU Cache Memories," *IEEE Transactions on Computers*, Vol. 36, No. 9, September 1987, pp. 1063–75.

[34] Stone, H.S., *High Performance Computer Architecture, Third Edition*, Reading, MA: Addison-Wesley, 1993.

[35] Strecker, W.D., "Transient Behavior of Cache Memories," *ACM Transactions on Computer Systems*, Vol. 1, No. 4, November 1983, pp. 281–93.

[36] Smith, J.E., and Goodman, J.R., "A Study of Instruction Cache Organizations and Replacement Policies," *Proceedings of the 10th Annual International Symposium on Computer Architecture*, June 1983, pp. 64–73.

[37] Thiebaut, D.F., "On the Fractal Dimension of Computer Programs and Its Application to the Prediction of the Cache Miss Ratio," *IEEE Transactions on Computers*, Vol. 38, No. 7, July 1989, pp. 1012–27.

[38]   Thompson, J.G., "Efficient Analysis of Caching Systems," Technical Report
         UCB/CSD 87/374, Computer Science Division, University of California,
         Berkeley, October 1987.

[39]   Thompson, J.G., and Smith, A.J., "Efficient (Stack) Algorithms for Analysis of
         Write-Back and Sector Memories," *ACM Transactions on Computer Systems*,
         Vol. 7, No. 1, February 1989, pp. 78–116.

[40]   Welch, T.A., "Memory Hierarchy Configuration Analysis," *IEEE Transactions
         on Computers*, Vol. C-27, No. 5, May 1978, pp. 408–13.

3

Virtual Caches

A virtual cache is indexed and tagged with the virtual address of the instructions or data being cached. This presents many complications to the operating system since the same virtual addresses can be used by different processes. Data cached by one process could be mistaken for data belonging to a different process. To prevent this from happening, the operating system must flush the cache before such ambiguities can occur. This chapter explains the operation of virtual caches, how ambiguities and aliases can occur, and how the operating system prevents them from affecting program execution in a uniprocessor environment.

3.1 Virtual Cache Operation

With a *virtual cache*, the program's virtual addresses are used to index the cache and to tag the data. The main advantage of this approach is that the cache can be accessed without the need to translate the virtual address to a physical address on every read or write operation. As Figure 3–1 depicts, a program executing on the CPU specifies the virtual address of the data it wishes to load or store, or of an instruction to fetch. The virtual address is sent to the cache, which does a look-up operation to see if the data is cached. If a miss occurs in the cache on a read operation, the physical address computed by the Memory Management Unit (MMU) is sent to the main memory, which returns the data. (Some implementations begin the address translation in parallel with the cache look-up.) The data is then loaded into the cache, so it is available for future references (locality), and returned to the CPU.

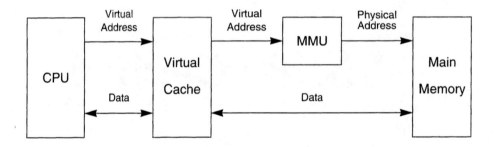

Figure 3–1: Virtual cache organization.

Systems using virtual caches may or may not use the MMU during read operations that hit in the cache. For example, the Intel i860 family uses virtual caches for its on-chip instruction caches. The MMU for these processors does not translate virtual addresses that generate a hit in the instruction cache during instruction fetches. This means that the hardware does not explicitly validate access permissions. The same is true for the virtual cache found on the Apollo DN4000 and Sun 3/200. These systems follow the model shown in Figure 3–1, where the MMU only translates virtual addresses after a miss has occurred in the cache. Systems that use virtual caches in this manner implicitly assume that if a program succeeded in reading the data during a miss operation, then it still has permission to read the data on later hits in the cache. As explained in later sections, the operating system must ensure that data the program no longer has permission to read is invalidated from the cache.

Stores work as follows: if the write-through policy is used, the data to be written and its virtual address are sent to the cache. The virtual address is immediately sent to the MMU for translation and for checking the permissions to ensure the process has permission to write to the address. If write access is allowed and a hit occurs in the cache, the new data is inserted into the cache line and written to main memory using the translated address from the MMU. If instead a miss occurs and write-allocate is used, the cache will first read the line from main memory using the translated address (but only if the line size of the cache is greater than the size of the data being written by the CPU, as explained on page 32). The new data from the store is then inserted into the line and written to the cache. If write-allocate is not used, then the cache contents do not change during a store operation that misses. In either case, the data from the store is written to main memory using the physical address. If write permission is not allowed for this address, then a trap is signaled to the CPU and neither the cache nor main memory is affected.

Ensuring that the access permissions are not violated is slightly more complicated if write-back caching is used. Assuming write-allocate is used (as is typical for write-back caches) and the virtual address misses in the cache on a write, then the MMU will need to translate the address and fetch the complete cache line from main memory as before. This provides an opportunity for the access permissions to be validated. If write permission is allowed, the new data is inserted into the cache line read from main memory and the modified bit for the line is set. If write-allocate is not used, then the behavior is the same as write-through without write-allocate when a miss occurs: the data is written to main memory alone, and the cache is not changed.

If instead a cache hit occurs during a store into a write-back virtual cache, and the line has already been modified (as indicated by the modified bit in the tags), then it can be implicitly assumed that the process still has write permission to the addressed data since it must have had such permission when it originally modified the line. In this scenario, no explicit validation is needed in the case of a hit on a modified line. As before, the operating system must flush the cache if the access permissions change during execution of the process.

The difficulty arises when a write that causes a hit on an unmodified line in the cache is attempted. It cannot be known whether write permission is allowed, so the address is sent to the MMU for validation. This is how the on-chip virtual write-back data cache for the Intel i860 XR functions. Its MMU checks the access permissions for all accesses to the data cache (both hits and misses). This validation occurs in parallel with the cache look-up to prevent the cache access from being slowed down. If write-access is allowed for a store, the new data is inserted into the cache line and the line's modified bit is set. It is not necessary to access main memory at all in this case since the line was already in the cache.

Implementations with write-back caches that translate virtual addresses and check access permissions only after a miss, such as the Apollo DN4000, get around the penalty of the serialized cache look-up/MMU validation operation in this case by adding a *writable* bit to the control portion of the tags. This bit is set whenever a new line is loaded during a cache miss and the process has write permission to the corresponding address. This bit is a copy of the write-permission bit in the page tables and allows the write validation to be handled completely by the cache itself, saving the overhead of an additional MMU operation. Such implementations are transparent to the operating system.

Since write-back caching leaves modified data in the cache, a line may have to be written back when it is replaced during miss processing, or explicitly flushed by the operating system (specifying that main memory should be validated with the modified data). If a write-back is necessary under these circumstances, the cache will send the virtual address of the data to be written back (which is stored in the tag) to the MMU. Once the physical address is computed, the modified line is written to main memory.

3.2 Problems with Virtual Caches

The virtual cache, while being able to return data quickly to the CPU by saving the address translation step, is the most difficult type of cache for an operating system to manage. The problems revolve around the fact that the virtual address is used to index and tag the lines. Virtual addresses do not uniquely identify a piece of data, since multiple processes can use the same range of virtual addresses. This causes *ambiguities* and *aliases* to occur in the cache unless the operating system takes steps to prevent them. The following two sections discuss these problems.

3.2.1 Ambiguities

An *ambiguity* occurs when *different* pieces of data have the *same* index and tag in a cache. This means that the cache will be unable to differentiate between the two different pieces of data, since the index and tag are the only means the cache has for identifying the data. References to such data are said to be ambiguous. For a virtual cache, ambiguities occur whenever a virtual address is used that has different physical address mappings at different points in time. For example (using the contents of physical memory as shown in Figure 3–2),

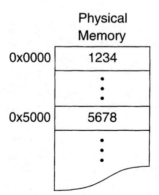

Figure 3–2: Contents of physical memory for ambiguity example.

if at time 1 virtual address 0x1000 is mapped to physical address 0x5000, then if that location is referenced, 5678 will be loaded into the cache, as shown in Figure 3–3. Further references to it will hit in the cache, and main memory will not be accessed. (Note that the entire virtual address is shown in the tags for clarity. An actual implementation would only store the upper bits of the address not used by the hashing algorithm (see page 39).)

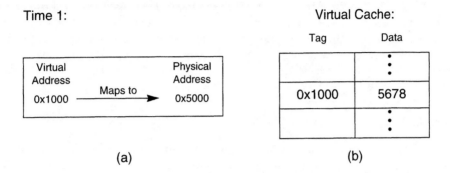

Figure 3–3: (a) Mapping at time 1.
(b) Cache contents after reference to 0x1000.

If at time 2 the mapping is changed to physical address 0x0000, then a reference to virtual address 0x1000 will still return the data for physical location 0x5000, since the virtual address will still generate a hit in the cache (see Figure 3–4). The cache look-up is based solely on the virtual address, and so the same index and tag are generated for the virtual address 0x1000 even though the physical address has changed.

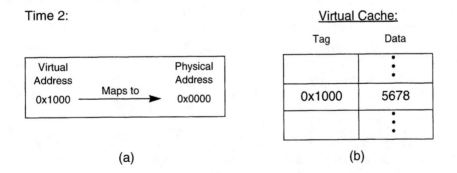

Figure 3–4: (a) Mapping at time 2.
(b) Cache contents unaffected by change in mapping.

The result is that the program will continue to get the wrong data (inconsistent with the contents of main memory) until the line containing the wrong data is replaced during miss processing or is explicitly flushed from the cache. The cache cannot do this automatically since it is dealing with the virtual addresses alone and is unable to tell that the physical mapping has changed.

It is the responsibility of the operating system to ensure that any old data is written back to main memory and invalidated prior to any changes in the virtual address space so that ambiguities cannot occur. If they are allowed to occur, then programs will sporadically read the wrong data from the cache, leading to unexpected and nondeterministic behavior. If ambiguities are allowed to develop for the operating system's own data, then the system will likely crash or at least run incorrectly.

3.2.2 Aliases

An *alias*, also known as a *synonym*, occurs when more than one virtual address is used to refer to the same physical memory location (the multiple virtual addresses are referred to as *aliases*). This can occur if a process has the same shared memory region attached at two different virtual addresses within its address space, or when two different processes use the same shared memory at different addresses in their respective address spaces. If each address hashes to produce a different line index, then the same data could be stored in two different locations in the cache. Unpredictable results will occur if the two versions get out of sync with one another.

Consider a process that has the page at physical memory location 0x3000 mapped at virtual addresses 0x2000 and 0x4000 as shown in Figure 3–5. (Assume pages are 0x1000 (4K) bytes long.) With such a mapping, the program will be able to read data from either virtual address 0x2000 or 0x4000 and expect the same result since both refer to the same physical page of memory. Assume the system in this example has a direct mapped, virtual cache that uses bits <15..4> of the virtual address as the index. This means that address 0x2000 will hash to line 0x200 and address 0x4000 will hash to line 0x400. If the first word at physical address 0x3000 is 1234, then if the process references both virtual address 0x2000 and then 0x4000, the value at physical location 0x3000 will be loaded into two different locations in the cache (as shown in Figure 3–6), since the addresses generate different indices.

So far the process has experienced no ill effects since the correct data is returned using either address. The process will continue to receive the correct data at these locations until it attempts to write to one of the addresses. If it now writes 5678 to virtual location 0x2000, line 0x200 will be updated but the alias at line 0x400 will not, causing the cache to contain inconsistent data for the two aliases. This is depicted in Figure 3–7.

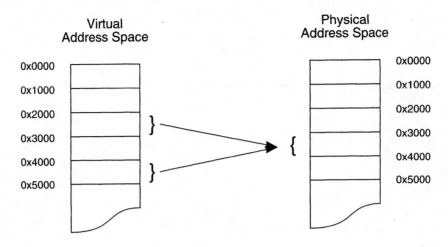

Figure 3–5: Two virtual address aliases for physical page at 0x3000.

Virtual Cache:

Line	Tag	Data
		$\vdots$
0x200	0x2000	1234
		$\vdots$
0x400	0x4000	1234
		$\vdots$

Figure 3–6: Virtual cache contents after references to 0x2000 and 0x4000.

References to virtual address 0x4000 will return the old, stale contents of physical location 0x3000. They will continue to do so until the line is replaced during miss processing or is explicitly flushed. Stale data in a cache will cause strange and unpredictable behavior in program execution. Stranger results will occur if the process writes a different value to virtual address 0x4000. Results will vary further depending on whether the cache is using the write-through or write-back policy (see Exercise 3.2).

Virtual Cache:

Line	Tag	Data
		• • •
0x200	0x2000	5678
		• • •
0x400	0x4000	1234
		• • •

Figure 3–7: Virtual cache contents after write to 0x2000.

The effects of aliases are completely different if the aliases generate the same cache line index. If the virtual addresses used in the preceding example were changed to 0x2000 and 0x12000, then both addresses would index line 0x200 of the cache. Since the cache is direct mapped, it can hold the data for only one of these two addresses at a time. If the process alternated reads between these two addresses, it would cause a cache miss each time (since the virtual address wouldn't match the current value of the tag) and the value would be reread from physical location 0x3000. The process would always get the correct data in this case because each reference to one alias would cause the line containing the other alias to be replaced in the cache.

The situation changes for writes. If the cache uses write-allocate, then the process will receive the correct data if it alternates writes to the two aliases. A miss will occur each time, and the line will be reread from main memory. If write-allocate is not used, then inconsistencies can arise. If a hit occurs when the process stores to 0x2000 with a write-through cache, then the data is stored in the cache and written to main memory. If a store is next done to 0x12000, then a miss occurs and the data is written to main memory alone. At this point, the cache is still holding the stale data from the first store, causing inconsistencies if the process were to read from 0x2000.

Now consider if the cache were two-way set associative instead of direct mapped. Both addresses would produce the same set index, but the cache would now be capable of caching both aliases simultaneously. The same problems that occurred when the aliases indexed different lines of the direct mapped cache would now occur here.

As stated previously, aliases can exist between address spaces. In our example, the virtual address aliases 0x2000 and 0x4000 could have been in two different processes, which would have caused the same inconsistencies as with the single address space case.

Aliases that cause different cache lines to be accessed result in erroneous data being returned to the process. The operating system must prevent these situations from occurring.

3.3 Managing a Virtual Cache

There are a number of situations that can cause ambiguities and aliases to occur in the UNIX system when using a virtual cache if they are not properly managed. The situations arise when changes occur to the process address space. The following sections detail these situations and the actions the kernel must take to keep a virtual cache and main memory consistent. In all cases, for those systems that use separate instruction and data caches (where both are virtual caches), the instruction cache should be invalidated at the same time the data cache is invalidated.

As will be seen in later chapters, it is possible to avoid having the operating system explicitly flush the cache by changing the organization of the cache to employ physical addresses in some manner. For example, the caches on the Intel i860 XP include the physical address in the tags in addition to the virtual address. This lets the hardware detect aliases and ambiguities in some cases. (This organization is covered in Section 6.2.6.) The discussion here, however, concentrates on the pure virtual cache: one in which only the virtual address is used.

3.3.1 Context Switch

Since each process has its own virtual address space, it is possible that two different processes will each use the same set of virtual addresses to refer to their text, data, and stack. On systems without a virtual cache, two such processes using the same virtual addresses will be able to access only their own address spaces, since the mapping of the virtual address space is changed at context switch time. The two virtual address spaces will each map to different physical pages, so neither process will be aware of the other's existence.

Ambiguities between two different processes' data occur when a virtual cache is added to the system. This happens because the processes may use the same virtual addresses to refer to different physical addresses before and after the context switch. A virtual cache is unable to distinguish between identical virtual addresses used by different processes and so may return the wrong data. Just as the example in Section 3.2.1 shows, any data the old process had cached prior to a context switch would be returned to the new process after the context switch, if the new process used a virtual address that generated the same index and tag in the cache. This would result in a cache hit, and the MMU operation that prevented such ambiguities in systems without virtual caches would never occur.

Not only does the new process receive the wrong data from the cache after the context switch, but some of the old process's data may be lost if write-back caching is used. If modified data is present in the cache before a context switch, then it could be written into the new process's address space if the line is replaced during miss processing. This corrupts the new process's address space and causes the data to be lost to the old process.

To prevent these problems from occurring, the kernel must flush everything the old process had cached (text, data, stack, etc.) from the virtual cache at context switch time. More specifically, if write-back caching is used, the kernel must validate main memory with any modified data in the cache. This modified data is part of the old process's state and thus must be saved prior to the context switch, or the data may be lost. Next, all lines in the cache must be invalidated. (As mentioned in Section 2.8, validating main memory and invalidating the line are usually performed as a single operation.) When the new process resumes its execution after the context switch, all memory references will miss in the cache, since all lines were invalidated, causing the process to fetch the correct data from its own address space.

Flushing a virtual cache on every context switch can be a time-consuming operation, especially if a large write-back cache is used. The time needed to flush the cache is proportional not only to the size of the cache, but to the number of modified lines as well, since all modified lines have to be written back to main memory. In addition to the overhead of flushing the cache itself, a side effect is that the new process will miss on all its initial memory references since the cache has just been completely invalidated. The locality of reference the process previously had will no longer be present in the cache, so the hit ratio will be low while the process reestablishes its cache locality. If context switches are too frequent, as can happen with highly interactive UNIX applications, then the benefit of having the cache in the system will be reduced because of the low hit ratio and the operating system overhead required to flush the cache. Large virtual caches are best suited for compute-bound, batch-oriented application environments where context switching is infrequent.

3.3.2 Fork

The semantics of the `fork` system call require that the child receive a complete copy of the parent's address space. If any modified data is cached in a write-back cache prior to the parent executing the `fork` system call, then this data must appear in the child's address space. This must be taken into account regardless of the type of cache being used.

Little additional cache management is needed for a virtual cache to handle the `fork` system call properly since the cache is already flushed during each context switch. This eliminates most inconsistencies between the parent's and child's data, but cache consistency during the copy operations and the effects of write-back caching must be considered.

If copy-on-write is not used by the system, then a copy of the parent's entire virtual address space must be made for the child during the fork. To do this, the kernel will typically map the physical pages the child will be using into an unused region of virtual memory in the kernel's address space, as shown in Figure 3–8.

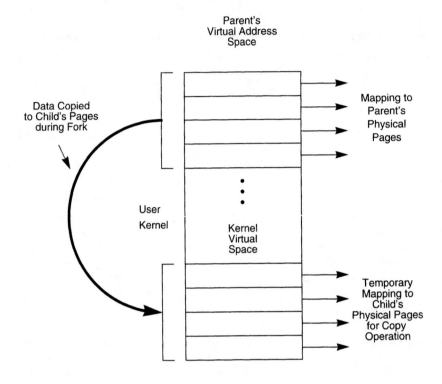

Figure 3–8: Memory mapping during address space copy for fork.

This enables the kernel to make the copy by simply referencing the child's pages from the context of the parent using a different set of virtual addresses. Data is copied in the direction of the large arrow in Figure 3–8, from the parent's user virtual addresses to the temporary kernel virtual addresses that map to the child's pages. Once the copy operation is complete, the mapping to the child's pages is removed.

Since the copy was made by using the parent's own virtual addresses as the source, it is guaranteed that any modified data that existed in the cache prior to the fork was copied to the child's address space because the addresses used as the source would have generated a hit on those cache lines. This then satisfies one of the requirements for cache consistency during a fork.

When the child begins execution, it must be ensured that main memory is up to date and that there is no stale data in the cache. If write-through caching is used, then even though the kernel virtual addresses used during the copy operation are aliases for the child's addresses, no special flushing is needed during `fork` since at least one context switch must occur before the child executes. Any data that remained in the cache tagged with the kernel virtual addresses will be eliminated when the cache is flushed at context switch time. However, if write-back caching is used, then main memory must be validated before the temporary mapping is removed so that the child's physical pages will be up to date. This must be done since the cache uses the virtual address during memory validation, and so the mapping must still be present in order for the MMU to translate the addresses.

If the cache is write-through and supports an uncached mode, it is beneficial to mark the kernel virtual addresses used during the copy as uncached. These destination addresses will only be written to once and never read again using those virtual addresses. Therefore, there is nothing to be gained by caching this data. Caching it may also cause useful data to be replaced. Note that if the cache doesn't use write-allocate, then the same effect is achieved without having to mark the pages explicitly as uncached. If the cache is write-back with write-allocate, then it may or may not be beneficial to use uncached stores for the copy. The benefits depend on the line size and the speed of main memory versus the cache. For example, if lines are short, then the overhead of reading the line on each store miss can be significant. However, if the lines are long, then the fact that consecutive stores will hit in the cache, thereby reducing the number of individual writes to main memory, may outweigh the overhead of reading the line on the first miss. Of course, if the cache lacks write-allocate, then the stores will all go to main memory.

If `fork` is implemented with copy-on-write, then no flushing is needed for write-through caches at `fork` time since no copying is done and the main memory copy of the data is always up to date. If write-back caching is used, then main memory must be validated during the `fork` operation to remove any modified data the parent may have in the cache. If modified data were left in the cache, then later write-backs of the modified lines (during line replacement or context switch) would incorrectly result in copy-on-write faults occurring. These would cause the parent to receive its own copy of the affected page, causing the modified data to be lost to the child. This is also true for caches like that of the Apollo DN-4000, which contain a writable bit. In this case, the bit could be set on a cache line prior to the `fork`. If no context switch occurs before `fork` returns to the parent, then the parent would be able to modify these lines without generating a copy-on-write fault (because a hit occurs, which means the MMU won't be used for that access). Both of these cases violate the semantics of the `fork` system call and must not be allowed to occur. Also, some architectures, such as the Intel i860 family, do not check for write permission during write-back operations. This means that lines written back after the `fork` but modified beforehand would not generate copy-on-write faults. Validating main memory during `fork` solves these problems.

When either the parent or the child later attempts to modify a page that it is sharing with copy-on-write, a copy of just that page is made by mapping a new physical page into the kernel's virtual space, similar to the example shown in Figure 3–8. The main difference is that just the one page is copied instead of the entire address space. As before, this generates an alias with the user virtual address for the page. However, in this case control could return to the user program without an intervening context switch. Therefore, the cache entries corresponding to the temporary region used for the copy must be written back to main memory (if the cache is write-back) and invalidated from the cache. Again, the use of uncached accesses for the destination of the copy prevents the alias from occurring.

Note that it is acceptable to allow what otherwise would be considered an ambiguity to occur between the parent's and the child's address space if copy-on-write sharing is used by `fork`. Since both processes are initially sharing the same physical pages immediately after the `fork`, the virtual addresses between the two processes will not be ambiguous even if a context switch is done that switches between the parent and the child, or vice versa. The kernel could then eliminate the cache flush in such circumstances. Note, however, that cache flushing would have to resume once one of the two processes modified its data, since this would end copy-on-write sharing for that page. References to that page would then be ambiguous. Few programs run for long without writing to their stack or data. Even if the child `exec`s immediately, any implementation that passes arguments on the stack would cause copy-on-write faults to occur before the `exec` could be done. So while it may seem appealing to try to eliminate the flush at context switch time in this case, it actually will save little overhead. In addition, this technique cannot be used at all if a context switch to any other process is needed.

3.3.3 Exec

The `exec` system call discards the process's current address space and replaces it with a new one for the new program the process will run. Since it is possible that the new program will reside in the same range of virtual addresses as the old program, ambiguities will result with any data the old program had cached once the new program begins execution. If ambiguities occur, the new program would receive some of the old program's data as if it were its own and it might even execute some of the old program's instructions if they were cached. To prevent this from happening, the kernel must invalidate all user data from the cache before execution of the new program begins. In the case of a write-back cache, main memory must not be validated with any modified data since the old program's address space has been discarded during the `exec` system call.

3.3.4 Exit

The address space of a process is discarded during the `exit` system call. The kernel must ensure that any cached data is also discarded so that ambiguities will not result when the next process is run. As it turns out, the last step in the processing of the `exit` system call is to perform a context switch that flushes the cache before running the next process. Therefore, a cache flush does not have to be explicitly added to the `exit` processing. However, the context switch code needs to know whether it is being invoked as part of `exit` if write-back caching is used. Normally, the context switch code must write back modified data in the cache. In the case of `exit`, however, the old address space has already been discarded and so there is no place to write back the data. Therefore, the write-back must be omitted during a context switch following an `exit` system call.

3.3.5 Brk and Sbrk

The `brk` and `sbrk` system calls are used to grow and shrink the process's bss segment. Growing the bss causes no cache problems since new virtual memory is allocated. The process could not have any stale data cached corresponding to the new virtual memory, since a fault would have occurred if it had attempted to write to a location outside of the segment. Also, the cache flush that occurs during each context switch prevents any ambiguities from arising with other processes' data that might have been in the same virtual address range.

Shrinking the bss segment is, however, a concern since the process must be prevented from accessing cached data corresponding to the region of virtual memory just released. Remember that not all implementations use the MMU for read operations that hit in the cache. So the process will still be able to read cached data from the released section of virtual memory unless the kernel explicitly invalidates this data from the cache. Note that as with `exit` and `exec`, it is incorrect to validate main memory with modified data if write-back caching is used, since that portion of the address space has been discarded.

As in all other cases, the instruction cache must be invalidated when shrinking the bss segment on systems that use separate instruction and data caches. While this may seem unnecessary since the bss is part of the program's data area, it is always possible that an interpreter has written and/or executed instructions from this area. If this happens, then those instructions could still be cached and must be invalidated. If this were not done and the bss was subsequently regrown (before the next context switch) and new instructions written into it, then the program could execute stale instructions left over from before the previous shrink operation.

3.3.6 Shared Memory and Mapped Files

The shared memory facility provides the potential for cache aliases to occur if different processes use different virtual addresses to share the same shared memory segment. No special cache management is needed, however, since the cache is already flushed at each context switch. This will automatically eliminate any aliases in shared memory, since the cache will have been flushed by the time the other process sharing memory is run.

Consider though what happens if a single process attaches a shared memory segment at different addresses within its own address space. This means that it can reference any of the aliases without an intervening context switch and cache flush, causing the problems described at the end of Section 3.2.2. The operating system must prevent these alias problems from occurring. It could set up the shared memory segment so that it was uncached, or it could simply disallow any attempts to attach the same shared memory segment to a process's address space more than once. Another alternative is possible if the cache is direct mapped and uses write-allocate. In this case, the operating system can allow the shared memory to be attached multiple times within a process's address if the starting addresses of each attachment all index the same cache line. As explained in Section 3.2.2, each reference to one of the aliases will force any previously cached alias to be replaced, thereby eliminating the alias problem. Restricting the attach addresses of the shared memory segment in this case is a better alternative than disallowing any attempt to attach the same shared memory multiple times within the same process. It also results in better performance than going to uncached accesses. Both the Sun and Apollo systems previously mentioned use this approach. As before, this solution does not work if the cache has two or more lines per set or does not use write-allocate.

An additional solution is possible by marking the pages from only one of the aliases to be valid at a time. This way, a page fault occurs when the program tries to access the other alias. At this point, the kernel can validate main memory, invalidate the cache for the previously used alias, and mark the pages from that alias to be invalid. The pages for the newly referenced alias can then be marked valid, allowing the process access to them. This procedure repeats each time the process accesses a different alias. The page fault that occurs each time a different alias is accessed allows the kernel to maintain cache consistency transparently, at the price of additional kernel overhead.

Stale data could remain in the cache if a process were to detach a shared memory region from its address space. This is similar to what happens when a shrinking sbrk system call is done. The cached data corresponding to the virtual memory that was occupied by the shared memory region must be invalidated from the cache. If the shared memory segment is still in use by other processes and write-back caching is used, then the main memory should first be validated. This step can be omitted if the shared memory segment is about to be destroyed.

3.3.7 I/O

Since the kernel runs within the process's address space during read and write system calls, I/O to buffered files will function correctly on a system with virtual caches. This is because the kernel uses the same virtual addresses to refer to the data being copied between the user and kernel buffers as the user program does. Therefore, no aliases or ambiguities occur.

I/O devices are typically connected directly to main memory and transfer data using DMA operations with physical addresses. Expanding Figure 3–1 to include I/O devices as shown in Figure 3–9, it can be seen that DMA operations will access main memory without going through the cache.

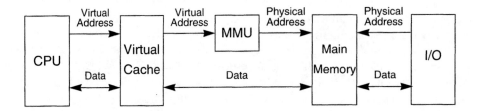

Figure 3–9: I/O access to main memory.

Therefore, unbuffered I/O generates a problem similar to aliasing, since the I/O subsystem is referencing data through DMA with a different address (a physical address instead of the virtual address) than the CPU uses when referencing the same data through the cache. DMA operations do not check the cache for hits since I/O devices are not connected to it and because DMA uses physical addresses (which cannot be used to index a virtual cache). Even the few systems that are capable of virtual DMA, where the I/O subsystem is given a virtual address instead of a physical one, will usually still choose to bypass the cache and go directly to main memory; otherwise, the DMA operations will compete with the CPU for access to the cache.

If a user process does an unbuffered `write` to a device and write-back caching is used, modified data corresponding to the I/O buffer may still be in the cache, meaning the data in main memory is stale. When the DMA occurs from main memory, it will get the stale data. To prevent this from happening, the kernel must validate main memory with modified data in the cache corresponding to the I/O buffer before the DMA operation starts.

Likewise, data corresponding to the I/O buffer could be cached prior to an unbuffered `read`. If the DMA operation were allowed to occur in such a case, the new data from the device would be placed in main memory and the cache would be unaffected. Nothing would prevent the user process from referencing the stale cached data. This would continue until the stale data was removed from the cache during miss processing. To prevent stale cache data from being used, the cache must be flushed (invalidated) of any data corresponding to the I/O buffer about to be read into via DMA. There would be no point in validating main memory with any modified data in the cache at this point, since it would be overwritten by the DMA.

It's possible to eliminate the explicit cache flushing for unbuffered I/O operations by combining it with the flushing done during context switch. The `read` and `write` system calls cause the process to be blocked until the I/O completes. This results in a context switch as soon as the I/O is initiated. Note that the flushing needed at context switch time correctly handles the unbuffered I/O case: main memory is validated for write-back caches, and the cache is invalidated. So no extra flushing is needed to maintain data consistency for I/O operations as long as the context switch flushing is performed *before* the DMA operation actually begins. For most systems, this simply means that the kernel performs the context switch flushing prior to initiating the I/O operation and then skips the flushing when the context switch actually occurs. This technique cannot be used in systems that support *asynchronous I/O*. This facility allows I/O to be done in parallel with process execution. Since the process is not necessarily blocked while the DMA is occurring, the context switch time flushing cannot be relied upon, and explicit flushing must be done.

The preceding discussion assumes that the virtual address of the raw (unbuffered) I/O buffer corresponds to a cache line boundary and that the buffer is a multiple of the cache line size. This is the simple case, as no other process data is contained within the cache lines occupied by the buffer. However, this need not be true. It is possible that other data will be adjacent to, and sharing cache lines with, the buffer. As Figure 3–10 illustrates, consider the following portion of a process's virtual address space (viewed as a linear array):

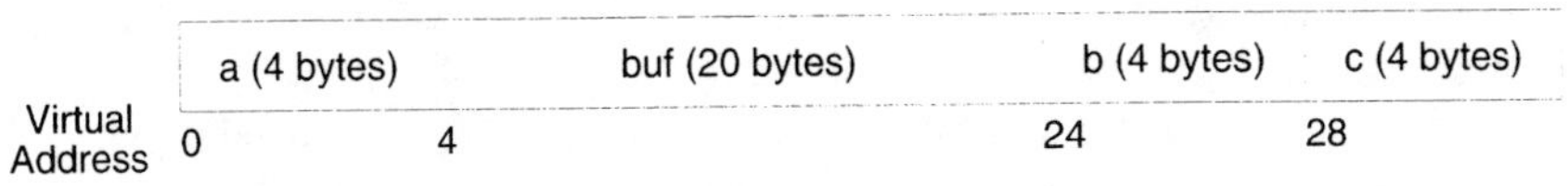

Figure 3–10: Virtual address space showing four variables.

This figure shows four variables beginning at virtual address 0: a, buf, b, and c. The variables a, b, and c are each four bytes long while buf is 20 bytes. If we now look at how these variables will appear in a cache with 16-byte lines (Figure 3–11), we see that buf spans two cache lines and shares the beginning and ending of the lines with a, b, and c (assume that virtual address 0 indexes cache line 0):

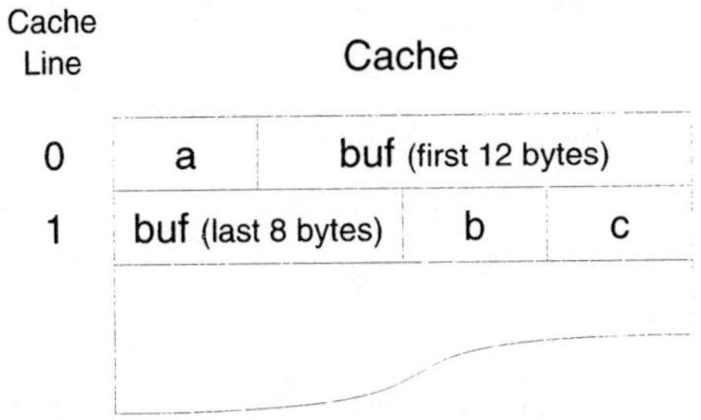

Figure 3–11: Layout in cache with 16-byte lines.

Now if the process does a raw `read` into `buf`, the contents of `buf` must be invalidated. The kernel cannot simply invalidate all lines occupied by `buf`, since this would also invalidate `a`, `b`, and `c`. If write-back caching were used, this could cause modified versions of these variables to be lost, causing the stale main memory versions to be used in future references. So when write-back caching is used, the kernel must first validate main memory with the contents of the first and last cache lines from I/O buffers that do not completely fill the cache lines, to be sure that adjacent variables are not affected. This need not be a concern if the context switch optimization previously discussed is used, but it is important to understand nonetheless.

A more complex problem arises if the I/O buffer pictured in Figure 3–10 lies within a shared memory region and write-back caching is used. (This can also occur if asynchronous I/O is used.) In this case, it is possible for another process sharing the same memory region to be accessing the variables surrounding the buffer (`a`, `b`, and `c`) at the same time that the DMA is occurring to `buf`. If a `read` into `buf` has been started by one process sharing memory and a second process sharing the memory is run, this second process could reference the variable `a`, for example, and cause the full cache line containing both `a` and the first 12 bytes of `buf` to be brought into the cache *before* the DMA operation begins. This means that the old contents of the first 12 bytes of `buf` would be cached. If the DMA were now to occur, it will replace the copy of `buf` in memory with the new data from the `read`. This will have no effect on the contents of the cache, which will continue to hold the old data from the beginning of the buffer. Now if the process modifies its cached version of `a`, the new data in the first 12 bytes of the buffer in memory will be overwritten with the old data from the cache when the full line is written back to memory, corrupting the memory copy of `buf`. Observe that this situation is highly dependent on the relative timing of the DMA operation and the cache accesses/write-backs of other processes sharing the same memory region. If the DMA occurs before another process can access the shared memory, then the problem will never occur.

The kernel must never allow such a data corruption problem to occur. The simplest solution to this problem is for the kernel to detect that the buffer is not evenly cache-line aligned (at either the beginning or the ending of the buffer, or both). In these cases, the kernel can allocate an alternative buffer in kernel memory where the DMA can be safely performed. When the DMA is complete, the kernel can copy the data back to the shared memory region without interference from other processes. While adding such a copy operation may seem to defeat the purpose of unbuffered I/O, it is better than risking corrupted data.

The problems described in this section must be taken into consideration when the kernel does its internal I/O operations. This includes both file I/O and I/O done during paging and swapping. In addition, device drivers must be aware of the existence of a cache in the system. An I/O device's control and status registers are typically *memory mapped*, meaning that they appear in the physical address space and can be referenced by normal load and store operations. These loads and stores must be done using uncached references so that stale status information is not read from the cache instead of from the device. Likewise, when a command is written to a control register, it must not be cached and held in a write-back cache, or else the device will not receive the command until the line is replaced. If the cache lacks an uncached mode, then the device driver will have to invalidate the cache explicitly after each load from a device register and validate main memory in the case of a store.

3.3.8 User–Kernel Data Ambiguities

It is important to prevent any ambiguities from occurring between kernel and user data. The cache is used both during kernel- and user-mode execution, and so it must be guaranteed both that any cached kernel data is inaccessible to users and that any cached user data is never mistaken as kernel data. This is crucial to ensuring the integrity and security of the system.

A virtual cache is particularly susceptible to such integrity problems since most systems do not use the MMU to validate accesses that hit in the cache. This means that if cached kernel data is left in the cache when a system call returns to user mode, it would be possible for the user to read this data by referring to the corresponding kernel address. To prevent cached kernel data from being accessed by the user process, the cache must be flushed (validating main memory if write-back caching is used and then invalidating the data in the cache) prior to returning to user mode after a system call or interrupt. This will become a very expensive operation if the cache is large, since UNIX programs tend to execute system calls frequently. Fortunately, cached user data won't be mistaken for kernel data upon entry to a system call if the process address space is divided between the user and the kernel as shown in Figure 1–2. This is because the kernel will use different virtual addresses to access its own data and so the cache will never return a hit, even if user data happened to be cached in the indexed line.

To get around the performance penalty of having to flush the cache on every return to user mode, some implementations, such as the Apollo DN-4000, add a bit to the tags to indicate if the data was fetched while in user or kernel mode. In order for a hit to occur on the line in user mode, the bit must indicate that the line contains user data. If the bit indicates kernel data, a normal miss occurs. This prevents the user from accessing cached kernel data and is similar in concept to the writable bit discussed on page 61. The user–kernel bit is ignored during kernel-mode cache accesses so that the kernel can access user data that might be in the cache (such data might be the system call parameters, for instance). Note that when the kernel copies data into user space (such as when returning the results of a system call), the data will be tagged as kernel data. This will prevent the user process from accessing it, so the range of addresses copied to must be flushed from the cache (main memory validated and cache invalidated). Even so, this technique will greatly reduce the amount of cache flushing that needs to occur by eliminating the cache flush described above, but it only works if write-through caching is used, unless additional hardware support is added.

Write-back caching cannot be used with this technique alone since, upon return to user mode, modified kernel data left in the cache could not be written back to main memory during line replacement caused by a cache miss in user mode. Writing back such a cache line would require that the user process be capable of translating the kernel virtual address and writing to the kernel's physical pages. Such a capability would violate the security of the system, since the user process could then write to any kernel address at will. To get around this problem, the Intel i860 does not check user–kernel access permissions during write-back operations from the cache. It does, however, validate access permissions on all cache accesses from the CPU, not just misses as the Apollo system does. The result is that user processes cannot access cached kernel data (nor modify it), but they can write back kernel data during line replacement. This approach maintains system security and eliminates the need for explicit cache flushing to prevent user–kernel ambiguities. Write-back caches that lack these capabilities must explicitly flush the data.

3.4 Summary

Virtual caches offer high-speed cache access by not requiring an MMU operation for references that hit in the cache, but they do require frequent flushing by the operating system. Ambiguities occur in the cache if the same virtual address is used to refer to different physical locations at different points in time. Aliases occur when multiple virtual addresses are used to reference the same physical location. The operating system must prevent ambiguities and aliases from occurring to make the presence of the cache transparent to user programs, which is essential for program portability. To do this, the cache must be flushed on context switch, `exec`, `exit`, shrinking `sbrk` operations, raw I/O operations, and possibly during transitions between user and kernel mode. Frequent flushing of large virtual caches is time consuming and can lead to poor system performance. In addition to the overhead of the flush operation, there is the additional disadvantage that flushing the cache causes the process's locality of reference to be discarded. Each time a process is resumed after a context switch, and potentially after each system call, the process will miss on all memory references, forcing an MMU translation and main memory access for each reference. If a separate instruction and data cache are used, then both the instruction and data cache must be invalidated whenever any of the situations just mentioned warrants an invalidation.

Two common modifications can be made to the virtual cache to reduce the amount of flushing that must take place. These are explored in the next two chapters.

3.5 Exercises

3.1   Consider a direct mapped, write-back virtual cache with 16,384 lines. Each line contains 16 bytes of data. The hashing algorithm uses bits <17..4> of the 32-bit virtual address to select the line. Bits <31..18> are stored in the tag for each line.

If a modified line is replaced during a miss operation, how does the cache determine the full 32-bit virtual address of the data being replaced if only the high-order 14 bits are stored in the tag?

3.2 Referring to the alias example in Section 3.2.2 (pages 64 - 65), complete the following exercises using the same cache organization and address space mapping. Add an additional address mapping where virtual address 0x92000 is mapped to physical address 0x1000. Assume that no flushing is done by either the application or the operating system and that no context switches are done. For each exercise, draw a small picture like that in Figure 3–6 showing the cache contents as they would appear after the listed operations are done. Also, indicate whether the cache contents are consistent with main memory. Assume the cache is initially empty at the start of each set of operations and that the main memory address 0x3000 contains 1234 and 0x1000 contains 5678. Use write-through and write-back caching as indicated. As usual, write-back caching uses write-allocate, and write-through does not.

a. Use write-through caching. The application reads 0x2000, writes 9876 to 0x2000, and reads 0x4000.

b. Use write-back caching. The application reads 0x2000, writes 9876 to 0x2000, and reads 0x4000.

c. Use write-back caching. The application reads 0x2000, writes 9876 to 0x2000, reads 0x92000, and reads 0x4000.

d. Use write-through caching. The application reads 0x4000, writes 9876 to 0x2000, reads 0x4000, and writes the result to 0x2000.

3.3 Does it matter whether the cache in the alias situation described on page 66, where virtual addresses 0x2000 and 0x12000 are mapped to the same address, uses write-through or write-back caching? Is it guaranteed that the process will always get the correct data? Explain.

3.4 The processing needed for the exec system call may require several I/O operations, each of which would require a context switch while the kernel waits for the I/O to complete. Describe what optimizations could be made in order to eliminate the need to explicitly flush the cache during the exec system call.

3.5 Do aliases or ambiguities occur between two or more threads sharing an address space?

3.6   A system uses a 64K direct mapped virtual cache with 16 bytes per line. If each
        of the following pairs of virtual addresses represents an alias to the same shared
        memory segment within an address space, which of the pairs require the kernel to
        take the special actions described in Section 3.3.6 in order to maintain consisten-
        cy? Explain.

        a.   0x1000 and 0x10000

        b.   0x1100 and 0x11100

        c.   0x52a40 and 0x53a40

        d.   0x8ffe90 and 0xfafe90

        e.   0x123450 and 0x1234560

3.7   Repeat the previous exercise using a fully associative cache instead.

3.8   In Section 3.3.8, a technique where a user–kernel mode bit is added to the tags to
        identify whether the data was fetched in user or kernel mode was presented. If the
        32-bit virtual address space is divided between the user and the kernel such that
        all kernel addresses have the high-order bit set and all user addresses have that bit
        clear, then suggest an alternate technique to resolve the ambiguities that does not
        require additional bits in the tags. Discuss how it would work.

3.9   Assume the kernel supports a message-passing facility where one process can
        pass an arbitrary length message to another. This is implemented by having the
        kernel copy the data into a kernel buffer when the message is sent. It is held in the
        buffer until the other process asks to receive the message, at which point it is cop-
        ied into the destination process's address space. If the system uses a virtual cache,
        what cache flushing, if any, must occur? Explain.

3.10   As explained in Section 1.3, the kernel dynamically allocates more stack as need-
        ed. What cache flushing, if any, must occur when this happens if the system uses
        a virtual cache? Explain.

3.11   What must be done to the cache when the kernel decides to swap out pages from
        a process's address space? Explain.

3.12   Referring back to Figures 3–3 and 3–4, assume a process has a page at virtual ad-
        dress 0x1000 in its address space initially mapped to physical address 0x5000.
        The kernel then swaps this page out. When the process faults on the page and the

kernel swaps it back in, the page is loaded into physical address `0x0000`, and the kernel changes the process's mapping to point to this new location. Does this represent an ambiguity in a system using a virtual cache? Must flushing occur?

3.13   Does cache size influence any of the situations described in this chapter where the kernel must flush a virtual cache to maintain consistency? How does it affect performance?

3.14   Most systems with virtual caches allow certain pages to be marked as uncached. This prevents data from being cached after a miss, forcing future references to miss as well. Uncached access is usually specified in the page tables. If this is the case, what happens if a page in main memory that was marked as cacheable is changed to be uncached? (Assume no context switches occur.) Should the cache be flushed at this point? Why?

3.6 Further Reading

[1]   Chao, C., Mackey, M., and Sears, B., "MACH on Virtually Addressed Cache Architectures," *Proceedings of the USENIX MACH Workshop*, 1990.

[2]   Cheng, R., "Virtual Address Cache in UNIX," *Proceedings of the Summer Usenix Conference*, June 1987, pp. 217–24.

[3]   Frink, C.R., and Roy, P.J., "The Cache Architecture of the Apollo DN4000," *Proceedings of the Spring COMPCON*, March 1988, pp. 300–2.

[4]   Frink, C.R., and Roy, P.J., "A Virtual Cache-Based Workstation Architecture," *Proceedings of the 2nd International Conference on Computer Workstations*, March 1988.

[5]   Goodman, J.R., "Coherency for Multiprocessor Virtual Address Caches," *Second International Conference on Architectural Support for Programming Languages and Operating Systems*, October 1987, pp. 72–81.

[6]   Inouye, J., Konuru, R., Walpole, J., and Sears, B., "The Effects of Virtually Addressed Caches on Virtual Memory Design and Performance," *Operating Systems Review*, Vol. 26, No. 4, October 1992, pp. 14–29.

[7]   Mogul, J.C., and Borg, A., "The Effect of Context Switches on Cache Performance," *Computer Architecture News*, Vol. 19, No. 2, April 1991, pp. 75–84.

4

Virtual Caches with Keys

This chapter presents a modification to the virtual cache implementation presented in Chapter 3. The tag field of each cache line is augmented to contain a process key that uniquely identifies a cache line as belonging to a particular process. The goals are to reduce the amount of flushing that must take place and to retain a process's locality of reference across context switches. In addition to instruction and data caches, this cache architecture is used in MMUs as well. The organization and effects of this type of cache on the UNIX kernel are explored in this chapter.

4.1 The Operation of a Virtual Cache with Keys

One way system designers have found to mitigate the flushing overhead of virtual caches is to add a *process key* to the tags of each line. Ideally each process is assigned a unique key so that the combination of the process's virtual address and key forms a unique identifier for a particular piece of data. The goal of using the keys is to prevent ambiguities from occurring between identical virtual addresses in different processes. This way, the cache does not have to be flushed as frequently as a pure virtual cache. The organization of such a cache is similar to that of the virtual cache in the previous chapter, with the addition of a special hardware register to hold the currently executing process's key, and additional bits in each tag to hold the key associated with the line (see Figure 4–1).

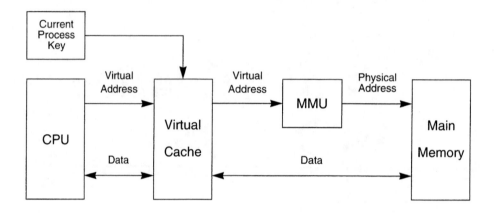

Figure 4–1: Organization of a virtual cache with keys.

The cache is still indexed with the virtual address but, for a hit to occur, not only must the virtual address match, but the current process key register must also match the key stored in the tag. The key of the currently executing process is loaded into this register by the operating system at context switch time. (The register may be located either in the CPU or in the cache controller.) This means that two different processes using the same range of virtual addresses no longer have the danger of referencing each other's data in the cache, as long as each process is given a unique key.

The process key itself is simply an integer value that is associated with each process. Some implementations refer to the key as a *task id* or *address space id* instead, but the meaning is the same. The process key should not be confused with the UNIX system process ID number or *pid*, which is a separate type of process identifier.

The actual value of the process key itself is unimportant. The only need is that it be unique for each process. This way the virtual addresses used by different processes will never be ambiguous. Unfortunately, the number of unique keys available is usually small, with some implementations having as few as three bits in the tags to store the key. If there are more processes in the system than there are keys, then the keys must be shared between multiple processes. If more than one process uses the same key, then the cache will be unable to distinguish between the cached data of those processes and ambiguities will again result. The operating system will have to flush the cache in these cases to prevent the ambiguities from occurring. This is discussed in more detail in Section 4.2.1.

Systems that have used this cache organization in the past are the Apollo DN4000 and Sun 3/200. Both systems were available in the late 1980s. The Apollo system used a combined 8K direct mapped instruction and data cache. The line size was 4 bytes and it used write-through with write-allocate. The Sun system's cache was 64K with 16-byte lines. It was direct mapped, combined instructions and data, and used write-back (with write-allocate). Both systems used three bits for the key, which allowed for eight different address spaces to be cached simultaneously.

4.2 Managing a Virtual Cache with Keys

Since the cache is still being indexed with the virtual address, aliases can occur. Ambiguities can also occur if more than one process uses the same key. The following sections detail the situations in which the kernel must flush the cache to prevent ambiguities and aliases from occurring. As with virtual caches, systems that use separate instruction and data caches must invalidate the instruction whenever the data cache needs invalidation.

4.2.1 Context Switch

There is normally no need to flush the cache at context switch if write-through caching is used, because the use of keys eliminates ambiguities in the cache between the same virtual addresses in different processes. As long as there are enough keys so that a unique key can be assigned to each process, the kernel must simply change the current process key register in the hardware to that of the key of the new process selected for execution. Note that since the cache has not been flushed, the old process's locality of reference will be left in the cache. It is therefore possible that its data will still be present when it is next chosen for execution. This is an important performance benefit since it means that a process may not miss as much as it would on systems using a pure virtual cache. This benefit can be lost to some degree if processes tend to use the same range of virtual addresses, since the cache index is generated from the virtual address. Processes using common virtual addresses will index the same cache lines. The keys will prevent ambiguities from occurring, but the lines loaded by previous processes will still be replaced with data from the currently executing process, thereby losing the previous process's locality of reference. This is particularly true for small direct mapped caches. (Techniques that attempt to preserve locality of reference across context switches are presented in Section 7.2.2.)

A difficulty with using keys arises when there are not enough keys for all processes in the system. This means that keys will have to be shared among multiple processes by reassigning a key from one process to another. When a reassignment is made, all entries in the cache tagged with the affected key must be flushed (main memory validated in the case of a write-back cache, and the cache lines invalidated). If this is not done, then ambiguities will occur between the virtual addresses of the process that previously used the key and the addresses of the new process.

It is important for the operating system to make good choices when reassigning the keys lest it end up in a position where it is reassigning a key on every context switch. Such a situation would eliminate the benefit of having keys, since the cache would be flushed as often as a pure virtual cache.

Most implementations of this cache organization prefer to use the write-through policy, as the Apollo system did. If write-back caching were used, then a process's modified data would be left in the cache after a context switch was made to the next process. If one of those modified lines was selected for replacement during miss processing, then the system would not know where to store the modified line since the old process's address space mapping has been replaced by that of the new process. The cache contains only the old process's virtual address of the data, but the MMU has been loaded with the address space mapping of the new process during the context switch, and so it cannot translate the old process's address. Using write-through caching eliminates this problem since no modified data is ever left in the cache.

To get around this problem, Sun used an MMU that was capable of storing the mappings associated with each process key simultaneously. Then, when a line needed to be written back, the cache passed both the virtual address and the key to the MMU, which used the key to determine how to translate the address. This is a more complex implementation, since it requires the MMU to manage multiple address space mappings at once, but it has the advantage that write-back caching can be used to help reduce the number of accesses to main memory.

If such hardware is not used, the only other alternative is to validate main memory with all modified data in the cache at context switch time. This ensures that no write-backs of a previous process's data will occur while another is running.

4.2.2 Fork

When a new process is created, it is appropriate to allocate a new process key to it so that its virtual addresses will not be ambiguous with those of the parent or any other process. (It is theoretically possible to share the same key between the parent and child in certain instances. See Exercises 4.6 and 4.8.) The kernel must ensure that modified data cached by the parent prior to the `fork` appears in the child's address space (if write-back caching is used) and that consistency is maintained during operations that copy all or a part of the address space.

Recall from Section 3.3.2 that if copy-on-write is not used with a pure virtual write-through cache, then there is no need to flush the kernel virtual addresses used during the address space copy to the child, since at least one context switch would occur before the child runs, eliminating the alias made during the copy (see Figure 3–8). Since a virtual cache with keys is not always flushed at context switch time, the alias would remain in the cache unless these entries are flushed (main memory validated if write-back caching is used, and the cache invalidated). As before, if write-back caching is used, then the child's physical pages would contain stale data corresponding to the lines that had not yet been written back to main memory. If it were to run, it could fetch this stale data since it would not generate a hit on the lines tagged with the kernel virtual addresses. Write-through caching or an explicit cache flush to validate main memory eliminates this problem. As before, the use of uncached references for the destination of the copy eliminates the alias and the need to flush the cache.

If copy-on-write is used in conjunction with a write-back cache, then main memory must be validated at `fork` time as described in Chapter 3. This prevents write-back operations due to line replacement from triggering copy-on-write faults.

It is interesting to see the behavior of cache operations while copy-on-write sharing occurs between the parent and child. Assume only two processes are running in the system, the parent and the child, and assume that they are sharing at least one page with copy-on-write. The parent process has been assigned key 1 and the child uses key 2. The cache is direct mapped and uses the write-through policy. Assume that virtual address $0x100000$ is within one of the shared pages, and that the cache hashing algorithm hashes this address to line $0x10$ of the cache. Assume the data at location $0x100000$ is 1011970. If the parent now runs and reads virtual address $0x100000$, cache line $0x10$ will be loaded with the data and tagged with that address and key 1 as shown in Figure 4–2 (as before, the entire address is shown in the tags for clarity):

If a context switch from the parent to the child is now done, the current process key will be changed to 2. If the child reads the same address, even though the address portion of the tag matches and the data portion of the line contains the correct data (since both processes

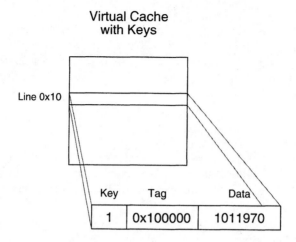

Figure 4–2: Cache contents after parent reads from address `0x100000`.

are sharing the same page), a miss will occur since the line is tagged with the wrong key. The miss causes the line to be replaced, which means the data from location `0x100000` must again be read. Line `0x10` is then replaced with the contents shown in Figure 4–3.

Key	Tag	Data
2	0x100000	1011970

Figure 4–3: Contents of line `0x10` after child reads from address `0x100000`.

Note that everything is the same except for the key (now 2 instead of 1). The mismatch on the key caused the cache to reread the data needlessly from main memory. So even though the same physical pages are being shared by the two processes, the data in the cache is not shared since each process accesses the cache with a different key. The correct data is always returned, but the cache has no way of knowing that the data should be shared. This is one of the disadvantages of using keys in a cache.

These effects are different if there are two or more lines per set in the cache. With such a cache, both the parent and the child would always index the same set when using the same virtual address. But since there is more than one line in the set, both processes could cache the same data in different lines, each tagged with a different key. Repeating this example with a two-way set associative cache, virtual address `0x100000` will still generate an index of `0x10`, but this will now be an index to a set of two lines. The contents of the set after the parent reads `0x100000` would then be as appears in Figure 4–4 (assume the second line of the set contains no data at present, indicated by "-" in all columns).

	Key	Tag	Data
Set 0x10	1	0x100000	1011970
	-	-	-

Figure 4–4: Contents of set `0x10` after parent reads from address `0x100000`.

If the child were to run now and to read virtual address `0x100000`, it would miss in the cache as before (since the key on the first line of the set does not match the child's). But with a two-way set associative cache, the replacement algorithm would choose the second line of the set to be replaced, since it is better to replace a vacant line than one containing valid data. The miss would be completed by reading the value from main memory and loading the cache as shown in Figure 4–5.

	Key	Tag	Data
Set 0x10	1	0x100000	1011970
	2	0x100000	1011970

Figure 4–5: Contents of set `0x10` after the child reads from location `0x100000`.

As with a direct mapped cache, the data had to be reread from main memory even though the physical pages are being shared. While this situation may look similar to an alias, it won't cause any consistency problems since neither process can access the other's data while it is in the cache (because the keys don't match). As soon as either process attempts to modify the page, copy-on-write sharing will end and each will have its own copy of the page.

4.2.3 Exec

It must be ensured that any cached entries corresponding to the old address space are invalidated from the cache before returning to user mode after an `exec` system call. A unique key must also be chosen for the new address space. The most straightforward implementation is to reuse the same process key for the new address space set up by `exec`. This way the process keys are associated with the process and not the program. This makes sense since `exec` discards the old program's address space. Therefore none of the cache lines tagged with the key will be needed any longer. This also saves the time it would otherwise take to find another unused key.

Since the same key will be used for the new address space, `exec` must invalidate all entries in the cache tagged with that key. This makes sure no ambiguities will be generated between the old and new address spaces.

4.2.4 Exit

With the pure virtual cache presented in the last chapter, it was not necessary to invalidate the cache at `exit` time, since the cache is always flushed during the context switch that will occur as the last step of an `exit`. Since a virtual cache with keys is not normally flushed at context switch time, cached data (all entries tagged with the process's key) from the exiting process's address space must be invalidated at `exit` time. This is necessary so that the key is available for reuse by a new process in the future.

An alternate approach would be to postpone the cache flush until the key is reallocated to a new process. There would be no danger of hitting on any of the terminated process's data that might have been left in the cache since all other processes use different keys. The stale entries only need to be invalidated when the key they're tagged with is reused by another process.

4.2.5 Brk and Sbrk

The cache management techniques needed to handle the `brk` and `sbrk` system calls for a virtual cache with keys are the same as those for a pure virtual cache (see Section 3.3.5).

4.2.6 Shared Memory and Mapped Files

A pure virtual cache relies on the fact that a cache flush is done during each context switch, which prevents aliases from occurring between different processes using the same shared memory region at different virtual addresses. This is not the case for a virtual cache with keys. The situation is further complicated by the fact that each process is using a different key. Maintaining cache consistency for shared memory and mapped files in a virtual cache with keys is therefore more complex than for a pure virtual cache. The ensuing discussion will first focus on direct mapped caches, since it is frequently possible to avoid explicit flushing to maintain consistency with this cache organization. Caches with two or more lines per set will be considered later. (The following discussion applies to both shared memory and mapped files.)

If all processes attach a shared memory region at the same virtual address in each process and direct mapped caching is used, then no aliases will occur. Here the effects are the same as in the first example in Section 4.2.2 (Figures 4–2 and 4–3), where each process forces any cached data belonging to others to be replaced, since they will all index the same line. Consistency is maintained even if write-back caching is used, as long as the cache uses write-allocate. In this case, a modified line from a shared page left in the cache by one process will be written back to main memory as part of miss processing for another. To see how this works, assume two processes both have a shared memory region attached at 0x100000, and that the processes have been assigned keys 1 and 2. Referring to Figure 4–6, assume the following modified line is held in the cache (the "M" in the "mod" column represents the modified bit for the line):

Key	Mod	Tag	Data
1	M	0x100000	1011970

Figure 4–6: Modified data from a shared memory region.

If the second process were to run and reference this address, it would miss (since the key doesn't match). The line would be written back to main memory and then replaced by reading from this same address, which would retrieve the proper value. The data is loaded into the cache and tagged with the current process's key (see Figure 4–7).

Key	Mod	Tag	Data
2	-	0x100000	1011970

Figure 4–7: Line contents after miss processing.

If write-allocate is not used, then inconsistencies are possible (similar to those explained on page 66). If the cache line contents are initially as shown in Figure 4–6, and the process using key 2 does a store to 0x100000, it will miss and store the data directly to memory. The data tagged with key 1, which is now stale, would not be affected, causing the process using key 1 to read the wrong data from the cache when it runs. This situation can be prevented by validating main memory during context switch when shared memory is used.

Now consider the case where two processes attach the same shared memory region to different virtual addresses in their address spaces. This would make it is possible for the two processes to index different lines in the cache, causing an alias problem to occur. This is similar to the example presented in Section 3.2.2, except that now the virtual addresses are coming from two different virtual address spaces instead of just one. The same end result occurs, namely that each process will end up caching data from the shared memory region in different locations of the cache, causing unpredictable results to occur.

There are several alternatives to prevent these aliases from occurring in the case of a direct mapped cache. One possibility is that the kernel could flush the region from the cache during context switch (validating main memory and invalidating the cache). This is not desirable since it ensures the process will always miss when referencing the shared memory after each switch, although it does allow different processes to attach the same shared memory region at any arbitrary page boundary. Alternatively, the kernel could choose to make the shared memory region uncached. Using uncached accesses is the least desirable method from a performance standpoint, since all references will always miss. Fortunately, there is another solution that works well in many cases.

If direct mapped caching is used, then the kernel could choose the restricted address technique. (This is similar to the technique presented in Section 3.3.6, where there were two aliases within one process's address space.) This would mean restricting the shared memory attach addresses so that all processes sharing the same region use addresses that index the same cache lines when referencing the same data. As far as the cache is concerned, the effect of this is just as if all processes had attached at the same address. Both the Sun and Apollo systems used this approach. For the reasons stated in the previous example, this will only work for caches with write-allocate.

To illustrate this, Figure 4–8 shows the logical representation of two different processes sharing a common physical page at different virtual addresses and how they map onto the cache. The cache is direct mapped with 1024 16-byte lines. Bits <13..4> of the virtual address are used to index the cache. Process A has the shared page mapped at address 0x10300 within its address space while Process B maps it at 0x40300. Both of these addresses hash to the same line index in the cache: 0x030. The shaded area in the figure represents the first 16 bytes of the shared page. Both processes will use the same cache line when they reference the page even though they are using different virtual addresses and different process keys.

Since each process is using its own key, it will not generate a hit on the shared data cached by the other process, but will instead cause the line to be replaced just as if it had been explicitly flushed. If the line had been modified by a previous process, then it will be written to main memory and reread by the current process and tagged with its key. This conveniently eliminates the need for an explicit flush, but again shows one of the main disadvantages of using keys in the cache: shared data cannot be shared while it is in the cache; it must be reread from main memory each time it is cache-resident but tagged with the wrong key. This will occur for all lines in the shared page. Note that this is still superior to using

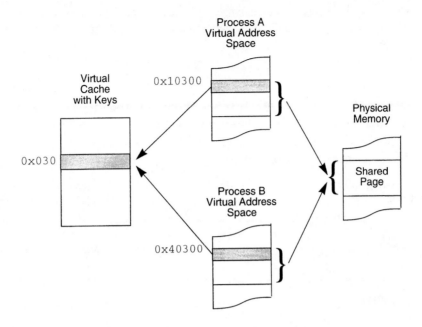

Figure 4–8: Shared memory address restriction example.

uncached accesses where all references to the shared memory region will always require a main memory access. As discussed previously, this technique works only if the cache uses write-allocate.

If the cache uses a modulo hashing algorithm (as defined in Section 2.3.1), then the only rule that the kernel must enforce on the processes sharing a region of memory is that the difference between the starting addresses of the shared memory region in all processes must all be an integer multiple of the cache size. This will cause the addresses used by each process to index the same cache line and replace any entries cached by the other processes. The use of restricted addresses prevents the data from the shared region from being loaded into more than one location in the cache and is guaranteed to prevent aliases from occurring.

These techniques work only for direct mapped caches. If the cache has two or more lines per set, then it could simultaneously cache shared data from two or more processes, even if they use the same virtual addresses. Unlike the example shown in Figure 4–5, this generates an alias since either line can be independently modified, possibly leading to inconsistent data. To prevent this from occurring, the kernel must flush the shared data from the cache at context switch time (validate main memory and invalidate the cache lines), or simply not cache the data. Again, the disadvantage of not being able to share data while it's in the cache is apparent.

4.2.7 I/O

The techniques the kernel must use to ensure consistency of I/O operations in relation to a virtual cache with keys are the same as those for a pure virtual cache (see Section 3.3.7).

4.2.8 User–Kernel Data Ambiguities

As discussed in Section 3.3.8, the Apollo system used a mode bit in the tags to differentiate cached user and kernel data. This allowed the kernel to eliminate the cache flush that otherwise had to occur to prevent the user from accessing cached kernel data. An analogous method used by Sun was simply to use a unique key when running in kernel mode (e.g., reserve key 0 for the kernel). This will cause all the kernel's cached data to be inaccessible to user processes as long as no one except the kernel uses the key. To implement this, the current process key register is changed on entry to kernel mode and restored to the user process key upon exit.

A distinct advantage of this approach is that cached kernel data will be accessible to all processes executing in the kernel. Kernel data is always shared among all the processes since there is logically only one kernel and one kernel address space in the Sun system. By using the same key for all kernel mode execution, kernel references made while executing within one process context will successfully hit on data cached while the kernel was executing in another. A miss will occur in the Apollo system in this case.

A disadvantage of using a separate key for the kernel is that hits cannot occur on cached user data when the kernel copies data to or from the user address space. This is the same as the problem with user shared memory (Section 4.2.6) and can be handled in the same manner: no flushing is needed if direct mapped caching is used; flushing is required if two-way or greater set associativity is used, or if the cache lacks write-allocate. Note that while the Apollo approach of using a user/kernel mode bit causes data copied out to the user's address space to be tagged with the correct key since the kernel runs with the same key as the user, a miss will still occur when the user process accesses that data. This will happen because the data will be tagged as kernel data. Since the cache is write-through and employs write-allocate, the correct data will automatically be returned in this case.

4.3 Virtual Cache Usage in MMUs

Caches are not limited to holding program instructions and data. A special-purpose cache, called either a *translation lookaside buffer* (*TLB*) or an *address translation cache* (*ATC*), is integrated into almost all MMUs. By caching the most recently used page mappings, those corresponding to the process's working set, it speeds up the virtual-to-physical address translation process due to locality of reference. The TLB itself is nothing more than a virtual cache. The entry to be used for the translation is found by using the virtual address. As such, it is indexed and tagged with this address. The "data" cached by a TLB is the physical page number and page access permissions. When a hit occurs in the TLB, the MMU can immediately compute the physical address and validate permissions from the data in the TLB. When a miss occurs, some implementations will read the page tables stored in main memory to acquire the relevant mappings. The new mapping is then automatically cached in the TLB for future use. This is the approach used by traditional processor architectures such as the Motorola 68040 and the Intel 80X86 family. It is also used by some RISC architectures, such as the Motorola 88000 and Texas Instruments SPARC line. Other RISC implementations generate a trap to the operating system when a TLB miss occurs. The operating system must then determine the proper mapping, check page permissions, and load the appropriate virtual-to-physical translation information into the TLB. This approach is used by the MIPS family.

If the virtual address alone is used to tag the data in a TLB, then it must be flushed on each context switch. This prevents ambiguities from occurring between the mappings of the old and new processes. The TLBs in the 68040, 88000, and 80X86 operate in this fashion. However, the TLBs for the MIPS family and the TI SPARC line utilize a virtual cache with keys. As with the data and instruction caches discussed in this chapter, allocating a unique TLB key to each process allows the TLB to cache entries from multiple processes simultaneously. This eliminates TLB flushing at context switch time. For example, the MIPS R4000 contains a 48-entry, fully associative TLB. Each entry includes an 8-bit address space identifier (key). A TLB with keys need only be flushed when the address translations change, such as during an `sbrk` system call that shrinks the bss, or when a key needs to be reused by a different process.

Keys are well suited for use in TLBs. Unlike data caches, for example, the entries cached by a TLB are read-only and are not shared. This avoids the inconsistency problems previously seen in this chapter relating to shared memory and copy-on-write pages. A TLB with keys preserves a process's translations across context switches, possibly reducing the TLB miss rate, while requiring little additional maintenance (flushing) from the operating system.

4.4 Summary

A virtual cache with keys tries to reduce the flushing overhead associated with pure virtual caches while still retaining the benefit of accessing the cache without an MMU operation. Since the cache is not normally flushed at context switch time, there is a chance that a process's locality of reference can still be cached when it is next selected for execution. This performance advantage is not possible with pure virtual caches.

While less flushing is needed, particularly at context switch time, there is the distinct disadvantage that shared data (either copy-on-write sharing during `fork`, shared memory, or mapped files) cannot be shared within the cache, since the processes will each be using a different key. By restricting the attach address for shared memory, explicit cache flushes are not needed as long as each process indexes the same line and direct mapped caching with write-allocate is used. Note, however, that the effect is the same as if an explicit flush had been done: a miss occurs and the line is replaced. If there are more than two lines per set, then explicit validation of main memory is needed to prevent stale data from being used. A virtual cache with keys does not eliminate the flushing needed during `exec`, `exit`, `brk`, `sbrk`, and I/O. These activities require the same flushing as a pure virtual cache does.

Additional performance penalties occur if there are not enough unique keys for all processes in the system, since the cache must be flushed when a key is reassigned. Systems that use separate instruction and data caches must invalidate both whenever invalidations are needed to maintain consistency. The amount of flushing needed can be reduced by tagging the lines with the physical address instead, as discussed in the next chapter.

4.5 Exercises

4.1   A system uses 32-bit addresses. It has a virtual cache with keys that uses 4 bits for the key and is two-way set associative. It contains 1024 lines, each with 16 bytes of data. How many bits are needed in the address portion of the tags? How many bits are needed in the address portion of the tags if the number of bits in the key is increased to 6? Why?

4.2   As stated in Section 2.8, cache implementations may allow flushing by line or address. What other type of flushing capabilities would be useful for a virtual cache with keys?

4.3   Explain the effect of changing a process's key without first flushing the cache if the old key was not used again by any other process in the system. Assume the process had data cached before the change was made and that no data in the cache is tagged with the new key. Would any other process in the system get incorrect data? What about the process whose key was changed? Consider both write-through and write-back caching.

4.4   If faced with a situation where there are more processes than keys, would an LRU algorithm for key reassignment be a good choice? Explain. Be sure to state any assumptions you're making.

4.5   On page 86 it says that a process's locality of reference is most likely to be lost across context switches when using small direct mapped caches. Why would this not be as true for large fully associative caches?

4.6   If `fork` was implemented with copy-on-write, would it be possible for the parent and child to share the same key? What effects would this have on the processes (including performance)? How long could they share the key? Explain.

4.7   In the examples shown in Figures 4–2 through 4–5, does it matter whether or not the cache uses write-allocate? Consider both direct mapped and two-way set associative caches.

4.8   Some UNIX system implementations support the `vfork` system call. Like `fork`, it creates a child process except that the child shares the parent's address space directly without copying it and without copy-on-write. This means that any modifications the child makes to the address space will be visible to the parent. `Vfork` is further defined to suspend the parent until the child either `exits` or `execs`. How should the kernel manage a virtual cache with keys when this system call is used? What needs to happen when the child `exits` or `execs`?

4.9   If the kernel is using a separate key while it is executing, how can it always fetch the correct data from a user process executing a system call if that process had cached data? Consider the effects of write-through versus write-back, and arbitrary set sizes.

4.10   If two different processes use the same set of virtual addresses, a virtual cache with keys will resolve the ambiguities, but the addresses will still generate the same index. If direct mapped caching is used, this will cause one process's data to replace the other's, reducing the hit ratio when the other runs again. One way to reduce such cache thrashing is to use the key as part of the hashing algorithm. If, for example, the key is exclusive-OR'ed with the virtual address when generating the index, then the same virtual address in different address spaces will index different lines in the cache (assuming they use different keys). Discuss the advantages and disadvantages of such an approach. How does it compare to caches that use the conventional hashing algorithm but have two or more lines per set?

4.11   If a process forks on a system that uses a TLB with keys, explain what the kernel should do with respect to the TLB.

4.12   Repeat Exercise 4.8, considering the effects of a TLB with keys instead of the instruction and data caches.

4.13   Consider a system that has a large number of keys for use by the cache (where keys are 10 bits or more, for example). What effect, if any, would this have on the algorithms and techniques presented in this chapter?

4.14   Should threads sharing an address space use the same key?

4.15   Consider a system with separate instruction and data caches. Both are virtual
        caches with keys. Discuss the advantages and disadvantages of an implementa-
        tion that had two separate current key registers, one for each cache. How should
        the operating system utilize this capability?

4.6 Further Reading

[1]   Chao, C., Mackey, M., and Sears, B., "MACH on Virtually Addressed Cache
        Architectures," *Proceedings of the USENIX MACH Workshop*, 1990.

[2]   Cheng, R., "Virtual Address Cache in UNIX," *Proceedings of the Summer
        USENIX Conference*, June 1987, pp. 217–24.

[3]   Frink, C.R., and Roy, P.J., "The Cache Architecture of the Apollo DN4000,"
        Proceedings of the Spring COMPCON, March 1988, pp. 300–2.

[4]   Frink, C.R., and Roy, P.J., "A Virtual Cache-Based Workstation Architecture,"
        Proceedings of the 2nd International Conference on Computer Workstations,
        March 1988.

[5]   Goodman, J.R., "Coherency for Multiprocessor Virtual Address Caches," *Second
        International Conference on Architectural Support for Programming Languages
        and Operating Systems*, October 1987, pp. 72–81.

[6]   Inouye, J., Konuru, R., Walpole, J., and Sears, B., "The Effects of Virtually
        Addressed Caches on Virtual Memory Design and Performance," *Operating
        Systems Review*, Vol. 26, No. 4, October 1992, pp. 14–29.

5

Virtual Caches with Physical Address Tags

This chapter presents a final enhancement to virtual caches that eliminates ambiguities and makes it possible to share data in the cache. This is done by removing the virtual address from the tags, which was the cause of the problems, and replacing it with the physical address of the data. With this approach, however, cache look-up can no longer occur independently from address translation by the MMU, since the physical address is needed to determine if a hit or miss occurs. The effects of this cache organization are explained in the following sections.

5.1 The Organization of a Virtual Cache with Physical Tags

A virtual cache with physical address tags is indexed in the same way as a pure virtual cache. The cache lines, however, are tagged with the physical address of the data. The virtual address is not used in the tags and is used only during indexing. With this type of cache organization, it is required that the virtual address be translated on every access since the physical address is needed to determine if the addressed data is cached. The logical organization of such a system appears in Figure 5–1.

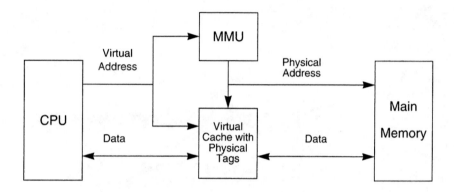

Figure 5–1: Virtual cache with physical tags organization.

In this type of system, the virtual address from the CPU is simultaneously sent to the cache and to the MMU. This way the address translation and cache access are overlapped. While the MMU is translating the address, the cache begins its look-up by hashing the virtual address to obtain the index. The cache can then read the contents of the indexed line or set to prepare for the tag comparison. The MMU sends the physical address to the cache as soon as it has translated the address. The cache then compares this address with that stored in the tags of the selected line(s) to determine if a hit or miss has occurred.

The benefit of such an organization is that ambiguities can never occur between unshared data in different processes, since each process's virtual address will translate to a distinct physical address that will uniquely identify the data. In this sense, the physical address tag behaves as the process keys did in the previous chapter. The improvement over keys is that shared data now can be efficiently shared in the cache. No longer will processes sharing data miss and force each other's lines out of the cache because the keys didn't match. Processes sharing data will generate the same physical addresses when their virtual addresses are translated and so will generate a hit when they index the shared data. This is explained in more detail ahead.

The disadvantage of this cache design is that the speed of the cache look-up operation is bounded by the translation time needed by the MMU. As will be seen, the appeal of this design is that it reduces the need for the kernel to flush the cache explicitly. So the trade-off is one of hardware overhead versus software overhead.

Since the physical address is available on every cache operation, two differences from the virtually tagged caches of the previous two chapters should be noted. First consider the case of a write-back cache. When a modified line is replaced, it is no longer necessary to translate the address, since the physical address is contained in the cache tags. The cache can send this physical address and the cache line contents directly to main memory, completely bypassing the MMU. As before, the assumption is that if the process had permission to modify the data in the cache, it must have permission to write the data back to main memory, and so the page access permissions do not need to be checked again by the MMU. This conveniently gets around the problem of write-back caching in virtual caches with keys (see page 86).

Also note that during the address translation, the MMU also has an opportunity to check the page access permissions. Therefore, a virtual cache with physical tags has no need to store redundant copies of the write permission bit, for example, as was done in other types of virtual caches (see page 61).

As with all caches, designers take advantage of the fact that it is not necessary to store the entire address in the tags, only those bits that cannot be inferred from the data's position in the cache. The low-order bits of the virtual address comprising the page offset within the virtual page will be the same in the physical address. These low-order bits do not have to be stored in the cache tags.

For example, consider a direct mapped cache with 512 lines, each 16 bytes long. Assume the page size is 2K and addresses are 32 bits. This means there are 11 bits in the page offset and 21 bits in the virtual page number (VPN). The interpretation of the address bits during a cache look-up would be as indicated in Figure 5–2.

Bits <3..0> will select the byte within the line after the lookup has occurred. The next nine bits, bits <12..4>, are sent to the cache and used to select one of the 512 cache lines to be read. Meanwhile, the virtual page number, bits <31..11>, is simultaneously sent to the MMU for translation to the physical page number (PPN). When the translation is complete, the MMU will output bits <31..11> of the physical address. If main memory needs to be accessed to fill a cache miss, these bits will be concatenated with bits <10..0> of the page offset to form the complete physical address. By the time the MMU has translated the ad-

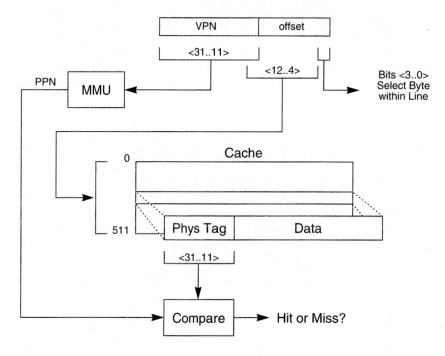

Figure 5–2: Interpretation of address bits during cache look-up.

dress, the cache has read out the indexed line and sends the contents of the tag to the comparator to see whether a hit or miss has occurred. A comparison is made between the physical page number (PPN) as translated by the MMU and the PPN stored in the tags. A hit occurs if they match.

Note that the entire PPN must be stored in the tags. This is different from the virtually tagged caches presented in the previous chapters. A virtually tagged cache would only need to store bits <31..13> of the virtual address in the tags since bits <12..0> were used to index the line and select the byte within the line. These caches derive both the tag and index from the same entity: the virtual address. It would be redundant to store the low-order two bits of the VPN, bits <12..11>, in the tags since these can be inferred from the line number. However, in a physically tagged virtual cache, there is no predetermined correspondence between the VPN and the PPN. Bits <12..11> of the PPN bear no relationship to bits <12..11> of the VPN. Therefore the entire PPN must be used to tag the line.

The physical address of the data in a line can later be reconstructed, if needed for a write-back operation, as follows. Bits <31..11> of the physical address are stored in the tags. Bits <10..4> of the physical address can be inferred from the line's position within the cache by taking the low-order seven bits of the line index. Finally, bits <3..0> can be set to select a specific byte or word as needed.

The on-chip caches of the MIPS R4000 are an example of this type of organization. It has separate instruction and data caches, each of which hold 8K and are direct mapped. Its data cache uses write-back with write-allocate.

For some designs, there is a subtle distinction between a virtual cache with physical tags and a physical cache. As will be seen in the next chapter, physical caches generate the index from the physical address alone, implying that an MMU translation must occur before cache look-up can proceed. Observe, however, that the look-up can begin immediately if the cache index is derived solely from bits in the page offset, since the offset is the same for the virtual and physical addresses. Such caches experience the performance benefit of a virtual cache with physical tags, where the MMU translation and cache look-up are over-lapped, in addition to the software benefits that pure physical caches provide. These caches should be considered as pure physical caches and will be covered in the next chapter. The overlap of the MMU translation and cache look-up can be considered as a hardware opti-mization that is transparent to software.

Note that the MIPS R4000 supports a selectable page size from 4K to 16M (in multiples of four). When used with 4K pages, the on-chip caches behave as virtual caches with physical tags because some bits from the virtual page number are required to index an 8K direct mapped cache. However, when the page size is 8K or greater, the cache behaves as a pure physical cache.

Finally, note that cache architectures that have both virtual and physical tags, such as the Intel i860 XP, do not qualify as the type of cache described in this chapter. On the i860, cache look-up for accesses from the CPU occurs using the virtual tags alone. This makes the cache behave as a pure virtual cache from the software's point of view. The physical tags are used for maintaining cache consistency with respect to DMA operations, as dis-cussed in the next chapter.

5.2 Managing a Virtual Cache with Physical Tags

The use of physical tags sharply reduces the cases where the kernel explicitly needs to flush the cache. The additional benefit of being able to share cached data will be seen shortly. As before, the use of separate instruction and data caches requires that each be invalidated in the situations described next.

5.2.1 Context Switch

Unrelated processes that are not sharing memory will use different physical pages for their data. Therefore, it is not normally necessary to flush the cache during context switch, since the physical tags will prevent ambiguities from occurring between different process's data. This is one of the main advantages of this cache architecture. A second advantage is that there are no keys to manage as required for the cache organization discussed in the previous chapter.

Note that when using a write-back cache, modified data from other processes will be present in the cache when the current process is running. If the current process causes a line modified by a different process to be replaced during miss processing, then this line must be written back to that process's address space. This does not pose a problem since the cache can generate the physical address without using the MMU. It can write the data directly into the physical pages corresponding to the address space of the process that modified it. This does not represent a security violation since the current process cannot alter or access the data. It could only do so if a hit were to occur, which cannot happen since the tags won't match (assuming shared memory is not being used).

Cache flushing at context switch time may be necessary when using shared memory. This is covered in Section 5.2.6.

5.2.2 Fork

No cache flushing is required for the `fork` system call in order to establish copy-on-write sharing. Unlike virtual caches with keys, this is true even if write-back caching is used (as described ahead). In addition, there is the added advantage that data can be shared in the cache itself, which was not possible with either of the other virtual cache architectures.

While the parent and child are sharing pages with copy-on-write, both will be using the same virtual addresses. These will be mapped to the same physical pages. Since the virtual addresses are the same, both processes will index the same line or set when using a given virtual address. Since the physical addresses are also the same, a hit will occur for either process if the data is in the cache. The data will continue to be shared between the two processes as long as it is cache-resident. This is much different from the effects of the virtual cache with keys, as shown on page 87, where each process would miss and force the data to be reread from main memory since their keys differed. The result is that fewer misses can be expected to occur with a virtual cache using physical tags than with one using keys.

Write-back caching and two-way or greater set associativity can also be used without the need for flushing. If modified data from the parent is present in the cache prior to the `fork`, then any references the child makes to the data while it is being shared with copy-on-write will hit in the cache and the correct data will be returned. Again, this is due to the fact that both are using the same virtual and physical address. Furthermore, write-backs of modified data to pages being shared with copy-on-write are not a concern as they were with the previous virtual cache architectures. In those, the write-back could generate a protection trap since the pages are shared read-only. This would incorrectly cause copy-on-write processing to occur. With a virtual cache with physical tags, the write-back will occur without using the MMU since the cache can generate the physical address itself. This allows it to transparently write back modified data into the shared pages. Both the parent and the child are guaranteed to read the correct data on later misses in this case.

Care must taken when making a copy of a page when either the parent or the child attempts to modify it. As stated above, modified data from the copy-on-write page may be present in a write-back cache while it is being shared. It must be assured that when copy-on-write sharing ends, both processes are given a copy of the modified version of the data rather than the stale data from main memory. The same technique presented in Section 3.3.2, where a temporary mapping is set up for the destination of the copy, should be used. If cached references are used for the kernel virtual addresses of the destination of the copy, then memory must be validated and the cache invalidated in order to eliminate the alias. The use of uncached references eliminates this flush.

Once the copy is made, no flushing is needed, since at that point the processes will be using different physical addresses. The physical tags mean that no aliases can occur and no flushing is needed even though both processes will be using the same virtual addresses.

5.2.3 Exec

When the old address space is deallocated during exec, stale entries will be left in the cache. The operating system could invalidate them during the system call or leave them in the cache until the physical pages they are associated with are reallocated. Since they are tagged with physical addresses that are not being used by any process, once exec deallocates the pages, there is no danger that another process could hit on the stale data. It must be ensured though that the stale data is removed prior to allocating the pages to a new process. This technique is described in more detail in Section 7.4.

5.2.4 Exit

As with exec, the address space that is deallocated during exit can be either flushed at system call time or postponed until the physical pages are reused, without any danger of ambiguities arising over the stale data that may be in the cache. This is similar to the effects of keys (Section 4.2.4) where no ambiguities could occur until the key was reused.

5.2.5 Brk and Sbrk

Cache management for the `brk` and `sbrk` system calls that shrink the bss segment is similar to that of `exec` and `exit` in that they deallocate part of the address space. The cache could be either flushed at system call time or postponed until the physical pages are later reallocated. Note that with this cache organization, the MMU is used during each reference and so will prevent the process from accessing any data from the deallocated region. (See Exercise 5.9.)

No cache flushing is needed when the bss is grown by `brk` or `sbrk` (although some flushing may be needed during page allocation if flushing was previously postponed during deallocation; see Section 7.4).

5.2.6 Shared Memory and Mapped Files

Cache consistency for shared memory is much easier to maintain when using physical tags than either of the other types of virtual caches. As was the case with `fork`, if all processes share memory with the same virtual addresses, then they will all index the same line or set in the cache. Since this memory is shared, the physical addresses will also match, allowing hits to occur on the data. In this case, no flushing is needed and data will be shared while it is in the cache. This is true for both write-through and write-back caching and any set size.

When modulo cache hashing is used, processes can also share memory at different virtual addresses without the need for cache flushing if the virtual addresses are the same color. As long as the different virtual addresses all index the same line or set, the common physical addresses will cause hits to occur and aliases will be prevented (see Section 4.2.6).

If processes try to share memory at different virtual addresses that do not cause the same line or set to be indexed, then the operating system will have to either flush the cache (validate main memory and invalidate the cache) when context switching between such processes, or simply cause the shared memory to be uncached. As an alternative, the operating system could of course disallow attempts to attach shared memory at virtual addresses that don't generate the same index. The case of a single process attaching the same shared memory region two or more times within its own address space is the same as described in the previous chapters (see Section 3.3.6).

It should be clear that a virtual cache architecture using physical tags will yield a better hit ratio for shared memory than either a pure virtual cache or one with keys. Not only is the data left in the cache across context switches, but shared cached data can be used by all processes sharing the data.

5.2.7 I/O

The techniques the kernel must use to ensure consistency of I/O operations for a virtual cache with physical tags are the same as those for a pure virtual cache (see Section 3.3.7).

5.2.8 User–Kernel Data Ambiguities

The use of physical tags eliminates any ambiguities between user and kernel data. Kernel and user data will always reside in separate physical pages of memory and therefore will always have different tags when it is cache-resident. Even if the kernel were to use a virtual address to reference its own data that matched a line of cached user data, no ambiguity would result since the physical tags would still be different.

Splitting the address space between the user and kernel as described in previous chapters is advantageous when using a virtual cache with physical tags. With this approach, cached kernel will be accessible to any process running in kernel mode, but inaccessible to user mode processes because the MMU will prevent accesses. The kernel will also be able to reference cached user data directly. This is a better situation than with a virtual cache with keys. For example, when a unique key is allocated to the kernel, accesses to user data will always miss, requiring explicit cache flushing in certain instances (see Section 4.2.8). With the split address space approach, flushing is unnecessary when the cache uses physical tags.

5.3 Summary

A virtual cache with physical tags is a great improvement over the previous two types of virtual caches in terms of the amount of management needed by the operating system. Physical tags eliminate ambiguities in nearly all cases, meaning that much less flushing will be needed. The use of physical tags retains all the benefits found in virtual caches with keys without the added overhead of key management. Furthermore, this is the only virtual cache architecture where shared memory can be cached and shared among the processes while the data is cache-resident. This can be a significant performance benefit for systems with large caches where shared memory or mapped file usage is high.

The main disadvantage of this architecture is that a virtual-to-physical address translation is needed during each cache access in order to determine if a hit or miss has occurred. If the MMU used in the system is slow, then this can reduce or eliminate the advantages of using physical tags. Even though multiple process contexts can be cached simultaneously, allowing the possibility that a process's data may already be cache-resident when a context switch is done to resume the process, the fact that processes tend to use the same range of virtual addresses reduces this possibility unless the cache is full associative or has a large number of lines per set. This is a problem with all types of virtual caches and is due to how the cache is indexed (as opposed to how the lines are tagged). A final disadvantage, albeit a small one, is that memory cannot be shared on arbitrary boundaries without cache flushing or uncached operation.

5.4 Exercises

5.1   Does it make sense to have a fully associative virtual cache with physical tags?

5.2   A cache has 16-byte lines, 256 sets, and is five-way set associative. Should this be considered a virtual cache with physical tags or a pure physical cache if the page is 4K?

5.3   A direct mapped cache with 512 lines has 32 bytes per line. If the page size is 8K, should this be considered a virtual cache with physical tags or a pure physical cache?

5.4   A system uses a 3-way set associative cache that has 64 bytes per line. If the page size is 64K, how large can the cache be made and still be considered a physical cache?

5.5   A system uses a 256K four-way set associative virtual cache with physical tags. Each line contains 16 bytes. If each of the following pairs of virtual addresses represents an alias to the same shared memory segment within an address space, which of the pairs require the kernel to flush the cache in order to maintain consistency? Explain.

        a.   0x1000 and 0x10000

        b.   0x1100 and 0x11100

        c.   0x52a40 and 0x53a40

        d.   0x8ffe90 and 0xfafe90

        e.   0x123450 and 0x1234560

5.6   Referring to Section 5.2.2, why is cache flushing not necessary to establish copy-on-write sharing, as it was for virtual caches with keys, when the set size is two or greater?

5.7   Draw a picture similar to Figure 5–2 for a 1M virtual cache with physical tags where virtual addresses are 48 bits and the page size is 64K. The cache is two-way set associative with 256-byte lines.

5.8   In Section 5.2.5 it states that flushing may be postponed in the case of releasing memory with `brk` or `sbrk` since the MMU prevents access to the pages even though the data may be cached. Can cache flushing also be postponed in the case of detaching a shared memory region or mapped file?

5.9   If a process has modified data in a virtual cache with physical tags that uses write-back, and it uses `sbrk` to release the pages that this modified data corresponds to, then what happens when those lines are later replaced if the cache flush is postponed as described in Section 5.2.5?

5.10   The kernel pages out a page from a process to the swap device and reallocates the physical page to a new use. Later, it brings the page back in, placing it in a different physical page. Describe the cache flushing that must occur when using a virtual cache with physical tags in order for consistency to be maintained.

5.11   A process does a raw I/O read operation into a buffer on its stack. Describe the cache flushing that must occur when using a virtual cache with physical tags. What must be done differently if a raw write operation is done instead?

5.5 Further Reading

[1]   Chao, C., Mackey, M., and Sears, B., "MACH on Virtually Addressed Cache Architectures," *Proceedings of the USENIX MACH Workshop*, 1990.

[2]   Frink, C.R., and Roy, P.J., "A Virtual Cache-Based Workstation Architecture," *Proceedings of the 2nd International Conference on Computer Workstations*, March 1988.

[3]   Goodman, J.R., "Coherency for Multiprocessor Virtual Address Caches," *Second International Conference on Architectural Support for Programming Languages and Operating Systems*, October 1987, pp. 72–81.

[4]   Inouye, J., Konuru, R., Walpole, J., and Sears, B., "The Effects of Virtually Addressed Caches on Virtual Memory Design and Performance," *Operating Systems Review*, Vol. 26, No. 4, October 1992, pp. 14–29.

6

Physical Caches

The final cache architecture to be examined is the *physical cache*. This type of cache abandons all use of the virtual address and uses the physical address to index and tag the lines. The advantage is the complete elimination of aliases and ambiguities at the cost of requiring an address translation for every access. This type of organization also allows a new technique—*bus watching*—to be used to maintain cache consistency for I/O operations. The chapter concludes with a discussion of multilevel caches.

6.1 The Organization of a Physical Cache

A physical cache is indexed and tagged with the physical address of the data. The virtual
address is never used by the physical cache in any way. Of course, this type of organization
requires that the virtual address be translated by the MMU for each cache look-up operation. Physical cache organization is diagrammed in Figure 6–1.

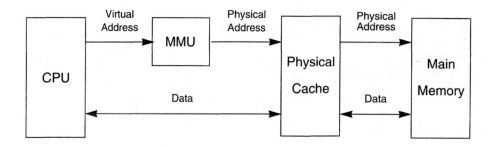

Figure 6–1: Physical cache organization.

The appeal of such a design is that neither ambiguities nor aliases can ever occur. Unrelated processes that are not sharing data will each be assigned different physical pages of
memory. Therefore, the physical tags from different processes will never match. Processes
that share data will be using the same physical pages, causing them to index the same line
or set and causing the tags to match and generate a hit. Aliases are not possible since no
virtual addresses are involved in the cache access. The end result is that there is generally
no need to flush the cache. If bus watching is used (explained in Section 6.2.6), then the
cache need never be flushed. In this case, the cache becomes completely transparent to the
operating system and user applications. This fact makes physical caches appealing for use
in systems that were not originally designed with caches in mind. This is true for the IBM
PC and compatibles, for example, where the early versions of the Intel 80X86 family
(80386 and earlier) had no on-chip caches. To retain compatibility with operating system
and application software that was written for previous versions of the microprocessor, the
80486 and the Pentium were both given on-chip physical caches. The 80486 has a single
8K write-through cache that is four-way set associative. The Pentium contains separate instruction and data caches, each of which is 8K and two-way set associative. The Pentium
data cache uses write-back.

As with virtual caches with physical tags, data in a physical cache can be shared while it is
cache-resident. In addition to this, the use of the physical address to index the cache causes
data from the same virtual address in different processes (which are not sharing memory)
to index different cache lines, since each will be using a different physical address. This
solves one of the potential performance problems of all types of virtual caches, where un-

related processes compete for the same cache lines, because these processes frequently use the same range of virtual addresses. This competition reduces the probability that cached data will still be present the next time the process is run. Physical caches have the potential to distribute such data throughout the cache evenly, leading to better performance.

In general, off-chip (external) caches are physical caches. This is the case for most processors that lack on-chip caches, such as the Intel 80386 and MIPS R2000/R3000. The address lines coming from both of these chips contain only the physical address. The virtual address is not available to the hardware off-chip. This makes a physical cache a natural match. Even though most processors now contain an on-chip cache, this is usually checked first before accessing an external cache. By that time, the virtual address will generally have been translated, allowing a physical cache to be used externally with no extra time penalty. The use of multiple caches is covered in detail in Section 6.3.

Depending on the size and organization of the cache, the look-up operation may begin before address translation is complete. As mentioned in Section 5.1, if all the bits used by the hashing algorithm to generate the index come from the page offset, then the look-up can begin immediately by taking these bits from the virtual address, since the page offset is the same in the virtual and physical addresses. This provides a beneficial hardware optimization, allowing the relevant cache line or set to be indexed and read while the MMU is translating the address. This provides the performance advantages of a virtual cache with physical tags, plus the software benefits of physical caches (little, if any, need for flushing). In all cases, however, translation must complete before the tags can be compared.

The caches for the 80486 and Pentium use this technique. For example, the Pentium has 32-byte lines meaning there are 128 sets (8K $\div$ 32 bytes per line $\div$ 2 lines per set). Therefore, bits <4..0> will select the byte within the line and bits <11..5> will select the set. Since 4K pages are used, the page offset is contained in bits <11..0>, allowing cache look-up to begin before the virtual address is translated.

If there is a sufficient number of lines per set, this technique can be used with caches that are larger than the page size. While the caches for the 80486 and Pentium are twice the page size, the caches for the Texas Instruments' SuperSPARC chip are larger still. Its data cache is five-way set associative with 64-byte lines, for a total of 20K of data. Bits <5..0> select the byte within the line, while bits <11..6> select the set. Since 4K pages are used, all index bits come from the page offset. Similarly, its instruction cache is 16K in size, four-way set associative with 32-byte lines. Bits <4..0> select the byte within the line, and bits <11..5> select the set, with all bits again coming from the page offset.

For larger physical caches where bits from the physical page number are needed to form the index, the address translation must complete before the cache look-up can begin. This is true for the MIPS R4000, which can have an external cache of up to 4M. This cache is direct mapped with a line size of up to 128 bytes. In this situation, bits <6..0> select the byte within the line, and bits <21..7> select the line. Therefore, bits <21..12> from the physical page number are needed before the cache index can be formed. Since the virtual address has already been translated during the look-up operation for the on-chip caches, there is no performance penalty for requiring the physical page number to index the external cache.

6.2 Managing a Physical Cache

Little or no cache flushing is needed for a physical cache. The reasons for this are explained in the following sections.

6.2.1 Context Switch

Since the physical tags prevent ambiguities, and indexing with the physical address prevents aliases, there is no need to flush the cache at context switch time. This is particularly beneficial to systems with large caches, as it can greatly reduce context switch time. A second benefit for large caches is that it is more likely that a process's data will remain cached while other processes are running, since physical indexing can more evenly distribute the data from different processes throughout the cache. A process can then expect a better hit ratio the next time it executes. This would not be true for a small physical cache (one that is less than or equal to the size of the typical process's locality of reference), however, since each process that runs will tend to replace the previous process's locality of reference with its own.

6.2.2 Fork

No flushing is needed at `fork` time in order to set up copy-on-write sharing, since the parent and child will both be using the same physical addresses to reference the shared data. This means they will both index and hit on the same lines when addressing the same data.

A physical cache also simplifies the task of copying a page when copy-on-write sharing ends (or when implementing `fork` without copy-on-write). With virtual caches with keys or physical tags, it was necessary to flush the address range of the temporary mapping in order to avoid aliases (see page 87). This is not necessary for a physical cache since the data will already be tagged correctly and be in the correct lines or sets when the copy to the new page is complete. The virtual address used for the temporary mapping is irrelevant to the cache.

6.2.3 Exec, Exit, Brk, and Sbrk

The memory deallocation that occurs during these system calls never requires any cache flushing when using a physical cache. When deallocation occurs, no process will be using the corresponding range of physical addresses; therefore, no process could ever generate a hit on any stale data that might be in the cache. When this memory is eventually reallocated to some process, one must ensure that any remaining stale cached data is not accessed. This will be true since the UNIX kernel will always fill the page either during an I/O read (such as satisfying a page fault) or through zero filling. If the page is zero-filled, as would happen when allocating new memory for stack growth, for example, the kernel would clear the memory through the cache, causing any remaining stale data to be replaced with zeros. Consistency for I/O operations is discussed in Section 6.2.6. In either case, the stale data is removed when the newly allocated page is initialized, and so no explicit cache flushing operations are needed.

6.2.4 Shared Memory and Mapped Files

No cache flushing is needed to maintain consistency of shared memory and mapped files when physical caching is used. As with a virtual cache with physical tags, data can be shared while it is cache-resident. Unlike physically tagged virtual caches, there are no restrictions on the virtual addresses the sharing processes use to access the shared memory since aliases cannot occur.

6.2.5 User–Kernel Data Ambiguities

When physical addresses are used in the cache, aliases and ambiguities between the user and kernel are not possible. Therefore, no cache flushing is needed to maintain consistency. As long as none of the kernel's pages are ever mapped into a user process's virtual address space, no user process can access kernel data since the MMU operation done for every cache access checks the page permissions.

6.2.6 I/O and Bus Watching

The previous virtual cache architectures all required cache flushing to maintain consistency for I/O operations since the DMA for I/O occurred independently of the cache. Physical caches, however, offer the ability to implement a technique called *bus watching* to maintain cache consistency for I/O operations without the need for flushing by the operating system. This is accomplished by having the cache monitor or "watch" the system bus for DMA operations from I/O devices in addition to performing look-ups from the CPU. The cache flushing the operating system previously performed is now handled automatically in hardware. Figure 6–2 depicts a high level view of such a system organization.

The system bus serves as a common interconnection between the CPU/MMU/cache, main memory, and I/O devices. It is a *broadcast*-based medium, meaning that any unit can receive information placed on the bus by any other unit connected to it. The CPU/MMU/cache reads memory by sending the physical address of the data out on the bus, as shown in Figure 6–3(a). Memory responds to the address by returning the requested data on the bus where the cache receives it (see Figure 6–3(b)).

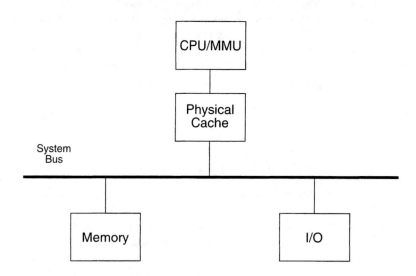

Figure 6–2: Cache, memory, and I/O interconnection on a system bus.

I/O devices perform DMA in the same manner. To write data to a device such as a disk, the I/O controller places the physical address of the data on the bus (see Figure 6–4(a)). The memory unit then responds by sending the corresponding data out on the bus, which the device then receives (see Figure 6–4(b)).

When data is to be written into memory by either the CPU or I/O, the physical destination address and the data are placed on the bus together. The address and data are captured by the memory unit, and the data is written into the addressed memory location.

Data is sent on the bus in one or more *bus transactions*. Each bus transaction can only send a limited amount of data, typically in the range of several words to several dozen words at a time. Therefore, if a large amount of data needs to be sent, such as when reading a page off a disk, the transfer will be broken down into multiple bus transactions, each containing the destination address and the data.

Since all bus transactions are visible to the cache, bus watching is straightforward to implement. When the cache is not using the bus to read or write memory itself, it monitors all bus activity by the I/O devices. This is commonly referred to as *snooping*. For each bus transaction of interest (as described ahead), the cache checks its contents to see if the physical address in the transaction is cache-resident (see Figure 6–5). The cache look-up operation for snooping is identical to that of a CPU access: the address is hashed, the corresponding line or set is indexed, and the tags are checked to see if a hit or miss has occurred. If a miss occurs, the cache does not need to do anything. In this case, the DMA for the bus

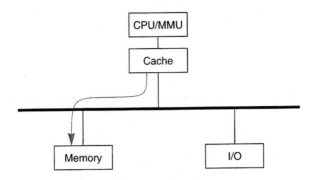

(a) CPU/MMU/cache sends address to main memory unit.

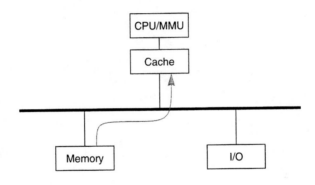

(b) Memory returns data to cache.

Figure 6–3: CPU/MMU/cache read operation.

transaction completes as if in a system without a cache. If the address hits in the cache, the action the hardware takes depends on whether the bus operation is a read or write of main memory, and whether the cache is write-through or write-back.

The case of write-through caching will be considered first since it is simpler. Here the cache can ignore all DMA main memory read operations from I/O devices. Since the cache is write-through, memory is always up to date, and so the I/O device will always read the correct version of the data from main memory. The cache must, however, snoop all DMA write operations from I/O to main memory. If a miss occurs, the cache does nothing and the data from the device is written to memory as usual. If a hit occurs, then the line is invalidated from the cache, and the DMA write to main memory completes unaffected. This ensures that the cache never contains stale data relative to main memory. When the CPU references the corresponding address later, it will cache-miss and read the new data from

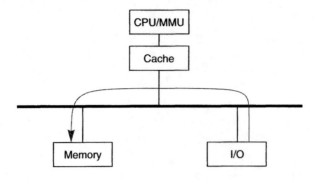

(a) I/O sends address to main memory unit.

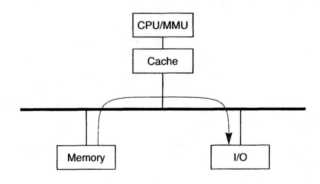

(b) Memory returns data to I/O device.

Figure 6–4: I/O DMA operation from memory to device.

main memory. Some implementations choose to replace the data in the cache with the new data from the device when a hit occurs during a DMA write to memory. This has the same basic effect of keeping the cache in sync with main memory. Such implementations assume that the CPU will soon need the data, so it is worthwhile to keep a copy in the cache.

The situation is more complex with a write-back cache, since such caches must snoop all bus transactions. In the case of a DMA read from memory, the cache may contain modified data, meaning that the corresponding data in memory is stale. This stale data must not be read by the I/O device, so the cache must snoop DMA reads. When a hit occurs on a modified line during such an operation, the cache returns its data to the I/O device and prevents main memory from responding with the stale data. This action is transparent to the I/O device. If a hit occurs on an unmodified line, then memory is in sync with the cache, and ei-

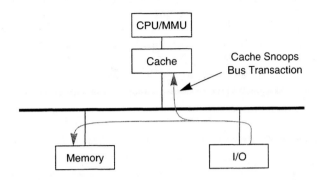

Figure 6–5: Cache snoops memory access by I/O.

ther could return the data. Whether the cache or memory returns the data in this case is implementation dependent. As stated, when a miss occurs during a DMA read, the cache need not do anything, allowing main memory to return the data.

As with write-through caching, a write-back cache need do nothing when a DMA write to main memory misses in the cache. The action taken when a hit occurs during a DMA write depends on the current state of the cache line. If the line is unmodified, then it can be invalidated as it was for a write-through cache. (Some implementations may load the new data into the cache as before.) If the line is modified and the DMA write is replacing the entire line (i.e., the line size is equal to the bus transaction size), then the line can be treated as if it were unmodified and it can be invalidated. In this case, the modified data in the cache is logically overwritten by the DMA write, so it is appropriate to discard the stale cache data. However, if the DMA write is not replacing the entire line, as can happen when the bus transaction size is smaller than the line size, then the cache must capture the new data from the DMA operation and update the cache line. It cannot invalidate the line in this case since it could lose modified data in the portion of the line not replaced by the DMA. For example, assume the cache line size is 32 bytes and the bus transactions are 16 bytes. Assume the cache contains modified data in line 5. A DMA write to memory, whose address corresponds to the data in the last half of line 5 of the cache, occurs. If the cache were now to invalidate the entire line, it would lose any modified data the CPU wrote into the first 16 bytes of the line. The cache must therefore load the new data into the last 16 bytes of the line. The line is left in the modified state so that the data will eventually be written back to main memory when the line is replaced. Situations where a partial line must be updated are common at the beginning and end of I/O buffers in memory. Such buffers are not constrained to start at addresses corresponding to cache line boundaries, nor are they required to be a multiple of the line size in length. This is the same situation as described in Section 3.3.7 (see Figures 3–10 and 3–11), where the kernel had to flush the cache to maintain consistency. Physical caches with bus watching perform this task in hardware automatically.

With the cache consistency of I/O operations now handled in hardware, no operating system intervention is required. Since none of the other situations described in this chapter require flushing, a physical cache with bus watching is completely transparent to the software. Because of this benefit, most modern processors support bus watching. This is true for the Intel 80X86 line, the MIPS R4000MC, the Motorola 68040 and 88000, and the TI SuperSPARC. If the cache lacks bus watching, such as the low-cost version of the MIPS R4000PC and the TI MicroSPARC, the same flushing as described in the previous chapters must occur to keep I/O DMA consistent.

Bus watching is generally found only with physical caches. A few implementations, such as the Intel i860 XP, support it in conjunction with virtual caches. The i860 XP does two things to support such a configuration. First, the caches can be indexed with either a virtual or physical address. This can be done since the 16K separate instruction and data caches are four-way set associative with 32-byte lines. Since there are 128 sets, bits <11..5> select the set, and bits <4..0> select the byte within the line. Since the page size is 4K, bits <11..0> are the same in both the virtual and physical addresses. Second, both caches have two address tags: one containing the virtual address and one for the physical address. This allows two separate paths for accessing the cache, as shown in Figure 6–6.

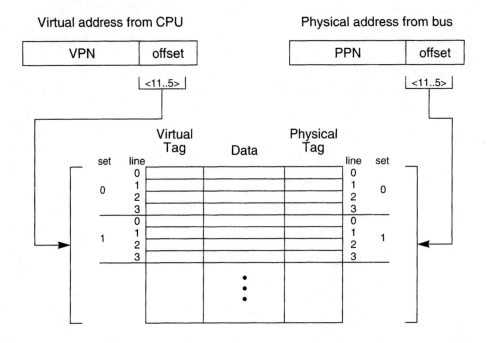

Figure 6–6: Intel i860 XP cache architecture.

As with a virtual cache, the CPU can complete a cache access without waiting for the MMU to complete the address translation. The CPU indexes the cache with bits from the page offset and checks the virtual tags for a hit. When a line is loaded during a miss, both the virtual and physical tags of the line are set to correspond to the virtual and physical addresses of the data just fetched. The physical address in the tags, therefore, represents the translation of the virtual address tag in the same line. Bus watching is supported by using the bits from the page offset of the physical address for the DMA operation to index the cache, and using the physical tags to check for a hit. Since the bits in the page offset are the same in both the virtual and physical addresses, the same set will be indexed when using either address. This guarantees the bus-watching hardware can locate any line cached by the CPU, even though the CPU uses a virtual address and bus watching uses a physical address. With this technique, bus watching on the Intel i860 XP operates the same as the physical caches of the Intel 80X86 and other processors described previously.

An additional benefit of the i860 XP cache architecture is that the hardware can automatically handle aliases. This is done during miss processing by checking the physical tags for an alias condition. For instance, assume that the physical page at 0xa000 is aliased to virtual addresses 0x15000 and 0x952000 within one process's address space. If the cache is initially empty (all lines marked invalid), then when the process references 0x15ff0, a line in set 127 will be loaded with the data at physical address 0xaff0. The virtual tag for the line will be set to 0x15 and the physical tag will be set to 0xa. (As usual, the bits used to index the cache are not stored in the tags since they can be reconstructed based on the line's position.) Now, assume the process references the other alias at 0x952ff0. Set 127 will be indexed again, but a miss will occur since none of the virtual tags matches this address. After the MMU has translated the address, the processor begins a read from main memory to fetch the data and simultaneously checks the physical tags within the indexed set for a hit. In this example a hit occurs, indicating that an alias has been encountered. To prevent both aliases from being loaded into the cache and possibly getting out of sync with one another, the i860 XP ignores the data returned from main memory and simply changes the virtual tag on the line. The physical tag is left unchanged. Thus, the line that used to have virtual tag 0x15 now has virtual tag 0x952. This activity is transparent to the software, relieving the operating system from having to flush the cache to prevent alias problems explicitly. In all other aspects, the caches of the i860 XP behave as virtual caches, requiring the other types of flushing described in Chapter 3.

6.3 Multilevel Caches

Some implementations may expand the memory hierarchy shown in Figure 2–1 to include more than one level of caching. The purpose of this is to increase performance further by providing a cache for the cache. An organization with two levels of caching is shown in Figure 6–7.

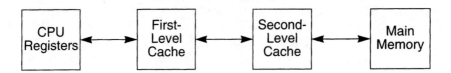

Figure 6–7: Two-level cache.

As before, each level of the memory hierarchy increases in speed and generally decreases in size the closer it is to the CPU. A hierarchy is used due to economic factors: high-speed memory is expensive and its density is low. The first-level cache (also known as a *primary* cache) is therefore faster and usually smaller than the second-level (or *secondary*) cache. This balances the cost and performance of the system by allowing a somewhat slower second-level cache to be used. The lower speed demands on this cache allow lower cost parts to be used, which in turn make a larger second-level cache economical. The higher speed of the first-level cache makes up for the slower speed of the second-level cache.

The organizations of these two caches need not be the same. A typical arrangement is to use a large physical second-level cache in conjunction with a small high-speed virtual cache of some sort. This means that the first-level cache can be accessed quickly, without even needing an MMU translation. If a miss occurs, the second-level cache is checked next. Such systems start the MMU translation in parallel with the first-level cache lookup. This means that the physical address will be ready if the second-level cache needs to be checked. This then combines the advantages of both types of cache architectures while also mitigating the disadvantages.

The use of multilevel caching does not change the circumstances under which the caches must be flushed. These are dictated by the respective cache architectures and must be done in the situations described in this and previous chapters. The following examples will illustrate this.

6.3.1 Primary Virtual Cache with Secondary Physical Cache

For the first example, an Intel i860 XR with an external physical cache will be used. The i860 XR has separate instruction and data caches, both of which are virtual caches. The data cache uses write-back. Note that the XR lacks the physical tags used by the XP, as described previously, and so does not support bus watching and alias detection. Assume that a single physical cache with bus watching is added externally to the i860. This cache will hold both instructions and data and is referred to as a *unified* cache. Figure 6–8 depicts this organization.

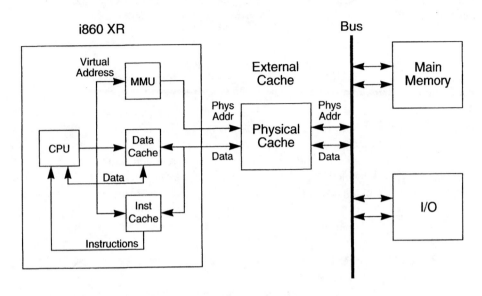

Figure 6–8: Intel i860 XR with external physical cache.

In this picture, the CPU inside the i860 chip issues the virtual address to the desired cache and MMU. The caches return their data or instructions to the CPU as requested. The physical address is sent to the external physical cache for look-up only when there is a miss in the internal caches. A miss in the external cache causes the physical address to be forwarded across the bus to main memory. This organization, where the cache is checked before accessing main memory, is called a *look-through* cache, which derives its name from the serial nature of the accesses. An organization where the physical address is sent to main memory at the same time that the cache is checked is called a *look-aside* cache. The advantage of look-aside is that the data from main memory is available sooner if a miss occurs. The disadvantage is that it wastes bus bandwidth in the case of a hit. In cases where the cache is large and the hit ratio is high, look-through is a better approach. The use of look-through versus look-aside is transparent to software.

Since the caches on the i860 are virtual, aliases and ambiguities can occur, and so the kernel must flush the caches under all the circumstances described in Chapter 3. For example, the data cache must be written back and invalidated at context switch time. Observe that since the secondary cache is physical, the primary data cache need only be written back to the secondary cache in order to maintain consistency. There is no need to write the data back to main memory. As expected, there is no need to flush the secondary cache at all since it is a pure physical cache. Even during I/O, the kernel need only write back and/or invalidate the i860's caches. Once the software takes care of the on-chip caches consistency, the hardware will maintain consistency in the secondary cache through bus watching. In short, the kernel must only concern itself with primary caches and can ignore the presence of the external cache.

Observe that there is no direct connection between the primary instruction and data caches. Therefore, the use of self-modifying code has the potential for causing stale instructions in the instruction cache. This can occur when the CPU has previously fetched the instructions that are to be modified, causing them to be cached in the instruction cache. When the CPU modifies them, it will store the new instructions into the data cache. This will have no effect on the instruction cache, which will continue to cache the stale instructions. In these cases, the stale instructions must be invalidated so that a miss will occur the next time they are fetched. Since a unified secondary cache is used, it is not necessary to write back the new instructions from the primary data cache to main memory. Instead, they need only be written into the external cache. When a miss occurs in the primary instruction cache, the secondary cache will be checked before accessing main memory.

6.3.2 Primary Virtual Cache with Physical Tags and a Secondary Physical Cache

This case will be illustrated using the MIPS R4000. It contains separate on-chip instruction and data caches and is capable of controlling an external combined instruction and data cache. (The R4000 can also support separate external caches, but a unified cache will be used for this example.) The on-chip caches are virtually indexed with physical tags, while the external cache is physical. All caches are direct mapped, and the data cache and external cache support write-back with write-allocate. In addition, the external cache supports bus watching. On the R4000, the kernel can enable bus watching on a per-page basis by setting a code in the page table entries. For this example, bus watching will be assumed to be on for all pages. A high-level view of this organization appears in Figure 6–9. (Note that this is a simplified conceptual model that shows the structure and data paths from the software's point of view. The external cache, for example, is not directly connected to the bus in actual systems. Instead the bus is connected to the R4000, which has a separate connection to the external cache. These hardware details have no effect on the discussion that follows.)

In this arrangement, the CPU sends the virtual address to the MMU and to the proper internal cache when it makes a memory reference (which can be either a load or store instruction, or an instruction fetch). While the primary cache performs indexing and accesses the desired line, the MMU translates the virtual address and sends the physical address to the cache for comparison with the tags of the indexed line. If a hit occurs, the data or instruction is returned to the CPU and the memory reference is complete. If a miss occurs, the external cache is accessed using the physical address, which has already been translated. If the data is found in the external cache, it is loaded into the proper primary cache and returned to the CPU. A miss in the external cache causes the physical address to be sent on

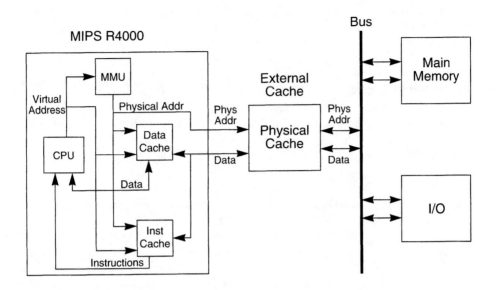

Figure 6–9: MIPS R4000 with external physical cache.

to main memory to retrieve the desired data. In this case, the data is loaded into both the primary and secondary caches, as well as sent to the CPU. Since the caches use write-allocate, both the primary data cache and the secondary cache will always be loaded during a miss, whether it occurs during a load or store operation. This guarantees that the primary caches are always a subset of the secondary cache. The importance of this will be seen shortly.

As with all cache architectures that have physical tags, there is little need for the operating system to flush the cache to maintain consistency. Ambiguities do not occur since they are resolved by the physical address in the tags. Since there are split instruction and data caches in this system, self-modifying code must be handled as described in the previous section. The two remaining cases to be handled are primary cache consistency with I/O, and primary cache aliases.

The R4000 provides assistance for handling both of these problems by storing the primary cache line index in the tags of each line in the secondary cache. Whenever the primary cache is loaded during a miss, the index of the line loaded is stored in the secondary cache line that holds the data from the same address. As stated, the primary cache is always a subset of the secondary, so it is impossible to have data in the primary cache and not have the data also cached by the secondary. This makes it possible for the hardware to detect primary cache aliases automatically. When a miss in the primary cache hits in the secondary, the primary cache index stored in the secondary cache tags is compared to the primary cache line indexed during the miss. If they differ, it indicates that an alias may be present in the primary cache, since the last miss satisfied by this secondary cache line was loaded into a different primary cache line than is being referenced during the current primary cache miss. Since the R4000 is a RISC processor, it does not contain the hardware to resolve the alias. Instead it generates a *virtual coherency exception* to the operating system, which must then flush the old primary cache line to eliminate any alias. The index in the second-ary cache line can then be set to point to the data's new primary cache location. With alias detection implemented in hardware, the kernel need only respond to the exceptions and flush the cache to handle all virtual alias situations. The various restrictions and techniques typically used with a virtual cache with physical tags (described in Section 5.2.6) are un-necessary with this design.

The index stored in the secondary cache lines is used during bus-watching operations as well. If an I/O device is performing a DMA read operation from main memory, then the caches must be snooped since they use the write-back policy. Since the secondary cache is physical, it can be indexed and checked using the physical address from the bus. The pri-mary data cache is write-back as well, and so it must also be checked during snoop opera-tions. Unlike the i860 XP, the physical address cannot be used to index the R4000's on-chip data cache since it requires bits from the virtual page frame number in order to form the cache index. Instead, the index in the secondary cache line is used. From the preceding discussion, this index points to the last primary cache line that referenced the secondary cache line. The indicated primary cache line is read, and its tag is checked against the phys-ical address. This is necessary since the primary cache is much smaller than the secondary, making it possible that the indexed primary line has been replaced with new data. When a primary line is replaced in this manner, the secondary cache tag corresponding to the old contents of the primary line is not updated. Because of this, snoop operations that hit in the secondary cache must check the tags in the indexed primary line to be sure it still contains the data associated with the secondary line. If a hit occurs, and the primary cache line is modified, then this data is returned to the I/O device. If a miss occurs in the primary, or the data is found to be unmodified but modified data was found in the secondary cache, then that data is returned. If a miss occurs in the secondary, then the primary need not be checked (since the primary is always a subset of the secondary), and the I/O device will read the data from main memory. Similar checks are performed for DMA writes to main memory. Overall, cache snooping on the R4000 is transparent to the software. No explicit cache flushing is needed to maintain consistency with any I/O operations.

6.4 Summary

Physical caches greatly reduce the need for maintenance by the operating system. If bus watching is used, then no cache flushing is ever needed since all consistency for I/O oper-ations is now handled in hardware. For these systems, it is as if the cache doesn't even exist (from the software's point of view). All that is seen is better performance from decreasing the memory access time for cached data. The disadvantage of physical caches is the need to perform an MMU translation on every access the CPU makes. Because of this, it can take longer for a physical cache than a virtual cache to return data to the CPU. This penalty is offset by eliminating the need to flush the cache explicitly. The performance disadvantages of a physical cache can be reduced by using it in conjunction with a virtual cache to form a multilevel cache. This allows the system to take advantage of the benefits of both architectures, while mitigating the disadvantages.

6.5 Exercises

6.1   Draw a picture similar to Figure 5–2 for a two-way set associative physical cache with 512 sets and 32-byte lines for a system with a 2K page size.

6.2   If bus watching is used, why not have the cache load all updates to main memory into the cache (i.e., for every bus transaction that transfers data from an I/O device to main memory, have the cache store the data into the cache as well even if a miss occurs)? After all, some process must intend to access the data from the CPU or else the data would never have been read in the first place. So why not have it available in the cache for faster access?

6.3   It is commonplace for systems to use separate instruction and data caches. If a system used physical caches for both, except that the data cache also had bus watching while the instruction cache did not, what operating system changes would be needed (i.e., under what circumstances does the instruction cache need to be flushed)? Be specific, explaining which system calls are affected, what type of flushing is needed, and when it must be done.

6.4   Draw a diagram similar to Figure 5–2 showing the interpretation of the address bits for a four-way set associative physical cache that has 128 sets and 8-byte lines. Assume the system has 4K pages.

6.5   Would the bus-watching technique the Intel i860 XP uses work if the cache size remained the same but was fully associative instead of four-way set associative? Assume the page and set sizes are unchanged.

6.6   Repeat the previous exercise but consider using a direct-mapped cache instead of a fully associative cache.

6.7   If a miss in the primary data cache on the R4000 causes a modified line to be replaced, where should the modified data be written? To the secondary cache or main memory?

6.8   Is it possible for both primary caches on the R4000 to contain a copy of the same data? If so, what must be true about the primary cache indexes?

6.9   Assume that the primary and secondary caches of the R4000 are caching data from location $0x1000$ in main memory. Assume the CPU references a different location that causes a miss in both caches. If this reference indexes a different line in the primary cache but the same line in the secondary cache as location $0x1000$, what must be done to complete the miss and also to maintain consistency?

6.10   Would the bus-watching technique of the Intel i860 XP still work if a key were stored along with the virtual tag (making it a virtual cache with keys from the CPU's perspective)? Would alias detection still work?

6.11   If the on-chip caches of the MIPS R4000 were virtual caches with keys instead of virtual caches with physical tags, would the bus-watching and alias detection technique of storing the primary cache index in the secondary cache still work?

6.12   If the on-chip caches of the MIPS R4000 were organized like those of the Intel i860 XP, would the bus-watching and alias detection technique of storing the primary cache index in the secondary cache still work?

6.13   If the on-chip caches of the MIPS R4000 were physical instead of virtual caches with physical tags, would it be necessary to store the primary cache line index in the secondary cache?

6.14   Are there any restrictions on the primary cache line size of the MIPS R4000 in relation to the secondary cache line size? Must they be equal, or can one be shorter than the other?

6.15   If a new version of the i860 XP is desired where the cache size is doubled, what must be done in order for the bus watching and alias detection to continue to work?

6.6 Further Reading

[1]   Azimi, M., Prasad, B., and Bhat, K., "Two Level Cache Architectures," *Proceedings of Compcon '92*, February 1992, pp. 344–9.

[2]   Baer, J.L., and Wang, W.H., "Architectural Choices for Multi-Level Cache Hierarchies," Technical Report TR-87-01-04, Department of Computer Science, University of Washington, January 1987.

[3]   Baer, J.L., and Wang, W.H., "On the Inclusion Property for Multi-Level Cache Hierarchies," Technical Report TR-87-11-08, Department of Computer Science, University of Washington, November 1987.

[4]   Bennett, B.T., Pomerene, J.H., Puzak, T.R., and Rechtschaffen, R.N., "Prefetching in a Multilevel Hierarchy," *IBM Technical Disclosure Bulletin*, Vol. 25, No. 1, June 1982, pp. 88–9.

[5]   Chiueh., T., and Katz, R.H., "Eliminating the Address Translation Bottleneck for Physical Address Cache," *SIGPLAN Notices*, Vol. 27, No. 9, September 1992, pp. 137–48.

[6]   Gecsei, J., "Determining Hit Ratios for Multilevel Hierarchies," *IBM Journal of Research and Development*, Vol. 18, No. 4, July 1974, pp. 316–27.

[7]   Goodman, J.R., "Coherency for Multiprocessor Virtual Address Caches," *Second International Conference on Architectural Support for Programming Languages and Operating Systems*, October 1987, pp. 72–81.

[8]   Gustavson, D.B., "Computer Buses — A Tutorial," *IEEE Micro*, August 1984, pp. 7–22.

[9]   Przybylski, S.A., *Cache and Memory Hierarchy Design: A Performance-Directed Approach*, San Mateo, CA: Morgan Kaufmann Publishers, 1990.

[10]   Short, R.T., and Levy, H.M., "A Simulation Study of Two-Level Caches," *Proceedings of the 15th Annual International Symposium on Computer Architecture*, June 1988, pp. 81–9.

Efficient Cache Management Techniques

The previous chapters have shown how a cache needs to be managed in order to maintain data consistency. The operating system design must go beyond this to manage the cache in an efficient manner, so that the maximum cache performance will be achieved. This chapter presents software techniques that can improve cache performance while maintaining data consistency.

7.1 Introduction

The overall performance of a cache is determined by three factors: the physical design of the cache, the locality of reference of the programs running on the system, and the operating system's effectiveness at managing the cache. Unfortunately, the operating system can do nothing to improve the cache performance of programs with poor locality of reference. Likewise, the physical design of the cache, in terms of the line size, set size, cache size, and so forth, is fixed when the hardware is built. The operating system, however, can be adapted to manage the cache effectively under varying conditions. This chapter will explore three techniques that reduce cache management overhead and increase overall cache performance. They are *address space layout*, *delayed cache invalidation*, and *cache-aligning data structures*.

7.2 Address Space Layout

7.2.1 Virtually Indexed Caches

Every UNIX system implementation has standard starting addresses for the three main regions in a process (text, data/bss, and stack). For effective cache utilization and even distribution of data, the effect of the cache hashing algorithm on the typical process address space must be considered when choosing these standard virtual addresses. This is true for any type of virtually indexed cache. The effect is best illustrated with an example.

Consider a 64K, direct-mapped, combined text and data virtual cache with 16-byte lines and 4096 lines. The cache uses a 12-bit line index by selecting bits <15..4> from the virtual address. Bits <3..0> select the byte within the line. Assume the page size on the system is 4K. For this example, we will consider the smallest possible process with one page each for text, data, and stack. For the first case, assume the addresses shown in Figure 7–1 were chosen as the standard region starting addresses.

Region	Address
Text	0x0
Data/bss	0x80000000
Stack	0xffff0000

Figure 7–1: Virtual region start addresses for case 1.

At first glance, these might seem like reasonable choices: the 32-bit virtual address space is evenly divided between text and data, and the stack begins near the top of the address space to give it the maximum amount of room to grow. (Assume stacks grow toward lower addresses in this system.) However, if we now consider the cache indexes that these three virtual addresses will generate, an undesirable result occurs as Figure 7–2 illustrates.

Text Address	Index		Data Address	Index		Stack Address	Index
0x0	0		0x80000000	0		0xffff0000	0
0x10	1		0x80000010	1		0xffff0010	1
0x20	2		0x80000020	2		0xffff0020	2
0x30	3		0x80000030	3		0xffff0030	3
⋮	⋮		⋮	⋮		⋮	⋮
0xff0	255		0x80000ff0	255		0xffff0ff0	255

Figure 7–2: Cache indexes generated using addresses from Figure 7–1.

Notice that the addresses of each of the three pages cause the same set of lines to be indexed: lines 0 to 255. This means that all the process's text and data references will only index the first 256 lines of the cache, leaving the remaining 3840 unused, as shown in Figure 7–3.

While the process is running, it will only utilize one sixteenth of the total cache size. All references from the three regions will compete for the same set of lines, causing a poor hit ratio due to cache thrashing. This situation is unnecessary since the process is only 12K in size and is running on a system with a 64K cache. There is more than enough space for the cache to hold the entire address space, if necessary, while the process is running.

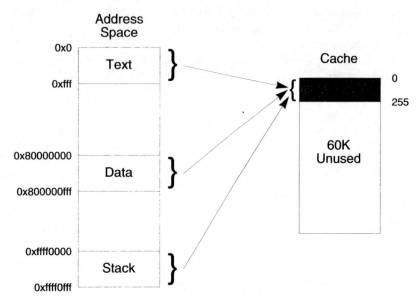

Figure 7–3: Address space mapping onto cache for case 1.

Taking the effects of the hashing algorithm into account, a new set of region start addresses can be formulated by choosing addresses that do not generate the same set of indexes. For example, the addresses shown in Figure 7–4 could be used.

Region	Address
Text	0x0
Data/bss	0x80006000
Stack	0xfffff000

Figure 7–4: Virtual region start addresses for case 2.

These addresses will generate the set of cache indexes shown in Figure 7–5. With this choice of addresses, none of the text or data from any of the pages will overlap in the cache, maximizing cache utilization for this process. Viewing the effect this has in Figure 7–6, it is easy to see that the cache has been partitioned among the text, data, and stack. The shaded areas mark the portion of the cache occupied by the text, data, and stack pages of a small, three-page process. Notice that a text region can be up to 24K in size before it overlaps with the lines occupied by the data region. Likewise, there is a 32K empty section in the cache between the bss and stack region to allow for growth there as well. By allowing for

Text Address	Index
0x0	0
0x10	1
0x20	2
0x30	3
⋮	⋮
0xff0	255

Data Address	Index
0x80006000	1536
0x80006010	1537
0x80006020	1538
0x80006030	1539
⋮	⋮
0x80006ff0	1791

Stack Address	Index
0xfffff000	3840
0xfffff010	3841
0xfffff020	3842
0xfffff030	3843
⋮	⋮
0xfffffff0	4095

Figure 7–5: Cache indexes generated using addresses from Figure 7–4.

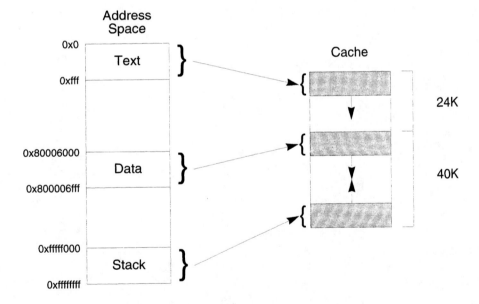

Figure 7–6: Address space mapping onto cache for case 2.

these areas of growth, the system can better support processes with larger address spaces. The choice of standard region start addresses is therefore highly influenced by the expected application region size for the system and can have a dramatic effect on overall cache performance.

This technique of properly choosing region start addresses for virtually indexed caches is important for large caches in order to utilize their space fully. The benefits decrease correspondingly as cache size decreases. The advantages will decrease rapidly for caches smaller than the minimum process size, since it is no longer completely possible to prevent cache contention from within a single process. No effect will be seen for caches that are less than or equal to the page size of the system. At this point, all three regions will contend for the same cache lines, so nothing can be done to prevent thrashing.

7.2.2 Dynamic Address Binding

Virtual caches with keys and virtual caches tagged with physical addresses both attempt to cache multiple process contexts simultaneously. One of the disadvantages of these types of cache organizations is that common virtual addresses in different processes index the same set of cache lines, causing a process's cached data to be replaced when the next process runs. This is especially true when all processes are bound to the same set of standard region start addresses at link time, as described in the previous section. For example, if two small processes were run using the address space layout shown in Figure 7–7, then both processes would compete for the same 12K in the cache.

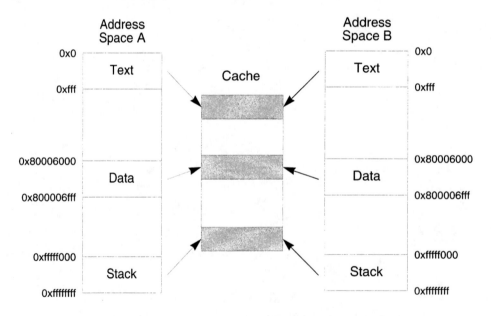

Figure 7–7: Multiple address spaces mapping onto the cache.

Once again, the cache is underutilized. Only 12K of the 64K of cache are being used. This disadvantage can be avoided by using dynamic binding.

A large virtual cache tagged with keys or physical addresses has the potential to cache data from many different processes simultaneously if the processes generate disjoint sets of cache indexes. While it is not completely possible to prevent different processes from indexing the same lines (since the cache is smaller than the combined sizes of the process address spaces), contention can nonetheless be reduced. One way to accomplish this is to bind the programs randomly to one of a set of region start addresses when the program is linked. Likewise, the address for the stack region can be randomly chosen at exec time. This increases the probability that the running processes on the system will have their data randomly distributed in the cache, avoiding contention with other processes. This technique, however, still has the disadvantage that the address bindings are statically fixed at link time, which prevents the operating system from dynamically adjusting to the varying mix of programs on a running system.

A second possibility is to use *position-independent code*. This refers to programs that are not bound to any particular virtual address when the program is compiled or linked. No hard-coded addresses appear in such programs (no absolute branch or data addresses are used). Instead, the operating system can load the program at any virtual address and begin execution. The program then references its data and branch destinations relative to the current PC or to the position where it was loaded. The advantage of this approach is that the operating system can dynamically choose a virtual address for the program during the exec system call. It can then choose an address range that will generate a set of cache line indexes that are disjoint from those of the other running processes. This permits the operating system to adjust to varying process mixes dynamically.

A disadvantage of dynamic address binding is that it removes an element of determinism, the fixed region starting addresses, from the program's execution environment. The lack of this element of determinism will mean that a program must undergo more extensive testing to be sure that it has no hidden dependencies on the virtual address at which it is loaded. Second, these techniques yield a measurable performance gain only on systems with very large caches: large enough to hold the locality of reference of several processes in the system. Smaller caches cannot hold the locality of reference from very many processes at once in any case, so the extra overhead of computing a load address that reduces cache line contention is not warranted. Finally, not all architectures efficiently support position-independent code. Therefore, there may be some performance degradation when compared to non–position-independent code. This must be weighed against the possible increase in cache performance.

7.2.3 Physically Indexed Caches

The region starting addresses do not affect the performance of physically indexed caches since the virtual address is never used when computing the cache index. Physically indexed caches are, however, affected by the addresses of the physical pages to which the virtual pages are mapped. Therefore, it is appropriate for the operating system to attempt to allocate physical pages such that physical cache line contention is minimized. Fortunately, this is relatively simple to achieve. What follows is one possible algorithm for allocating physical pages that can distribute cache references throughout the cache to reduce contention.

With modulo cache indexing, consecutive pages of physical memory will map to consecutive locations in the cache. For example, Figure 7–8 depicts a 16K cache on a system with 4K pages and shows how the physical pages will map onto the cache. (Each shaded area represents one page.)

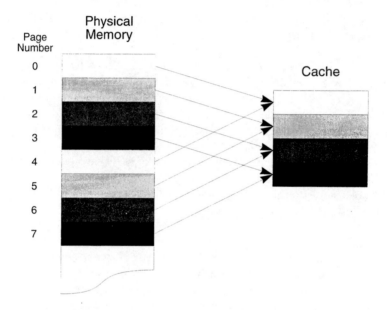

Figure 7–8: Physical page mapping to cache.

As can be seen, every fifth page (e.g., page number 4 in the figure) "wraps around" back to the beginning of the cache. All physical pages with the same shading map to the portion of the cache with the corresponding shading. The different shades are frequently referred to as *colors*. Each physical page is then referred to as having a certain color.

A straightforward way to distribute cache references evenly is to divide the physical pages into n groups, where n is equal to the cache size divided by the page size (i.e., the number of colors in the cache). All pages that index the same portion of the cache (those that have the same color) are then placed in the same group (i.e., sorted according to their color). In the above example, n would be 4 and pages 0, 4, 8, 12, 16, . . . would be in group 0 since they all index the first 4K of the cache. Likewise, pages 1, 5, 9, 13, 17, . . . would be in group 1, and so on. Whenever physical memory is allocated, a page is selected using round-robin allocation from the four groups. For example, the first page would be allocated from group 0, the second from group 1, the third from group 2, the fourth from group 3, then returning again to group 0, group 1, etc. This way the pages in use by the system have cache indexes that should be evenly distributed throughout the cache. This algorithm will consume little operating system overhead.

This technique can be taken a step further if the operating system tracks which colors have been allocated to a particular process so that each process's pages are evenly distributed for best process-level performance. Ideally, a process with only three pages (text, data, and stack) would have each page allocated from a different group, allowing the process to execute without any cache line contention among its own references.

The techniques discussed in this section work well on large caches that are several times the page size or more. They do little, however, to improve performance for small caches since random chance alone would evenly allocate the pages. For example, if the cache were only twice the page size, there would be a 50 percent chance that a physical page allocated at random off the free page list would come from the other group as the previously allocated page without any extra work by the operating system. Furthermore, no improvements can be gained when the cache size is smaller than the page size, because all pages will map to the same cache lines since there is only one color.

7.3 Cache Size Bounded Flushing

The maximum amount of data that needs to be flushed from a cache, for either validating main memory or invalidating the cache, is always bounded by the size of the cache. For example, if an I/O write operation is requested by a process on a system using a write-back cache, then main memory must first be validated with any modified data from the I/O buffer that may still be in the cache (this is true for all types of caches that lack bus watching). If the cache is 2K in size and the I/O buffer is 4K, then at most 2K of data, the maximum amount of data that could have been cached, needs to be flushed from the cache to ensure that the entire 4K I/O buffer in main memory has been updated with any modified data from the cache. Using the fact that cache flushing is bounded by the size of the cache, for all types of caches and in all situations, can provide a great deal of savings in flushing overhead. This is particularly true for small caches, as the amount of data that logically needs to be flushed from large I/O operations or when a large process exits, for example, can easily exceed the cache size. This technique can be further enhanced as will be seen next.

7.4 Delayed Cache Invalidations

As discussed in previous chapters, there are many potential circumstances where the operating system must invalidate the cache to maintain consistency of data. While some cache invalidation must be done immediately (to maintain I/O consistency or prevent a user–ker-

nel ambiguity from occurring), other types of invalidation may be postponed if the particular cache implementation ensures that the inconsistent or stale data will not be referenced.
For example, when a process exits on a system using a virtual cache with keys, it is guaranteed that no other process can hit on the defunct process's stale data as long as the other
processes are using different keys. Therefore, it is not necessary to invalidate the cache at
exit time.

Delaying cache invalidation operations is an important consideration as frequent cache invalidation can dramatically reduce system performance. Part of the reduction comes from
the overhead of the invalidate operation itself. Cache invalidation is time consuming, requiring at the minimum a write to the cache tags to invalidate the line. This operation must
typically be repeated for each line being invalidated, as few cache architectures can flush
more than one line at a time.

Another part of the reduction in system performance is caused by attempting to invalidate
lines that do not even contain the data that the operating system is trying to remove. Typically only a fraction of a process's address space (its locality of reference) will be cached
at any given time. Unfortunately, the operating system has no way to know which portions
are resident in the cache. Therefore, when it comes time to invalidate the cache upon exit,
for example, the operating system must assume the worst case and flush the entire range of
addresses that were in use by the process. So if a 16K cache were used on a system with a
4K page size, and a small process with three pages (text, data, and stack) exited, the operating system would have to invalidate the entire 12K of address space to be sure that all of
the process's data was removed from the cache. Fortunately, nearly all cache architectures
check for a cache hit before actually flushing a line. This prevents the invalidate operation
from removing data from other processes, but still requires a line-by-line check for the 12K
of data.

An improvement is to delay invalidation in those instances where the cache architecture
prevents stale data from being referenced, and later eliminate the stale data with a single
flush operation. It is easy to see the benefits. With a 12K virtual cache with physical tags
and 4K page size, 12K would have to be invalidated on each exit of the smallest possible
process. If ten such processes exited in a row, this would result in 120K of data that the
operating system would have to invalidate from the cache. If the operating system were to
wait until the tenth process exited, it would only need to invalidate the 12K cache once and
be guaranteed that all stale data from the defunct processes had been removed. This results
in a 90 percent savings in invalidations over the ten exit operations. The exact implementation of this technique depends on the cache organization, but is typically inexpensive.

Delayed invalidation cannot be used with virtually tagged caches. (See Exercise 7.9.)
Also, physical caches with bus watching do not require any of these techniques, since they
never need any flushing (refer to Section 6.2.6).

7.4.1 Virtual Caches with Keys

For virtual caches with keys, invalidations from `exit` system calls can be delayed until the system has used all available free keys and needs to reuse the key associated with a defunct process. The operating system can simply maintain two lists of keys: unused keys that contain no associated stale cache data and used keys from defunct processes. When new processes are created, a key is taken from the first list. When that list becomes empty and there are keys on the second list and write-through caching is used, the operating system simply invalidates the entire cache and moves the contents of the second list to the first. The system then has a new pool of free keys to use.

The procedure for write-back caching is complicated since the operating system must not invalidate the modified data of running processes. There needs to be a way to invalidate the data associated with stale keys while not affecting other data (the details of this depend on the particular cache implementation). One cannot simply write back and then invalidate all data from the cache, because the physical pages that were associated with the stale entries may have been reallocated. One possibility would be to change the mappings in the MMU so that all virtual pages associated with any stale key map to an unused physical page of memory. At that point, the entire cache can be written back and invalidated. The write-back of stale data is needless but causes no harm since the corresponding physical pages are not in use. In any case, if there are no keys on either list, then the cache will still have to be flushed (validating main memory if it is write-back) in order to reassign a key from one running process to another.

7.4.2 Physically Tagged Caches without Bus Watching

For virtual caches with physical tags and pure physical caches without bus watching, the operating system needs to maintain two free lists of physical memory (similar to the two lists of keys mentioned in the previous section) one that contains physical pages with no stale cache entries (the clean list) and one for pages that may have stale entries (the dirty list). When processes `exit`, their physical pages are placed on the dirty list. When physical memory needs to be allocated for some new use, it is taken from the clean list. If the clean list is empty and there are pages on the dirty list, then the cache is invalidated once (if write-through caching is used) and all pages on the dirty list are moved to the clean list.

Write-back caching is easier to handle for these two cache organizations since it is known that the physical pages are not in use. Therefore, the entire cache can be written back to memory and invalidated without taking further measures. As before, this may needlessly cause some stale data to be written to memory, but this does no harm since the pages are not in use.

Since the MMU is validating memory accesses on every operation for virtual caches with physical tags and pure physical caches, the delayed cache invalidation technique can be expanded beyond its use during `exit`. Any time memory is deallocated (from shrinking sbrk system calls, shared memory detach, etc.), the freed physical pages can be placed on the dirty list. It is not possible for any process to access any of the stale entries as long as no page tables contain a valid mapping to the deallocated pages. This provides an additional performance boost for these systems that is not possible when using virtually tagged caches.

7.5 Cache-Aligning Data Structures

A final technique for maximizing cache performance is to *cache-align* data structures in memory. Here data structures within a program, and possibly the program itself, are modified to increase the cache efficiency of the data storage. The goal is to arrange the program's data so that frequently accessed data structures fit evenly within cache lines to minimize cache misses and compact the program's locality of reference. While such modifications are not always portable, since knowledge of the cache line size must be "built-in" to the program, they can increase performance in situations where portability of the object code is not as important as the program's performance. A good example of such a program is the operating system itself.

To see how this benefits cache performance, it best to think of memory as an array of cache lines, as Figure 7–9 illustrates.

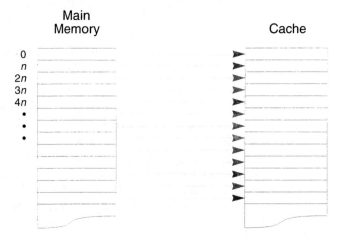

Figure 7–9: Memory viewed as an array of cache lines.

If a physical cache with line size n is used, then the first n bytes starting at physical address 0 map to the first line of the cache. The next n bytes map to the next cache line, and so on. So the n bytes of data beginning at physical addresses 0, n, $2n$, $3n$, etc. will each fit completely within one cache line. (Note that the same is true when using virtual addresses and virtually indexed caches.) With this knowledge, data structures can now be laid out in memory so that they fit as efficiently as possible into the cache lines.

For example, one of the most frequently accessed data structures in the UNIX operating system is the *process table*. The process table is an array of structures, one for each process in the system and contains such things as the process ID, the user and group IDs. If the line size is greater than the size of an individual process table entry but less than twice the size, then an array of process table entries would be laid out in the cache as shown in Figure 7–10.

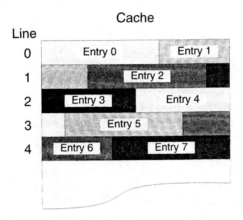

Figure 7–10: Layout of process table array in cache.

Notice how process table entries 1, 3, 4, and 6 span two cache lines while the rest fit completely within a single line. There is a very high degree of locality within a single process table entry while the process it represents is executing. Therefore, we can expect the entire entry to be cache-resident during those periods. Entries 0, 2, 5, and 7 in Figure 7–10 can be loaded into the cache with a single cache miss. Entries 1, 3, 4, and 6 will generate two misses and will occupy two cache lines. The extra misses can affect system performance because of the high degree of locality within a process table entry. Additionally, little is to be gained by caching pieces of other processes' table entries, since processes typically only access their own process table entry while they are running. It is desirable to have each entry occupy only one cache line rather than two, as in the cases of entries 1, 3, 4, and 6. One way to accomplish this is to pad each entry to the cache line size (in circumstances where the line size is greater than the data structure size but less than twice the size). This results in the layout shown in Figure 7–11.

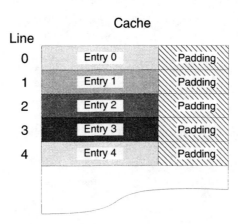

Figure 7–11: Layout of process table array with padding in cache.

Now each entry occupies only one line, meaning that only a single cache miss need be processed to load a complete entry. The trade-off, of course, is wasted memory for the padding at the end of each entry. Also note that fewer process table entries will now fit in the cache at any one time. These considerations must be taken into account when deciding whether to use this technique. If the size of the padding is very small, then it is well worthwhile. However, as the padding size increases, more cache space is wasted and may result in lower performance. Likewise, padding will reduce performance when used on data structures where multiple entries will be part of the locality of reference (such as an array of pointers to hash buckets). Benchmarks must be run in each circumstance to determine the best approach.

Cache-aligning data structures can also help cases where multiple data structures are involved. By placing related data together in memory, one can improve a program's locality of reference and have it require fewer cache lines (and therefore fewer cache misses) to run efficiently. The benefits of cache-aligning data structures are more significant in multiprocessor systems as will be seen in Part III.

7.6 Summary

This chapter has shown several techniques to manage a cache efficiently. Address space layout is important as it affects cache utilization and cache line contention. Cache performance can be increased by carefully choosing region start addresses for virtually indexed caches and choosing physical pages for physically indexed caches to distribute the colors evenly. Since all cache flushing is bounded by the cache size, the technique of delayed cache invalidation can be used to optimize the task of removing stale cache data. Finally, cache-aligning data structures can help reduce cache misses by coalescing the data for a particular locality of reference so that it fits within a single cache line. All of these techniques should be used whenever possible to improve cache performance, especially since all are easy to implement.

7.7 Exercises

7.1   A system has the following separate instruction and data caches: the data cache is a 16K, four-way set associative virtual cache with physical tags and 16-byte lines; the instruction cache is a direct-mapped 8K virtual cache with physical tags and 16-byte lines. The system uses a 4K page size and indexes the data cache with bits <11..4> of the virtual address. The instruction cache is indexed with bits <10..4>. Choose the standard region starting virtual addresses for text, data, and stack if the typical application has between 4K and 16K of text, between 4K and 8K of data, and between 8K and 16K of stack (stacks grow downward). Explain your choice.

7.2   Repeat the previous exercise for a system with the following caches: a 16K direct-mapped virtual data cache, and a 20K direct-mapped physical instruction cache. Both use 16-byte lines.

7.3   Repeat Exercise 7.1 for a system with an 8K two-way set associative unified primary cache and a 4M direct-mapped physical secondary cache. Both use 32-byte lines.

7.4   Why aren't the techniques described in Section 7.2.2 applicable to pure virtual and physical caches?

7.5   How many colors does a 16K four-way set associative cache with 8-byte lines contain if the page size is 4K?

7.6   The MIPS R4000 can support a 4M direct-mapped external physical cache with 128-byte lines. Using the algorithm from Section 7.2.3, how many groups of physical pages should the kernel maintain if the page size is 8K?

7.7   Using the multilevel cache organization from Section 6.3.1 and the technique described in Section 7.3, how much data must be flushed when a process detaches a 1M shared memory region? The on-chip instruction cache is 4K, and the data cache is 8K. Assume the external cache is 256K.

7.8   Explain why delayed cache invalidation cannot be used on I/O buffers associated with DMA read operations that do not use bus watching.

7.9   Explain why delayed cache invalidation cannot be used with pure virtual caches.

7.10   The end of Section 7.4 states that delayed invalidation can be expanded to include such things as shared memory detaches and shrinking `sbrk`s. Explain why delayed invalidation cannot be used in these cases with a virtual cache with keys.

7.11   How should the delayed cache invalidation algorithm described in Section 7.4.2 be modified for a system with a primary virtual cache with physical tags and secondary physical cache?

7.12   How much padding (in bytes) should be added to each data structure in an array if the cache line size is 128 bytes and the existing data structure size is 60 bytes? Assume that, as with process table entries, the locality of reference includes only one array element at a time. Explain your answer.

7.13   Repeat the previous question using a line size of 32 bytes and an existing data structure size of 120 bytes.

7.8 Further Reading

[1]   Gupta, R., and Chi, C., "Improving Instruction Cache Behavior by Reducing Pollution," *Proceedings of Supercomputer '90*, pp. 82–91.

[2]   Lynch, N.L., Bray, B.K., and Flynn, M.J., "The Effect of Page Allocation on Caches," *SIGMICRO Newsletter*, Vol. 23, No. 1-2, December 1992, pp. 222–5.

[3]   McFarling, S., "Program Optimization for Instruction Caches," *Proceedings of the Third International Conference on Architectural Support for Programming Languages and Operating Systems*, April 1989, pp. 183–91.

[4]   Mogul, J.C., and Borg, A., "The Effect of Context Switches on Cache Performance," *Computer Architecture News*, Vol. 19, No. 2, April 1991, pp. 75–84.

[5]   Thiebaut, D.F., and Stone, H.S., "Footprints in the Cache," *ACM Transactions on Computer Systems*, Vol. 5, No. 4, November 1987, pp. 305–29.

[6]   Thompson, J.G., "Efficient Analysis of Caching Systems," Technical Report UCB/CSD 87/374, Computer Science Division, University of California, Berkeley, October 1987.

Part II

Multiprocessor Systems

8

Introduction to Multiprocessor Systems

This chapter introduces the tightly coupled, shared memory, symmetric multiprocessor, which will become the focus for the remainder of the book. It is the type of multiprocessor most commonly used with UNIX systems, since it parallels the execution environment assumed by standard uniprocessor UNIX kernel implementations. The following sections describe its organization in preparation for subsequent chapters that examine how the UNIX operating system can be adapted to run on this type of hardware. Starting with a detailed description of the memory model, this chapter goes on to introduce the problems of providing mutual exclusion on these systems and explains how these problems were solved in uniprocessor kernel implementations. All multiprocessor systems presented in this part of the book operate without caches, to illustrate better the fundamental issues that multiprocessor operating systems must solve. Multiprocessor caching is covered in detail in Part III.

8.1 Introduction

Users continue to demand faster, more economical computer systems. One way designers can meet this demand is by building faster individual CPUs, thus increasing the amount of processing that can be done per unit time. The disadvantage of this approach is that once a certain threshold in CPU performance is passed, hardware and development costs increase at a greater rate than the resulting increase in CPU speed. Building very high-speed CPUs requires balancing many trade-offs. For instance, high-speed silicon technologies have lower component density, have increasingly critical signal synchronization and propagation delay constraints, require more power, and dissipate more heat (sometimes even requiring liquid cooling). Because of these difficulties, designers frequently look to multiprocessors as an alternate approach for increasing the overall performance of a computer system.

A multiprocessor (MP) consists of two or more CPUs combined to form a single computer system. With the multiprocessor approach, the designer alleviates the need to build higher speed CPUs by instead making multiple CPUs available. The workload can then be distributed across all available CPUs. If we compare a uniprocessor (UP) system and a multiprocessor system designed with the same CPU, the multiprocessor will typically not perform any one task faster than the uniprocessor, since the CPU speeds are the same, but it can perform more tasks in parallel per unit time. This is the primary appeal of a multiprocessor: more tasks performed per unit time using more economical CPU technology than if one tried to build a uniprocessor capable of processing the same task load in the same amount of time. In addition, some applications can be rewritten to make use of the inherent parallelism of an MP system. The application can be divided into a set of cooperating subprograms, each of which executes on different processors. In this case, the time required to run the application can be reduced. Scientific applications, for example, can frequently be sub-divided in this manner, with some compilers performing the parallelization automatically.

Multiprocessing provides advantages from a marketing standpoint as well. Multiprocessor systems can be scaled by adjusting the number of CPUs to fit the application environment. This is appealing to end users and customers who can start out with a one- or two-processor system, for example, and upgrade it by adding CPUs as their computing needs expand. In addition, there is the possibility of increased system availability. If one CPU were to fail, the remaining CPUs may be able to continue functioning (depending on the system design), maintaining system availability but at reduced performance. This provides a degree of *fault tolerance*, which is required in environments such as on-line transaction processing where system down-time results in lost revenue.

8.1.1 MP Operating Systems

The operating system for a multiprocessor must be designed to coordinate simultaneous activity by all CPUs. This is a more complex task than managing a uniprocessor system. As will be seen in the following chapters, the extent of the modifications needed to adapt a uniprocessor UNIX kernel implementation to run on an MP system varies greatly. Nevertheless, each implementation must address three main areas: *system integrity*, *performance*, and the *external programming model*.

All MP kernel implementations must maintain system integrity. This means that the CPUs' parallel activity is properly coordinated so that the kernel's data structures are not compromised. This ensures the correct functioning of the system under all possible situations, regardless of the timing of external events and activities by the CPUs in the system. (See Section 8.4 for a discussion of these problems.)

Once integrity is achieved, the implementation can be modified and tuned to maximize performance. While there are many different ways to arrive at an MP kernel that fulfills the system integrity requirement, the different techniques that may be used vary in how efficiently the CPUs are managed and therefore affect the overall performance of the MP system. The next several chapters will highlight several different MP implementations, that vary greatly in performance.

The third factor, the external programming model, determines how the presence of multiple CPUs affects the system call interface (which is part of the *application program interface*, or *API*). The operating system designer for an MP system has to choose whether or not to "disguise" the MP system to appear as a UP system. If the system call interface is compatible with that of a UP, then existing uniprocessor application programs can be run on the MP without change. If, on the other hand, the system call interface is not compatible, then programs will have to be written with explicit knowledge of the multiple CPUs in the system and may be required to use special system calls to communicate with, or pass data to, processes running on other processors.

For example, consider the UNIX process ID number. In a uniprocessor system, any process can refer to any other process by this number. An MP kernel implementation that does not maintain the uniprocessor system call interface may require that a CPU number be given in addition to the process ID in order to refer to a process running on a different processor. The disadvantage of such an approach is that it eliminates application portability.

Because of the high cost of rewriting programs to conform to a new system call interface, most implementations choose to maintain the uniprocessor system call interface so the presence of the multiple CPUs is entirely transparent. This is the only type of implementation considered in this book. This is not to say that the operating system is forbidden from offering new interfaces that allow programmers to make use of the inherent parallelism in an MP; it means that the kernel must provide all the uniprocessor system call interfaces and facilities that have become standard.

Before approaching the subject of the kernel modifications needed to enable the UNIX system to run on an MP, it is important to understand the architecture of multiprocessor systems so that effects on the operating system can be seen.

8.2 The Tightly Coupled, Shared Memory, Symmetric Multiprocessor

The multiprocessor architecture of interest for the remainder of the book is the *tightly coupled, shared memory, symmetric multiprocessor*, frequently abbreviated as the *SMP*. (As the SMP is the only type of multiprocessor presented in this book, "SMP" and "MP" will be used interchangeably.) As mentioned earlier, this is the most commonly used type of MP since it readily supports the implementation of an operating system that retains the uniprocessor external programming model. A high-level view of such a system with four CPUs appears in Figure 8–1.

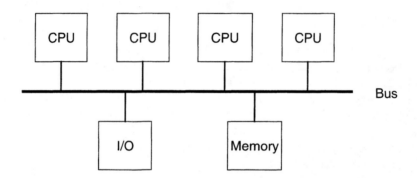

Figure 8–1: Example SMP block diagram.

There are several important factors to understand about this type of multiprocessor architecture. First, all CPUs, memory, and I/O are *tightly coupled*. There are several ways to achieve this, but the simplest and most commonly used method is for all units to be directly interconnected by a common high-speed bus (which is the type of interconnect that this book focuses on). Recall from Section 6.2.6 that a bus is a broadcast-based communication medium capable of transferring one or more words of data at a time. This allows any unit connected to the bus to communicate at high speeds with any other unit. Because a bus transfers many bits in parallel at high speed, its length is very limited. Another meaning of *tightly coupled* refers to the fact that all components are located within a short distance of one another (usually within the same physical cabinet).

The *shared memory* aspect is easy to see in Figure 8–1: there is a single, globally accessible memory module used by all CPUs and I/O devices. The CPUs themselves have no local memory (except possibly for caches) and store all their program instructions and data in the global shared memory. The important factor here is that data stored by one CPU into memory is immediately accessible to all other CPUs. As will be seen in Part III, each CPU may have its own local cache but no other nonshared memory.

The final aspect of importance in the SMP architecture is that memory access is *symmetric*. This means that all CPUs and I/O devices have equal access to the global shared memory. The contents of memory are fully shared, and all CPUs and devices use the same physical address whenever referring to the same piece of data. Access to the bus and memory is arbitrated, so that all CPUs and devices are guaranteed fair access. In addition, their accesses do not interfere with one another. For example, it is not necessary for a program running on one CPU to be concerned with programs running on other CPUs that are reading and writing different portions of memory. Any simultaneous accesses to the same portions of memory by multiple CPUs are arbitrated so they will not interfere with one another. (This is discussed further in Section 8.3.)

Note that due to their location, the I/O devices are also shared in a symmetric fashion by all CPUs. This allows any CPU to initiate I/O operations as needed. Also note that the I/O devices still have complete access to the global memory for DMA purposes. This means that data written by any CPU can be sent to an I/O device via DMA, and the result of a DMA operation from a device to memory is accessible by all CPUs. Since I/O devices access memory over the same shared bus, all discussion describing how CPUs access memory is directly applicable to DMA-based I/O devices.

It is easy to see now that the architecture of an SMP is a logical extension of the UP system structure presented in Section 6.2.6: the bus, memory, and I/O structure are the same in both. The UP system is converted to an SMP with the addition of more CPUs, much like adding additional I/O cards to the system.

The maximum number of CPUs that can be used for practical work in an SMP is limited by the bandwidth of the shared bus and main memory. This bandwidth, which is fixed when the system is designed, must be sufficient to supply the needs of all CPUs and I/O devices in the system, or the overall performance of the system will suffer. For example, if the bus and main memory bandwidth is 20 Mb/sec and the I/O devices need to perform 5 Mb/sec of DMA for a given application environment, then this leaves 15 Mb/sec available for the CPUs. If each CPU requires 3 Mb/sec in order to continue executing instructions without delay, then the system can support a maximum of 5 CPUs. If additional CPUs are added beyond this limit, then there will be more total memory requests than the bus and main memory can supply, causing requests to be delayed. If we consider the case where a CPU is fetching instructions from main memory, then it is apparent that any delay will cause the CPU to execute instructions slower, since it will sit idle while waiting for memory to supply the next instruction. As a result, the additional CPUs will not increase the performance of the system.

The design of an SMP system bus and main memory subsystem that supplies the proper bandwidth to the CPUs and I/O devices is an important aspect in the design of a high-performance system. From the operating system's point of view, though, it has no effect on the problems faced in order to maintain the uniprocessor external programming model, or on ensuring the correct functioning of the operating system itself. The chapters that follow will therefore concentrate on the operating system issues SMP systems present.

8.3 The MP Memory Model

The *memory model* for an MP system defines how the CPUs, and hence the programs running on them, access main memory, and how they are affected by simultaneous accesses by other CPUs. Since main memory is accessed with physical addresses, the effects of virtual address translation, including any exceptions that might occur when an unmapped virtual address is used, are not considered as part of the memory model. The individual CPUs handle these activities. The memory model is instead concerned with the transfer of physical addresses and data between the CPUs and main memory.

It is possible for different MP hardware systems to implement different memory models. The operating system programmer must thoroughly understand the model of a particular machine, so that the operating system can be made to run correctly and ensure system integrity. The primary differences between memory models on different machines center on how the hardware orders the execution of load and store instructions. Changing the order of execution is done to improve performance. The memory model also specifies how simultaneous accesses to the same memory location by multiple processors behave. Different implementations of the bus arbitration and/or main memory subsystems, which may be chosen to reduce cost or improve speed, are the chief factors that alter the memory model as seen from the CPU's point of view.

The memory model for an SMP includes those characteristics mentioned in the previous section: memory is globally accessible, tightly coupled, and symmetric. The model then goes on to define load–store ordering and the effects of simultaneous access to memory by multiple CPUs. (The reader may wish to review the introductory system bus discussion in Section 6.2.6 before continuing.)

8.3.1 The Sequential Memory Model

The simplest and most commonly used memory model is the *sequential memory model* (also known as *strong ordering*). In this model, all load and store instructions are executed in *program order,* the order in which they appear in the program's sequential instruction stream, by each CPU. Furthermore, the effects of load and store instructions on main memory are sequential from the viewpoint of the main memory subsystem and other CPUs. This model is used by the Motorola MC68000 and MC88000 processor lines, the Intel 80X86 family, as well as the MIPS RISC processor line. To contrast this, architectures such as SPARC Version 8, which may send the data associated with store instructions to main memory in a different order than the stores were executed, are nonsequential since another CPU reading the same data will not see the contents of main memory change in the same order as the program storing the data executed the instructions. (Other memory models and the effect they have on the operating system will be explored in Chapter 13.)

Along with defining the order of memory operations to be in program order, the sequential memory model also defines them to be *atomic*, as described in the following two sections. For simplicity and because of its common usage, this book will focus on the sequential memory model for the next several chapters. All examples and discussion will assume this model is used. Assume further that the compiler or optimizer does not change the order of instructions within a program. The description in Sections 8.3.2 and 8.3.3 covers the core aspects of a simplified memory model needed to understand its effects on the operating system. Most systems employ various optimizations to improve performance without affecting the software. These are beyond the scope of this book.

8.3.2 Atomic Reads and Writes

The sequential memory model defines an individual read or write operation from a CPU or I/O device (through DMA) to main memory to be atomic. Once begun, such an operation cannot be interrupted or interfered with by any other memory operation, from any CPU or I/O device, on the system. (Special hardware implementation techniques, such as "split reads," that allow multiple bus operations to proceed in parallel, are not considered, since they are transparent to the operating system.) The atomicity of memory operations is easily guaranteed by virtue of the single shared bus that must be used to access main memory. The bus can be used by only one CPU (or I/O device) at a time. If multiple CPUs wish to access memory simultaneously, special hardware in the bus *arbitrates* between the multiple requestors to determine which will be allowed to use the bus next. When one is chosen, the bus is *granted* to it, and that CPU is allowed to complete a single read or write operation atomically involving one or more physically contiguous words in main memory. During this single operation, all other CPUs and I/O devices are inhibited from performing any of their own read or write operations. After the completion of each operation, the cycle repeats: the bus is rearbitrated and granted to a different CPU. The choice of which CPU gets the next turn on the bus may be done using *first-in-first-out*, *round-robin*, or whatever other type of scheduling is implemented in the bus hardware. Eventually, all CPUs that wish to access main memory are granted a cycle, so that none are prevented from accessing memory forever. (Remember that the SMP architecture specifies that there be equal access to main memory among all CPUs.) I/O devices arbitrate for the bus in the same manner as CPUs.

Figure 8–2 shows an SMP system with two processors (I/O has been omitted for simplicity). Assume processor A wishes to read data from main memory. If the bus is idle, it will be allowed to begin its bus cycle immediately by sending the address to be read to main memory (see diagram (a) in Figure 8–2). If CPU B tries to begin a write operation while the data is being returned to CPU A, its operation will be inhibited until A completes its cycle (diagram (b)). Once A's cycle is complete, the bus arbitrator will grant the bus to B, which will then be allowed to complete its memory operation (diagram (c)).

The amount of data that can be transferred in a single operation is limited to prevent one processor from hogging the bus. While the typical transfer size in actual machines is usually equal to the cache line or subline size, the transfer size is not directly visible to the operating system. Since only MP systems without caches are being considered now, assume that, for simplicity, the transfer size is a single word.

As just seen, delays may be introduced while waiting for the bus to be granted to the CPU. From the software's viewpoint, an instruction that accesses memory merely seems to take longer to execute if it is delayed while waiting for its turn on the bus. This is why it is important for the bus and memory bandwidth to be greater than or equal to the sum of the memory traffic that all CPUs and I/O devices are capable of generating. If this is not the case, then the CPUs will not be able to execute at peak performance since they will be frequently delayed when trying to access memory. In any event, bus-induced delays are transparent to the software running on the system (except for performance).

Given the preceding definition, it is clear that if each CPU accesses only a portion of main memory that is unique and independent of the portions accessed by the other CPUs, then each CPU will execute as if it were the only processor on the system, from the software's point of view. The fact that multiple CPUs access the same shared main memory unit is irrelevant, since each CPU's accesses are to locations that are never accessed by the other processors. (This again shows how the SMP is a logical extension of the UP system model.) Now we must consider the effects of simultaneous access to the same location by multiple CPUs.

In the sequential memory model, even simultaneous access to the same word in main memory by multiple CPUs is guaranteed to be atomic. If all CPUs in a system were to simultaneously issue a write to the same word, for example, then the bus arbitration hardware would inhibit the writes of all but one of the CPUs. The chosen CPU would be granted the bus and allowed to complete its write. When complete, the bus arbitrator would choose a different CPU to go next, and that CPU would be allowed to perform its write. As before,

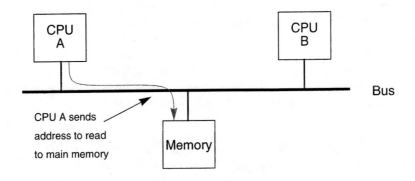

(a) CPU A begins read bus cycle.

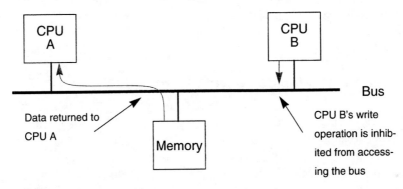

(b) Memory returns data to CPU A while CPU B waits.

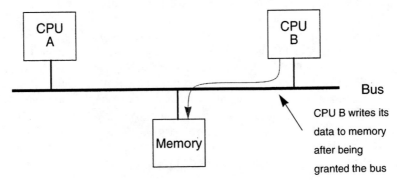

(c) CPU B is granted bus for its memory operation.

Figure 8–2: Bus arbitration example.

this continues until all write requests are satisfied. The net result is that simultaneous accesses to memory, whether to the same location or not, are *always* sequentialized by the bus arbitrator. From the perspective of the main memory subsystem, only a single memory operation occurs at any point in time. It is *never* possible for two or more CPUs to be actually writing into the same main memory at exactly the same time since all operations are sequentialized by the bus. (Special hardware techniques such as multiported memory and multiple memory banks can allow certain memory operations to proceed in parallel, but any system supporting the sequential memory model will still maintain the atomicity of memory operations described here.)

While memory operations are atomic and sequentialized, the relative ordering of simultaneous memory operations from multiple CPUs is nondeterministic. If two CPUs try to write to the same location at exactly the same time, the software cannot make any assumptions about which one will go first. Likewise, if one CPU is reading from a memory location while another is writing to that location, the CPU performing the read will get either the old or new value of the location, since one cannot guarantee whether the read or the write operation will occur first. Such situations are called *race conditions* and are discussed in more detail in Section 8.4.

8.3.3 Atomic Read-Modify-Write Operations

Since the need to synchronize access to shared memory locations is so common on SMP systems, most implementations provide the basic hardware support for this through atomic *read-modify-write* operations. Such operations allow a CPU to read a value from main memory, modify it, and store the modified value back into the same memory location as a single atomic bus operation. These are a separate type of operation from the regular atomic reads and writes used by the normal memory and instruction fetch operations described previously. Read-modify-write operations are implemented as special instructions in the CPU and are only used when such synchronization is necessary.

The type of modification that may be done to the data during a read-modify-write operation is implementation specific, but the most common is the *test-and-set* instruction. The Motorola MC68040 and the IBM 370 architecture are examples of processors that use this operation. This instruction reads a value from main memory (usually a byte or word), compares it to 0 (setting the condition code in the processor accordingly), and unconditionally stores a 1 into the memory location, all as a single atomic operation. It is not possible for any other CPU or I/O device to access main memory once a test-and-set instruction begins its bus cycle. With this one basic operation, the operating system can build higher level synchronization operations, as will be described in later chapters.

While more complex operations, such as an atomic increment or decrement operation, are possible, modern RISC systems tend to offer simpler operations. For example, probably the most basic single atomic read-modify-write instruction is the *swap-atomic* operation.

This type of operation is used in the Sun SPARC processor and in the Motorola MC88100 RISC processor, which lacks the test-and-set instruction of the MC68040. Such an instruction merely swaps a value stored in a register with a value in memory. One can then construct a test-and-set operation by setting the value in the register to 1, performing the atomic swap, and then comparing the value in the register (the old contents of the memory location) to 0 afterwards. Figure 8–3 illustrates this in C.

```c
int
test_and_set(volatile int *addr)
{
        int old_value;

        old_value = swap_atomic(addr, 1);

        if (old_value == 0)
                return 0;

        return 1;
}
```

Figure 8–3: Test-and-set implemented using swap-atomic.

The `test_and_set` function takes the address of a word to operate on. The `volatile` declaration tells the compiler that the integer `addr` points at can change while the function is executing even if the function itself has not changed the value. In this case, another processor could be doing a test-and-set operation to the same location at the same time. Declaring a variable as `volatile` disables code optimizations the compiler might otherwise make, such as collapsing redundant loads or stores into a single operation. While not strictly necessary for this example, it is good programming practice to declare all variables subject to simultaneous modification by multiple processors as volatile. (Volatile declarations are also used when accessing I/O device registers.)

To continue the test-and-set example, assume that the `swap_atomic` function simply executes the swap-atomic hardware instruction on the word addressed by its first parameter. It returns the old contents of that location after swapping it with its second parameter. This implementation shows that the test-and-set operation is really two separate operations combined into one instruction. The first phase of a test-and-set is to fetch the current value of the word and replace it with 1 atomically. The second phase is to test the value fetched in the first phase. The RISC approach to this is to use separate, simpler instructions, thereby simplifying the hardware design. (See Exercise 8.9 at the end of the chapter for another example of the usage of swap-atomic.)

Some RISC architectures simplify this a step further and provide a pair of instructions that together can be used to perform an atomic read-modify-write operation. The pair is the *load-linked* and *store-conditional* instructions. This is the approach taken by the MIPS R4000 RISC processor. (Previous versions of the MIPS processor did not implement any atomic read-modify-write instructions.) The load-linked instruction performs the first half of an atomic read-modify-write operation by loading a value from memory (usually a word), and sets a flag in the hardware that indicates that a read-modify-write operation is in progress to that location. (The flag is usually maintained by the cache controller and is invisible to the software.) The read-modify-write operation is completed by using the store-conditional instruction to store any desired value back to the memory location loaded from, but it does so *only* if the hardware flag is still set. Any stores done to this location by any CPU or I/O device since the load-linked instruction was executed will cause this flag to be cleared. Therefore, if the store-condition instruction finds the flag still set, it will be guaranteed that the location hasn't changed since the load-linked instruction was done and that the entire sequence of instructions starting with the load-linked and ending with the store-conditional have been executed atomically with respect to the associated memory location. These two basic instructions can then be used to construct more sophisticated atomic operations (the details of which are left as an exercise).

Synchronization is still achievable without any atomic read-modify-write operations at all using a software technique known as *Dekker's Algorithm*. It can operate using only individual atomic read and atomic write operations. Dekker's Algorithm is covered in detail in Section 13.2.

8.4 Mutual Exclusion

Since the sequential memory model does not guarantee a deterministic ordering of simultaneous reads and writes to the same memory location from more than one CPU, any shared data structure cannot be simultaneously updated by more than one CPU without the risk of corrupting the data. The lack of deterministic ordering causes a race condition to occur. This happens whenever the outcome of a set of operations in an SMP depends on the relative ordering or timing of the operations between two or more processors. Such nondeterministic behavior can be catastrophic to the integrity of the kernel's data structures and must be prevented.

To illustrate this problem, consider the case where there is a global counter that is incremented at various points in time by either CPU in a two-CPU system. Assume that the counter must accurately reflect the sum of all increments by either CPU (i.e., none can be lost). Further assume the system uses the *load–store* architecture, meaning that operands and results for arithmetic instructions (as well as most other instructions) must be in registers and are moved between registers and main memory with load and store instructions. (This is typical of most RISC systems.) Therefore, in order to increment a memory location, the three-instruction sequence shown in Figure 8–4 is needed. The sequence is shown in pseudo-assembly language, where the notation %r0 is used to indicate a reference to register 0 and counter refers to global counter value in main memory. As each CPU in an MP system has its own set of registers, %r0 refers to register 0 of the CPU that is executing the instruction.

```
load    %r0,counter
add     %r0,1
store   %r0,counter
```

Figure 8–4: Assembly language instructions to increment a counter in memory.

The time line in Figure 8–5 shows the contents of counter in main memory as well as the contents of register 0 of each CPU. Assume one instruction is executed by each CPU in each time interval. For the first example, consider the case where CPU 1 executes all three instructions in Figure 8–4's code fragment first, followed by CPU 2 (a dash appearing in a column indicates that the value at that point in time is irrelevant to the example).

	CPU 1			CPU 2	
Time	Instruction Executed	Register %r0	Value of Counter	Instruction Executed	Register %r0
1	load %r0,counter	0	0		-
2	add %r0,1	1	0		-
3	store %r0,counter	1	1		-
4		-	1	load %r0,counter	1
5		-	1	add %r0,1	2
6		-	2	store %r0,counter	2

Figure 8–5: Results if both CPUs execute the code sequence sequentially.

In this case, the resulting value of counter is correct: the value was initially 0 and was incremented twice (once by each CPU), yielding a final value of 2. The value of counter will always be correct as long as the CPUs never execute the three-instruction sequence at the same time. If they do, the results shown in Figure 8–6 will occur.

Here we see that the final value of counter in main memory is incorrect. The value is 1 instead of 2, meaning that one of the increments has been lost. This happened because both CPUs fetched the original value of counter from main memory, unaware that a simulta-

	CPU 1			CPU 2	
Time	Instruction Executed	Register %r0	Value of Counter	Instruction Executed	Register %r0
1	load %r0,counter	0	0	load %r0,counter	0
2	add %r0,1	1	0	add %r0,1	1
3	store %r0,counter	1	1	store %r0,counter	1

Figure 8–6: Results if both CPUs execute the code sequence simultaneously.

neous increment operation was in progress on the other CPU. In such instances, the processors are said to race with one another, since the outcome depends on which one gets through the code sequence first.

Any sequence of instructions that updates variables or data structures shared between two or more processors can lead to a race condition. The sequence of instructions themselves is referred to as a *critical section*, and the data they operate on is the *critical resource*. A critical section can be as short as the three-instruction sequence in Figure 8–4, or can involve extensive regions of code. In order to eliminate the race condition caused by multiple processors simultaneously executing the critical section, at most one processor may be executing within the critical section at one time. This is referred to as *mutual exclusion* and can be implemented in a variety of ways.

Before going on to show how mutual exclusion can be implemented in MP systems, it is useful to review how it was achieved in uniprocessor UNIX systems and why these techniques fail on MPs. The following chapters will then describe several techniques that can be used on MP systems.

8.5 Review of Mutual Exclusion on Uniprocessor UNIX Systems

It is possible to have race conditions even in uniprocessor operating systems. Any system that permits multiple threads of control, such as multiple processes, needs to consider mutual exclusion between the threads. It is also possible for the instructions executed by interrupt handlers to race with the code they interrupt.

The following sections review the important aspects of the implementation of mutual exclusion on uniprocessor UNIX systems. These systems divide their handling of this problem into three categories according to the type of mutual exclusion. They are *short-term mutual exclusion, mutual exclusion with interrupts,* and *long-term mutual exclusion.*

8.5.1 Short-Term Mutual Exclusion

Short-term mutual exclusion refers to preventing race conditions in short critical sections, such as the one presented in Section 8.4. These critical sections occur when the kernel is in the midst of updating one of its data structures. Since the kernel data structures are shared among all executing processes, a race condition would be possible if two or more processes executing in kernel mode were to update the same data structure at the same time. Since a uniprocessor can only execute one process at a time, these race conditions are only possible if one process executing in the kernel can be preempted by another. This is why the designers of the UNIX kernel chose to make the kernel nonpreemptable while executing in kernel mode. Recall from Section 1.2 that processes executing in kernel mode are not timesliced and cannot be preempted. A context switch to another process occurs only when a kernel mode process allows it.

The nonpreemptability rule for processes executing in kernel mode greatly reduces the complexity of uniprocessor UNIX kernel implementations. Since only one process is allowed to execute in the kernel at a time and is never preempted, race conditions while examining and updating kernel data structure cannot occur. Therefore, nothing more need be done to maintain data structure integrity in cases such as the counter example presented in Section 8.4.

8.5.2 Mutual Exclusion with Interrupt Handlers

If the code executed by an interrupt handler accesses or updates the same data structures used by noninterrupt code (usually referred to as *base-level* code), then a race condition can occur. For example, a process executing in kernel mode may be executing the code sequence in Figure 8–4 when an interrupt occurs. If the interrupt handling code were to attempt to increment the same counter, then the wrong result might occur just as in the MP scenario. Fortunately, processes executing in kernel mode are permitted to disable interrupts temporarily. Therefore, whenever the base-level code is about to update a data structure that is shared with an interrupt handler, it first disables interrupts, executes the critical section, and then reenables interrupts. The act of disabling and reenabling interrupts implements mutual exclusion. In uniprocessor UNIX kernels, the *spl* functions provide the means to enable and disable interrupts. "Spl" stands for "Set Priority Level" and refers to setting the interrupt priority level below which interrupts are ignored by the processor. For example, the C code that properly protects the increment of counter from all possible interrupts is displayed in Figure 8–7.

```
s = splhi();
counter++;
splx(s);
```

Figure 8–7: Protecting a critical section from interrupts.

The `splhi` function blocks all interrupts (sets the interrupt priority level to the highest level). They remain blocked until another explicit call to an `spl` function unblocks them. Since interrupts from different devices can occur at different priority levels, the `spl` functions used to block interrupts return the old priority so that it can be restored at the completion of the critical section. The counter can now be safely incremented without racing with code in an interrupt handler. The previous priority level, returned by `splhi`, is restored with the `splx` function.

It is important to understand how this implementation of mutual exclusion differs from that of short-term mutual exclusion. With short-term mutual exclusion, implementing the general policy of nonpreemptability of kernel mode processes solved the problem without having to code it into the kernel explicitly. With interrupts, mutual exclusion had to be explicitly coded into the algorithms by use of the `spl` functions.

8.5.3 Long-Term Mutual Exclusion

Most of the UNIX system calls provide services that are guaranteed to be atomic operations from the viewpoint of the user program. For example, once a `write` system call to a regular file begins, it is guaranteed by the operating system that any other `read` or `write` system calls to the same file will be held until the current one completes. (This mutual exclusion of file operations makes it easier to write deterministic user programs that share files.) A `write` system call may require one or more disk I/O operations in order to complete the system call. Disk I/O operations are relatively long operations when compared to the amount of work that the CPU can accomplish during that time. It would therefore be highly undesirable to use nonpreemptability for such long operations, because the CPU would sit idle waiting for the I/O to complete. To avoid this, the process executing the `write` system call needs to allow itself to be preempted so other processes can run. Once preemption is allowed, however, a technique is needed to prevent other `read` and `write` system calls to the same file from beginning. Uniprocessor UNIX kernels implement this type of mutual exclusion with the `sleep` and `wakeup` functions.

The `sleep` function is an internal kernel routine (which can only be used by processes executing in kernel mode) that causes the process calling it to be suspended until a specified event occurs. This is the primary means by which a process executing in kernel mode voluntarily relinquishes control and allows itself to be preempted. The `wakeup` function is used to signal that a particular event has occurred, and it causes all processes waiting for that event to be awakened and placed back on the run queue. The event is represented by an arbitrary integer value, which is usually the address of a kernel data structure associated with the event. The technique for using `sleep` and `wakeup` to implement long-term mutual exclusion is illustrated with the following example.

Each object within the kernel that requires long-term mutual exclusion is represented by an instance of a data structure. To implement atomic operations on the object, the object is "locked" so that only one process can access it at a time. This is done by adding a flag to the data structure that is set if the object is presently locked. For simplicity, assume the flag is stored in a byte in the object's data structure, so that each has a unique flag. One possible way to implement mutual exclusion on an arbitrary object is shown Figure 8–8 (the actual details vary in different versions of the UNIX system and are not relevant to the discussion here).

```
void
lock_object(char *flag_ptr)
{
        while (*flag_ptr)
                sleep(flag_ptr);

        *flag_ptr = 1;
}
```

Figure 8–8: Code to lock an object.

In this example, the flag is set to 1 to indicate that a process currently has the object locked. At the beginning of an atomic operation, the `lock_object` function is called to lock the object by passing a pointer to the flag byte associated with it. If the object is not presently locked, the condition in the *while* statement will fail and the process will lock the object by setting the flag (the need to use a *while* loop is explained ahead). The process can now continue the operation and voluntarily preempt itself, while waiting for disk I/O to complete in the case of atomic file operations for instance, and be assured that no other process can successfully lock the object until the first process explicitly unlocks it. Any other process that attempts to access the same object will use the same data structure and attempt to lock it by calling the `lock_object` function with the address of the same flag byte. This time, however, the condition in the *while* statement will be true, and the process will execute the `sleep` call, which will suspend the process.

It is important to understand that the operations of testing the flag, finding it to be clear, and setting it form a critical section and must be done with mutual exclusion. Otherwise a race condition would be possible, resulting in cases where two or more processes would think they had the object locked. Fortunately, this race condition is prevented by the uniprocessor nonpreemptability policy.

Notice that the event being slept on is the address of the flag itself. The general convention of using an address within the data structure associated with the object to identify the event is used throughout the kernel. This is convenient as it easily allows processes waiting for the locks on different objects to sleep on different events. That way, only the processes waiting for a particular lock are awakened when the lock becomes free (as opposed to awakening all processes waiting for any lock).

The `sleep` function itself needs to perform only a few simple operations to suspend the calling process. It first records the event in a table so that a later `wakeup` operation can identify which processes to awaken. It then performs a context switch, causing another process to be selected for execution. The process that calls `sleep` is not run again until it is awakened. (Note that the `sleep` function in actual UNIX kernel implementations takes a second parameter that specifies the priority at which the process should be run when it is awakened. This has been omitted for simplicity as it does not affect mutual exclusion.)

When the process holding a lock has completed its atomic operation on the object, it would call the function shown in Figure 8–9.

```
void
unlock_object(char *flag_ptr)
{
        *flag_ptr = 0;
        wakeup(flag_ptr);
}
```

Figure 8–9: Code to unlock an object.

Here the flag is cleared and all processes that were waiting for the lock are awakened using the `wakeup` function. The event passed to `wakeup` must match that used with the `sleep` function in order for the correct processes, those waiting for this particular lock, to be awakened. To awaken a process, `wakeup` searches the table where `sleep` recorded which processes were sleeping on which events, and places all those that match the given event on the run queue. An important aspect of the `wakeup` function is that there is no "memory" of the event saved. This allows the `unlock_object` function to call it without having to know whether or not any processes are actually sleeping on the event. If `wakeup` finds no processes waiting on an event, it simply returns without doing anything. A process that sleeps on the same event in the future will always be suspended, regardless of what happened during previous `wakeup` operations.

When a process that was sleeping in the code shown in Figure 8–8 is awakened and later chosen for execution by the scheduler, it simply resumes execution where it had left off, namely inside the `sleep` function at the point where the context switch occurred. At this point, `sleep` returns to the caller. The *while* loop condition is retested, and if the desired lock is still free, the loop terminates and the process acquires the lock for itself. If the object is again found to be locked, the process goes back to sleep and waits to be reawakened by the new holder of the lock. This can happen in two different situations. The first is if another process came along and locked the object while the process that had been awakened was waiting on the run queue for its time slice. The second is if there were multiple processes waiting for the same lock. Since there is no memory of a wakeup operation, `wakeup` must awaken all processes sleeping on the same event. They are all placed on the run queue and are run sequentially as the scheduler selects them. The first one to run will find the lock free and will successfully lock it. If one of the other processes awakened for this same event runs before the first releases the lock, it will find it locked and go back to sleep. It will try to acquire the lock again when it is reawakened. This is why the `lock_object` function must contain a *while* loop.

It can now be seen that the `lock_object` and `unlock_object` functions provide long-term mutual exclusion around the section of code that they bracket. Unlike short-term mutual exclusion provided by the nonpreemptability policy, this type of mutual exclusion must be explicitly coded into the kernel.

8.6 Problems Using UP Mutual Exclusion Policies on MPs

To achieve a high-performance MP system, it is desirable to allow system calls and other kernel activity to occur on any processor. This way, the kernel's workload can be distributed throughout the system. Unfortunately, the techniques presented in the previous sections, which enable a uniprocessor kernel implementation to avoid race conditions, fail to work properly when more than one processor on an MP system can execute kernel code at the same time. The reasons for this follow, while solutions to these problems are presented in the following chapters.

The primary difficulty that prevents a uniprocessor kernel from running properly on an MP system is that multiple processors executing in the kernel simultaneously violates the assumptions that support short-term mutual exclusion. Using the nonpreemptability policy for kernel processes, UP systems avoid many race conditions. Even though the kernel on an MP system can prevent a process on a particular processor from being preempted by another, a process that begins a system call on another processor can cause the same race conditions described in Section 8.4 to occur. Once more than one processor begins executing in the kernel, the kernel data structures can be corrupted unless additional steps are taken to prevent races.

Mutual exclusion with interrupt handlers may not function properly on an MP system either. The `spl` functions only affect the processor priority on the processor they are executed on and do not affect interrupts delivered to other processors. Depending on the design of the hardware, interrupts may be delivered to any CPU in the system, or they may always be directed to one CPU. In either case, a process executing on one processor that is using the spl functions to implement mutual exclusion on data structures shared with interrupt handlers will not be properly protecting the data if the interrupt handler begins execution on a different processor.

Finally, the coding technique used to implement long-term mutual exclusion with the sleep and wakeup functions will not work correctly on MP systems. Recall from Section 8.5.3 that the implementation of lock_object relies on short-term mutual exclusion to prevent race conditions between the time the flag is tested and the process either goes to sleep or sets the flag itself. Since the short-term mutual exclusion policy is no longer effective on MPs, these code sequences now contain races. For example, consider the case where two processes on different processors begin to execute the lock_object function in Figure 8–8 at the same time. Assuming the lock is currently free, they will both test the flag and find it to be clear. They will then both go on to set the flag and continue their execution. Each process will then think it had acquired the lock, thus violating the mutual exclusion policy.

There can also be race conditions between lock_object and unlock_object. It is possible for one process executing lock_object to test the flag and see it set just as another process is about to release the lock. Imagine the second process releasing the lock between the time the first process tests the lock and starts executing the sleep function. In this case, the wakeup function called when the lock is released would do nothing, since the process locking the object hadn't gone to sleep yet. When the first process does call sleep, it will be suspended even though the lock is now free. Note that there is now no process to wake it up (no process has the lock, therefore no process will call unlock_object). The process will continue to sleep until another process tries to acquire the same lock. This new process will find the lock free and will be able to acquire it without sleeping. When it eventually releases the lock, wakeup will cause the first process to run again. Since there is no guarantee on how long the first process will have to wait for this to occur, such situations must be prevented by eliminating the race condition.

Three main techniques for preventing these problems are presented in the next three chapters. They vary in the degree to which the kernel must be modified to prevent all possible race conditions.

8.7 Summary

The SMP is the most commonly used type of multiprocessor system since it parallels the execution environment of uniprocessor systems. The important aspects of such MP systems are that all CPUs and I/O devices are tightly coupled, share a common global main memory, and have symmetric and equal access to memory. Most MP kernel implementations preserve the uniprocessor external programming model so that application programs do not have to be modified to run on an MP.

The memory model for an MP describes the ordering of load–store instructions within a program and how simultaneous access to main memory by multiple CPUs results. The sequential memory model provides for atomic read and write operations that are executed according to program order on each CPU, but it does not specify the relative ordering of simultaneous operations to the same memory location from different CPUs. Because of this, the sequential memory model usually provides some type of atomic read-modify-write operation that CPUs can use for synchronization purposes.

The lack of deterministic ordering of memory operations to shared locations allows race conditions to occur. Any multiple instruction operation to a shared memory location or data structure, such as an increment operation or adding a new element to a linked list, is subject to races since multiple processors could be attempting the operation at the same time. To prevent races, the kernel must implement mutual exclusion to sequentialize access to shared data and prevent it from being corrupted.

To simplify their design, uniprocessor UNIX kernel systems have relied on the fact that processes executing in kernel mode are nonpreemptable. This eliminates most race conditions since no other process can access any kernel data until the currently executing process voluntarily relinquishes the CPU. Long-term mutual exclusion, needed to support atomic file operations, for instance, is done using explicit locks and calls to the `sleep` and `wakeup` functions. Mutual exclusion with interrupt handling code is implemented by explicitly blocking and unblocking interrupts for the duration of the critical regions in the base-level kernel code. However, these policies fail to provide mutual exclusion on MP systems when kernel code can be executed simultaneously on more than one processor.

8.8 Exercises

8.1   What happens if a CPU and an I/O device both try to read or write the same main memory location at exactly the same time?

8.2   If three CPUs all store different values into the same memory location at the exact same time, can you predict what value will be in that location after all three stores have completed if strong ordering is used? (Assume CPU 1 stores a 1, CPU 2 stores a 2, and CPU 3 stores a 3.)

8.3   If memory location 0x100 initially contains the value 10, and CPU 1 stores the value 1 into that location at the exact same time that CPU 2 reads from that location, then what will be the value in that location after both operations have finished? What value will CPU 2 read and why? Assume the system uses the sequential memory model.

8.4   How many bus transactions can be in progress on the bus at the same time? Assume the sequential memory model defined in Section 8.3.1 is used.

8.5   Consider an SMP system that contains ten CPUs and five I/O devices that can per-
       form DMA. The bus is arbitrated using the round-robin technique, meaning that
       each CPU or I/O device is allowed one bus transaction at a time until all CPUs and
       devices have had a turn. The cycle then repeats, granting each requestor a second
       cycle, and so on. If a bus transaction takes one unit of time (including arbitration),
       what is the minimum and maximum times that an arbitrary CPU or I/O device
       must wait between the time it requests the bus and the time it is granted the bus?

8.6   Write a C function with the following prototype that implements an atomic test-
       and-set operation:

       ```
       int test_and_set(int *addr);
       ```

       The function should unconditionally store a 1 into the addressed location. It
       should return 1 if the previous contents were nonzero; otherwise, it should return
       0. The addressed location should be updated atomically. Implement this function
       using the following C subroutines that have been coded for you:

       ```
       int load_linked(int *addr);
       int store_conditional(int *addr, int value);
       ```

       where load_linked performs a *load-linked* operation on the word at address
       addr and returns the word, and store_conditional conditionally stores val-
       ue into location addr and returns 1 if the store occurred and 0 otherwise.

8.7   Write a C function with the following prototype that implements an atomic-swap
       operation:

       ```
       int swap_atomic(int *addr, int new_value);
       ```

       The old value at location addr is atomically swapped with new_value, and the
       old value is returned. Use the load_linked and store_conditional func-
       tions defined in Exercise 8.6.

8.8   Write a C function with the following prototype that implements an atomic incre-
       ment operation:

       ```
       void inc_atomic(int *addr);
       ```

       addr points to a word in memory that is atomically incremented. Use the
       load_linked and store_conditional functions defined in Exercise 8.6.

8.9   Implement the inc_atomic() function from the previous question, but this time
       using the swap-atomic primitive (described in Section 8.3.3) as the only read-
       modify-write operation (i.e., test-and-set, load-linked, and store-conditional may

not be used for this problem). Use the atomic-swap function written in Exercise 8.7. For this problem, assume that the value to be incremented is always greater than or equal to zero and that it never overflows. It is permissible to require the use of a separate function to read the value of the counter, if necessary, to avoid race conditions while the count is being incremented. Show this function as well if your solution needs it.

8.10   Does the following function to insert a new element onto a linked list contain a race condition? Assume that the linked list is shared among all the processors of an SMP system but that the new element is not shared until it is on the list. Explain why a race condition does or does not exist.

```
struct element_t {
        element_t     *next;
        int           data;
};

void insert(element_t *list, element_t *new)
{
        new->next = list;
        list = new;
}
```

8.11   Repeat the previous exercise, assuming a uniprocessor environment instead. Explain why a race condition does or does not exist. What happens if the insert function is used in both interrupt handlers and base-level code?

8.12   Consider two CPUs executing the code shown below:

```
            CPU 1                                    CPU 2

int                              void
get_wait_count(int *lock_ptr)    lock_object(int *lock_ptr)
{                                {
    return lock_ptr[1];              while (lock_ptr[0]){
}                                        lock_ptr[1]++;
                                         sleep(lock_ptr);
                                         lock_ptr[1]--;
                                     }

                                     lock_ptr[0] = 1;
                                 }
```

Only CPU 1 executes the get_wait_count functions and only CPU 2 executes lock_object. The lock_object function has been modified from the version shown in Figure 8–8 to keep count of the number of processes that are sleeping for the lock. This has been implemented by passing in a pointer to an array of two words, the first of which holds the lock flag and the second of which holds the count of the number of processes waiting for the lock. Are there any race conditions here? Explain.

8.13   What can be done to guarantee that a process that has slept while trying to acquire a lock with the code shown in Figure 8–8 will eventually be able to do so if there is a continuous stream of other processes all competing for the same lock? Assume a uniprocessor environment.

8.9 Further Reading

[1]   Adve, S., and Hill, M., "Weak Ordering — A New Definition," *Proceedings of the 17th Annual Internation Symposium on Computer Architecture*, May 1990, pp. 2–14.

[2]   Adve, S., and Hill, M., "Implementing Sequential Consistency in Cache-Based Systems," *Proceedings of the 1990 International Conference on Parallel Processing*, August 1990, pp. I:47–50.

[3]   Dewan, G., and Nair. V.S.S., "A Case for Uniform Memory Access Multiprocessors," *Computer Architecture News*, Vol. 21, No. 4, September 1993, pp. 20–6.

[4]   Dubois, M., Scheurich, C., and Briggs, F., "Memory Access Buffering in Multiprocessors," *Proceedings of the 13th Annual International Symposium on Computer Architecture*, June 1986, pp. 434–42.

[5]   Dubois, M., and Scheurich, C., "Memory Access Dependencies in Shared-Memory Multiprocessors," *IEEE Transactions on Software Engineering*, Vol. 16, No. 6, June 1990, pp. 660–73.

[6]   Gharachorloo, K., Lenoski, D., Laudon, J., Gibbons, P., Gupta, A., and Hennessy, J., "Memory Consistency and Event Ordering in Scalable Shared-Memory Multiprocessors," *Proceedings of the 17th Annual International Symposium on Computer Architecture*, May 1990, pp. 15–26.

[7]   Gharachorloo, K., Gupta, A., and Hennessy, J., "Performance Evaluation of Memory Consistency Models for Shared-Memory Multiprocessors," *Proceedings of the Fourth International Conference on Architectural Support for Programming Languages and Operating Systems*, April 1991, pp. 245–57.

[8]   Gillford, P., Fielland, G., and Thakkar, S., "Balance: A Shared Memory Multiprocessor," *Proceedings of the Second International Conference on Supercomputing*, May 1987.

[9]   Lamport, L., "How to Make a Multiprocessor Computer that Correctly Executes Multiprocess Programs," *IEEE Transactions on Computers*, Vol. C-28, No. 9, September 1979, pp. 241–8.

[10]   Lamport, L., "The Mutual Exclusion Problem: Part I — A Theory of Interprocess Communication," *Journal of the ACM*, Vol. 33, No. 2, 1986, pp. 313–26.

[11]   Lamport, L., "The Mutual Exclusion Problem: Part II — Statement and Solutions," *Journal of the ACM*, Vol. 33, No. 2, 1986, pp. 327–48.

[12]   Miya, E.N., "Multiprocessor/Distributed Processing Bibliography," *SigArch News*, Vol. 13, No. 1, March 1985, pp. 27–9.

[13]   Mosberger, D., "Memory Consistency Models," *ACM SIGOPS Operating Systems Review*, Vol. 27, No. 1, January 1993, pp. 18–26.

[14]   Peterson, G.L., "Myths About the Mutual Exclusion Problem," *Information Processing Letters*, Vol. 12, No. 3, June 1981, pp. 115–6.

[15]   Sawyer, B.B., "Multiprocessor UNIX Utilizing the SPARC Architecture," *UniForum Conference Proceedings*, February 1989, pp. 107–19.

[16]   Scheurich, C., "Access Ordering and Coherence in Shared Memory Multiprocessors," Ph.D. thesis, University of Southern California, May 1989.

[17]   Stone, H.S., *High-Performance Computer Architecture, Third Edition*, Reading, MA: Addison-Wesley, 1993.

9

Master–Slave
Kernels

This chapter presents the simplest technique for modifying a uniprocessor kernel implementation to run on an SMP system without race conditions: the *master–slave* kernel. An SMP mutual exclusion primitive, called a *spin lock*, is also presented. These are used to reestablish short-term mutual exclusion which then prevents the problems described at the end of the last chapter from occurring. The causes of *deadlocks* in MP kernels are presented next, along with techniques used to avoid them. Finally, the kernel changes necessary to implement a master–slave system are presented, followed by a discussion of the performance effects.

9.1 Introduction

The short-term mutual exclusion implementation technique presented in Section 8.5.1 is one of the main foundations upon which uniprocessor UNIX kernel implementations are built. It eliminates the need to code explicit locking into the kernel in many places. Without it, race conditions can occur when accessing and updating kernel data structures. This technique alone is insufficient to prevent race conditions on SMP systems when two or more processes are executing in the kernel simultaneously on different processors. Even if no preemption of kernel processes is allowed, the simultaneous kernel activity by multiple processors causes races nonetheless. Several methods can be used to prevent such races, some requiring extensive kernel modification. This chapter considers the simplest technique of reinstating the uniprocessor assumptions on MP systems as a primer to more complex implementations.

The short-term mutual exclusion technique from Chapter 8 relies on the fact that there is never more than one process executing in the kernel at the same time. A simple technique for doing this on an MP system is to require that all kernel execution occur on one physical processor, referred to as the *master*. All other processors in the system, called *slaves*, may execute user code only. A process executing in user mode may execute on any processor in the system. However, when the process executes a system call, it is switched to the master processor. Once the system call completes, the process may again run on any processor. Any traps generated by a user-mode process running on a slave (such as page faults or arithmetic exceptions) also cause a context switch to the master, so that the mutual exclusion requirements of the kernel trap handlers are also maintained. Finally, all device drivers and device interrupt handlers run only on the master processor.

The master–slave arrangement preserves the uniprocessor execution environment from the kernel's point of view. This allows a uniprocessor kernel implementation to run on an MP system with few modifications and works for any number of processors. One of the main areas of modifications is in how processes are assigned to individual processors. A simple technique for this is to have two separate run queues, one containing kernel-mode processes that must be run on the master, and one containing user-mode processes for the slaves. At each context switch, each slave selects the highest priority process on the slave run queue, while the master processor selects the highest priority process on the kernel process queue. A process running on a slave that executes a system call or generates a trap is placed on the run queue for the master processor. When the master processor performs a context switch, the old process it was executing is placed on the slave queue if it was executing in user mode; otherwise, it goes back on the master queue.

Since there could be multiple processors enqueuing, dequeuing, and searching the run queues at the same time, a way to prevent race conditions is needed. The run queues are the only data structures that require an explicit MP short-term mutual exclusion technique, since all other data structures are protected by running all kernel code on the master. The easiest way to provide such short-term mutual exclusion is with spin locks.

9.2 Spin Locks

A *spin lock* is an MP short-term mutual exclusion mechanism that can be used to prevent race conditions during short critical sections of code. As with the functions from Chapter 8 that block interrupts and implement long-term mutual exclusion, a spin lock is acquired prior to entering the critical section and released upon completion. Spin locks derive their name from the fact that a processor will busy-wait (spinning in a loop) when waiting for a lock that is in use by another processor.

Spin locks are the only MP primitive operation needed to implement a master–slave kernel. As will be seen in the following chapters, other types of primitives may be used by different kernel implementations. The simplicity and efficiency of spin locks for protecting short critical sections make them useful in these implementations as well.

Spin locks are implemented using a single word in memory that reflects the current status of the lock. A lock is acquired for exclusive use by a particular processor when that processor is able to change the status of the spin lock from the unlocked to the locked state atomically. This must be done as an atomic operation to ensure that only one processor can acquire the lock at a time. For the examples that follow, a value of zero will be used to represent the unlocked state of a spin lock. All routines take a pointer to the spin lock status word to be acted upon. A spin lock can then be initialized with the routine shown in Figure 9–1.

```
typedef int lock_t;

void
initlock(volatile lock_t *lock_status)
{
        *lock_status = 0;
}
```

Figure 9–1: Initializing a spin lock.

Using the test-and-set instruction presented in Section 8.3.3, the function in Figure 9–2 can be used to lock a spin lock atomically (the definition of the `test_and_set` function is as given in Exercise 8.6, where it returns 1 if the previous state was nonzero, otherwise it returns 0).

```
void
lock(volatile lock_t *lock_status)
{
        while (test_and_set(lock_status) == 1)
                ;
}
```

Figure 9–2: Atomically locking a spin lock.

The function in Figure 9–2 locks a spin lock by atomically changing its state from 0 to 1. If the lock status is already 1 (meaning the lock is in use by another processor), then the `test_and_set` function returns 1, and the processor spins in the loop until the lock is released. A spin lock is released by simply setting the lock status to 0, as the code in Figure 9–3 shows.

```
void
unlock(volatile lock_t *lock_status)
{
        *lock_status = 0;
}
```

Figure 9–3: Unlocking a spin lock.

Spin locks work correctly for systems with any number of processors. If multiple processors try to acquire the same lock at exactly the same time, the atomic nature of the `test_and_set` function allows only one processor at a time to change the lock status from 0 to 1. The other processors will see the lock is already set and will spin until the processor owning the lock releases it. The kernel can now form a critical section by surrounding it with `lock` and `unlock` function calls (see the code in Figure 9–4).

```
lock(&spin_lock);
perform critical section
unlock(&spin_lock);
```

Figure 9–4: Implementing a critical section with spin locks.

Spin locks work well if the critical section is short (usually no more than a few hundred machine instructions). They should not be used as a long-term mutual exclusion technique, because processors waiting for the lock do not perform any useful work while spinning. Overall system performance will be lowered if the processors spend too much time waiting to acquire locks. This can also happen if too many processors frequently contend for the same lock. (These points will be further illustrated in Chapter 10.)

Two things can be done to reduce lock contention. First, the kernel can use different spin locks for different critical resources. This prevents processors from being held up by other processors when there is no threat of a race condition. Second, the `lock` and `unlock` functions should be enhanced to block interrupts while the lock is held. Otherwise, an interrupt occurring while the processor holds a spin lock will further delay other processors waiting for that lock (and might result in a deadlock, as explained in the next section).

9.3 Deadlocks

When one processor tries to acquire exclusive use of more than one resource at a time, it must be done with care, otherwise a deadlock becomes possible. A deadlock occurs when two or more processors are each holding a resource needed by another, and each is waiting for the resource held by the other to be released. For example, consider a data structure where each element is on two separate linked lists. Assume a separate spin lock is used to protect each list so that they may be accessed independently. Further assume that certain operations require that an element found by traversing one list must be unlinked from both lists, and that this must be done as a single, atomic operation. This means that the locks for both lists must be held simultaneously while unlinking the element. If this is implemented by acquiring the lock for the list to be traversed first and then attempting to acquire the lock for the other list, a deadlock could result. This can occur when two processors each begin such an operation by traversing the opposite list, as shown in Figure 9–5.

Processor 1	Processor 2
`lock(&lock_a);`	`lock(&lock_b);`
`find element to unlink on list a`	`find element to unlink on list b`
`lock(&lock_b);`	`lock(&lock_a);`
`unlink element from both lists`	`unlink element from both lists`
`unlock(&lock_b);`	`unlock(&lock_a);`
`unlock(&lock_a);`	`unlock(&lock_b);`

Figure 9–5: Potential deadlock situation.

If both processors begin their respective code fragments at exactly the same time, then processor 1 will acquire `lock_a` and processor 2 will acquire `lock_b`. Processor 1 will then busy-wait for `lock_b` and processor 2 will busy-wait for `lock_a`. Since neither processor will ever relinquish the lock it is already holding, the two processors will spin forever trying to acquire the other lock. The two processors have now deadlocked. This particular deadlock situation is called the *AB–BA deadlock*, which refers to the fact that the two processors have tried to acquire the locks in the opposite order from one another. This action will always invite a potential deadlock.

Note that whether a deadlock actually occurs depends on the relative timing between the two processors. If either processor 1 or processor 2 can complete its code sequence (as shown in Figure 9–5) before the other begins, then no deadlock will result.

To prevent such deadlocks from occurring, all processors must acquire *nested locks*, locks that are acquired in sequence and held simultaneously, in the same order. Correcting the code from the previous example results in the common code sequence in Figure 9–6 to be executed by any processor whenever it begins an operation requiring an element to be atomically unlinked from both lists.

```
lock(&lock_a);
lock(&lock_b);
find element to unlink on list a or b
unlink element from both lists
unlock(&lock_b);
unlock(&lock_a);
```

Figure 9–6: Modified algorithm to prevent deadlocks.

Note that either list can still be traversed by holding only that list's lock in the cases where an atomic unlink is not going to be performed. No deadlock is possible even if another processor is simultaneously performing an atomic unlink.

To summarize, the key to preventing AB–BA deadlocks is for all processors to acquire and release nested locks in exactly the same order. The same is true when three or more locks are involved: as long as the same ordering is maintained when acquiring and releasing locks, no deadlocks will occur.

Deadlocks can occur when using spin locks in other situations. For example, if a process holding a spin lock were to perform a context switch, then any processor that attempted to acquire the same lock would spin until the process holding the lock was run again and released the lock. Such situations are undesirable from a performance standpoint, since the other processors could spin for an arbitrarily long period of time, but even worse, they can also lead to a deadlock. This can happen if all processors in the system try to acquire a spin lock held by a process that has context-switched. Once the processors begin spinning for the lock, they no longer perform context switches. This means that it is not possible for the process holding the spin lock to be run, and hence it will never have a chance to release the lock. All processors will spin forever, deadlocking the system. To prevent this deadlock from occurring, no process must ever hold a spin lock across context switches.

Another situation where deadlocks can occur with spin locks is if base-level kernel code and an interrupt handler use the same spin lock. If a processor has locked the spin lock and an interrupt occurs on that same processor, a deadlock will result if the interrupt handler tries to acquire the same lock. The processor will spin forever at interrupt level since the process that was interrupted will never get a chance to release the lock. For this reason, the base-level kernel code must block interrupts from occurring when holding a spin lock used by an interrupt handler.

A process can also cause a deadlock with itself by attempting to acquire the same lock more than once. As with the preceding case, the process will spin forever on the second attempt to acquire the same lock. Some implementations modify the spin lock primitives to check for a process locking the same lock more than once (called *recursive locking*), and skip the lock operation if the process has already acquired the lock. The process keeps a count of the number of recursive lock attempts that have been made so that an equal number of unlocks must occur before the spin lock is actually released. This allows nested procedures to acquire locks without knowledge of what locking has been done at previous levels. The implementations and examples in this book do not rely upon such techniques, and so these will not be considered further.

9.4 Master–Slave Kernel Implementation

With a master–slave kernel implementation, the only critical resources are the two run queues. The operations of enqueuing and dequeuing processes from them must be done with mutual exclusion to prevent the queues from being corrupted. This is easily accomplished by protecting each queue with a spin lock.

9.4.1 Run Queue Implementation

Assume that each run queue is implemented as an unsorted linked list. (A priority queue would be a better implementation, but the simplicity of an unsorted linked list allows the examples to concentrate on the mutual exclusion aspects of the problem.) The list is made by linking together the process table entries of the processes on the queue. Among other information, the process table entry contains the process's priority and a pointer to the next element on the list. To prevent unnecessary contention, a separate spin lock is used for the master and slave run queues. Figure 9–7 shows the definitions for these data structures.

```
typedef struct proc proc_t;
typedef struct queue queue_t;

struct proc {
        proc_t *p_next;         /* next process on run queue */
        int     p_pri;          /* process priority          */
        ...
};

struct queue {
        lock_t q_lock;          /* lock protecting queue     */
        proc_t *q_head;         /* head of run queue         */
};

queue_t master_queue;
queue_t slave_queue;
```

Figure 9–7: Declarations for master–slave run queues.

The definition of the queue structure exhibits a typical coding technique used in MP kernels: combining a critical resource and the lock that protects it into a single data structure.

The two queues are initialized at system start-up time with the routine in Figure 9–8.

```
void
init_queue(queue_t *q)
{
        initlock(&q->q_lock);
        q->q_head = NULL;
}

init_queue(&master_queue);
init_queue(&slave_queue);
```

Figure 9–8: Initializing a run queue.

A process can then be placed on one of the queues with the code shown in Figure 9–9. The enqueue function can be called at any time by any processor in the system, since the spin lock prevents all possible race conditions when dealing with the run queue.

```
void
enqueue(queue_t *q, proc_t *p)
{
        int s;

        s = splhi();
        lock(&q->q_lock);
        p->p_next = q->q_head;
        q->q_head = p;
        unlock(&q->q_lock);
        splx(s);
}
```

Figure 9–9: Enqueuing a process on a run queue.

The call to splhi blocks all interrupts while the spin lock is held. This prevents races with interrupt handlers that may make processes runnable. This can happen when an I/O operation completes, for instance, that causes a process waiting for the I/O to be placed back on the run queue. As stated previously, a deadlock would result if an interrupt occurred while the run queue spin lock was held and the interrupt handler called the enqueue function. (Some implementations combine the calls to splhi and lock into a single operation. See Section 12.4.1.)

The dispatch function shown in Figure 9–10 selects and removes the highest priority process from a queue, or returns null if the queue is empty. Assume that the lowest p_pri value represents the highest priority process on the queue. If more than one process has the same p_pri value, and that value is the lowest, then the oldest such process (the one closest to the end of the queue) is selected.

The spin lock for the queue must be held for the entire search operation and while the chosen entry is dequeued. It would be incorrect to search the list without holding the lock, since the state of the queue could change if another processor added or deleted an entry. This also ensures that two processors that are simultaneously trying to dispatch a process do not pick the same one. Once the chosen process is removed from the queue, the lock can safely be released.

As before, interrupts must be blocked to prevent deadlocks that could happen if an interrupt occurred while executing the critical region in dispatch and the handler called the enqueue function.

```
proc_t *
dispatch(queue_t *q)
{
    proc_t **p;
    proc_t **highest_ptr;
    proc_t *highest;
    int s;

    highest_ptr = NULL;
    s = splhi();
    lock(&q->q_lock);

    for (p = (proc_t **)&q->q_head; *p; p = &(*p)->p_next)
        if (highest_ptr == NULL ||
            (*p)->p_pri <= (*highest_ptr)->p_pri)
                highest_ptr = p;

    /* Unlink the highest priority process unless the queue
     * was empty
     */

    if (highest_ptr != NULL) {
        highest = *highest_ptr;
        *highest_ptr = (*highest_ptr)->p_next;
    } else
        highest = NULL;

    unlock(&q->q_lock);
    splx(s);
    return highest;
}
```

Figure 9–10: Selecting a process from a run queue.

9.4.2 Process Selection for Slaves

The slave processors can only execute processes that are on the slave run queue. When a slave needs to select a new process for execution, it would execute the code fragment in Figure 9–11.

```
while ((newproc = dispatch(&slave_queue)) == NULL)
    ;
```

Figure 9–11: Slave processor code to select a new process to run.

If there are no processes on the queue, the slave simply busy-waits in the loop until one becomes available. There is no harm in busy-waiting in this case, since there is nothing for it to do anyway. Note however, that as the slave repeatedly calls dispatch while waiting for a process to run, it will acquire and release the queue lock each time. While the overhead of doing this on the slave is irrelevant, the combined overhead of all slave processors holding the lock could needlessly delay the processor that is trying to enqueue a process. This is not a critical issue for master–slave implementations, since the critical section of code in the dispatch routine is small when the queue is empty. Even so, it is useful to see how to avoid unnecessary lock contention, as the technique can be applied in other situations. To reduce contention, the dispatch routine shown in Figure 9–10 can be modified to test the state of the queue before acquiring the lock. The code in Figure 9–12 can be added to the beginning of the routine to return early when the queue is empty.

```
proc_t *
dispatch(queue_t *q)
{

        . . .

        if (q->q_head == NULL)
                return NULL;


        . . .
```

Figure 9–12: Modified dispatch routine.

It is safe to examine the state of the queue as shown without holding the lock even if other processors are simultaneously enqueuing or dequeuing processes from the queue. The resulting race conditions are no different from what could happen if the lock were held. For example, assume that between the time the queue was found to be empty in the code in Figure 9–12 and before the return was executed, another processor enqueued a process on the queue. This case is no different from the case where the queue lock is released in the code in Figure 9–10 after the queue was found to be empty, and another processor enqueues a process before the return statement could be executed.

Second, there is no danger of two different processors racing with each other when only one process is on the queue. Assume two slaves both begin execution of the modified dispatch code in Figure 9–12 at the same time. If there's one process on the queue, both slaves will find the queue nonempty and will proceed to acquire the queue lock. One will get the lock first and will successfully dequeue the sole entry on the list. The other will then run, find the queue empty, and simply return null. The key factor here is that the queue state is retested after acquiring the queue lock. The code cannot assume that the queue has at least one process on it even though the test at the top of the function showed it to be non-empty. Another important factor is that the code in Figure 9–11 continues calling dispatch until it finds a process. This eliminates any races that might occur when a new process is added to the queue just after the dispatch routine finds the queue to be empty.

When a process running on a slave executes a system call or generates a trap, it is simply switched over to the master processor by using the enqueue function to place it on the master_queue. The code in Figure 9–11 is then used to choose a new process to execute on the slave.

9.4.3 Process Selection for the Master

Since the master processor can run either kernel- or user-mode processes, it can select processes from either queue, as shown in Figure 9–13.

```
do {
        if ((newproc = dispatch(&master_queue)) == NULL)
                newproc = dispatch(&slave_queue);
} while (newproc == NULL);
```

Figure 9–13: Master processor code to select a new process to run.

The code gives preference to choosing a process off the master run queue since those processes can only be run on the master. User-mode processes can run on any processor, so those can be left for the slaves to run (unless there are no kernel-mode processes to run).

9.4.4 Clock Interrupt Handling

Each processor in a master–slave implementation receives and handles its own clock interrupts. This allows each processor to keep track of the currently executing process's time quantum. To keep the uniprocessor short-term mutual exclusion policy in place, all the usual kernel activity associated with a clock interrupt, such as keeping track of the time of day, performing alarm system call timeouts, recalculating process priorities, and so forth is handled by the master processor. The clock interrupt handler on the slaves simply has to check for situations where a context switch should be performed. This can happen in three instances: when the current process's time quantum expires, when a higher priority process is added to the slave run queue (traditional UNIX implementations communicate this by setting a flag, which can be checked in the clock interrupt handler), or when a signal has been posted to the process. In the first two cases, the currently executing process is put back on the slave run queue. In the third case, the process must be switched to the master processor so that the kernel code required to handle the signal can run without the risk of race conditions.

9.5 Performance Considerations

As seen in the preceding sections, the implementation of a master–slave MP kernel is straightforward and conceptually simple. It satisfies the system integrity requirement and preserves the uniprocessor external programming model discussed in Section 8.1.1. An important question, though, is how it will perform.

Ideally, the overall system throughput of an SMP will increase linearly as more processors are added and will equal the product of the number of processors and the throughput of a single processor. Thus a two-processor system should be able to handle twice the throughput of a UP, a three-processor system should have three times the throughput, and so on. How close an MP implementation can approach this ideal depends on three main factors: the hardware architecture, the application job mix, and the kernel implementation.

If the hardware design is not suitable for an SMP system, then no amount of software tuning will allow an implementation to approach the ideal goal of linear performance increase as additional processors are added. For example, if the memory subsystem does not provide sufficient bandwidth for all processors (see Section 8.2), then the extra processors will not be fully utilized. For the purposes of this book, MP performance will focus on the software architecture and will assume that the hardware is not the limiting factor.

The application job mix refers to the number and type of applications that are run on the system. By using the same application mix on different kernel implementations, a benchmark can be formed by which system performance can be measured and compared with other kernel implementations. It is important to understand the application job mix of any benchmark in order to interpret the results correctly. For example, a benchmark composed of a single program that is run once will never show any performance gain on an MP system over a UP system, since it provides no work for the other processors to do. The most useful benchmark results are obtained when the benchmark closely models the intended use of the system.

To show how disparate benchmark results for the same kernel implementation can be, consider two different benchmarks run on a master–slave MP implementation. The first benchmark consists of a group of processes that are completely compute bound. Once started, they generate no page faults, traps, nor system calls, and perform no I/O. Such a benchmark will show a nearly ideal linear increase in system throughput as additional processors are added to the system. Since the benchmark spends all its time in user mode, all the slave processors can be fully utilized. On the other hand, a second benchmark that consists of the same number of processes, except that the processes are system call bound, will show the opposite result. If each process merely executes a trivial system call, such as getpid or time, continuously in a tight loop, with as little user-level processing as possible, this benchmark will show no performance improvement over a UP system, regardless of the number of processors present in the MP system. In this scenario, all processes in the benchmark require continuous service by the kernel. Since only the master processor can provide this service, the slaves will sit idle throughout the benchmark. Likewise, I/O bound benchmarks will show no performance improvement on MP systems with master–slave kernels, since the increased CPU throughput available from the slaves doesn't speed up I/O.

It can be concluded from this that a master–slave implementation is a poor choice for highly interactive (or otherwise I/O intensive) application environments because of the high system call and I/O activity of these applications. It would be a good choice for compute bound scientific application environments. The usefulness of this type of MP kernel implementation for other application job mixes can be shown with the following example.

Application mixes that lie between the extremes of compute bound or system call bound may still be able to benefit from additional slave processors. If an application mix is run on a UP and found to spend 50 percent of its time executing in the kernel, 40 percent executing at user-level, and 10 percent waiting for I/O to complete, for example, then the 40 percent at user-level can be distributed to the slave in a two-processor master–slave MP system. This will result in, at most, a 40-percent performance improvement. This assumes that all the user-level work can be done in parallel with the kernel and I/O activities. If this is not true, then there will be less performance improvement. It is typical for some portion of the user-level work to depend on the results of system calls or I/O operations. So if it turns out that only half of the user work can be done in parallel with the kernel and I/O work, then a 20-percent performance improvement will be seen. Adding additional processors will not increase performance any further because they can do nothing to reduce the 50 percent of the time the application mix spends running on the master, nor can they reduce the time spent waiting for I/O. This is the primary problem with master–slave kernels when used in non-compute bound environments: the master quickly becomes a bottleneck and prevents throughput from increasing when additional processors are added. It may not be economical to add a second processor for only a 20-percent performance improvement. Anything beyond a two-CPU master–slave MP system is almost always uneconomical for situations such as these.

9.5.1 Master–Slave Improvements

The master–slave kernel implementation can be improved by relaxing the requirement that *all* system calls execute on the master. Any system call that merely returns a single piece of kernel information can be safely executed by a slave. The `getpid` system call is an example, since it only returns a value that cannot change for the life of the process. Other system calls in this category are `getpgrp`, `getppid`, `getuid`, `geteuid`, `getgid`, `getegid`, `getrlimit`, `time`, `times`, and `uname`.

Similarly, any system call that modifies only data that is private to one process (i.e., never modified by any other process) can also be run on the slaves. No races can result if only one process modifies the data. Examples of system calls in this group are `alarm`, `nice`, `profil`, `setpgrp`, `setuid`, `setgid`, `setrlimit`, `ulimit`, and `umask`. (A further discussion of situations where locking can be omitted is presented in Section 10.3.)

While these modifications are easy to make, they are unlikely to have a significant effect on the overall performance of a master–slave system. These system calls are not frequently used, nor are they the ones that consume any significant amount of CPU time in the kernel.

Since tying all the kernel activity to one processor is the limiting factor in a master–slave implementation, the only way to improve system performance is to make it possible for multiple processors to execute in the kernel simultaneously. This may require a significant amount of work to modify the kernel so that race conditions cannot occur. These techniques are explored in the next chapter.

9.6 Summary

A uniprocessor kernel cannot be run on an SMP system without modification. The short-term mutual exclusion technique used by UP kernels relies on the fact that there is never more than one process executing in the kernel at the same time. One way an MP system can keep this policy in effect is to restrict all kernel activity to one processor in the system. This master processor services all system calls, interrupts, and any other kernel activity. The other processors in the system, the slaves, can execute processes only while they are running in user mode. Once a process running on a slave begins a system call or generates a trap, it must be switched to the master for servicing.

In such an implementation, the only critical resource is the run queue. A technique is needed to serialize access to the run queues by multiple processors so that race conditions are prevented. Spin locks, a simple MP mutual exclusion primitive, can be used for this. Spin locks can be implemented by atomically updating a memory location so that only one processor can successfully acquire the lock at any point in time. Once a processor acquires a spin lock, all other processors attempting to acquire the lock will busy-wait until it is released.

Deadlocks can result if locks are used in a nested fashion and are not locked in the same order by all processors. To prevent deadlocks, all processors must lock nested locks in the same order. A deadlock can also result if a process holding a spin lock performs a context switch, or if an interrupt handler attempts to acquire a spin lock already held by the process that was interrupted.

In a master–slave kernel, the master tends to be the limiting factor in the overall performance of the system. Once the master processor is saturated, adding additional slaves will not improve performance since they cannot share the kernel load in the general case. A number of simple system calls can be run on the slaves, since no other process could simultaneously be modifying the data referenced by these calls. But since these are not the system calls that consume most of the time on the master, running them on the slaves will not appreciably improve performance. Performance can be significantly improved only by allowing parallel kernel activity on multiple processors.

9.7 Exercises

9.1   Rewrite the spin lock functions `lock` and `unlock` from Section 9.2 using the `load_linked` and `store_conditional` functions described in Exercise 8.6.

9.2   Repeat the previous exercise using swap-atomic instead. Use the C function for `swap_atomic` as prototyped in Exercise 8.7.

9.3   Write the following set of C functions (using the given prototypes) to implement an unsorted, singly linked, null-terminated list. The list is composed of elements of the following structure:

```
struct element {
        struct element   *next;
        int              tag;
        int              data;
};

typedef struct element elem_t;

void initlist(list_t *list);
int search(list_t *list, int tag);
void add(list_t *list, elem_t *element);
elem_t *remove(list_t *list, int tag);
```

The `initlist` function initializes the fields of the `list_t` structure as necessary. The `search` function searches the list for an element with a given tag and returns the data in the element. It returns zero if no element with the given tag is found. (You may assume there are never any duplicate tags.) The `search` function must allow multiple processors to search the same list at the same time (multiple simultaneous readers). The `add` function adds new elements to the front of the list. The `remove` function searches for a given tag, unlinks it, and returns a pointer to the element if found. It returns null otherwise. The `add` and `remove` functions must operate with mutual exclusion from each other and from any search operations (single writer at a time, which excludes all readers). Use spin locks to implement the necessary mutual exclusion. Define the `list_t` data structure to contain all locks and data necessary to implement the list head. Since readers and writers may arrive in any order, be sure your implementation avoids deadlocks in all circumstances.

9.4   Consider an application that is composed of two processes that communicate via shared memory. Are there any differences in the way the two processes must synchronize with one another when running on a UP versus running on an MP? Consider the cases where the processes must atomically update a portion of the shared memory. Remember that the two processes could run simultaneously on different processors.

9.5   Can a deadlock result between the following routines? Either routine may be called at any time by one or more processors in the system (but preemptions and interrupts never occur while one of the functions is executing). Assume no other locks are held before the functions are called, and that no further locks are used by the critical sections. Explain your answer. If a deadlock can occur, describe the situation that makes it possible.

```
func1() {
        lock(&lock_a);
        lock(&lock_b);
        /* do critical section */
        unlock(&lock_b);
        unlock(&lock_a);
}

func2() {
        lock(&lock_c);
        lock(&lock_a);
        /* do critical section */
        unlock(&lock_a);
        unlock(&lock_c);
}
```

9.6   Repeat the previous problem, including the following third routine. Now any of
          the three routines may be executed on any processor at any time.

```
func3() {
        lock(&lock_b);
        lock(&lock_c);
        /* do critical section */
        unlock(&lock_c);
        unlock(&lock_b);
}
```

9.7   Sending a signal to a process with the kill system call requires that a data struc-
          ture associated with the receiving process be updated. Can this system call be ex-
          ecuted by a slave? What if the process is sending a signal to itself?

9.8   Assume that a new facility is added to the kernel that records how many page
          faults have occurred on each page in a process's address space. A new system call
          is added to retrieve this information. Can this system call be run on a slave?

9.9   If a process running on the master processor kills a process that is presently run-
          ning on a slave with the SIGKILL signal, which always causes the process to be
          terminated, how long will the process on the slave continue to execute before it
          terminates? Does the master processor need to do anything to notify the slave pro-
          cessor? What if the process on the slave is executing in an infinite loop?

9.8 Further Reading

[1]   Arnold, J.S., Casey, D.P., and McKinstry, R.H., "Design of Tightly Coupled
          Multiprocessor Programming," *IBM Systems Journal*, Vol. 13, No. 1, 1974, pp.
          60–87.

[2]   Clark, B.E.J., and Shirnia, A., "Hardware and Software Aspects of Tightly
          Coupled Symmetrical UNIX Multiprocessors," *Proceedings of the Autumn 1988
          EUUG Conference*, pp. 345–55.

[3]   Coffman, Jr., E.G., Elphick, M.J., and Shoshani, A., "System Deadlocks,"
          Computing Surveys, Vol. 3, No. 2, June 1971, pp. 67–78.

[4]   Finger, E.J., Krueger, M.M., and Nugent, A., "A Multiple CPU Version of the
          UNIX Kernel," *USENIX Conference Proceedings*, January 1985.

[5]   Goble, G.H., and Marsh, M.H., "A Dual Processor VAX 11/780," *Purdue
          University Technical Report*, TR-EE 81-31, September 1981.

[6] Habermann, A.N., "Prevention of System Deadlocks," *Communications of the ACM*, Vol. 12, No. 7, July 1969, pp. 373–77, 385.

[7] Havender, J.W., "Avoiding Deadlock in Multitasking Systems," *IBM Systems Journal*, Vol. 7, No. 2, 1968, pp. 74–84.

[8] Holley, L.H., Parmelee, R.P., Salisbury, C.A., and Saul, D.N., "VM/370 Asymmetric Multiprocessing," *IBM Systems Journal*, Vol. 18, No. 1, 1979, pp. 47–70.

[9] Holt, R.C., "Comments on the Prevention of System Deadlocks," *Communications of the ACM*, Vol. 14, No. 1, January 1971, pp. 36–8.

[10] Holt, R.C., "Some Deadlock Properties of Computer Systems," *Proceedings of the Third ACM Symposium on Operating System Principles*, October 1971, pp. 64–71.

[11] Isloor, S.S., and Marsland, T.A., "The Deadlock Problem: An Overview," *IEEE Computer*, Vol. 13, No. 9, September 1980, pp. 58–78.

[12] Kameda, T., "Testing Deadlock-Freedom of Computer Systems," *Journal of the ACM*, Vol. 27, No. 2, April 1980, pp. 270–80.

[13] Korth, H.F., "Deadlock Freedom Using Ege Locks," *ACM Transactions on Database Systems*, Vol. 7, No. 4, December 1982, pp. 562–632.

[14] Lomet, D.B., "Subsystems of Processes with Deadlock Avoidance," *IEEE Transactions on Software Engineering*, Vol. SE-6, No. 3, May 1980, pp. 297–304.

[15] Minoura, T., "Deadlock Avoidance Revisted," *Journal of the ACM*, Vol. 29, No. 4, October 1982, pp. 1023–48.

[16] Newton, G., "Deadlock Prevention, Detection, and Resolution: An Annotated Bibliography," *ACM Operating Systems Review*, Vol. 13, No. 2, April 1979, pp. 33–44.

[17] Noguchi, K., Isao O., and Hiroshi M., "Design Considerations for a Heterogeneous Tightly Coupled Multiprocessor System," *AFIPS Conference Proceedings, 1975 National Computer Conference*, pp. 561–5.

[18]   Paciorek, N., LoVerso, S., and Langerman, A., "Debugging Multiprocessor Operating System Kernels," *Proceedings of the Second Symposium on Experiences with Distributed and Multiprocessor Systems*, March 1991, pp. 185–201.

[19]   Parnas, D.L., and Haberman, A.N., "Comment on the Deadlock Prevention Model," *Communications of the ACM*, Vol. 15, No. 9, September 1972, pp. 840–1.

[20]   Probert, D., Berkowitz, J., and Lucovsky, M., "A Straightforward Implementation of 4.2BSD on a High-Performance Multiprocessor," *USENIX Conference Proceedings*, January 1986.

[21]   Rypka, D.J., and Luciado, A.P., "Deadlock Detection and Avoidance for Shared Logical Resources," *IEEE Transactions on Software Engineering*, Vol. SE-5, 1979, pp. 465–71.

[22]   van de Goor, A.J., Moolenaar, A., and Mulder, J.M., "Multiprocessor UNIX: Separate Processing of I/O," *EUUG Conference Proceedings*, April 1988, pp. 123–34.

[23]   Zobel, D., "The Deadlock Problem: A Classifying Bibliography," *Operating Systems Review*, Vol. 17, No. 4, October 1983, pp. 6–16.

10

Spin-Locked Kernels

This chapter presents one of several methods that adapt a uniprocessor kernel implementation to allow multiple processors to execute in the kernel simultaneously. Race conditions are prevented by adding spin locks to protect the kernel data structures. A variation of the master–slave kernel is presented first, followed by multithreading techniques. The chapter also discusses design and performance trade-offs.

10.1 Introduction

Master-slave kernel implementations are insufficient for application environments that require more than a modest amount of kernel services. Applications that are interactive, perform large amounts of file I/O, generate frequent page faults, and so forth, all require moderate to significant amounts of kernel activity. To make SMP systems cost effective for these types of applications, the kernel must be made to support simultaneous system calls from different processes running on different processors. Such a kernel implementation allows multiple threads of kernel activity to be in progress at once and is referred to as a *multithreaded* kernel. To multithread an operating system, all critical regions must be identified and protected in some way. Spin locks are one such mechanism that can provide this protection. (Other techniques are presented in the following chapter.)

When spin locks are used, the *granularity* of the locks must be decided. This refers to how many spin locks are used and to how much data is protected by any one lock. A *coarse-grained* implementation uses few locks, each of which protects a large amount of the kernel, perhaps an entire subsystem. A *fine-grained* implementation uses many locks, some of which may protect only a single data structure element. The choice of using a coarse- or fine-grained implementation is both a space and time trade-off. If each lock requires one word, then an extremely fine-grained implementation will probably add one word to every instance of every data structure in the system. At the other extreme, a very coarse-grained implementation uses little extra space but may hold locks for long periods of time, causing other processors to spin excessively while waiting for the locks to free. Even fine-grained implementations may waste time if too many locks are used. This can happen when multiple locks must be acquired and released in order to perform simple activities. In these cases, the overhead of manipulating the locks themselves becomes significant.

In the following sections, both coarse- and fine-grained implementations will be examined. We begin with the highest degree coarse-grained implementation possible.

10.2 Giant Locking

The use of only a handful of spin locks throughout the kernel is referred to as *giant locking* (where each lock protects a "giant" amount of data). The easiest giant-locked kernel to implement is one that uses only a single lock. At this extreme, the lock protects all kernel data and prevents more than one process from executing in kernel mode at a time. While the use of a single lock does not result in a true multithreaded kernel, since only one process can hold the lock at once, the concepts and lessons learned here can be applied to more complex implementations. The same basic types of lock contention can occur in any implementation.

In a giant-locked kernel with only a single lock, the lock is acquired on any entry to the kernel, such as via a system call or trap, and released only when the process context-switches or returns to user mode. The lock must be held while a context switch is in progress, since it is protecting the state of the run queue. Once a processor has selected a new process to run and has removed it from the run queue, it must check to see if the process is executing in kernel or user mode. If the process is running in user mode, the processor can then release the kernel giant lock and run the process. If it is in kernel mode, it retains the lock so that kernel execution of the new process may continue.

Interrupts may occur on any processor and at any time. Minimally, each processor will receive clock interrupts, but may also receive I/O interrupts. The protection given by the spl routines is insufficient on MP systems, since they only affect the interrupt priority level of the processor on which they are executed. The interrupt might still occur on a different processor, resulting in a race condition if the device driver is running elsewhere. Therefore, interrupt handlers must also acquire the kernel giant lock, since they represent an entry point into the kernel as well. Note, however, that a deadlock will result if an interrupt occurs on a processor that is already holding the kernel spin lock (as explained in Section 9.3). One way to prevent this is to block all interrupts on the processor that is holding the kernel giant lock. If an interrupt occurs on a different processor (one that isn't holding the lock), then it will simply spin while waiting to acquire the lock in the same way that a process executing a system call would. While this maintains the integrity of the operating system, it will increase interrupt latency. Since any interrupt may be delayed for an arbitrarily long period of time, the performance of the I/O subsystem will suffer. This can be avoided by protecting each device driver with separate spin locks. When an interrupt occurs, the interrupt handler acquires the spin lock for the respective device driver. Having separate locks increases the chances that the interrupt handler will be able to acquire the lock for its driver without the excessive delays that might occur when using the kernel giant lock. Solving performance problems in this manner is taking the first step toward a finer-grained implementation.

The giant-locking technique presented here is similar to master–slave kernels. In both implementations, all kernel activity is restricted to a single processor, which preserves a uniprocessor-like environment for the kernel to run in. Other processors in the system are free to execute user-mode processes at any time. The difference is that with a giant-locked kernel any processor can execute kernel code, making context switching to the master unnecessary. This may seem like an advantage at first, but a giant-locked kernel may perform worse than a master–slave kernel. With a giant-locked kernel, if a process executes a system call while another processor is holding the kernel lock, then the processor on which the new system call is being made will sit idle while spinning for the lock. In a master–slave kernel, the processor could have selected another user-mode process to run instead of simply sitting idle. If the processor holding the kernel lock is performing a lengthy system call, then the other processors could end up spinning for a long period of time. This situation is made worse by the fact that the processor already holding the lock continues to hold it if it context-switches to another kernel-mode process, making it possible to lock other processors out of the kernel for indefinite periods of time. Situations like these must be avoided in any practical MP kernel implementation.

It is possible to make up for these shortcomings by using additional spin locks. First, it is undesirable to have processors idly spin while waiting for the kernel lock when they could be executing another user-mode process instead. To do this, a new type of spin lock operation that *conditionally* acquires the lock can be used. This is implemented by the code in Figure 10–1.

```
int
cond_lock(volatile lock_t *lock_status)
{
        if (test_and_set(lock_status) == 1)
                return FALSE;
        else
                return TRUE;
}
```

Figure 10–1: Conditionally locking a spin lock.

The `cond_lock` function makes one attempt to acquire the spin lock. If the lock is free, `cond_lock` acquires it and returns true. If the lock is already in use, it returns false. Now a processor can detect when the kernel lock is in use and, if so, context-switch to another user-mode process instead of waiting for the kernel lock. The concept of conditionally acquiring locks is a generally useful technique in SMP kernel implementations.

Second, the run queues must be protected by a separate lock from the normal kernel giant lock. This is necessary so that when a processor is unable to acquire the kernel giant lock, it can still acquire the run queue lock within a brief period of time, so that it may enqueue the process it was running and select a new user-mode process for execution.

Note that these improvements bring the performance of a giant-locked kernel only up to the level of a master–slave kernel. The only difference between the two approaches is that now any processor can become the master instead of permanently designating one processor as such. Since the giant-locking approach is more complex to implement, there is little point in using it. To move beyond the performance limitations of master–slave systems, more kernel parallelism must be made possible.

10.3 Multithreading Cases Requiring No Locks

The first step to multithreading a kernel is to identify those instances where locking is not necessary. This avoids the use of extraneous locks, saving both time and space. It also eliminates any possible lock contention in these cases, since no locks are used. All the system calls mentioned in Section 9.5.1 can run without locks. The conditions that make this possible occur when only data structures that are private to a process are used, as explained ahead. (Note that even a process's private data structures may be examined or modified by another process if the process is being debugged. The debugged process is typically suspended before access to its private data is permitted. This prevents race conditions between the debugger and the debugged process, and so this case need not be considered further.)

Each UNIX process has a *user area* (abbreviated as *u-area*), which is a kernel data structure containing the majority of a process's private data. It holds such things as the current signal handler settings, the arguments to the current system call, a register save area to hold the user's register values while a system call is in progress, and other private data. Only the process associated with the u-area manipulates this data. Processes never share a u-area and, except in the case of debugging, no process accesses the u-area of another. Therefore, no locking is needed when the process is reading or writing data in its own u-area.

Another private data structure is the process's kernel stack. Each process has its own kernel stack that is used while executing system calls on behalf of the user process. Since no process ever accesses another one's kernel stack, no locking is needed when using any data located on the kernel stack. This conveniently includes all C local variables (also called *automatic* variables) and function arguments.

Lastly, some system calls dynamically allocate additional space for private data. This is done in cases where the amount of data needed is larger than will fit on the kernel stack or is more than is desirable to permanently allocate in the u-area. Examples of such supplementary data areas are space to hold path names that are part of the arguments to a system call, and the argument list passed to the `exec` system call. Such data can be considered to be a temporary extension of the process's private kernel stack or u-area, and thus needs no locking as long as no other process can access it.

Each process also has a *process table entry*. Unlike the u-area, parts of the process table entry may be accessed and modified by other processes in the system (in cases other than debugging). Most of these cases require locking, but there are some where locking is still not necessary, even though the data structure is shared among all processes. For example, the process table entry holds the process ID, and the process's user and group IDs. The process ID never changes for the life of the process; therefore, any process can read this value at any time without any locking. Similarly, the user ID and group ID can be modified only by the process associated with the process table entry (by executing a `setuid`, set-

`gid`, or other such system call). Other processes may read these values (to see if they have permission to send signals to the process, for instance), but no other process will ever modify them. Therefore, any process can read these without locking as well.

Note that there is an inherent race condition between other processes reading a process's IDs while that process is changing them. Even if locking were added to prevent the values from being read while they were being changed, the same race condition would result: a process that read the values before they were changed would see the old values, while one that reads them afterward would see the new values. Locking will have no effect on this race. Therefore, it is best to forgo locking completely, saving space and eliminating needless lock contention. Generalizing this case, locking can be omitted anytime there is only a single writer to a single piece of data in any one word of memory. This is true for any number of simultaneous readers. The ability to omit locking relies on the fact that the sequential memory model guarantees that memory operations to any one word of memory are atomic.

Inherent race conditions similar to this one occur elsewhere in the kernel. Locking can be avoided in these cases as well. Locking cannot, however, be omitted when more than one word must be updated atomically or when read-modify-write operations are required. For these critical sections, one must choose between coarse- or fine-grained locking.

10.4 Coarse-Grained Locking

The giant-locking technique that employs only a single lock can be expanded to allow some additional parallelism by adding more locks. By using separate locks for each subsystem within the kernel, for example, processes on different processors can be simultaneously performing system calls if they affect only different kernel subsystems.

Following this level of granularity, one lock would be allocated for the process management subsystem and would protect all changes to the data stored in the process table entries in the system. To see how this would work, consider the case where one process is sending a signal to another. A process's pending signals are represented by a bit mask stored in the process table entry on most UNIX kernels. In order to send a signal, the mask must be updated with a read-modify-write operation that sets the bit corresponding to the signal being sent. This requires locking, since multiple processes may be attempting to send a signal to the same process at the same time. By requiring all processes that are sending signals to lock the common process management lock, the race conditions are eliminated. This is true for all other fields in the process table entry that can be modified by other processes.

Continuing in this manner, one spin lock would protect the file management subsystem. This would be acquired and held during all file system related system calls such as `open`, `read`, `write`, and `close`. Another lock could be used to protect the virtual memory subsystem. This brings up the problem of deadlocks when one operation affects more than one subsystem in the kernel. For example, satisfying a page fault may require reading data from a file. Such an operation would start by locking the virtual memory subsystem lock. Then, to read the data from the file system, it would also have to acquire the file subsystem lock. Similarly, if another process begins a file truncation operation, for instance, it would begin by locking the file subsystem lock, and it then may have to lock the virtual memory subsystem lock in order to invalidate any pages from the truncated portion of the file that may have been mapped into some process's address space. If these two operations occur at the same time, a deadlock would result between them, because they are acquiring the locks in the opposite order. (See Section 9.3.)

To prevent these deadlocks, a lock ordering must be defined and used consistently throughout the kernel. For example, the policy could be that when both the file system and virtual memory subsystem locks are needed at the same time, the file system lock is always acquired first. Since the file truncation code acquires the locks in this order, no changes to the code are needed. The code for the virtual memory subsystem must, however, be modified to conform to the defined lock ordering. There are several ways to accomplish this.

The simplest way is to lock the file subsystem lock first before beginning any virtual memory operation. The file lock can then be released once it is known that a file system operation will not be required. While easy to implement, this approach is undesirable since it tends to defeat the purpose of having separate locks for the two subsystems. It offers little additional parallelism over using a single lock to protect both subsystems.

A second solution is to lock only the file subsystem lock when the virtual memory subsystem finds that it is needed. To avoid a deadlock, the code must first release the virtual memory lock, then lock the file lock. Once the file operation is complete, the virtual memory lock can be reacquired. Such a technique of releasing one lock so that proper lock ordering can be maintained is not uncommon in MP kernels. The disadvantage, however, is that all the virtual memory subsystem data structures must be in a consistent state before the lock is released. Once released, another process on a different processor will be free to begin a virtual memory operation. These effects must be taken into consideration and may require other modifications to the code to prevent race conditions between different processes. It might be necessary, for instance, to restart the virtual memory operation once the file subsystem finishes its part of the task. This would occur when other processes could have altered the virtual memory data structures so that the previously examined state was no longer valid.

A third technique is to make use of the conditional lock operation to try to avoid the need to release the virtual memory lock. This is done by having the virtual memory code conditionally acquire the file system lock when it finds it must perform a file operation. If the lock is free, then it will acquire the lock and can continue without releasing the virtual memory lock. In this case, it won't be necessary to ensure the virtual memory data structures are consistent, nor will it be necessary to restart the operation later, since the virtual memory lock is never released. However, in the case where the conditional lock operation fails, the virtual memory lock will have to be released as before.

To summarize, the use of conditional locking avoids deadlocks when locks are acquired out of order, because the possibility of spinning forever while waiting for the lock cannot occur. If the conditional attempt to acquire the lock fails, the process can take alternate action, which would be the same as described in the previous solution. While this principle is valid in general, it is unlikely to be useful on coarse-grained systems when there is a high rate of system calls. In these cases, the subsystem locks will be locked on an almost continual basis, making it highly unlikely that a conditional locking operation will ever succeed.

Each kernel subsystem can be locked in the manner just described. A remaining problem is when a process executing in the kernel must sleep. As stated in Section 9.3, processes cannot sleep (context-switch) while holding spin locks, since this can result in a deadlock. Therefore, any subsystem locks that a process is holding must first be released. Since this will allow other processes to access the data structures protected by these locks, one must ensure that they are in a consistent state prior to sleeping, or that the appropriate long term lock is kept held. One of these two situations will be true in any cases where the uniprocessor version of the kernel slept. Context switching on a uniprocessor brings the same potential of race conditions as on an MP, since other processes can run and access the same data. Thus, adapting this code for the MP environment only requires handling the spin locks properly.

One way to implement this is to record the locks a process is holding, and the order in which they were acquired, in the process's u-area. The context switch code can then release the locks for the process that is being suspended. When the process resumes execution after sleeping, it must reacquire any locks it was previously holding. This can be handled by the context switch code as well.

While a coarse-grained MP kernel implementation begins to allow parallel kernel activity on more than one processor, it is still too restrictive for system-call–intensive workloads. It will not generally provide much performance increase over master–slave kernels to those application job mixes that require large amounts of kernel services. For example, if applications require file I/O, then all such activity will still be single-threaded in a coarse-grained kernel because of the single file system lock, even if each process uses a different file.

10.5 Fine-Grained Locking

10.5.1 Short-Term Mutual Exclusion

The goal of fine-grained locking is to increase the amount of parallel kernel activity by different processors. While many processes may want to use the same kernel subsystem, it is frequently the case that they will be using separate portions of the associated data structures. By having separate locks for each file, for example, it is possible for several processes to be simultaneously executing within the file system if they are using different files. In this way, each subsystem can be divided into separate critical resources, each with its own lock. This requires an analysis of all data structures that were protected by the uniprocessor short-term mutual exclusion technique, and adding the appropriate spin locks. Describing the locking for all such possible separate critical resources in the UNIX kernel is beyond the scope of this book. What follows are some examples of fine-grained locking using spin locks, the concepts from which can be applied throughout the kernel.

Applying fine-grained locking to the previous signal example, we can allocate one spin lock in the process table entry of each process to protect the bit mask of pending signals. This will allow signal operations involving different processes to be in progress simultaneously on different processors in the system. To send a signal, the sending process must first lock the receiving process's signal lock. It can then perform the critical section of modifying the process's signal mask to include the signal being sent.

Continuing this example, each process must periodically check to see if it has any pending signals. There is no need for the process to hold its signal lock while doing so, since it will not solve the inherent race condition that exists between processes sending signals and the receiving process checking its mask for new signals. With or without locking, a new signal could be delivered just before or just after the receiving process checks its mask (another inherent race condition). However, a process must hold its signal lock while it is updating its own signal mask. This occurs when a process sends itself a signal, or when it is processing a signal sent to it and is clearing the corresponding bit in the mask. Both of these are read-modify-write operations that must be done atomically, which requires locking.

Spin locks are also suitable for protecting many of the kernel's global data structures and lists. For example, each mounted file system is represented by a data structure, with all the structures maintained on a linked list. The operations of searching, adding, or removing entries from this list are critical sections. One spin lock can be allocated to protect this list. Similarly, the kernel also maintains free lists of various data structures (buffers, physical page frames, etc.). Each of these can be protected by an individual spin lock as well.

As a further example, consider the case where a new process is being created and a new process ID (*pid*) must be allocated. It must be ensured that the new pid is unique. This is typically implemented by having a counter that holds the next pid to use. Some implementations use 30,000 as the maximum value of the pid, so the counter can periodically wrap-around. Therefore, the next pid value represented in the counter must be checked to ensure it is not still in use by a previously created process. This can be done by scanning all the process table entries in the system to make sure none have that value. Since two processors could be trying to create a new process at the same time, the code to allocate a unique pid must be a critical section to guarantee that both don't allocate the same pid. This can be done by protecting the counter with a spin lock. Each time the counter is used, the spin lock is acquired and the current counter value is taken as the next pid to attempt to use. Then, before releasing the lock, the counter is incremented. This way, each processor will always read a unique value from the counter.

After getting a new pid from the counter, a search must be made to ensure that no process is using that value. If the process table is a simple fixed-size array, then all processors can simultaneously scan the array without holding any locks. No race conditions can result, since scanning a fixed array does not rely on the data in it. If the process table entries are kept on a linked list instead, then a spin lock must be used while traversing the list to prevent the list from changing (such as when a terminated process is removed from the list). This will single-thread access to the list, allowing only one process to scan the list at a time. Because of this, the spin lock used to protect the counter can be eliminated, and the counter can instead be protected by the process table list spin lock. There is no advantage to guarding the counter value as a separate critical resource, since all processors will be serialized by the process table lock in any event. As stated before, superfluous locks should be avoided to save both space and locking overhead. (The operation of scanning the process table is a good candidate for a *multireader* lock, which will be explained in the next chapter.)

10.5.2 Long-Term Mutual Exclusion

Another area where uniprocessor short-term mutual exclusion is used to prevent race conditions is in the code that acquires long-term mutual exclusion locks, such as the object locks from Section 8.5.3. Refer back to the code in Figure 8–8 and note that the `lock_-object` function relies on the fact that only one process can be executing the function at once. This way, the function can test the flag and then set it (if the lock was free), or go to sleep, as an atomic operation. This critical region can be reestablished on a multithreaded kernel by adding a spin lock as shown in Figure 10–2.

The use of the `object_locking` spin lock properly protects the critical section in the `lock_object` function. In the case where the long-term lock is free, the flag can be tested and set atomically.

Remember that spin locks cannot be held while a process is sleeping. However, the spin lock cannot be released prior to calling `sleep`, since a race would result between the sleep and the wakeup in the `unlock_object` function (see Section 8.6). The decision to sleep and the work necessary to place the process in that state must be done atomically, which

```
void
lock_object(char *flag_ptr)
{
        lock(&object_locking);

        while (*flag_ptr)
                sleep(flag_ptr);

        *flag_ptr = 1;
        unlock(&object_locking);
}
```

Figure 10–2: MP code to lock an object.

means that the spin lock must be held throughout the procedure. The same solution presented in Section 10.4, where the locks are recorded in the u-area and released by the context switch code, can be used. As before, the locks are reacquired when the process is awakened. This is needed since the process will still be executing in the critical region of the lock_object function and therefore needs to hold the spin lock while testing the state of the flag and deciding which action to take (either sleeping again or setting the lock for itself).

An alternate solution is to pass the address of the spin lock to be released and reacquired to the sleep function directly. (See Section 12.4.3 for an example of an MP primitive that does this.) This is a more structured approach, as it eliminates the need to use process global data in the u-area. The restriction here, though, is that the process can be holding only one spin lock when it calls sleep. This is likely to be the case when lock_object calls sleep, since the kernel would not be holding other spin locks when it attempts to acquire a long-term lock.

The unlock_object code needs to hold the spin lock as well, since clearing the flag and waking up any processes waiting for the long-term lock is a critical region (see Figure 10–3).

```
void
unlock_object(char *flag_ptr)
{
        lock(&object_locking);
        *flag_ptr = 0;
        wakeup(flag_ptr);
        unlock(&object_locking);
}
```

Figure 10–3: MP code to unlock an object.

The use of the `object_locking` spin lock solves the race conditions pertaining to long-term mutual exclusion described in Section 8.6. Once the `lock_object` function returns, the process is guaranteed exclusive use of the object just as in uniprocessor implementations. It can now modify fields within the object's data structure without the need for further locking. It can also sleep while waiting for things such as disk I/O, without the risk of race conditions. Any instances of long-term mutual exclusion can be protected in the same way.

10.5.3 Mutual Exclusion with Interrupt Handlers

The uniprocessor technique of blocking interrupts to prevent race conditions when data structures shared between base-level driver code and interrupt handlers, as described in Section 8.5.2, is not sufficient in a multithreaded MP kernel. If the critical section shown in Figure 8–7 were to execute on one processor, then only interrupts on that processor would be blocked. If the interrupt were to occur on a different processor, then the critical resource would simultaneously be accessed, and possibly updated, by two processors at once. Such race conditions must not be allowed to occur. The master–slave implementation avoided this problem by executing all kernel code and all interrupt handlers on a single processor. Further steps must be taken in a multithreaded kernel.

Since these critical sections require short-term mutual exclusion, a spin lock can be used to prevent races from occurring. The UP code shown in Figure 8–7 can be enhanced as shown in Figure 10–4.

<table>
<tr><td><u>Base Level Code</u></td><td><u>Interrupt Handler Code</u></td></tr>
<tr><td>

```
s = splhi();
lock(&driver_lock);
counter++;
unlock(&driver_lock);
splx(s);
```

</td><td>

```
lock(&driver_lock);
counter++;
unlock(&driver_lock);
```

</td></tr>
</table>

Figure 10–4: Interrupt handler mutual exclusion.

The spin lock and the `spl` protection work together to solve the two possible race conditions. The `spl` protection prevents race with the interrupt handler if the interrupt occurs on the same processor that executes the base-level code fragment, just as it does on a UP system. The spin lock protects against races if the interrupt handler executes on a different processor than the one executing the base-level code. In this case, the interrupt handler will simply spin until the other processor finishes the critical section. Note that the use of a spin lock alone is insufficient. The `spl` level must be raised as well by the base-level code. Unless interrupts are blocked, the interrupt could occur on the process holding the spin lock, causing a deadlock as the interrupt handler tries to acquire the same lock.

10.5.4 Lock Granularity

Once spin locks are added throughout the kernel as described in the preceding sections, any processor will be able to execute any process, whether it is executing in user or kernel mode. In such a multithreaded kernel, each processor will simply choose the highest priority process from the run queue at each context switch. The next question is how fine should a fine-grained implementation be?

As stated, locking granularity can range from coarse to fine. In deciding how fine an implementation should be, one must consider not only performance, but the semantics of the operations themselves. For example, I/O to regular files, in terms of individual `read` and `write` system calls, is guaranteed to be atomic by the definition of the UNIX external programming model. Traditional UNIX kernel implementations have done this by use of the previously described object-locking techniques that allow only a single process to be operating on a file at a time. However, the lock can be legitimately made finer by allowing multiple processes that are merely reading the file to perform simultaneous `read` system calls. This can be advantageous in cases where a file is frequently read, such as the password file (since translating user names to IDs, and vice versa, is a frequent operation), or in the case of looking up files in a directory. It is also possible to allow simultaneous processes to be both reading and writing the same file if they are operating on independent portions of the file. The only operations that actually need to be completely atomic are those where there are two or more processes simultaneously operating on the same portion of a file, and at least one is writing to the file. This can happen when multiple processes are trying to append information to a log file, for example. This shows where the limit of lock granularity occurs: it cannot be made any finer than the semantics of the operation permit.

Next, there is a distinction between the number of separate locks used in the implementation versus the amount of data each lock protects. For example, the previous section described an implementation for signals where there was a separate spin lock protecting the bit mask of pending signals in each process table entry. This finer level of granularity over a single process management subsystem lock allows signal operations to proceed in parallel with other process management operations, such as allocating unique process IDs for new processes. Note that this same goal can be achieved by using a single lock protecting all signal bit masks in all processes as opposed to having a separate lock for each process. In both cases, such unrelated operations as sending signals and allocating process IDs can proceed in parallel. The difference is whether multiple operations of the same type, sending signals in this case, can occur simultaneously. Similarly, one can use a separate spin lock in each object subject to long-term locking, or one can use a single spin lock, as was shown in the `lock_object` and `unlock_object` functions, regardless of which object is being operated on. Either implementation maintains both the external programming model and the integrity of the operating system. They may, however, differ in performance.

When deciding what level of granularity to use, one must consider both the number of processors in the system and the expected applications. In general, systems with a small number of processors (e.g., two to four) will not benefit much from the added granularity of having a separate spin lock for signals in each process table entry over having a single global spin lock for the same purpose. Because the critical region is so small, it becomes unlikely that two or more processors will be executing it at the same time. Even if they do, the shortness of the critical region ensures that other processors will be only briefly delayed while awaiting the spin lock. As the number of processors increases, the likelihood of multiple processors simultaneously sending signals increases. This is particularly true if the applications are making heavy use of signals (as an interprocess communication mechanism, for example). In such cases, contention for a single global spin lock could be too high, so it would make sense to consider separate locks for each process. Note that the performance is the same in the case where there is little or no contention for the signal spin lock. One set of spin lock operations is required whether there is one global lock or whether there is a separate lock per process. The only difference is the extra space needed for separate locks and the possibility of reduced lock contention.

Deciding this degree of granularity is separate from deciding between giant locking and multithreading. The decision to multithread leads to the choice of protecting signal masks with a separate lock. The next decision is how many separate locks should be used to accomplish this: one global lock or one lock per process. Whichever granularity choice is made, it is still possible that unrelated kernel operations may occur in parallel. It is this characteristic that gives multithreaded kernels the potential to outperform master–slave and giant-locked implementations.

10.5.5 Performance

To compare the performance of a multithreaded kernel with that of the master–slave implementation from Chapter 9, the two extreme application job mixes of compute bound processes and system call bound processes will again be used. As before, compute bound jobs can run in parallel on all processors without contention. Not surprisingly, a multithreaded kernel will neither help nor hinder the performance of such applications. The difference lies in the performance of the system when running system-call–intensive applications. If the processes in the application job mix use separate kernel resources, each of whose data structures are protected by separate locks, then these processes will not contend for the same locks and will be able to run simultaneously on different CPUs, whether they are in user or kernel mode. This is the best possible situation, as the application load can be increased linearly as the number of processors in the system is increased. Unfortunately, it is rarely the case that applications will run without any lock contention, even in a fine-grained implementation. There will always be some shared data structure that must be used by all processors. The run queue is a good example, as are data structure free lists.

Similarly, processes that are using separate files, all protected by different locks, may still find themselves contending for a shared resource, the disk drive itself, if all the files are stored on the same drive. These factors will limit the performance of a multithreaded kernel and make it difficult to achieve the goal of linear performance improvement as additional processors are added. The implementation must be tuned for a specific application job mix in order to maximize performance.

10.5.6 Kernel Preemption

The original uniprocessor UNIX kernel was nonpreemptable by design to simplify the implementation of short-term mutual exclusion. As seen, all cases where short-term mutual exclusion is required must be explicitly protected by a spin lock in order for a multithreaded kernel implementation to function correctly on an MP system. Since short-term mutual exclusion has now been made explicit, the old UP approach of not preempting processes executing in kernel mode can be relaxed. Anytime a process is not holding a spin lock and has not blocked any interrupts, then it is not executing in a critical region and can be preempted. When a kernel process is preempted under these circumstances, it is guaranteed that it is only accessing private data. This observation is useful on real-time systems, for example, as it can reduce the dispatch latency when a higher priority process becomes runnable. Note that the preempted process may be holding a long-term lock but that this does not represent a violation of the associated critical region, since no other process can acquire the long-term lock until the preempted process releases it.

10.6 Effects of Sleep and Wakeup on Multiprocessors

In Section 8.5.3, it was seen that the `wakeup` function causes all processes sleeping on the corresponding event to be awakened and made runnable. In the case of multiple processes waiting for a long-term mutual exclusion lock, the first process to run would find the lock free and would obtain it. In some cases, the process will be able to complete the critical region and release the lock before context switching. With file locks, this could happen when the needed file data is already in the buffer cache, for instance. This means that on a uniprocessor, the next process to run from the group that was previously awakened will also be able to immediately obtain the lock. This is the desired behavior since, if the other processes that were awakened were to run before the first process had released the lock, then they would find the lock busy again and go back to sleep (the processes thrash). Since the uniprocessor kernel ensures that only one process can execute at a time, and since it cannot be preempted, the possibility exists that it can release the lock before context switching, thereby avoiding the thrashing.

On a multiprocessor, however, once a set of processes sleeping on a common event are awakened, they are all eligible for execution and may be selected off the run queue by different processors and run simultaneously. Fortunately, the use of spin locks in the `lock_-object` code prevents race conditions from occurring if this happens. One process will be able to acquire the spin lock first, and so it will have the first chance at acquiring the object lock for itself. The other processes will spin while waiting for the first to release the spin lock. When this happens, the next process will be able to acquire the spin lock and will find the object locked, and so it will return to sleep. This will continue until all processes in the group return to sleep. The result is that more thrashing can occur when using `sleep`/`wakeup` on a multiprocessor, since it is unlikely that the first process to acquire the lock will release it before the others that were awakened are scheduled to run on other processors. The competition for the lock and the thrashing that results is commonly referred to as the *thundering herd* phenomenon.

This problem can be avoided by using a variation of `wakeup`, which will be called `wakeup_one`, that wakes up only a single process when it is called. If there are multiple processes sleeping on the same event, then the highest priority process should be chosen. If all are of equal priority, then they should be awakened in first-in, first-out order. As before, there is no memory of a wakeup operation, so if `wakeup_one` is called and no processes are sleeping on the event, it returns without doing anything. All cases where `wakeup` was used in implementing long-term mutual exclusion can be changed to use this new function instead, thereby eliminating the thrashing that could otherwise result.

Note that it would not be correct to reimplement `wakeup` itself to have the functionality of `wakeup_one`. The problem here is that some portions of the uniprocessor kernel depend on the characteristic of `wakeup` that all processes sleeping are awakened. This is true in situations where `sleep`/`wakeup` are being used for process synchronization as opposed to implementing long-term mutual exclusion. For example, there may be many processes waiting to write data into a pipe that is full. (A pipe is a UNIX interprocess communication mechanism that passes a byte stream of data between processes.) When a reader drains the pipe, it awakens all processes that were waiting to write data into the pipe. This is the simplest implementation since it frees the reader from having to know how many writers are waiting and whether the total amount of data from all their writes will again fill the pipe or not. Instead, the reader can simply awaken them all and allow the writers to compete for the pipe among themselves. With such an implementation, waking up only a single writer would cause the others to be blocked from execution. The problem here is that the implementation doesn't cause other writers to be awakened when one writer completes its write, even if there was space available in the pipe.

It is, of course, possible to reimplement the parts of the kernel that rely on the behavior of `wakeup`. This will usually be for the better, since the semantics of `wakeup` can cause thrashing whenever multiple processes are sleeping on the event. In the case of pipes, the pipe itself has a long-term mutual exclusion lock, which each writer must hold. So if a number of writers were simultaneously awakened, then only one would be able to acquire the lock at a time. The rest would return to sleep but would be sleeping on a different event now: the lock itself instead of waiting for space to become available in the pipe. This again causes thrashing.

If all parts of the kernel are rewritten to use `wakeup_one`, then the old functionality of `wakeup` can be eliminated. The disadvantages of the uniprocessor `wakeup` function lead some implementations to replace `sleep`/`wakeup` with new primitives that are more suitable for MP environments. These are covered in the next two chapters.

10.7 Summary

A uniprocessor kernel implementation can be modified to run on a multiprocessor by the addition of spin locks. These are added to protect the critical regions that the short-term mutual exclusion technique implicitly guarded. There are a number of places where locking is not necessary at all. Any time data that is private to one process is used, locking is not needed since there can be no race conditions. Access to the process's kernel stack, and hence all local variables and function arguments, and the process's u-area, are examples of private data structures that do not require locking.

The amount of concurrent kernel activity that is possible across all the processors is partially determined by the degree of multithreading. A coarse-grained implementation uses few locks, but can suffer the same drawbacks as a master–slave kernel implementation when the applications require frequent kernel service. A fine-grained implementation attempts to overcome these drawbacks by protecting different data structures with different locks. If the applications tend to use kernel facilities that have disjoint data structures, such as using different files, then multiple processors may execute in kernel mode simultaneously. Note that is not always necessary to use a separate spin lock in each instance of a data structure in order to achieve a high-performance multithreaded kernel. The goal is to ensure that unrelated processes can perform their kernel activities without contention, not merely to sprinkle many locks throughout the kernel.

An advantage of a multithreaded kernel is that all critical sections are protected either by a long-term lock or a spin lock, or by raising the interrupt priority level. This makes it possible to preempt kernel processes that are not holding any spin locks and that do not have any interrupts blocked. This capability is important for real-time systems.

The effect of the uniprocessor `wakeup` function, to awaken all processes sleeping for the event, is generally undesirable for an MP system, since it is possible for these processes to all run simultaneously on different processors. Since the processes will likely compete for a common lock when they run, this can lead to thrashing if most of them must sleep again after failing to acquire the lock. This problem can be solved by introducing a new wakeup function that wakes up a single process at time. It is also possible to rewrite the portions of the kernel that relied on the uniprocessor behavior of `wakeup`.

10.8 Exercises

10.1   Explain how clock interrupts can be handled when using the giant-locked kernel technique from Section 10.2. Be sure to consider both cases: when a clock interrupt occurs on the processor that is currently holding the kernel spin lock and when it occurs on a processor running user-mode code.

10.2   In the conditional locking code shown in Figure 10–1, is it worth trying more than once to acquire the lock before returning failure?

10.3   Consider an MP system that does not support the sequential memory model. Assume that simultaneous reads from the same location still work properly, but that a read that occurs while a write is in progress to the same location may cause incorrect results to be returned. Assume, however, that the hardware guarantees that the test-and-set instruction always works properly, even when simultaneous test-and-set operations are performed to the same word of memory. What effect would such a memory model have on the MP kernel techniques presented in this chapter?

10.4   Rewrite the uniprocessor code shown here to execute correctly on an MP using the fine-grained locking techniques presented in this chapter. This code implements a simple mailbox-style interprocess communication facility. Processes send a message by posting it in a mailbox using send_msg. Other processes can retrieve messages using recv_msg. Only a single message can be held in the mailbox at a time. Once there is a message in the mailbox, other senders must wait until it is empty. In addition to modifying the code, answer the following questions. Is it possible for both senders and receivers to be sleeping on the address of the mailbox at the same time on a uniprocessor? Consider the effects of having both functions sleep on the same address. Will the wakeup call in send_msg wake up processes sleeping in recv_msg, send_msg, or both? Likewise, will the wakeup call in recv_msg wake up processes sleeping in recv_msg, send_msg, or both? Should the MP version use wakeup or wakeup_one? Explain.

```
void *mailbox = NULL;

void
send_msg(void *msg)
{
        while (mailbox != NULL)
                sleep(&mailbox);

        mailbox = msg;
        wakeup(&mailbox);
}
```

```
void *
recv_msg()
{
        void *msg;

        while (mailbox == NULL)
                sleep(&mailbox);

        msg = mailbox;
        mailbox = NULL;
        wakeup(&mailbox);
        return msg;
}
```

10.5   Given a multithreaded UNIX kernel implementation, suggest a technique where-
        by device drivers written for a uniprocessor system can be used in the MP envi-
        ronment without requiring any source code changes to the device driver itself.

10.6   Consider the coarse-grained kernel implementation presented in Section 10.4
        where one lock is allocated to each subsystem. Assume that it may be necessary
        to hold any two locks simultaneously. Write a C function that acquires a second
        lock in a deadlock free manner when the process is already holding any other lock.
        The takes two arguments: the address of the lock already held and the address of
        the new lock to be acquired. The function must return with both locks held. It is
        permissible for the function to release the lock already held and then reacquire it,
        if necessary, to prevent a deadlock.

10.7   When using the function from the previous exercise, is it necessary to have a spe-
        cial function to release the locks so that they're released in whatever order they
        were acquired?

10.8   Consider the `alarm` system call when implemented on a multithreaded kernel.
        The alarm time-out value is stored in the process table entry so it can be updated
        by both the process itself and the clock interrupt handler. The clock interrupt han-
        dler decrements the time-out value once each second and sends the process a sig-
        nal when its value reaches zero. In a multithreaded kernel, the clock interrupt han-
        dler may be running on one processor and updating the time-out values while a
        process on a different processor is executing an `alarm` system call to change the
        current value. Is a lock needed to protect the time-out value, or is this simply an
        inherent race condition?

10.9   The following code finds an element on a linked list, and then atomically exchanges the value in the list element with a new value passed in. What can be improved regarding the MP aspects of this implementation? Assume the function find_and_replace can be called from any processor, but that swap is only called from find_and_replace. Assume all spin locks have been properly initialized.

```
struct element {
        lock_t          e_lock;
        int             e_tag;
        int             e_value;
        struct element *e_next;
};

struct element *list;
lock_t list_lock;

int
find_and_replace(int tag, int new_value)
{
        struct element *ep;
        int old_value;

        lock(&list_lock);

        for (ep = list; ep; ep = ep->e_next)
                if (ep->e_tag == tag) {
                        old_value = swap(ep, new_value);
                        unlock(&list_lock);
                        return old_value;
                }

        unlock(&list_lock);
        return -1;
}

int
swap(struct element *ep, int new_value)
{
        int old_value;

        lock(ep->e_lock);
        old_value = ep->e_value;
        ep->e_value = new_value;
        unlock(ep->e_lock);
        return old_value;
}
```

10.9 Further Reading

[1]   Anderson, T.E., "The Performance of Spin Lock Alternatives for Shared-Memory Multiprocessors," *IEEE Transactions on Parallel and Distributed Systems*, Vol. 1, No. 1, January 1990, pp. 6–16.

[2]   Beck, B., Kasten, B., and Thakkar, S., "VLSI Assist for a Multiprocessor," *Second International Conference on Architectural Support for Programming Languages and Operating Systems*, October 1987, pp. 10–20.

[3]   Beck, R.D., and Kasten, R.A., "Multiprocessing with UNIX," *Systems and Software*, October 1984.

[4]   Black, D.L., Tevanian Jr., A., Golub, D.B., and Young, M.W., "Locking and Reference Counting in the MACH Kernel," *Proceedings of the 1992 International Conference on Parallel Processing*, August 1992, pp. II:167–73.

[5]   Boykin, J., and Langerman, A., "The Parallelization of Mach/4.3BSD: Design Philosophy and Performance Analysis," *Proceedings of the USENIX Workshop on Experiences with Distributed and Multiprocessor Systems*, October 1989, pp. 105–26.

[6]   Campbell, M., Barton, R., Browning, J., Cervenka, D., Curry, B., Davis, T., Edmonds, T., Holt, R., Slice, J., Smith, T., and Wescott, R., "The Parallelization of UNIX System V Release 4.0," *USENIX Conference Proceedings*, January 1991, pp. 307–23.

[7]   Campbell, M., and Holt, R.L., "Lock Granularity Analysis Tools in SVR4/MP," *IEEE Software*, March 1993, pp. 66–70.

[8]   CaraDonna, J.P., Paciorek, N., and Wills, C.E., "Measuring Lock Performance in Multiprocessor Operating System Kernels," *Proceedings of the USENIX Symposium on Experiences with Distributed and Multiprocessor Systems*, September 1993, pp. 37–56.

[9]   Clark, B.E.J., and Shirnia, A., "Hardware and Software Aspects of Tightly Coupled Symmetrical UNIX Multiprocessors," *Proceedings of the Autumn 1988 EUUG Conference*, pp. 345–55.

[10]   Conde, D. S., and Hamilton, G., "An Experimental Symmetric Multiprocessor Ultrix Kernel," *USENIX Conference Proceedings*, February 1988, pp. 283–90.

[11]   Curran, S., and Stumm, M., "Scheduling a UNIX Workload on Small-Scale, Shared Memory Multiprocessors," *Computer Systems*, Vol. 3, No. 4, October 1990, pp. 551–79.

[12]   Keating, C., and White, G., "The Transformation of UNIX to Support Multiple 80386 Processors," *UniForum Conference Proceedings*, February 1989, pp. 121–9.

[13]   Langerman, A., Boykin, J., and LoVerso, S., "A Highly Parallelized Mach-based Vnode Filesystem," *USENIX Conference Proceedings*, Winter 1990.

[14]   Paciorek, N., LoVerso, S., and Langerman, A., "Debugging Multiprocessor Operating System Kernels," *Proceedings of the Second Symposium on Experiences with Distributed and Multiprocessor Systems*, March 1991, pp. 185–201.

[15]   Peacock, J.K., "File System Multithreading in System V Release 4 MP," *USENIX Conference Proceedings*, Summer 1992.

[16]   Peacock, J.K., Saxena, S., Thomas, D., Yang, F., and Yu, W., "Experiences from Multithreading System V Release 4," *Proceedings of the Third Symposium on Experiences with Distributed and Multiprocessor Systems*, March 1992, pp. 77–91.

[17]   Pike, R., Presotto, D., Thompson, K., and Holzmann, G., "Process Sleep and Wakeup on a Shared-memory Multiprocessor," *EurOpen Conference Proceedings*, Spring 1991, pp. 161–6.

[18]   Sinkewicz, U., "A Strategy for SMP ULTRIX," *USENIX Conference Proceedings*, June 1988, pp. 203–12.

[19]   Stum, M., Unrau, R., and Krieger, O., "Designing a Scalable Operating System for Shared Memory Multiprocessors," *Proceedings of the USENIX Workshop on Micro-Kernels and Other Kernel Architectures*, April 1992, pp. 285–303.

[20]   Test, J.A., "Concentrix — A UNIX for the Alliant Multiprocessor," *USENIX Conference Proceedings*, January 1986.

11

Semaphored Kernels

This chapter presents a new MP primitive, the semaphore, that replaces the functionality of the uniprocessor `sleep`/`wakeup` facility. Semaphores can be used for both mutual exclusion and synchronization. Since they were invented to function correctly without the need for external locking and nonpreemptability assumptions, unlike sleep/wakeup, they are generally simpler to use. As will be seen, semaphores are not designed to replace spin locks for protecting short critical sections, and so spin locks are still used in semaphored kernels. The implementation of semaphores and their use in the operating system are presented. A variety of other MP primitives is shown in the next chapter.

11.1 Introduction

The previous chapter showed how spin locks can be added to a uniprocessor kernel to make it run correctly on an MP system. Spin locks are required around uses of the `sleep` and `wakeup` functions since there would otherwise be race conditions in the code that uses them. By themselves, `sleep` and `wakeup` are not suitable for MP systems because of these races. In addition, the behavior of `wakeup`, where it wakes up all processes sleeping on a particular event, is frequently undesirable for MP systems.

Because of these considerations, operating system designers have turned to other primitives to replace `sleep` and `wakeup` in multiprocessor UNIX systems. As with spin locks, these primitives are designed to function correctly in an MP environment regardless of the number of processors in the system. They differ from spin locks in that they allow a process to be suspended if certain criteria cannot be immediately satisfied (such as trying to acquire a long-term lock that is already in use). While a variety of such primitives has been invented for use in MP systems (some of which are described in the next chapter), one of the simplest is the Dijkstra *semaphore*. It can be used to implement both mutual exclusion and inter-process synchronization.

An MP implementation of the UNIX operating system done by AT&T Bell Labs in the early 1980s used semaphores. It was implemented on a dual-processor SMP system called the 3B20. The source code for this implementation was made available for license and subsequently became the initial base upon which many companies, including Silicon Graphics, Sequent, and Pyramid Technologies, developed their own MP systems. Kernels that have evolved from this base have been used on MP systems ranging from microprocessors to mainframes, and some are still in use today.

The state of a semaphore is represented by a signed integer value upon which two atomic operations are defined. The *P(s)* operation decrements the integer value associated with semaphore *s* by 1 and blocks the process if the new value is less than zero. If the new value is greater than or equal to zero, the process is allowed to continue execution. The converse is the *V(s)* operation, which increments the semaphore value by one and, if the new value is less than or equal to zero, unblocks one process that was suspended during a *P* operation on that semaphore. The process executing the *V* operation is never blocked. A queue of processes blocked on the semaphore is maintained as part of the semaphore state, in addition to the integer value. When the value of the semaphore is negative, the absolute value indicates the number of processes on the queue.

The distinguishing factor between *P* and *V* and the uniprocessor `sleep` and `wakeup` functions is that semaphores are higher level operations that make both the decision to block and the act of blocking the process an atomic operation. This is analogous to the `lock_object` function that tested the state of the object and either locked the object for itself or slept, all as an atomic operation. In addition, the *V* operation has the desired effect of unblocking only a single process at a time as `wakeup_one` did. Since semaphores have state associated with them (the integer value updated by each operation), it is unnecessary to keep external flags to record the state of the lock as the `lock_object` function did. Furthermore, this state information means that semaphores retain a "memory" of past operations, unlike `wakeup` (for which there is no memory of the operation if no process was sleeping on the event).

11.1.1 Mutual Exclusion with Semaphores

By initializing the semaphore value to 1, long-term mutual exclusion locks can be implemented. A critical section is then protected by using a P operation before entering it, and using V upon exiting (see Figure 11–1). This will allow only one process in the critical region at a time. Once the first process enters the critical region, it will decrement the semaphore value to zero. The process will be allowed to proceed, but any other processes following it will block when they execute the P operation. When the first process exits the critical region, the V operation will allow another to enter by unblocking a waiting process if there is one.

```
P(s)
perform critical section
(process is free to context switch at any time)
V(s)
```

Figure 11–1: Critical region protected by a semaphore.

Semaphores used for mutual exclusion in this fashion are called *binary semaphores*. This refers to the fact that the binary semaphore logically has only two states: locked and unlocked. The semaphore value for a binary semaphore is never greater than 1, as this would allow more than one process to be in the critical section at a time.

As with all uses of long-term mutual exclusion, the process is allowed to block while in the critical region (while waiting for I/O to complete, for instance). As in uniprocessor kernels that use the `lock_object` function to implement long-term mutual exclusion, this does not cause the lock to be released. It is released only when the process performs the V operation. This is different from the use of spin locks in the coarse-grained kernels discussed in the last chapter, where the spin locks (but not the long-term locks themselves) were automatically released and reacquired around context switches (see Section 10.4).

11.1.2 Synchronization with Semaphores

Semaphores can be used for process synchronization by initializing the value to zero. This allows one process to wait for an event to occur by using a P operation. Since the semaphore value is initially zero, the process will block immediately. Completion of the event can be signaled by another process using a V operation. The V operation causes a process waiting for the event to be awakened and run (see Figure 11–2). Because the semaphore is incremented by a V operation even if no processes are blocked on the semaphore, an event that is signaled before the first process can perform the P operation causes that process to continue without waiting. This is a desirable situation since it requires no additional coordination to handle the inherent race condition between a process waiting for the event and the one signaling its completion.

Process 1   Process 2

```
P(s) /* wait for event */                       .

                                                .

                                                .
                             V(s) /* signal event */
```

Figure 11–2: Synchronization with semaphores.

11.1.3 Resource Allocation with Semaphores

Finally, semaphores can be used to control the allocation of resources from a finite pool. For example, assume there is a pool of special-purpose buffers in the system that processes must periodically allocate. If no buffers are presently available, a process requesting one will wait until one becomes available. By initializing a semaphore to the number of buffers in the pool, a P operation can be done to reserve a buffer. As long as the semaphore value remains greater than zero, each process reserving a buffer will be allowed to proceed without blocking. A V operation is done when a buffer is released. Once all buffers are in use, new processes reserving a buffer are blocked. When a buffer is released, a process waiting for a buffer is awakened and allowed to continue (see Figure 11–3).

Note that the P operation does not allocate a buffer, but merely reserves one. Allocation and deallocation must be implemented separately. Deadlocks can result if processes attempt to reserve more than one resource from the pool at a time. This is discussed in the following section.

```
P(s) /* reserve buffer */
allocate and use buffer
...
return buffer to pool
V(s) /* release reservation */
```

Figure 11–3: Resource reservation with semaphores.

11.2 Deadlocks

Some of the potential deadlock situations described in Section 9.3 are also possible with semaphores. To summarize these briefly, the problems of lock ordering and the *AB–BA* deadlock apply to semaphores in the same way they did to spin locks. Likewise, a process that attempts to acquire a semaphore used for mutual exclusion more than once will deadlock with itself. Once it attempts to lock the semaphore a second time (known as *recursive locking*), it blocks forever. These two deadlock problems are the same as they were when using spin locks. Furthermore, these situations are applicable to any MP primitive that implements mutual exclusion.

Context switching while the process holds a binary semaphore is permissible. It does not lead to a potential deadlock as it did with spin locks, because processes trying to acquire the semaphore lock will block and allow other processes to run. This way processes waiting for the lock do not prevent the process holding the lock from running and releasing the lock, as they did with spin locks.

While it is safe to acquire a spin lock in an interrupt handler (assuming the interrupted code was not holding the same lock), semaphore *P* operations cannot be used at interrupt level just as the `sleep` function cannot be used. Interrupt handlers have no process context, and so there is no process to block if a *P* operation is done and the semaphore value is less than or equal to zero. Blocking the interrupted process is incorrect, especially since it may be the process that would have performed the *V* operation to release the semaphore. This is analogous to the case where the interrupt handler spins forever trying to acquire a spin lock that was in use by the interrupted process.

It is possible for a process to perform multiple *P* operations on semaphores used for synchronization. This does not cause a deadlock because the event is always signaled by a different process. To illustrate this, consider a producer–consumer relationship between two processes. Process 1 waits for a buffer of data, and processes it when it arrives. Process 2 prepares the data and alerts process 1 when it is ready using a semaphore. (See Figure 11–4.) So even though process 1 performs repeated *P* operations on the same semaphore, no deadlock occurs. Because the semaphore is used for synchronization purposes, this is not considered recursive locking.

Process 1

```
for (;;) {
    P(s); /* wait for data */
    process data from process 2
}
```

Process 2

```
for (;;) {
    prepare data for process 1
    V(s); /* data ready */
}
```

Figure 11–4: Producer–consumer model.

Deadlocks can occur when using semaphores for resource reservation if processes attempt to reserve more than one resource at a time (which is done by using multiple P operations). To see how this can happen, imagine a pool contains four resources and there are two processes that each wants to use three of them at once. If these processes run on different processors and begin their sequence of three consecutive P operations at the same time, then they will deadlock as soon as each takes two of the resources. This depletes the pool before either process satisfies its need, causing both processes, and any others that try to allocate from the pool, to block forever. As is typical with deadlock situations, the relative timing of the two processes determines whether a deadlock will actually occur. If either of the two processes is able to complete its sequence of P operations to reserve the resources it needs before the other starts, then no deadlock will occur.

There are several algorithms for allocating multiple resources in a deadlock-free manner. They all avoid deadlocks by preventing a process from partially acquiring the resources it needs. If the entire allocation is not available, the process is not given any resources and is blocked until the complete reservation it requested can be made. This way a process does not consume resources needed by others while it is waiting. The *banker's algorithm* utilizes this technique. Instead of performing multiple P operations to acquire the resources, processes use a new primitive where they specify the number of resources needed. They are then allocated on an all-or- nothing basis. (See references [11], [14], [23], and [31] in Section 11.9 for more details.)

Finally, notice that deadlocks, with respect to the resource allocation request itself, will never happen as long as processes never attempt to utilize more than one resource from the pool at a time. If the pool is empty, the process blocks until one is available without holding any of the resources, which prevents the deadlock from occurring.

11.3 Implementing Semaphores

The advent of RISC processors means that operations like semaphores, which require multiple memory accesses to be done atomically, are rarely implemented in hardware. Instead, semaphores must be built on top of the basic hardware atomic operations by software. This is easily done using spin locks.

Each semaphore requires a small data structure to maintain the current value and the queue of blocked processes (see Figure 11–5). A singly linked list will be used for the queue, with pointers to both the first and last elements on the list. A process that blocks on a semaphore is added to the tail of the list, and processes unblocked by a *V* operation are removed from the head. (Alternately, processes may be awakened according to their priorities.) A spin lock is added to provide mutual exclusion while the data structure is being updated.

```
struct semaphore {
        lock_t          lock;       /* protects other fields   */
        int             count;      /* current semaphore value */
        proc_t          *head;      /* ptr to 1st blocked proc */
        proc_t          *tail;      /* ptr to last blocked proc */
};

typedef struct semaphore sema_t;
```

Figure 11–5: Semaphore data structure.

The semaphore data structure must be initialized before it is used. This will usually be done at system initialization time or when a data structure that contains a semaphore is allocated. A semaphore can be initialized to any given value with the function in Figure 11–6.

```
void
initsema(sema_t *sp, int initial_cnt)
{
        initlock(&sp->lock);
        sp->head = NULL;
        sp->tail = NULL;
        sp->count = initial_cnt;
}
```

Figure 11–6: Initializing a semaphore.

The semaphore *P* operation can be implemented as shown in Figure 11–7. A process's u-area contains a pointer to its process table entry. This pointer is referenced as u.u_procp. As with the implementation of run queues (see Section 9.4.1), the p_next element of the proc structure is used to link together processes blocked on the same semaphore. A process can never be on the run queue and blocked on a semaphore at the same time, so the same pointer can be used for both. Likewise, a process cannot be blocked on more than one semaphore at a time.

```
void
p(sema_t *sp)
{
        lock(&sp->lock);
        sp->count--;

        if (sp->count < 0) {
                if (sp->head == NULL)
                        sp->head = u.u_procp;

                else
                        sp->tail->p_next = u.u_procp;

                u.u_procp->p_next = NULL;
                sp->tail = u.u_procp;
                unlock(&sp->lock);
                swtch();
                return;
        }

        unlock(&sp->lock);
}
```

Figure 11–7: The semaphore *P* operation.

The swtch() function performs a context switch. It causes the state of the currently executing process to be saved and a new process selected for execution. (This is the same function used internally by sleep.) When the process is later awakened (after being made runnable by a *V* operation), it will resume execution inside the swtch function at the point where its state was saved. It then simply returns to the p() function. At this point, the process has been granted the semaphore. Since the semaphore count was adjusted when the process first entered the p() function, no further action is necessary and it merely returns to the caller.

The semaphore *V* operation can be implemented as shown in Figure 11–8. If a process had blocked during a previous *P* operation, the *V* operation removes the oldest such process from the queue and adds it to the run queue. As such, this implementation favors overall fairness by awakening processes in FIFO order. It could also be made to awaken the highest priority process, but with the side effect that a low-priority process may be blocked for an arbitrarily long amount of time, if higher priority processes continuously block while performing *P* operations. (Note that this is the desired behavior for real-time systems.)

```
void
v(sema_t *sp)
{
        proc_t *p;

        lock(&sp->lock);
        sp->count++;

        if (sp->count <= 0) {
                p = sp->head;
                sp->head = p->p_next;

                if (sp->head == NULL)
                        sp->tail = NULL;

                unlock(&sp->lock);
                enqueue(&runqueue, p);
                return;
        }

        unlock(&sp->lock);
}
```

Figure 11–8: The semaphore *V* operation.

There is an inherent race condition between the time the semaphore's internal spin lock is released during a *P* operation that blocks the process, and the time the process finishes the context switch inside the swtch function. It is possible for another processor to be spinning on the lock while waiting to do a *V* operation. As soon as the *P* operation releases the spin lock, the *V* operation will be able to proceed. If the only process on the semaphore queue is the one still executing within swtch, then the *V* operation will remove it and add it to the run queue. It is then possible for another processor to select this process for execution and attempt to run it before it is able to finish its context switch inside the *P* operation on the first processor. If this were to happen, abnormalities could occur since one processor would be restoring the process's state before it was completely saved on the other processor. This race condition becomes more likely if a lengthy interrupt occurs just before `swtch` is called. Figure 11–9 contains a time line showing the sequence of events leading to this race.

Time	Processor 1	Processor 2	Processor 3
	process A does a *P* operation that blocks the process	• • •	
	process A is placed on semaphore queue	process B starts a *V* operation—waits for spin lock	
	semaphore spin lock released	process B gets spin lock—finds process A on semaphore queue and places it on run queue	• • •
	swtch called — process A's context save is begun		current process blocks, process A is chosen from run queue, but the context save on processor 1 hasn't finished yet!
	• • •		
	context save finishes—process stops running		

Figure 11–9: Semaphore implementation race condition.

To prevent this race condition, the state of the process can be changed from *running* to *blocked* by the `swtch` routine after it has completely saved the process's state. Whenever a processor selects a process for execution, it checks the process state before attempting to run it. If the state is marked as *running*, then it means some other processor is still saving the process's state. The new processor can simply busy-wait on the state until it changes to *blocked* before continuing. Normally, the process will already be marked blocked since this race condition is rare. However, the kernel must be prepared to handle the case in order to maintain system integrity.

11.4 Coarse-Grained Semaphore Implementations

It is possible to use semaphores instead of spin locks to implement the coarse-grained kernels presented in the last chapter (see Sections 10.2 and 10.4). Binary semaphores are more convenient for this than spin locks, since they block the process when the lock is already taken. With spin locks, a conditional lock operation was needed to avoid spinning when other user-mode processes could be executed instead. This is not needed when using semaphores.

Other aspects of the implementation are unchanged: giant locks must still be released prior to sleeping inside the kernel, and separate run queue locks are still needed so that context switches can occur without acquiring one of the giant locks. The resulting performance of the system will be the same because semaphores simply provide a more convenient MP primitive for implementing giant locks than spin locks do, and they do not affect the degree of parallelism that is possible within the kernel. While semaphores make better giant locks, spin locks remain a useful primitive in coarse-grained kernels in situations such as protecting the run queues.

11.5 Multithreading with Semaphores

The principles presented in the last chapter for multithreading with spin locks apply equally when multithreading a kernel with semaphores. For example, it is still highly desirable to avoid unnecessary locking whenever possible (Section 10.3). Likewise, lock granularity still needs to be considered (Section 10.5.4). The main difference seen when multithreading with semaphores is that the semaphore primitives replace `sleep` and `wakeup`. In the previous chapter, spin locks were used to augment the old mechanisms so that they would work without race conditions on MP systems. The following sections discuss this in more detail.

11.5.1 Long-Term Mutual Exclusion

Long-term mutual exclusion is easily implemented with semaphores. Since the semaphore value maintains the state of the lock (a value of 1 means unlocked, less than or equal to 0 means locked), there is no need for the external flag that was passed to the uniprocessor `lock_object` function to indicate the lock status. Furthermore, since semaphores already perform the tasks of blocking and unblocking processes as needed, `sleep` and `wakeup` are not needed either. The result is that `lock_object` and `unlock_object` can be eliminated and replaced with semaphore operations. Instead of maintaining the lock status flag in the data structure to be locked, a semaphore is associated with it instead. Then wherever `lock_object` was used, the semaphore P operation is used instead, passing a pointer to the semaphore in the data structure to be locked. Similarly, all calls to `unlock_object` are replaced with semaphore V operations.

In addition to eliminating the need for a separate status flag, the following differences between using semaphores and traditional uniprocessor techniques for implementing long-term mutual exclusion should be noted.

First, the `while` loop inside the `lock_object` function is not needed when using semaphores. The loop was necessary in the case where there were multiple processes sleeping for the lock. Since `wakeup` awakens all processes sleeping for the same event, the uniprocessor kernel had to ensure that only one such process could acquire the lock while the rest returned to sleep. Processes could therefore wake up, find the lock still locked, and return to sleep an arbitrary number of times before finally acquiring the lock for themselves, hence the need for the `while` loop.

The loop was still necessary even when `wakeup_one` was used in the last chapter, since a new process calling `lock_object` for the first time competes for the lock with processes that have just been awakened. The new process could acquire the lock before processes that have been sleeping for an arbitrary amount of time, causing these processes to loop and sleep again.

These situations cannot happen with semaphores as implemented in this chapter. New processes arriving at the semaphore will always sleep if the lock has already been taken. They are awakened in FIFO order so that a continuous stream of new processes cannot prevent waiting processes from acquiring the lock. Processes are also awakened one at a time, which eliminates the need for them to compete for the lock each time they wake up. A process awakened by the *V* operation is guaranteed to have the lock.

11.5.2 Short-Term Mutual Exclusion

While semaphores could be used to implement short-term mutual exclusion (except in interrupt handlers), spin locks are a better choice. Just as spin locks are inefficient if the critical section they protect is too long, semaphores are inefficient if the critical section is too short. This is due to the context switch overhead incurred if a process blocks on the semaphore. If this overhead is greater than the time that the process would have spent spinning on a spin lock, then the critical region is too short to use semaphores. Therefore, the spin lock examples from previous chapters showing run queue manipulation, signal handling, and so on should not be changed to use semaphores. It is common for MP kernels to use more than one type of primitive operation, where each is suited to a different situation.

11.5.3 Synchronization

As shown at the beginning of the chapter, *P* and *V* operations can be used for process synchronization, just as the uniprocessor `sleep` and `wakeup` functions were used. To illustrate this, consider the synchronization done between parent and child processes when the parent is using the `wait` system call, which blocks the parent process until a child exits. If a child exits before the parent executes the `wait` call, then `wait` returns immediately. In either case, `wait` returns the exit status of the child (the value it passed to the `exit` system call or the signal number that caused it to terminate).

One way to implement the synchronization between exit and wait is by adding a semaphore to the process table entry (which will be called p_waitsema). The semaphore is initialized to zero when the process is created. When the process performs a wait system call,
it does a *P* operation on the semaphore. Figure 11–10 shows this in pseudo-code.

```
wait()
{
        if (no children)
                return ESRCH;

        p(&u.u_procp->p_waitsema);
        find a child that has exited
        return child's exit status
}
```

Figure 11–10: Algorithm for wait.

When a process exits, it performs a *V* operation on its *parent's* semaphore as shown in Figure 11–11.

```
exit()
{
        save exit status
        release address space
        close files
        etc.
        .
        .
        .
        v(&u.u_procp->p_parent->p_waitsema);
}
```

Figure 11–11: Algorithm for exit.

Notice that the algorithm for wait must first check to see if there are any children. If there
aren't any, then this is an error and ESRCH is returned. It would be incorrect for wait to
perform the *P* operation before checking this since, if there were no children, the process
would deadlock with itself. Without children, no process would ever perform the *V* operation on the semaphore to cause the first process to run again.

Also note that the algorithm works correctly for any number of children and regardless of
the relative ordering of the wait and exit system calls. For example, if a process has five
children and three exit before the parent waits for any of them, then the semaphore value

will be three at that point. This means that the next three `wait` system calls that the parent executes will return without blocking. If neither of the remaining two children exits before the parent performs another `wait` system call, then the next `wait` call will block.

This example shows a case where there is a single "consumer" process (the parent) that waits for an event to occur (a child exits). There are situations where there may be multiple processes waiting for an event to occur and all processes should be awakened when it does (similar to the semantics of `wakeup`). For instance, if multiple processes have generated a page fault on a shared page, then all will want to be unblocked when the I/O to read the page has completed. This can easily be implemented by using a variation of the *V* operation, called *broadcast-V*, that unblocks all processes on the semaphore queue. The code is the same as shown in Figure 11–8, except that it loops until the semaphore value reaches zero. It differs from a regular *V* operation in that it does nothing if no processes are blocked on the semaphore. This is the desired behavior of broadcast-type operations, since processes arriving after the event occurs generally don't need to block. To illustrate this in the context of the previous example, if the page is already in memory, then a new process faulting on that page wouldn't need to wait for the I/O to complete and so it wouldn't perform the *P* operation in the first place.

As in the case of long-term mutual exclusion, semaphores can replace all uses of `sleep` and `wakeup` in the uniprocessor kernel that were used for synchronization purposes. These are too numerous to list here, but all follow the guidelines described in this section.

11.6 Performance Considerations

11.6.1 Measuring Lock Contention

In order to benefit the most from fine-grained, multithreaded MP kernels, the areas of high lock contention must be identified and fixed. Excessive contention reduces the amount of parallel kernel activity and will diminish overall system performance. To find where the performance bottlenecks are, measurements of the system can be made while it is running the expected application job mix. The results can be used to identify areas of lock contention, and the kernel can be modified to eliminate or reduce them.

It is easy to identify contention for binary semaphores since a *P* operation is done as the critical region is entered. The implementation of the *P* operation can be modified to record various statistics, which can be conveniently stored in the semaphore data structure itself. The data can then be gathered for analysis after a benchmark run is complete. At a minimum, the following statistics are of interest for each binary semaphore:

- total number of *P* operations performed

- number of *P* operations where the process had to block

- maximum and average lengths of the queue of processes blocked on this semaphore

The degree of contention for a semaphore is then shown by the ratio of the number of times the P operation caused the process to block (because the lock was already in use) and the total number of operations. The higher the ratio, the higher the contention. The number of processes affected by the contention can then be seen by the queue length statistics. The worst contention points will be those where the percentage of operations that had to block and the queue lengths are both high.

Statistics can be gathered for spin locks as well. Since processes spin instead of block on locks that are already in use, the average and maximum number of spins needed to acquire a lock can be recorded instead of the number of blocking operations and queue lengths. This generates data similar to that in the preceding paragraph.

11.6.2 Convoys

A *convoy* of processes occurs when there is a persistent queue of processes waiting on a binary semaphore. This happens when the number of P operations where the process had to be blocked is nearly the same as the total number of P operations. It means that there is too much contention for the semaphore and/or that the lock is being held too long. Convoys are typical in coarse-grained implementations when the application job mix executes frequent system calls.

For example, consider the case where the file system is protected by a single giant lock. Any process doing a file operation will hold the lock even while it is blocked waiting for disk I/O to complete. During this time, it is possible for many other processes to try to begin file operations of their own. These will be blocked, since the lock is already in use, marking the beginning of a convoy. If the applications are file I/O intensive, then it is likely that the convoy will persist indefinitely. The bottleneck is caused by many processes attempting to be in a long critical section at once but the implementation allowing only one process at a time to be there. This situation is pictured in Figure 11–12, where process A is executing within the critical section protected by a binary semaphore while the other processes are blocked, waiting to enter.

At first glance, it may seem helpful to partition the critical section into two or more sequential sections, each protected by a separate lock. In the case of a giant-locked file system, it would be possible to have the initial steps of translating the user's file descriptor into the internal file representation, computing the file offset, and preforming various error checks all done under a separate lock from the later activities of checking the buffer cache for the necessary data and performing disk I/O if needed. This would change the picture to appear as that shown in Figure 11–13.

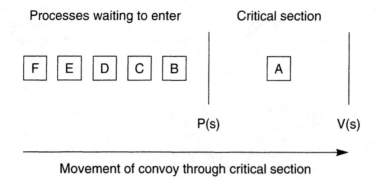

Figure 11–12: Convoy forming behind critical section.

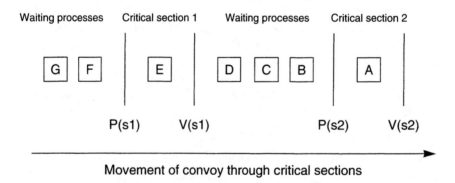

Figure 11–13: Dividing a lengthy critical section in two.

Here processes A and E are in the critical sections while processes B, C, D, F, and G are waiting to enter.

This arrangement is not guaranteed to eliminate a convoy. Consider the case where the first critical section is shorter than the second (which is true in this example, since the disk I/O done in the second critical section is likely to be the longest operation). This means that processes will quickly pass through the first critical section and form a convoy while waiting to enter the second. If convoys form on both semaphores, then the performance will be worse than the initial case, since each process must now context-switch at least twice in order to complete a single operation.

The way to eliminate a convoy is to parallelize the code so that multiple processes can execute in what was a single critical region. Instead of merely going from one process within the critical region at a time to two processes, as in Figure 11–13, it is necessary to allow all of the processes that were waiting in the convoy to execute in parallel. To accomplish this, the algorithms and data structures must be organized so that processes can complete their work without high contention for the same locks. In the case of file systems, this can be done by using separate locks for each file. This allows processes doing I/O to different files to proceed in parallel while still retaining the semantics of the uniprocessor kernel (guaranteeing atomic file operations). This can be pictured as in Figure 11–14, where processes A, B, and C are doing file I/O to different files, and s1, s2, and s3 are separate semaphores for each of these files.

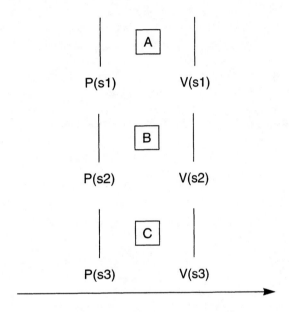

Movement of processes through critical sections

Figure 11–14: Parallelizing a critical section.

This implementation eliminates the convoys shown previously as long as the processes use different files. If many processes need to do I/O to the same file at once, a convoy could again form. Parallelizing the critical sections can be taken a step further in this example by recognizing that allowing multiple processes to read the same file at the same time does not violate the uniprocessor system call semantics for file operations. This type of locking can be done with a multireader lock.

11.6.3 Multireader Locks

In some cases, critical sections can be parallelized by allowing multiple processes that need merely to read various data structures to do so concurrently. As long as none of the processes modify any of the data structures, no races can occur. When a process does need to make a modification, it can do so by waiting for the reader processes to finish and then make its modifications with mutually exclusive access from all other readers and writers. Such a locking scheme is termed a *multireader, single-writer* lock (or simply a multireader lock for short). This could be useful for file operations, for example, since files tend to be read more frequently than they are written. This is particularly true of the directories along commonly used search paths. Even in cases where there are multiple writers and few, if any, readers, such as a group of processes continuously writing to a log file, this type of locking has little additional overhead compared to binary semaphores, so it won't adversely affect performance even when the application job mix can't take advantage of it. Multireader, single-writer locks can be easily implemented with semaphores as follows.

The data structure shown in Figure 11–15 will be used to record the state of a multireader lock. A spin lock is used to protect the counter fields in the multireader data structure. The data structure keeps track of both the number of processes currently in the critical section, as well as the number of processes waiting to enter. These counts are divided between readers and writers.

```
struct multi_reader {
    lock_t    m_lock;   /* protects cnt fields below    */
    int       m_rdcnt;  /* # of rdrs in critical section */
    int       m_wrcnt;  /* # of wrtrs in critical section*/
    int       m_rdwcnt; /* # of waiting readers         */
    int       m_wrwcnt; /* # of waiting writers         */
    sema_t    m_rdwait; /* sync sema where readers wait */
    sema_t    m_wrwait; /* sync sema where writers wait */
};

typedef struct multi_reader rdwrlock_t;
```

Figure 11–15: Multireader lock structure.

Before using the lock, it must be initialized by calling the routine in Figure 11–16.

The strategy for controlling access to the critical resource protected by the multireader lock is to allow readers to enter the critical section at any time, as long as no writers are waiting or currently in the critical section. Once a writer arrives, subsequent readers are blocked.

```
void
init_rdwrlock(rdwrlock_t *mp)
{
        initlock(&mp->m_lock);
        initsema(&mp->m_rdwait, 0);
        initsema(&mp->m_wrwait, 0);
        mp->m_rdcnt = 0;
        mp->m_wrcnt = 0;
        mp->m_rdwcnt = 0;
        mp->m_wrwcnt = 0;
}
```

Figure 11–16: Initializing a multireader lock.

This ensures that a continuous stream of new readers arriving at the lock does not starve out the writers forever. Processes that wish to acquire the multireader lock for reading use the routine in Figure 11–17.

```
void
enter_reader(rdwrlock_t *mp)
{
        lock(&mp->m_lock);

        /*
         * If a writer has the lock presently or there are
         * writers waiting, then we have to wait.
         */

        if (mp->m_wrcnt || mp->m_wrwcnt) {
                mp->m_rdwcnt++;
                unlock(&mp->m_lock);
                p(&mp->m_rdwait);
                return;
        }

        mp->m_rdcnt++;
        unlock(&mp->m_lock);
}
```

Figure 11–17: Acquiring a multireader lock for reading.

A reader leaving a critical section protected by a multireader lock calls the routine shown in Figure 11–18. Once all the readers have left the critical section, a single writer is awakened, if any are waiting.

```
void
exit_reader(rdwrlock_t *mp)
{
        lock(&mp->m_lock);
        mp->m_rdcnt--;

        /*
         * If we're the last reader, and a writer is waiting,
         * then let the writer go now.
         */

        if (mp->m_wrwcnt && mp->m_rdcnt == 0) {
                mp->m_wrcnt = 1;
                mp->m_wrwcnt--;
                unlock(&mp->m_lock);
                v(&mp->m_wrwait);
                return;
        }

        unlock(&mp->m_lock);
}
```

Figure 11–18: Reader releasing a multireader lock.

When a writer wishes to acquire the lock (see Figure 11–19), it must wait for all processes using the lock to leave the critical region. If no processes are currently using it, the writer can acquire the lock immediately. Note the m_wrcnt field can never be greater than 1 by definition of the multireader, *single*-writer lock.

Releasing a multireader lock that is held by a writer is the most complex operation. To ensure a degree of fairness, readers are awakened first when both readers and writers are waiting for the lock. This prevents a continuous stream of writer processes from arriving at the lock and starving out the readers. Since subsequently arriving readers are blocked when one or more writers are waiting, it is guaranteed that writers will not be blocked indefinitely either. In this way, the lock rotates between readers and writers when both types of processes are waiting. Since readers can use the critical section in parallel, all readers are awakened whenever a writer leaves. The code to implement this is shown in Figure 11–20.

It is possible to implement multireader locks with spin locks as well (see Exercise 9.3). These are useful for protecting critical sections that are too short for semaphores. Together, spin locks, semaphores, and multireader locks provide a useful base set of primitives for resolving contention in multithreaded kernels.

```
void
enter_writer(rdwrlock_t *mp)
{
        lock(&mp->m_lock);

        /*
         * Block if any processes are already using the lock.
         */

        if (mp->m_wrcnt || mp->m_rdcnt) {
                mp->m_wrwcnt++;
                unlock(&mp->m_lock);
                p(&mp->m_wrwait);
                return;
        }

        mp->m_wrcnt = 1;
        unlock(&mp->m_lock);
}
```

Figure 11–19: Acquiring a multireader lock for writing.

11.7 Summary

Semaphores provide a useful MP primitive that can replace all uses of the uniprocessor sleep/wakeup mechanism. A semaphore can implement either mutual exclusion or process synchronization and works correctly for any number of processors in the system, including the uniprocessor case. The advantage of semaphores over the sleep/wakeup mechanism is that they update the status of the semaphore and block or unblock a process, all as an atomic operation. It is unnecessary to maintain a separate flag as was required in the lock_object function when sleep/wakeup was used. Second, semaphores awaken only a single process at a time, which eliminates unnecessary thrashing. Consequently, semaphores are good for implementing long-term mutual exclusion. They are also superior to spin locks when implementing giant locks in coarse-grained kernels (since giant locks are long-term mutual exclusion locks). Semaphores should not, however, be used as a complete replacement for spin locks. Spin locks are still preferable for implementing mutual exclusion in short critical sections. Attempting to use semaphores in these cases introduces unnecessary context switching overhead, which can be greater than the time that would have been spent spinning.

As with any locking scheme, excessive contention for a lock limits the amount of parallel kernel activity, and hence limits overall system performance. In extreme cases, persistent queues of processes, called convoys, can form at the entry to the critical section. Splitting a lengthy critical section into two or more pieces will not appreciably improve the situation,

```
void
exit_writer(rdwrlock_t *mp)
{
        int rdrs;

        lock(&mp->m_lock);

        /*
         * Let readers go first if any are waiting.
         */

        if (mp->m_rdwcnt) {
                mp->m_wrcnt = 0;

                /*
                 * Awaken all readers that are presently
                 * waiting.
                 */

                rdrs = mp->m_rdwcnt;
                mp->m_rdcnt = rdrs;
                mp->m_rdwcnt = 0;
                unlock(&mp->m_lock);

                while (rdrs--)
                        v(&mp->m_rdwait);

                return;
        }

        /*
         * No readers waiting, let one writer go if there is one.
         */

        if (mp->m_wrwcnt) {
                mp->m_wrwcnt--;
                unlock(&mp->m_lock);
                v(&mp->m_wrwait);
                return;
        }

        /*
         * Nobody waiting.  Release lock.
         */

        mp->m_wrcnt = 0;
        unlock(&mp->m_lock);
}
```

Figure 11–20: Writer releasing multireader lock.

since it introduces the possibility of extra context switches. Instead, a way must be found to parallelize the critical section. This can be done by partitioning the data structures such that separate locks can be used to protect them. Another possibility is to use a multireader, single-writer lock that allows multiple processes to access a shared data structure at once, as long as none of them needs to modify it (which is a common operation in operating systems). Writers are granted mutually exclusive access so that the integrity of the data structures is maintained. These techniques can be used to increase the amount of parallel kernel activity, which can improve overall system performance.

11.8 Exercises

11.1   Does each semaphore require its own spin lock or can unrelated semaphores share the same spin lock? What effect would sharing the same lock have?

11.2   Could the UNIX kernel originally have been written using semaphores instead of the `sleep/wakeup` facility? If so, discuss the trade-offs.

11.3   Use semaphores to implement a double buffering scheme between two processes. Process A fills buffer 1 with data. When it is done with this, it awakens process B, which uses the data. In parallel with this, process A fills buffer 2. When complete, it waits until B is done with buffer 1, then fills it with new data while B uses buffer 2, and so on. Show C code fragments for processes A and B.

11.4   In the multireader lock implementation shown in Section 11.6.3, what happens when a new reader arrives just as an exiting writer starts awakening readers?

11.5   Assume that a multireader lock is in use by a writer and that there are readers already waiting for the lock. Now, a new reader invokes `enter_reader` and acquires the spin lock just before the writer calls `exit_writer`. Assume further that an interrupt occurs just after the new reader releases the spin lock, but before it can perform the *P* operation on `m_rdwait`. This allows the exiting writer that was spinning on the multireader lock's spin lock to acquire the lock and proceed. What happens if the exiting writer starts awakening readers at this point (before the new reader can execute the *P* operation)?

11.6   Could the `exit_writer` routine make use of the *broadcast-V* operation when awakening readers instead of doing the *V* operation in the while loop?

11.7   Rewrite the multireader lock implementation to add an additional degree of fairness in the case where there are both readers and writers waiting for a writer to exit the critical section. Instead of awakening all readers in this case, awaken readers and writers in order of arrival. If a group of readers arrives before a writer, then that whole group of readers should be awakened, but not the readers that arrived after the writer. For example, if process A has the lock for writing, and other processes arrive in the following order: processes B and C for reading, process D for writing, and process E for reading, then when A exits the critical section, only B and C will be awakened (E will not be awakened at this point). Any new readers arriving are blocked. Once both B and C exit the critical section, process D is awakened, then process E runs after D is complete.

11.8   Write a modified version of the *P* and *V* functions that take a count of the number of resources that should be atomically acquired. Use the banker's algorithm to prevent deadlocks.

11.9   In the `exit_reader` code shown in Figure 11–17, why must the `m_wrcnt` field be set to 1 when a writer is awakened instead of having the writer do it itself in the `enter_writer` function immediately after the *P* operation?

11.9 Further Reading

[1]   Bach, M.J., and Buroff, S.J., "Multiprocessor UNIX Systems," *AT&T Bell Labs Technical Journal*, Vol. 63, No. 8, October 1984, pp. 1733–50.

[2]   Bach, M.J., *The Design of the UNIX Operating System*, Englewood Cliffs, NJ: Prentice Hall, 1986.

[3]   Beck, B., Kasten, B., and Thakkar, S., "VLSI Assist for a Multiprocessor," *Second International Conference on Architectural Support for Programming Languages and Operating Systems*, October 1987, pp. 10–20.

[4]   Black, D.L., Tevanian, Jr., A., Golub, D.B., and Young, M.W., "Locking and Reference Counting in the MACH Kernel," *Proceedings of the 1992 International Conference on Parallel Processing*, August 1992, pp. II:167–73.

[5]   Blasgen, M.W., Gray, J.N., Mitoma, M., and Price, T.G., "The Convoy Phenomenon," *IBM Research Report*, RJ2516, May 1977, revised January 1979.

[6]   Campbell, M., Barton, R., Browning, J., Cervenka, D., Curry, B., Davis, T., Edmonds, T., Holt, R., Slice, J., Smith, T., and Wescott, R., "The Parallelization of UNIX System V Release 4.0," *USENIX Conference Proceedings*, January 1991, pp. 307–23.

[7]   Campbell, M., Holt, R., and Slice, J., "Lock Granularity Tuning Mechanisms in SVR4/MP," *Proceedings of the Second Sympoisum on Experiences with Distributed and Multiprocessor Systems*, March 1991, pp. 221–8.

[8]　　　Campbell, M., and Holt, R.L., "Lock Granularity Analysis Tools in SVR4/MP," *IEEE Software*, March 1993, pp. 66–70.

[9]　　　CaraDonna, J.P., Paciorek, N., and Wills, C.E., "Measuring Lock Performance in Multiprocessor Operating System Kernels," *Proceedings of the USENIX Symposium on Experiences with Distributed and Multiprocessor Systems*, September 1993, pp. 37–56.

[10]　　Courtois, P.J., Heymans, F., and Parnas, D.L., "Concurrent Control with Readers and Writers," *Communications of the ACM*, Vol. 14, No. 10, October 1971, pp. 667–8.

[11]　　Deitel, H.M., *An Introduction to Operating Systems*, Reading, MA: Addison-Wesley, 1990.

[12]　　Denning, P.J., Dennis, T.D., and Brumfield, J.A., "Low Contention Semaphores and Ready Lists," *Communications of the ACM*, Vol. 24, No. 10, October 1981, pp. 687–99.

[13]　　Dijkstra, E.W., "Solution of a Problem in Concurrent Programming Control," *Communications of the ACM*, Vol. 8, No. 5, September 1965, p. 569.

[14]　　Dijkstra, E.W., "Cooperating Sequential Processes," in *Programming Languages*, F. Genuys (ed.), Academic Press, New York, 1968, pp. 43–112.

[15]　　Dijkstra, E.W., "The Structure of the T.H.E. Multiprogramming System," *Communications of the ACM*, Vol. 11, No. 5, May 1968, pp. 341–46.

[16]　　Easton, W.B., "Process Synchronization without Long-Term Interlock," *ACM Operating Systems Review*, Vol. 6, No. 1, June 1972, pp. 50–95.

[17]　　Eisenber, M.A., and McGuire, M.R., "Further Comment on Dijkstra's Concurrent Programming Control Problem," *Communications of the ACM*, Vol. 15, No. 11, November 1972, p. 999.

[18]　　Eykholt, J.R., Kleiman, S.R., Barton, S., Faulkner, R., Shivalingiah, A., Smith, M., Stein, D., Voll, J., Wekks, M., and Williams, D., "Beyond Multiprocessing: Multithreading the SunOS Kernel," *USENIX Conference Proceedings*, Summer 1992.

[19]　　Garg, A., "Parallel STREAMS: A Multiprocessor Implementation," *USENIX Conference Proceedings*, January 1990, pp. 163–76.

[20]   Graunke, G., and Thakkar, S., "Synchronization Algorithms for Shared-Memory Multiprocessors," *Computer*, June 1990, pp. 60–9.

[21]   Gray, J.N., "Notes on Data Base Operating Systems," *IBM Research Report*, RJ2188(30001), February 1978, p. 83.

[22]   Gurwitz, R.F., and Teixeira, T.J., "Stellix: UNIX for a Graphics Supercomputer," *USENIX Conference Proceedings*, June 1988, pp. 321–30.

[23]   Habermann, A.N., "Prevention of System Deadlocks," *Communications of the ACM*, Vol. 12, No. 7, July 1969, pp. 373–7, 385.

[24]   Hartman, J.H., and Ousterhout, J.K, "Performance Measurement of a Multiprocessor Sprite Kernel," *USENIX Conference Proceedings*, Summer 1990, pp. 279–87.

[25]   Kelley, M.H., "Multiprocessor Aspects of the DG/UX Kernel," *USENIX Conference Proceedings*, January 1989, pp. 85–99.

[26]   Korty, J.A., "Sema: A Lint-like Tool for Analyzing Semaphore Usage in a Multithreaded UNIX Kernel," *USENIX Conference Proceedings*, Winter 1989, pp. 113–23.

[27]   Lamport, L., "A New Solution to Dijkstra's Concurrent Programming Problem," *Communications of the ACM*, Vol. 17, No. 8, August 1974, pp. 453–55.

[28]   Lamport, L., "Concurrent Reading and Writing," *Communications of the ACM*, Vol. 20, No. 11, November 1977, pp. 806–11.

[29]   Lauesen, S., "A Large Semaphore-Based Operating System," *Communications of the ACM*, Vol. 18, No. 7, July 1975, pp. 377–89.

[30]   Lee, T.P., and Luppi, M.W., "Solving Performance Problems on a Multiprocessor UNIX System," *USENIX Conference Proceedings*, Summer 1987, pp. 399–405.

[31]   Madduri, H., and Finkel, R., "Extension of the Banker's Algorithm for Resource Allocation in a Distributed Operating System," *Information Processing Letters*, Vol. 19, No. 1, July 1984, pp. 1–8.

[32]   Paciorek, N., LoVerso, S., and Langerman, A., "Debugging Multiprocessor Operating System Kernels," *Proceedings of the Second Symposium on Experiences with Distributed and Multiprocessor Systems*, March 1991, pp. 185–201.

[33] Patil, S.S., "Limitations and Capabilities of Dijkstra's Semaphore Primitive for Coordination among Processes," *M.I.T. Project MAC Computational Structures Group Memo 57*, February 1971.

[34] Sawyer, B.B., "Multiprocessor UNIX Utilizing the SPARC Architecture," *UniForum Conference Proceedings*, February 1989, pp. 107–19.

[35] Saxena, S., Peacock, J.K., Yang, F., Verma, V., and Krishnan, M., "Pitfalls in Multithreading SVR4 STREAMS and Other Weightless Processes," *USENIX Conference Proceedings*, Winter 1993, pp. 85–96.

[36] Torrellas, H., Gupta, A., and Hennessy, J., "Characterizing the Caching and Synchronization Performance of an MP Operating System," *SIGPLAN Notices*, Vol. 27, No. 9, September 1992, pp. 162–74.

12

Other MP Primitives

This chapter presents a sampling of some other MP primitives: monitors, eventcounts, and sequencers. It also covers the set of primitives that are used in an MP version of UNIX System V from UNIX Systems Laboratories. The semantics and use of these primitives are compared to the primitives and techniques of the previous chapters.

12.1 Introduction

A myriad of MP primitives have been invented over the years. All primitives provide either mutual exclusion, synchronization, or both. As will be seen, they differ primarily in how convenient or flexible they are in particular situations. To illustrate these differences, the following sections describe a sampling of other primitives, including those used in the System V Release 4.2 MP software product (abbreviated as *SVR4.2 MP*) from UNIX Systems Laboratories. The use of these primitives to multithread an operating system is the same as presented in the last two chapters. Therefore, this chapter will concentrate on the semantics of these primitives.

12.2 Monitors

A *monitor* provides mutual exclusion for a critical resource and all critical sections that access or modify the resource. It also provides a means of synchronization among processes using the monitor. A monitor can be thought of as a compartment that contains the resource. In order for a process to access the resource, it must first *enter* the compartment. Mutual exclusion is achieved by only allowing one process in the compartment at a time. If another process tries to enter the monitor while it is already in use, it is blocked until the process using it *exits* the monitor or *waits* on an event associated with the monitor. Each monitor may have one or more events on which processes can wait. Processes remain blocked on these events until another process executing within the monitor *signals* the event. By definition, signaling can only be done from within the monitor. This eliminates the need to add extra synchronization to solve race conditions where one process might be on the verge of waiting just as another process tries to signal it.

When an event is signaled, one process blocked on the event is awakened. Since only one process can execute within a monitor at a time, the signaled process will not resume execution until the process that signaled it exits the monitor. At that point, the signaled process resumes execution inside the monitor at the point where it waited. The semantics of a monitor guarantee that the process just signaled will execute within the monitor next. Other processes waiting to enter the monitor will continue to wait until all signaled processes have finished. If an event is signaled and no processes are waiting, then the signal has no effect, just as with `wakeup`. Since monitors have no memory of past signal operations, a wait operation always causes the process to be blocked.

In the literature, monitors are shown using special programming language constructs that associate the data in the critical resource with subroutines that form the critical sections. Calling one of these subroutines causes the monitor to be entered implicitly. When they return, the monitor is implicitly exited. The data associated with the monitor cannot be accessed in any way except by calling these routines. Since standard C provides no direct facilities to support this, monitors must be explicitly coded in much the same way as semaphores. Subroutines can be provided that implement the enter, exit, wait, and signal func-

tions. For example, assume there a linked list that needs to be modified by multiple processors. The routines in Figure 12–1 can be used to add and remove elements from the list
using a monitor to protect the critical resource. Assume that if the list is empty, the remove
function waits until an element is added to the list. (Since pseudo-code is used, the declarations for the linked list and list elements are omitted for brevity.)

```
monitor_t list_monitor;

enum list_events { LIST_NOTEMPTY };

void
add(elem_t *new)
{
    mon_enter(&list_monitor);
    add new element to list
    mon_signal(&list_monitor, LIST_NOTEMPTY);
    mon_exit(&list_monitor);
}

elem_t *
remove(void)
{
    mon_enter(&list_monitor);

    if (list empty)
        mon_wait(&list_monitor, LIST_NOTEMPTY);

    remove element from list
    mon_exit(&list_monitor);
    return element;
}
```

Figure 12–1: Example monitor usage in C.

As with semaphores, each monitor is represented by a small data structure, called a
monitor_t in this example. The routines add and remove are critical sections, and so
they must enter and exit the monitor as shown. The events associated with a monitor are
listed in an enumerated type. In this example, there is only one event, but there may be an
arbitrary number of events in the general case. As stated previously, the act of waiting on
an event blocks the process and allows others to enter the monitor. Since a signaled process
has priority over other processes trying to enter the monitor, the remove function does not
have to test the status of the list again before removing an element, as it is guaranteed that
the element just added will be there. As a final note, in order to conform to the definition
of a monitor, the routines mon_signal and mon_wait must be called only from within a
mon_enter and mon_exit pair.

12.3 Eventcounts and Sequencers

An *eventcount* is a positive, nondecreasing integer value upon which three operations are defined. The *advance(E)* operation adds 1 to the value of the eventcount *E*, which is said to *signal* the event. The *await(E, V)* operation causes the calling process to be blocked until the value of eventcount *E* reaches the value *V*. If the value of the eventcount is greater than or equal to *V* when *await* is called, then the process continues without blocking, since the event was signaled in the past. The current value of an eventcount can be read with *read(E)*. Eventcounts are initialized to zero when created and never decrease in value. It is assumed that the memory location holding the eventcount's value is large enough so that it never overflows throughout the lifetime of the eventcount. (A 32-bit unsigned integer is generally sufficient.)

Related to an eventcount is a *sequencer*, which is a positive, nondecreasing integer value upon which one operation is defined. *Ticket(S)* increments the sequencer by 1 and returns the new value, all as an atomic operation. It is guaranteed, therefore, that multiple simultaneous callers to *ticket* for the same sequencer will all receive unique return values. As with eventcounts, sequencers are initialized to zero and must never overflow during their lifetime. Eventcounts and sequencers were used in at least one MP version of the UNIX system: Data General's DG/UX 4.00. (See reference [17] in Section 12.8.)

Eventcounts and sequencers can be used to implement mutual exclusion and synchronization in a variety of ways. For example, it is possible to implement mutual exclusion like that of binary semaphores with the data structure shown in Figure 12–2. Simple mutual exclusion locks like these are frequently called *mutex* locks for short.

```
struct mutex {
        eventcount_t  event;    /* eventcount to wait on */
        sequencer_t   seq;      /* determines ordering    */
};

typedef struct mutex mutex_t;

void
init_mutex(mutex_t *mp)
{
        init_eventcount(&mp->event);
        init_sequencer(&mp->seq);
        advance(&mp->event);
}
```

Figure 12–2: Mutex locks implemented with eventcounts and sequencers.

Eventcounts and sequencers are represented by the `eventcount_t` and `sequencer_t` data structures, respectively. They are initialized by calling `init_eventcount` and `init_sequencer`. These initialize the eventcount or sequencer to zero. (The implementation of eventcounts and sequencers is left as an exercise.) Acquiring and releasing a mutex lock can be done with the code in Figure 12–3.

```
void
lock_mutex(mutex_t *mp);
{
        int my_turn;

        my_turn = ticket(&mp->seq);
        await(&mp->event, my_turn);
}

void
unlock_mutex(mutex_t *mp)
{
        advance(&mp->event);
}
```

Figure 12–3: Locking and unlocking a mutex lock.

The strategy here is to use the sequencer to give each process a unique ticket, and then allow the processes to enter the critical section in order according to the value of their tickets. This is analogous to the service counter in a store where customers take a number when they arrive and are serviced in order of arrival. The sequencer hands out unique sequential numbers, while the eventcount determines who goes next (similar to the "now serving number n" sign in the store). So each process calling `lock_mutex` takes the next ticket from the sequencer and awaits its turn. Since the first ticket returned by the sequencer will be 1, the eventcount must be advanced once by the initialization code in Figure 12–2. This allows the first process calling `lock_mutex` to acquire the lock immediately, since the eventcount will equal the first ticket causing the `await` call to return without blocking the process.

The eventcount is advanced when the lock is released, allowing the process with the next ticket value to acquire the lock. Notice that there is no need for a spin lock as there was in the `lock_object` code implemented using `sleep/wakeup` (see Figure 10–2). This is because the eventcount maintains its state, the value of the counter, even if no process is awaiting the next value. This eliminates the race condition caused by `wakeup` having no effect if no processes are sleeping on the event. Also note that sequencers enforce a strict FIFO ordering among processes competing for the lock. Semaphores, on the other hand, could be implemented to allow processes to acquire the lock according to their process priorities.

Eventcounts can also be used in situations requiring only process synchronization. Consider double buffering between a producer and consumer process. The strategy will be to use two eventcounts: one to signal when a buffer is full, and one to signal when a buffer is empty. The declaration and initialization code follows in Figure 12–4.

```
buf_t          buffer[2];
eventcount_t   full;
eventcount_t   empty;
...
init_eventcount(&full);
init_eventcount(&empty);
advance(&empty);
advance(&empty);
```

Figure 12–4: Initialization for double buffering example.

Figure 12–5 shows the code for the producer and consumer processes.

```
         Producer                    |              Consumer

int cur_buf;                         |  int cur_buf;
int next;                            |  int next;

cur_buf = 0;                         |  cur_buf = 0;

for (next = 1; ; next++) {           |  for (next = 1; ; next++) {
    await(&empty, next);             |      await(&full, next);
    fill buffer[cur_buf]             |      use buffer[cur_buf]
    advance(&full);                  |      advance(&empty);
    cur_buf = !cur_buf;              |      cur_buf = !cur_buf;
}                                    |  }
```

Figure 12–5: Producer–consumer implementation with eventcounts.

Each time a process finishes its work with a buffer, it signals the other process by advancing the corresponding eventcount. Each process keeps track of the value the eventcount must reach before it can use the next buffer of data in the variable next. Since both buffers are initially empty, the empty eventcount is advanced twice by the initialization code so that the producer process will fill both buffers before it blocks waiting for the consumer to empty the first one.

12.4 The MP Primitives of SVR4.2 MP

SVR4.2 MP is a fine-grained, multithreaded operating system that runs on SMP architectures. As such, it uses the locking strategies illustrated in the preceding chapters. SVR4.2 MP provides a variety of primitives, a subset of which have been publicly documented. The semantics and function prototypes of the primitives presented in the sections that follow are derived from the SVR4.2 Device Driver Reference Manual listed in reference [10] in Section 12.8. This manual is provided so that developers can write multithreaded device drivers that can be linked with the base operating system.

12.4.1 Spin Locks

The spin lock implementation SVR4.2 MP provides is similar to spin locks as presented in this book, with the addition of parameters to block interrupts and to aid in debugging. Spin locks are declared to be of type `lock_t` and are allocated by calling `LOCK_ALLOC` as shown below in C function prototype format. `LOCK_ALLOC` dynamically allocates space for a spin lock, initializes it, and returns a pointer to it. This is provided both as a convenience and so that separately compiled kernel modules are not dependent on the size of the `lock_t` structure.

```
lock_t *LOCK_ALLOC(uchar_t hier, pl_t minpl, lkinfo_t
                   *lkinfop, int slpflg);
```

By convention, all MP primitive interfaces are in upper case to show that they are represented by `#defines` instead of functions. This allows their implementation to be easily redefined (in order to substitute debugging or statistics-gathering versions, for example).

The parameters, except for `slpflg`, are present for debugging and statistics-gathering purposes only. The kernel must be specially compiled in order to use them, since they add overhead to each operation; otherwise, these parameters are ignored.

The `hier` parameter is a small integer indicating the lock's position in the *lock hierarchy*. (The type `uchar_t` is an unsigned character.) Because of the AB–BA deadlock problem (see Section 9.3), a lock ordering is defined by the system implementers for all instances of lock nesting. The lock at each nesting level is then given a unique number in the hierarchy, with the outermost (or first level) given the lowest number. The hierarchy number increases at each subsequent nesting level. By storing the lock's hierarchy number with the lock when it is initialized, it can be checked each time the lock is acquired and released to make sure locks are not being used in the incorrect order. The system can then alert the kernel developer of a potential deadlock situation should this happen.

Another deadlock situation occurs if an interrupt handler tries to acquire a lock that has already been locked on the same processor (also described in Section 9.3). To help detect these situations, a minimum interrupt priority level, the `minpl` parameter, specifies the lowest interrupt priority level the processor should be at while the corresponding spin lock is held. Interrupts at or below this level will be blocked, so it is safe to use the same spin lock in interrupt handlers associated with those levels. Interrupts above `minpl` can still occur, and so none of the spin locks that the processor may be holding can be used in those interrupt handlers. Values for `minpl` are implementation dependent, but are generally small integer values, with increasing values indicating higher priority levels. The value defined by `plbase` means all interrupts are enabled.

The `lkinfop` parameter is a pointer to a *lock information* structure that contains the lock's type (spin lock in this case) and an ASCII string holding a mnemonic name for the lock. It is used to make debugging output and statistical reports more readable.

Finally, the `LOCK_ALLOC` routine needs to allocate memory to hold the spin lock and debugging information. The `slpflg` parameter is a flag indicating whether the calling process can be blocked in order to allocate this memory in the case where it is not immediately available. Interrupt handlers that initialize spin locks should pass the `KM_NOSLEEP` flag, since they have no process context to block.

If a spin lock is only needed temporarily, it can be deallocated with the following function after it is no longer needed:

```
void LOCK_DEALLOC(lock_t *lockp);
```

Spin locks are locked with the following function:

```
pl_t LOCK(lock_t *lockp, pl_t ipl);
```

The `ipl` parameter specifies the interrupt priority to block. All interrupts at or below this level will be blocked until the spin lock is released. It must be greater than or equal to the `minpl` that was specified when the lock was initialized. The `LOCK` function returns the interrupt priority level that was in effect before it was raised to `ipl`. As stated in Section 9.2, blocking interrupts while holding spin locks is important for performance reasons, since an interrupt that occurs while a lock is held lengthens the time other processors will spend spinning for that lock. There is also the need to prevent deadlocks that can occur if an interrupt handler tries to acquire a spin lock already held by the processor. For these reasons, the SVR4.2 MP interfaces combine spin locks and interrupt blocking into a single operation.

Spin locks are released by calling:

```
void UNLOCK(lock_t *lockp, pl_t ipl);
```

The `ipl` argument should be the value that `LOCK` returned. This restores the interrupt priority to what it was prior to the lock being acquired.

Since it is occasionally desirable to acquire a spin lock only when it is not in use (in cases where the implementation doesn't want to spin for an arbitrarily long period of time, or it needs to acquire locks out of order), a conditional lock function is provided:

```
pl_t TRYLOCK(lock_t *lockp, pl_t ipl);
```

It raises the interrupt priority level to `ipl` and acquires the lock in the same manner as the `LOCK` function does, but only if the lock is free. If it's already locked, it returns the value of the symbol `invpl` (an implementation-dependent symbolic constant defined in a header file) instead of the old `ipl` level.

12.4.2 Sleep Locks

SVR4.2 MP does not use semaphores, monitors, or eventcounts. Instead, the designers chose to separate mutual exclusion from synchronization and provide different primitives for these two needs. *Sleep locks* provide the functionality of binary semaphores and, as such, are used for long-term mutual exclusion. Their name comes from the fact that a process that attempts to acquire the lock will sleep if the lock is already in use.

Sleep locks are declared to be of type `sleep_t` and are allocated with the following function:

```
sleep_t *SLEEP_ALLOC(int arg, lkinfo_t *lkinfop, int slpflg);
```

This allocates and initializes the sleep lock to the *unlocked* state. As with the spin lock implementation, `lkinfop` is used only during debugging. The meaning of this parameter is the same as in Section 12.4.1. The parameter `arg` is reserved for future implementations.

A sleep lock can be deallocated with:

```
void SLEEP_DEALLOC(sleep_t *slp);
```

A sleep lock is acquired with the following function:

```
void SLEEP_LOCK(sleep_t *slp, int pri);
```

As with binary semaphores, if the lock is available, the process acquires the lock and continues executing. If the lock is already in use, it sleeps. In this case, the `pri` argument specifies the scheduling priority at which the process wishes to run when it is awakened after having been granted the lock. This allows the implementation to control the relative priorities of processes competing for locks within the system. For example, high-contention locks are given higher priorities so that the process holding the lock will be scheduled soon after it is awakened. This allows it to run and finish the critical section soon, so it can release the lock for others to use. If the priority of processes waiting for critical locks is set too low, convoys can quickly form while the process holding the lock waits on the run queue for its turn to execute.

A variation of the `SLEEP_LOCK` call is provided that allows interaction with UNIX signals. Since signals may arrive asynchronously, the receiving process may be executing a system call when a signal arrives. Typically, the signal will be ignored until the system call is complete, as this simplifies the design of the kernel. There are a few system calls where the arrival of a signal causes the system call to be aborted. This is true of system calls that can take arbitrarily long to complete, such as waiting for data to arrive on a pipe or from a terminal during a `read` system call. In the case of terminal I/O, input may not arrive for minutes or hours if the terminal is not in use. Postponing all signals that long would not be productive, particularly if someone were trying to terminate such a process by sending it a signal. Therefore, all UNIX kernel implementations provide a means to indicate that long-term sleeps can be interrupted by signals. In the uniprocessor implementations, this is done by passing low-priority `pri` arguments to the `sleep` call. Priorities numerically greater than the threshold defined by `PZERO` are considered interruptible by a signal. Other values cause signals to be ignored.

SVR4.2 MP provides this functionality through separate interfaces. The `SLEEP_LOCK` interface ignores all signals while sleeping for the lock. The `SLEEP_LOCK_SIG` interface causes the sleep to be aborted if a nonheld, nonignored signal arrives while the process is waiting for the lock. (Processes may choose to ignore or hold the delivery of certain signals. The arrival of such signals therefore does not affect the process.) The prototype for this function is as follows:

```
bool_t SLEEP_LOCK_SIG(sleep_t *slp, int pri);
```

If the lock is available, or if the process must sleep for the lock and no signals occur, then this function returns `TRUE` (a nonzero value) and the effect of this call is identical to `SLEEP_LOCK`. If a signal is received while the process is sleeping, then the process is awakened and the function returns `FALSE` (zero) to indicate that it did not acquire the lock. The kernel can then take whatever recovery action is needed to abort the system call. The important point is that the process has not been granted the lock when `FALSE` is returned. It therefore must not enter the critical region protected by the lock, since it is likely that some other process is executing within it.

Sleep locks are unlocked with the following function. It does not matter whether the lock was acquired with `SLEEP_LOCK` or `SLEEP_LOCK_SIG`.

```
void SLEEP_UNLOCK(sleep_t *slp);
```

Conditional locking operations are occasionally useful with sleep locks. SVR4.2 MP provides this through the following function:

```
bool_t SLEEP_TRYLOCK(sleep_t *slp);
```

It returns TRUE if the lock was acquired, otherwise it returns FALSE (meaning the lock is in use by another process). As before, the process must not enter the critical region when FALSE is returned. Since this call is guaranteed not to block, it may be used in interrupt handlers.

Overall, sleep locks are identical in functionality and use to binary semaphores. Therefore, the same deadlocks and restrictions apply: lock ordering is required to avoid AB–BA deadlocks, processes that lock the same sleep lock twice in a row will deadlock with themselves, and interrupt handlers may not use the `SLEEP_LOCK` and `SLEEP_LOCK_SIG` interfaces.

12.4.3 Synchronization Variables

SVR4.2 MP provides a separate primitive that performs process synchronization called *synchronization variables*. These can be thought of as an MP variation of `sleep`/`wakeup` since synchronization variables maintain no state. Any needed state information is instead maintained in external flags or counters. The same race conditions that occurred when testing or updating the state information used with `sleep`/`wakeup` on MP systems can occur with synchronization variables. As was shown in Section 10.5, the use of spin locks prevented these races. Therefore, synchronization variables are designed to work in conjunction with spin locks. (As will be seen in Section 12.5, the usage of synchronization variables tends to be like that of monitors.)

Synchronization variables are declared to be of type `sv_t` and are allocated and initialized with the following function:

```
sv_t *SV_ALLOC(int slpflag);
```

As usual, `slpflag` indicates whether the process can be blocked if needed to allocate memory for the synchronization variable. Synchronization variables are deallocated by calling

```
void SV_DEALLOC(sv_t *svp);
```

Each event that the kernel wishes to wait on separately is represented by a different synchronization variable. This is analogous to how unique event arguments were used with `sleep`. To wait for an event to occur on a synchronization variable, the following function is used:

```
void SV_WAIT(sv_t *svp, int pri, lock_t *lockp);
```

As with sleep locks, `pri` specifies the priority at which the process will run when the event occurs and the process is awakened. The `lockp` parameter specifies a spin lock that *must* be held by the process prior to calling `SV_WAIT`. The `SV_WAIT` call then unlocks the spin lock and suspends the process on the specified synchronization variable as an atomic operation. The importance of this will be illustrated shortly. Since the `SV_WAIT` function unlocks the spin lock, the caller must reacquire it after `SV_WAIT` returns if it still needs the lock. When the spin lock is released by `SV_WAIT`, it also unblocks all interrupts.

To signal an event on a synchronization variable, the following function is used (the `flags` argument is currently unimplemented):

```
void SV_SIGNAL(sv_t *svp, int flags);
```

This function awakens one process sleeping on the synchronization variable. Despite its name, this call has nothing to do with the UNIX signal mechanism discussed in the previous section. (It does *not* generate a UNIX signal.) `SV_SIGNAL` is similar to `wakeup` in that if no processes are sleeping on the variable, there is no memory that the operation has been performed, and the call does nothing. This is one of the primary differences between synchronization variables and other MP primitives such as semaphores and eventcounts, as a *V* or *advance* operation increments the semaphore or eventcount value whether or not any processes are waiting.

Together, `sv_wait` and `sv_signal` behave very much like `sleep/wakeup`. For example, the `lock_object` and `unlock_object` routines can be implemented with them as shown in Figure 12–6. (While one would not implement long-term mutual exclusion with synchronization variables, since sleep locks are more convenient, this example provides a good contrast with `sleep/wakeup`.)

Comparing this code to that of Figure 10–2, which uses `sleep`, many similarities can be seen. First, since synchronization variables maintain no state, a flag is still needed in the object's data structure to indicate the state of the lock. Second, a spin lock is still needed so that there are no races between testing the flag and either setting the flag or sleeping. Note that the spin lock must be explicitly reacquired after the call to `SV_WAIT`. In the example from Figure 10–2, it was assumed that the kernel automatically released and reacquired spin locks when a process slept. Synchronization variables require this to be done explicitly.

```
lock_object(char *flag_ptr, sv_t *svp)
{
        lock(&object_locking);

        while (*flag_ptr) {
                sv_wait(svp, PRI, &object_locking);
                lock(&object_locking);
        }

        *flag_ptr = 1;
        unlock(&object_locking);
}
```

Figure 12–6: Locking an object with synchronization variables.

The code to unlock the object, shown in Figure 12–7, is similar to that of the sleep/wake-up version as well.

```
unlock_object(char *flag_ptr, sv_t *svp)
{
        lock(&object_locking);
        *flag_ptr = 0;
        SV_SIGNAL(svp, 0);
        unlock(&object_locking);
}
```

Figure 12–7: Unlocking an object using synchronization variables.

As with the code in Figure 10–3, the spin lock is required so that there are no races between signaling a synchronization variable and a process about to wait on it. The main difference between this version of the code and the previous version that uses wakeup is that SV_SIGNAL awakens only a single process (as wakeup_one did), whereas wakeup awakens all processes sleeping on the event. The latter effect can be achieved with synchronization variables by using this function:

```
void SV_BROADCAST(sv_t *svp, int flags);
```

As was the case with sleep locks, there are instances where the kernel cannot wait indefinitely for the event to occur. The following variation of SV_WAIT awakens the process if a UNIX signal occurs before the event is signaled:

```
bool_t SV_WAIT_SIG(sv_t *svp, int pri, lock_t *lkp);
```

The return code indicates which event happened: it returns FALSE if a UNIX signal occurred and returns TRUE if an SV_SIGNAL or SV_BROADCAST occurred.

12.4.4 Multireader Locks

SVR4.2 MP also provides multireader, single-writer locks. These locks are declared to be of type rwlock_t and are allocated and deallocated with the following functions:

```
rwlock_t *RW_ALLOC(uchar_t hier, pl_t minpl, lkinfo_t *lkp,
                   int sleep);

void RW_DEALLOC(rwlock_t *lockp);
```

The arguments to RW_ALLOC are defined to be the same as for LOCK_ALLOC. A multireader lock is acquired for reading or writing with:

```
pl_t RW_RDLOCK(rwlock_t *lockp, pl_t ipl);

pl_t RW_WRLOCK(rwlock_t *lockp, pl_t ipl);
```

It is implementation dependent whether these functions will block the process or spin if the lock cannot be immediately acquired. Both reader and writer locks are released with:

```
void RW_UNLOCK(rwlock_t *lockp, pl_t ipl);
```

The meaning of the parameters to these functions are the same as described in previous sections.

12.5 Comparison of MP Synchronization Primitives

This section will show through an example how semaphores compare with the synchronization primitives presented in this chapter.

Consider the case of logging errors detected by the kernel to a file. Assume that the system uses a separate logging process to write the errors to a disk file. The errors are communicated to the logging process through a queue in memory. When an error occurs, a queue entry is added and the logging process is notified by calling the log_error function. The error logging process can then write the entries on the queue out to disk (or take other appropriate action). This frees the process that encountered the error from having to wait for the I/O to complete or acquire any locks that may be needed in order to perform the I/O to the file, and avoids any possible lock ordering problems that might occur if an error was detected while executing inside the file or disk I/O subsystems.

To implement the notification of the logging process with eventcounts, the `log_error` function will advance an eventcount each time it adds an error to the queue. Pseudo-code for the function and logging process is shown in Figure 12–8. (Assume the eventcount is initialized to zero as usual.)

Logging Process

```
log_error(error)                for (next = 1; ; next++) {
{                                   await(&err_event, next);
    lock(&err_queue);               lock(&err_queue);
    add error to queue              remove entry from queue
    unlock(&err_queue);             unlock(&err_queue);
    advance(&err_event);            write error to disk
}                               }
```

Figure 12–8: Error logging notification with eventcounts.

The queue itself is protected by a spin lock. The eventcount is only used for synchronization purposes and provides no mutual exclusion in this example. The logging process waits for the arrival of an entry on the queue to process by awaiting the next consecutive value of the eventcount. It then processes the error and waits for the next one to occur. If several new errors are added to queue while it is already processing one, then subsequent calls to *await* won't block until it has processed all pending errors.

The code shown in Figure 12–9 reimplements the previous algorithm using synchronization variables instead.

Logging Process

```
log_error(error)                for (;;) {
{                                   lock(&err_queue);
    lock(&err_queue);
    add error to queue              if (queue empty) {
    SV_SIGNAL(&err_syncvar, 0);         SV_WAIT(&err_syncvar, PRI,
    unlock(&err_queue);                     &err_queue);
}                                       lock(&err_queue);
                                    }

                                    remove entry from queue
                                    unlock(&err_queue);
                                    write error to disk
                                }
```

Figure 12–9: Error logging notification with synchronization variables.

Notice how the programming paradigm changes. Since synchronization variables maintain no state themselves, the spin lock must now be held while the logging process tests the state of the queue and decides whether to wait for an entry or to remove one from the queue. Similarly, log_error must hold the spin lock while sending the signal. This ensures that either the logging process has reached the SV_WAIT call (which releases the spin lock and blocks the process atomically), or that it is performing disk I/O. In the first case, the signal will awaken the logging process, which will find the new error on the queue. In the latter case, it will find the error on the next iteration of the for loop. Either way, the race condition is avoided. Note that it is guaranteed that the logging process will find at least one entry on the queue when it is awakened, since it is the only one removing entries from the queue. It must also check the state of the queue before calling SV_WAIT, since additional errors could have been added while it was writing the previous one. If it were to call SV_WAIT on each iteration, it would have to wait until yet another error was added, causing it to temporarily ignore errors already on the queue.

These steps were unnecessary when using eventcounts because an advance operation permanently changes the state of the eventcount. The relative timing of the advance and await operations is irrelevant. The state of the eventcount eliminates the race condition that exists when using synchronization variables.

Monitors will be used for the next version of this algorithm, as shown in Figure 12–10. The algorithm is basically the same as with synchronization variables, except that the monitor's enter and exit functions have replaced the need for a spin lock. The fact that the logging process awakens with exclusive access to the critical section simplifies the code slightly. As before, the lack of state with monitor events requires that the queue be retested during each iteration in the logging process.

Logging Process

```
log_error(error)
{
    mon_enter(&err_mon);
    add error to queue
    mon_signal(&err_mon,
            NEWENTRY);
    mon_exit(&err_mon);
```

```
for (;;) {
    mon_enter(&err_mon);

    if (queue empty)
        mon_wait(&err_mon,
                NEWENTRY);

    remove entry from queue
    mon_exit(&err_mon);
    write error to disk
```

Figure 12–10: Error logging notification with monitors.

Repeating the example again using semaphores yields the code in Figure 12–11. Remember that semaphores used for synchronization are initialized to zero (which is not shown in the example).

	Logging Process

```
log_error(error)
{
    lock(&err_queue);
    add error to queue
    unlock(&err_queue);
    V(&err_sema);
}
```

```
for (;;) {
    P(&err_sema);
    lock(&err_queue);
    remove entry from queue
    unlock(&err_queue);
    write error to disk
}
```

Figure 12–11: Error logging notification with semaphores.

The algorithm is similar to the one using eventcounts. As with eventcounts, note that there is no need to signal the logging process while holding the spin lock. The state of the semaphore eliminates these races. Since the semaphore value is incremented each time an error is added to the queue, the logging process can simply perform one P operation for each error. As can be seen, this simplifies the code, as there is not even the need to keep track of the next expected eventcount value as was done in Figure 12–8. This points out the main difference between these four synchronization primitives: it changes the programming paradigm complexity of the code needed to implement the algorithm. Different primitives are better suited for easy use in different circumstances. In these examples, semaphores yielded the simplest code, but there is no appreciable difference in performance between the four versions of the algorithm. Systems that provide multiple primitives do so only for coding convenience. So, in general, any situation requiring synchronization can be implemented in terms of any such primitive. The same is true for primitives that provide mutual exclusion. In most cases, the main concern will be whether a spin, sleep, or multireader version of a particular primitive is appropriate for a particular algorithm.

12.6 Summary

There are many different types of MP primitives. All can be used to implement mutual exclusion, synchronization, or both. Other than requiring spin versus sleep semantics for a particular situation, the primary difference between the primitives is the convenience of their use in specific circumstances.

Monitors provide both mutual exclusion and synchronization and can be thought of as a compartment that one must enter before accessing the critical resource. Only one process is allowed in a monitor at a time, which enforces mutual exclusion. While in the monitor, a process can wait for an event to occur, or can signal an event other processes may be waiting on. Since all synchronization occurs from within the monitor, no additional locks are needed to eliminate race conditions between processes about to wait on an event and one about to signal it.

An eventcount is a nondecreasing, positive integer value that is initially zero. The eventcount can be incremented by 1 using the advance function. A process can wait for a particular eventcount value to be reached using the await function. A sequencer is similar to an eventcount, except that only a single operation may be done. The ticket function causes the sequencer to be incremented by 1 and returns the new value as an atomic operation. It is therefore guaranteed that each caller of the ticket function will receive a unique value, regardless of the number of simultaneous callers. Eventcounts and sequencers can be used to implement both mutual exclusion and synchronization.

SVR4.2 MP is an MP version of the UNIX operating system from UNIX Systems Laboratories. It provides a variety of MP primitives for the developer: spin locks, sleep locks, synchronization variables, and multireader locks. Sleep locks provide mutual exclusion in a manner similar to binary semaphores. Synchronization variables function similarly to the uniprocessor `sleep/wakeup` mechanism in that there is no memory of previous operations.

12.7 Exercises

12.1   Using spin locks, show an implementation in C for the `mon_enter`, `mon_exit`, `mon_signal`, and `mon_wait` functions as described in Section 12.2. Show the internal data structure and initialization code as well.

12.2   How would in the code in Figure 12–1 have to be written if the monitor did not guarantee that a signaled process runs before other processes trying to enter the monitor? Is this desirable?

12.3   Is it possible to implement a version of monitors where processes spin instead of block when waiting to enter the monitor? Would this be useful? How should the wait operation function in this case (i.e., should it spin or sleep)?

12.4   Using spin locks, show an implementation in C for the `advance`, `await`, `read`, and `ticket` functions as described in Section 12.3. Show the internal data structure and initialization code as well.

12.5   How would you implement a broadcast-type operation with eventcounts using only advance, await, and read? Assume that you want to awaken all processes that are awaiting any value of the eventcount.

12.6   Rewrite the code shown in Figure 12–1 using spin locks and semaphores. Discuss the advantages and disadvantages of each approach.

12.7   Repeat the previous exercise with eventcounts and sequencers.

12.8   Show a C code implementation of sleep locks. Define the contents of `sleep_t` data structure, and write functions for `SLEEP_ALLOC`, `SLEEP_DEALLOC`, `SLEEP-_LOCK`, `SLEEP_TRYLOCK`, and `SLEEP_UNLOCK`. Ignore debugging parameters and priority arguments. Model the implementation after that of semaphores shown in Figures 11–5 through 11–8 using the SVR4.2 spin lock primitives. Use `malloc` and `free` to allocate and deallocate space, respectively, for the `sleep_t` structure.

12.9   Show a C code implementation of synchronization variables. Define the contents of the `sv_t` data structure, and write functions for `SV_ALLOC`, `SV_WAIT`, `SV_SIGNAL`, and `SV_BROADCAST`. Ignore debugging parameters and priority arguments.

12.10   Repeat Exercise 11.3 using synchronization variables instead of semaphores.

12.11   Repeat Exercise 12.10 using eventcounts.

12.12   Rewrite the code shown in Exercise 10.4 using eventcounts instead of `sleep/-wakeup`.

12.8 Further Reading

[1]   Brinch, H.P., "Structured Multiprogramming," *Communications of the ACM*, Vol. 15, No. 7, July 1972, pp. 574–78.

[2]   Brinch, H.P., *Operating System Principles*, Englewood Cliffs, NJ: Prentice Hall, 1973.

[3]   Brinch, H.P., "The Solo Operating System: Processes, Monitors, and Classes," *Software—Practice and Experience*, Vol. 6, 1976, pp. 165–200.

[4]   Campbell, M., Barton, R., Browning, J., Cervenka, D., Curry, B., Davis, T., Edmonds, T., Holt, R., Slice, J., Smith, T., and Wescott, R., "The Parallelization of UNIX System V Release 4.0," *USENIX Conference Proceedings*, January 1991, pp. 307–23.

[5]   Campbell, M., Holt, R., and Slice, J., "Lock Granularity Tuning Mechanisms in SVR4/MP," *Proceedings of the Second Sympoisum on Experiences with Distributed and Multiprocessor Systems*, March 1991, pp. 221–8.

[6]   Campbell, M., and Holt, R.L., "Lock Granularity Analysis Tools in SVR4/MP," *IEEE Software*, March 1993, pp. 66–70.

[7]   CaraDonna, J.P., Paciorek, N., and Wills, C.E., "Measuring Lock Performance in Multiprocessor Operating System Kernels," *Proceedings of the USENIX Symposium on Experiences with Distributed and Multiprocessor Systems*, September 1993, pp. 37–56.

[8]   Deitel, H.M., *An Introduction to Operating Systems*, Reading, MA: Addison-Wesley, 1990.

[9]   Dijkstra, E.W., "Hierarchical Ordering of Sequential Processes," *Acta Informatica*, Vol. 1, 1971, pp. 115–38.

[10]   Hines, R.M., and Wilcox, S., editors, *Device Driver Reference: UNIX SVR4.2*, Englewood Cliffs, NJ: Prentice Hall, 1992.

[11]   Hoare, C.A.R., "Monitors: An Operating System Structuring Concept," *Communications of the ACM*, Vol. 17, No. 10, October 1974, pp. 549–57.

[12]   Hoare, C.A.R., "Communicating Sequential Processes," *Communications of the ACM*, Vol. 21, No. 8, August 1978, pp. 666–77.

[13]   Hoare, C.A.R., *Communicating Sequential Processes*, Englewood Cliffs, NJ: Prentice Hall, 1985.

[14]   Howard, J.H., "Proving Monitors," *Communications of the ACM*, Vol. 19, No. 5, May 1976, pp. 273–9.

[15]   Howard, J.H., "Signaling in Monitors," *Second International Conference on Software Engineering*, San Francisco, October 1976, pp. 47–52.

[16]   Keedy, J., "On Structuring Operating Systems with Monitors," *Operating Systems Review*, Vol. 13, No. 1, January 1979, pp. 5–9.

[17]   Kelley, M.H., "Multiprocessor Aspects of the DG/UX Kernel," *USENIX Conference Proceedings*, January 1989, pp. 85–99.

[18]   Kessels, J.L.W., "An Alternative to Event Queues for Synchronization in Monitors," *Communications of the ACM*, Vol. 20, No. 7, July 1977, pp. 500–3.

[19]   Korth, H.F., "Locking Primitives in a Database System," *Journal of the ACM*, Vol. 30, No. 1, January 1983, pp. 55–79.

[20]   Lampson, B.W., and Redell, D.D., "Experience with Processes and Monitors in MESA," *Communications of the ACM*, Vol. 23, No. 2, February 1980, pp. 105–117.

[21]   Lister, A.M., and Maynard, K.J., "An Implementation of Monitors," *Software—Practice and Experience*, Vol. 6, No. 3, July 1976, pp. 377–86.

[22]   Reed, D.P., and Kanodia, R.K., "Synchronization with Eventcounts and Sequencers," *Proceedings of the 6th ACM Symposium on Operating System Principles*, 1977, p. 91.

[23]   Reed, D.P., and Kanodia, R.K., "Synchronization with Eventcounts and Sequencers," *Communcations of the ACM*, Vol. 22, No. 2, February 1979, pp. 115–23.

[24]   Wegner, P., and Smolka, S.A., "Processes, Tasks, and Monitors: A Comparative Study of Concurrent Programming Primitives," *IEEE Transactions on Software Engineering*, Vol. SE-9, No. 4, 1983, pp. 446–62.

13

Other Memory Models

This chapter presents a discussion of nonsequential memory models. These change the order in which memory operations occur in order to boost the performance of the memory system. Both total store ordering and partial store ordering as implemented in the SPARC architecture are covered, including their effects on both UP and MP kernels.

13.1 Introduction

All of the preceding examples in this book have assumed that the hardware implements the sequential memory model (strong ordering). This is the most widely used memory model in both past and present computer systems. The sequential model dictates that memory operations, such as loads and stores, are executed in *program order*: the sequential order in which these instructions appear in the instruction stream as the program executes. It also specifies that loads and stores done by different processors are ordered in some sequential, but nondeterministic, fashion. To illustrate this, the code fragment in Figure 13–1, executed by two processors, can be used to test for the presence of the sequential memory model. (Note that this and the other examples that follow are shown in simplified assembly language, as opposed to the assembly language of any particular processor, to avoid obscuring the examples with syntactic details.)

```
        Processor 1                          Processor 2

        store    %r1,A                        store    %r1,B
        load     %r2,B                        load     %r2,A
```

Figure 13–1: Code fragment to test for sequential memory model.

Both processors begin execution at the same time, but since the bus sequentializes access to memory, one of the stores will complete first (which one completes first is nondeterministic). There are only three possible ways in which the processors may execute their code fragments and conform to the sequential memory model: one store from each processor may be done followed by the two loads in some order; both instructions from processor 1 may execute before any instructions from processor 2; or both instructions from processor 2 may execute before any from processor 1. The result is that *at least one* of the loads will load the new value stored by the other processor. Both loads may return the new values, but it is impossible for both to return the old values, as this would imply that neither of the stores reached memory before the loads executed. This would violate the sequential nature of the code. An example of an algorithm that requires the behavior just described is *Dekker's Algorithm*.

13.2 Dekker's Algorithm

Dekker's Algorithm is a technique used to implement critical sections in the absence of atomic read-modify-write memory operations in hardware. It works using loads and stores alone, but requires the sequential memory model to function. The reasons for this will be discussed later. The following paragraphs describe how the algorithm functions on systems with sequential ordering.

The code shown in Figures 13–2 through 13–4 implements spin locks for a two-CPU system using Dekker's Algorithm instead of atomic-swap or test-and-set. The algorithm eliminates race conditions by recording the status of the lock from each CPU's point of view separately, and by providing a way to break the tie that occurs when both processors try to acquire the lock simultaneously. Such ties do not occur when using atomic instructions since the hardware resolves the ties. The data structure defined in Figure 13–2 maintains the status of the lock.

```
enum state { UNLOCKED, LOCKED };

typedef struct {
    char status[2];       /* status byte for each CPU */
    char turn;            /* which CPU goes next during ties */
} lock_t;

void
initlock(lock_t *lock)
{
    lock->status[0] = UNLOCKED;
    lock->status[1] = UNLOCKED;
    lock->turn = 0;
}
```

Figure 13–2: Spin lock structure and initialization for Dekker's Algorithm.

When acquiring a spin lock, each CPU must make sure that the other CPU is neither currently using the lock nor currently trying to acquire the lock for itself. This is accomplished with the function shown in Figure 13–3. Here, the function cpuid() returns the CPU number of the processor it is executing on (either 0 or 1 for this example), and the function othercpu() returns the CPU number of the other processor.

The algorithm shown in Figure 13–3 is straightforward if the lock is currently unlocked and only one CPU tries to acquire it. In this case, it sets its own status to LOCKED and checks the status of the other CPU. If it's unlocked, then no races have occurred and the lock has been successfully acquired. If the other CPU now tries to acquire the lock, it will find that the first CPU currently has it and will spin in either the inner or outer while loops, depending on the value of the turn variable. Regardless of the setting of turn, the other CPU will not be able to acquire the lock for itself until the first releases it.

When both CPUs enter the lock function at the same time to acquire the same lock, both will set their lock status to the locked state. They will then notice that the other processor is also trying to acquire the lock and will use the turn field to determine which one actually

```
void
lock(volatile lock_t *lock)
{

    /* Try to take the lock for ourselves */

    lock->status[cpuid()] = LOCKED;

    /* Check to see if the other cpu is using the lock */

    while (lock->status[othercpu()] == LOCKED) {

        /* If it's not my turn, back-off until the other cpu */
        /* is out of the critical section */

        if (lock->turn != cpuid()) {
            lock->status[cpuid()] = UNLOCKED;

            while (lock->turn == othercpu())
                ;

            lock->status[cpuid()] = LOCKED;   /* try again */
        }
    }
}
```

Figure 13–3: Acquiring a spin lock using Dekker's Algorithm.

acquires the lock. The loser of the tie will relinquish its attempt to acquire the lock and will spin until the other finishes. A key element of this algorithm is that it never returns until the other processor's lock status indicates that it is not using the lock.

A spin lock is released using the function in Figure 13–4. Both the lock status and the turn value must be set accordingly so that the other CPU will be able to exit both `while` loops in the `lock` function.

```
void
unlock(lock_t *lock)
{
    lock->status[cpuid()] = UNLOCKED;
    lock->turn = othercpu();
}
```

Figure 13–4: Unlocking a spin lock using Dekker's Algorithm.

13.3 Other Memory Models

While the sequential memory model is the most natural memory model from the programmer's point of view, higher performance can be achieved by changing the order in which certain operations are performed during execution. For memory operations, the availability of data at different levels in the memory hierarchy means that load and store instructions will take varying amounts of time to execute. As a simple example, consider the program fragment shown in Figure 13–5, which loads two values from memory, adds them together, and stores the result back to memory.

```
load    %r1,A
load    %r2,B
add     %r3,%r1,%r2    /* add A and B */
store   %r3,C          /* store result */
```

Figure 13–5: Example program fragment to show instruction reordering.

Assume that the value of B is cached and A is not. The first load instruction will therefore take longer to execute, since it involves a cache miss and a main memory operation to complete. Instead of waiting for the first load to complete, some processors will prefetch and begin execution of the second load while the first is waiting for main memory to return the results. Since the second load causes a cache hit, it is likely that it will complete execution before the first load. The advantage of this scheme is that the overhead of the second load has been completely hidden by the latency of the first. The hardware can then execute the add instruction as soon as the first load finishes.

Multiple instruction execution is common in present-day processors. For instance, the MIPS R4000 can issue (begin execution of) up to two instructions per clock cycle, and there can be up to eight instructions in the processor's eight-stage pipeline at one time. The programmer, however, need not be directly aware of this when writing a program. By providing *interlocks*, the hardware automatically keeps track of the progress of each instruction and the data dependencies between instructions. While the R4000 does not execute instructions out of order, in the general case, the interlocks on a processor that does reorder instructions would not allow the add instruction in Figure 13–5 to execute until the prior two loads have completed, for example. Likewise, the final store would not occur until the add completed. This maintains the sequential nature of the program while allowing some instructions to be reordered.

By further relaxing the strict ordering imposed by the sequential memory model, additional performance can be achieved, but it may not be transparent to the software. First, notice that an arbitrary sequence of loads from main memory can be allowed to execute in any order, assuming that they all use separate registers. This has no effect on the program as long as the hardware interlocks ensure that the register is not used by subsequent instructions until the load finishes.

The ability to reorder load instructions transparently at execution time does not apply to stores, however. For example, an arbitrary sequence of store instructions may contain multiple stores to the same location, such as updating a loop counter. The semantics of sequential programs dictate that the stores be done in program order, otherwise the wrong value will be stored at the wrong time, causing subsequent loads to retrieve the wrong value.

The relative ordering of stores, even to different locations, is an important concern for the kernel on MP systems. Referring back to Figure 9–3, it can be seen that a spin lock is released by simply storing a 0 in the lock. Since the instructions preceding the store that releases the lock are part of the critical region the lock protects, one must ensure that the results have been committed to memory before this store completes.

To illustrate this, consider the example in Figure 13–6, which shows the last portion of a critical section. The last operation is to increment a counter and then release the spin lock protecting the critical section. To simplify the example, the code to acquire the lock has been omitted for brevity. Likewise, the procedure call to the `unlock` function is not shown either so as not to obscure the example with subroutine linkage. This leaves the sequential instruction stream to increment the counter and release the lock.

```
                .
                .
                .
        load    %r1,counter     /* get old counter value */
        add     %r2,%r1,1        /* increment counter */
        store   %r2,counter      /* store new value */
        clear   %r3
        store   %r3,lock         /* release spin lock */
```

Figure 13–6: Critical section instruction stream.

For this code to operate properly on an MP, the store of the updated counter value must occur before the store to release the lock. If the hardware were to re-order the execution of these two stores, the spin lock would be released first, allowing another processor to acquire the lock. That processor could then load the old value of the counter before the first processor completes the store of the updated value. This violates the critical section and so must never be allowed to occur. The need to control the ordering of store instructions is required whenever spin locks, semaphores, or any other MP primitives are used.

A special case where loads and stores must always be done in the order issued is when I/O and processor control registers are addressed instead of physical memory. Since the program must sequentially read status registers and write to command registers in order to perform I/O, one must ensure that the hardware does not reorder these types of operations. The particulars of this are described in the following sections.

With these concerns in mind, two new memory models will be examined. These models are used starting with version 8 of the SPARC architecture as well as on other systems. They define the relative ordering of load and store instructions and are called *total store ordering* and *partial store ordering*. (Strict sequential ordering is not used by the SPARC, which uses total store ordering by default.) The goal of these models is to allow the implementation of high-speed memory systems, with the greatest potential speed offered by using partial store ordering. As will be seen, not all programs written for the sequential memory model are portable to machines using partial store ordering. So this memory model is optional and enabled via a bit in a processor control register.

13.4 Total Store Ordering

To increase the performance of the memory system, the SPARC architecture includes a *store buffer* (also known as a *write behind buffer*) in the CPU. Its purpose is to buffer the data for stores so that the CPU doesn't have to wait for main memory (or even the cache) to respond. This allows the CPU to continue program execution while the store buffer handles the task of moving data to memory. The store buffer operates in conjunction with the CPU and is separate from any cache that may be present. (For simplicity, assume that there are no caches in the systems presented ahead.) Each CPU in an MP system has its own store buffer. The size of the buffer is implementation dependent, but is on the order of a few words. The store buffer on the TI SuperSPARC contains eight double words, for example. Figure 13–7 shows the architecture of a two-processor system.

Logically, each CPU has separate connections for instruction fetches, loads, and stores. Despite this, each CPU still has only a single connection to the system bus. This connection can be thought of as a switch that is thrown to allow either an instruction fetch, load, or store operation to access the bus. The bus can be used for only one such operation by one CPU at a time.

In this model, instruction fetches always go to main memory. The address and data from store instructions are placed in the store buffer, which is guaranteed to send the data to main memory in FIFO order (all stores are ordered, hence the name total store ordering). Loads check the contents of the store buffer (as if it were a small cache) before accessing main memory. If a hit in the store buffer occurs, the data associated with the most recent store to the address is returned to the CPU. Note that main memory is not accessed in this case, which in itself gives some additional performance improvement just as a cache does. If the data required to complete the load is not present in the store buffer, main memory is

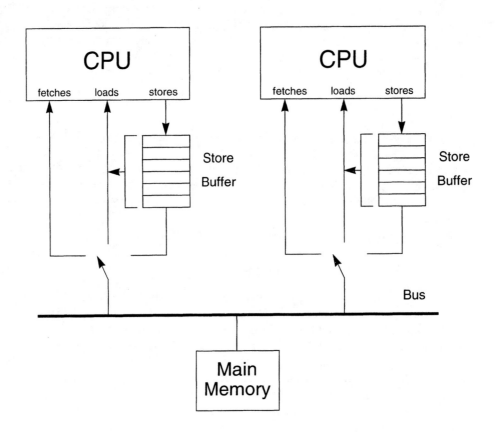

Figure 13–7: SPARC store buffer architecture.

accessed instead. Once a load instruction that requires a main memory access begins, no further memory operations are issued by the CPU. This ensures that sequentiality is maintained to a degree.

SPARC provides an atomic-swap instruction that performs both a load and a store to a single location as an indivisible operation. The hardware handles these specially. When issued, an atomic-swap instruction is placed in the store buffer to be handled in FIFO order relative to previously issued stores, but it also blocks further memory operations from being issued by the CPU. The effect of this is to postpone further memory operations until the store buffer is empty and the atomic swap is completed.

SPARC automatically reverts to sequential ordering for loads and stores done to I/O or processor control registers. These are detected when the loads and stores are done to specially designated address spaces (listed in the architecture manual), or to pages specially marked via the page tables. Since these accesses adhere to the familiar sequential model, no kernel changes are needed in relation to them.

The primary two differences between this memory model and the sequential memory model are that stores are not immediately committed to main memory, and loads are not guaranteed to access main memory. Note that the effects of total store ordering is not a concern for UP systems, since there is only one store buffer that is checked by every load the processor issues. This, in conjunction with the FIFO nature of the store buffer, makes total store ordering behave the same as sequential ordering for these systems.

In an MP system, however, the data stored by one processor will not be immediately available to a load done by another. A load checks only the store buffer for its processor, and not the store buffers on other processors. A load that misses in its own store buffer accesses main memory, which may contain stale data if there is a pending store in the buffer of another processor. Referring back to the code shown in Figure 13–1, it can be seen that it does not behave the same way as it did when run on the sequential memory model. When the two processors execute their respective stores, both will be placed in the processor's store buffer. The loads that follow will both access main memory, causing both to retrieve the old values of A and B. This was the case that could never occur with strong ordering, and so the effects of this new behavior on the software must be considered.

Overall, the results of simultaneous loads and stores to the same location in memory by multiple processors using total store ordering are nondeterministic. This is true for the sequential memory model as well. The locking constructs from the previous chapters were used to implement critical sections to eliminate the nondeterministic behavior. By definition, these critical sections allowed only one processor to execute within them at a time, preventing simultaneous loads and stores to the critical resource. Therefore, as long as the locking primitives still function correctly under total store ordering, the critical sections will remain in effect, and the kernel need not be modified further to support this memory model.

Let us first consider how spin locks function with total store ordering. The code to acquire a spin lock using the atomic-swap instruction is shown in Figure 13–8. The function swap_atomic stores its second argument into the location addressed by the first, and returns the location's previous value. As before, a value of 1 in the lock word means it is locked. Therefore, a lock is acquired by attempting to set the lock word to 1 until the previous value indicates it was unlocked. The atomic nature of the instruction allows only one processor to acquire the lock at a time.

```
void
lock(volatile lock_t *lock_status)
{
        while (swap_atomic(lock_status, 1) == 1)
                ;
}
```

Figure 13–8: Locking a spin lock using atomic swap.

Now assume that two processors using total store ordering simultaneously attempt to acquire a lock that is presently unlocked. When the atomic swap is issued by the CPU, it causes all pending stores in the store buffer to complete and prevents subsequent memory operations from being issued. Any prior stores the processor may have done to the lock word will have been written to memory before the atomic swap reaches the head of the store buffer FIFO. At this point, the store buffer is empty, so the processor behaves as if the store buffer doesn't exist. Contention for the lock proceeds the same as it does with sequential ordering. Only one processor will be able to acquire the lock at a time, preserving the semantics of the operation. Furthermore, one can ensure that subsequent instructions in the instruction stream that access the critical resource will not be issued until the lock is acquired, since the atomic-swap operation prevents further memory operations from being issued until it completes.

Next, assume that one processor has acquired the lock and has updated a data structure it protects. The other processor is still waiting to acquire the lock by spinning in the loop inside the `lock` function. When the processor owning the lock releases it, it does so by storing a zero into the lock word. This store is placed in the store buffer and is handled in FIFO order along with any others. This guarantees that all updates to the critical resource are committed to memory before the lock word is updated, and therefore satisfies the concern discussed in the previous section. When the store that releases the lock reaches the head of the store buffer, it is written to main memory, allowing the other processor to acquire the lock.

For the next case, assume the processor that just released the lock attempts to acquire it again before the store to clear the lock word makes its way through the store buffer. The processor will perform an atomic swap to reacquire the lock, which will go in the store buffer behind the store that releases the lock. This means the store clearing the lock will go to memory first, followed by the atomic swap, which will load the value back from main memory. This way, all processors contending for a lock are guaranteed to use the up-to-date value in memory, and never the value in their own store buffer. Since the value of the lock word in memory is consistent, the semantics of spin locks remain in effect. The key elements that make this work are that the atomic-swap operation synchronizes the store buffer with main memory, and that subsequent loads and stores are not issued until the lock has been acquired.

Since spin locks have been shown to function correctly, higher level primitives built on top of them, as coded in previous chapters, will also function correctly. Finally, the algorithms and data structures for the kernel's critical sections will function correctly as well.

The only algorithms that don't function correctly on machines implementing total store ordering are those where multiple processors perform simultaneous loads and stores to the same locations without using some type of locks for mutual exclusion. This can be illustrated with Dekker's Algorithm.

This algorithm fails under total store ordering. Consider the case where both processors begin execution of the `lock` function shown in Figure 13–3 at the same time, attempting to acquire a spin lock that is presently free. Both CPUs will set their lock status to 1, then both will check the lock status of the other. Since the previously executed stores to set the lock status are held in each processor's store buffer, both processors will load the stale value of the other processor's lock status from memory. This stale information still indicates that the processor does not hold the lock, leading both processors to think they have successfully acquired the lock. Notice that the `lock` function here begins with the same basic code sequence as shown in Figure 13–1: a store to a location that will be read by another processor, followed by a load from a location written by another processor. As stated previously, sequential memory ordering is required for this type of algorithm to function correctly.

Note that the algorithm can be fixed to run under total store ordering by replacing the simple assignment statements to the lock status words with calls to `swap_atomic()`. This forces the store buffer to be synchronized with memory before allowing subsequent loads to proceed, eliminating the problems just described.

None of the algorithms presented in previous chapters rely on memory ordering the way that Dekker's algorithm does. Therefore, no further kernel changes are needed to support these algorithms under total store ordering other than using the atomic-swap instruction to implement spin locks.

User programs that use shared memory can be affected by total store ordering as well. As with the kernel, stores done to shared memory by one user program on one processor will not be immediately seen by a user program running on another. User programs that utilize shared memory must synchronize in some way in order to avoid race conditions. This is true for sequential memory models as well. As long as the primitives they use function correctly under total store ordering, whether it be a synchronization facility provided by the kernel, or Dekker's algorithms in shared memory, then the higher level code will function as well.

Finally, note that instruction fetches do not check the store buffer for hits. Self-modifying code may therefore not function properly. SPARC provides a special `flush` instruction that synchronizes stores and instruction fetches if needed.

13.5 Partial Store Ordering

Partial store ordering uses the same architecture as shown in Figure 13–7, except that the store buffer is *not* guaranteed to be processed in FIFO order. If there are multiple stores to the same location in the store buffer, these alone are guaranteed to be done in FIFO order, but the relative ordering of stores and atomic swaps to other locations is nondeterministic. Loads still check the store buffer for hits and return the data associated with the most recent store to that location, if there is one. Otherwise, they go to memory as before. Atomic swaps behave as described for total store ordering.

No code changes are needed to support partial store ordering for uniprocessor systems (except possibly in the case of DMA operations described ahead). As with total store ordering, loads return the data from the most recent store to the location, if present in the store buffer; otherwise, they go to memory. Therefore, the store buffer is transparent to any loads the processor issues. Second, stores to the same location are always done in FIFO order, so the result is the same as with sequential memory ordering.

On multiprocessor systems, attempts by multiple processors to acquire the same lock function mostly as discussed in the last section. The atomic swap prevents further memory operations from being issued, but the store buffer is not guaranteed to be empty when the atomic swap executes. Since the store buffer isn't processed in FIFO order, the atomic swap may be done before stores issued before it. This does not impact the critical section the lock protects, since loads and stores that affect it have not been issued yet, and will not be issued until the lock is acquired. Therefore, the code in Figure 13–8 works correctly with partial store ordering. Complications occur, however, when a lock is released.

One of the concerns with nonsequential memory models is the need to ensure that critical resources are up to date in memory before the lock protecting them is released. Consider again the code fragment in Figure 13–6. It performs two sequential stores: the first to update the counter value, and the second to release the lock protecting the counter. These will be placed into the store buffer sequentially, but the order in which the data reaches memory is nondeterministic with partial store ordering. As stated before, if the store associated with releasing the spin lock reaches memory first, then another processor could acquire the lock and read the stale value of the counter from memory.

Since this must never be allowed to occur, the SPARC architecture includes a special instruction called a *store-barrier* (assembler mnemonic `stbar`) to force a degree of sequentiality. When the CPU issues the store-barrier instruction, it is placed in the store buffer and forces all stores that were issued before the store-barrier to complete before any stores that are issued after it. The store-barrier instruction separates groups of stores in the buffer but does not affect the ordering of stores in each group (hence the name partial store ordering). So if there are multiple stores in the store buffer before the store barrier is issued, for example, then their completion order is still nondeterministic. The same is true for the

stores that follow the store-barrier. If a program has a sequence of stores that must be sent
to memory in the order they were issued, then it is necessary to place a store-barrier instruction after each store. This shows the trade-off partial store ordering presents: it has the potential for greater performance, but it requires changes to programs that require sequential
ordering to function correctly.

In the special case of loads and stores to I/O and processor control registers, sequential ordering is used as was done for total store ordering. This avoids having to code store barrier
instructions explicitly throughout such code.

Figure 13–9 shows the correct way to release a spin lock when using partial store ordering
(this is a modified version of the code from Figure 9–3).

```
void
unlock(volatile lock_t *lock_status)
{
        store_barrier();
        *lock_status = 0;
}
```

Figure 13–9: Unlocking a spin lock with partial store ordering.

The call to the `store_barrier` function (which simply executes a store-barrier instruction and returns) ensures that any stores associated with the critical resource the lock protects will have been written to memory before the store that releases the lock.

As with total store ordering, higher level MP primitives, and the critical resources they protect, need not be changed to support partial store ordering. Since the other primitives are
built on top of spin locks, the store-barrier used when releasing a spin lock synchronizes all
previous stores as well. This is advantageous, as it allows the potential for performance
improvement with only a trivial code change. If the kernel contains any primitives or algorithms that do not use spin locks, such as Dekker's algorithm, then explicit store-barrier
instructions must be incorporated. For example, the spin lock implementation shown in
Figures 13–3 and 13–4 can be made to function with partial store ordering by including the
enhancement needed for total store ordering (replacing stores to the lock status fields with
atomic swaps) and by adding a store-barrier to the beginning of the `unlock` function.

Partial store ordering introduces a new problem during context switching. Consider the
case shown in Figure 11–9 where a race condition occurs when releasing a semaphore.
This race was eliminated by making a processor that selects a process off the run queue wait
until the process's state becomes *blocked*. This ensures that the process's context has been
completely saved on the previous processor before trying to restore it on the new processor.
Since the store buffer is not FIFO, the store that changes the process state to blocked may

occur before the stores that complete the process context save. This would cause stale data to be loaded on the new processor. To prevent this, a store barrier must be placed before the process state is changed to blocked. This way, all the stores that save the context will be committed to memory before the store that allows another processor to begin reading the context. This case isn't a problem with total store ordering because it will always do the store to change the process state last.

A similar problem can occur when data is stored to memory, immediately followed by a store to an I/O register that begins a DMA operation to that memory. While SPARC guarantees that loads and stores to I/O locations are done sequentially among themselves, it does not guarantee sequentiality between mixed loads and stores to I/O locations and physical memory. So it is possible for the data associated with the store to memory to be in the store buffer when the store issued afterward to start the DMA operation is sent to the I/O register. If this were to happen, then the DMA operation would access the stale data in memory, since DMA operations do not check the store buffer. As before, the insertion of a store barrier instruction before the store to initiate I/O solves the problem. Due to the small size of the store buffer and the relatively large number of memory operations device drivers normally perform to set up an I/O operation, this case is unlikely to occur in normal situations, but it should be understood and considered nonetheless. Again, this problem cannot occur with total store ordering, since the stores to memory and the I/O registers are always done sequentially.

13.6 The Store Buffer as Part of the Memory Hierarchy

The store buffer is simply another level in the memory hierarchy of a system. When caches are present in the system, the store buffer fits between the CPU's registers and the first-level cache. The store buffer itself behaves much like a small cache, since loads can hit in the buffer. Updating Figure 6–7 to include the store buffer yields the hierarchy depicted in Figure 13–10.

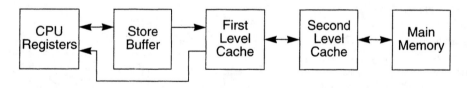

Figure 13–10: Memory hierarchy with a store buffer.

The problems that occur when using a store buffer on an MP system begin to show the general problem of MP caching. Since the store buffer of each processor operates independently, there is the potential for one processor to read stale data from memory, or its own store buffer, when there is a pending store in the buffer of another processor. Just as the store buffer requires changes to the implementation of spin locks to ensure stores are synchronized, the challenge of handling the general case of MP caching is to synchronize the caches of all processors so that stale data is not accessed. This is the subject of Part III of this book.

13.7 Summary

The sequential memory model has been used in the majority of both past and present systems. While the ordering of loads and stores from different processors is nondeterministic, it does guarantee that the results of previously issued store operations by one processor have been committed to memory before that processor issues new operations. Furthermore, loads always read from memory. Dekker's Algorithm relies on these semantics in order to function properly.

The SPARC architecture uses different memory models in order to achieve higher performance. A store buffer is added so that the CPU can continue execution while the results of store instructions are being sent to memory. The store buffer is another level in the memory hierarchy of a machine. Under total store ordering, the contents of the store buffer are sent to memory in FIFO order. With partial store ordering, only stores to the same location are done in FIFO order. The ordering of other stores is nondeterministic. In either of these models, loads check the store buffer for the requested address and return the data associated with the most recent store to that location.

As long as spin locks can be shown to function correctly, higher level MP primitives and the critical regions they protect will also function correctly. The atomic-swap instruction used to lock a spin lock forces the store buffer to be synchronized with memory by causing any prior stores to the lock word to complete first. It also prevents further memory instructions from being issued. This ensures that all CPUs will access the lock word in memory directly instead of a possibly stale copy in their store buffers. It also prevents loads and stores from the critical section from being issued until the lock is acquired.

Releasing a spin lock with partial store ordering requires the inclusion of a store-barrier instruction. This forces all previously issued stores to reach memory before the lock itself is released. A store-barrier is also needed during context switch to ensure that the process's state is completely saved before it is chosen for execution on another processor. Store-barrier instructions are not required with total store ordering.

13.8 Exercises

13.1   Implement Dekker's Algorithm for an arbitrary number of CPUs.

13.2   What would be the effect on the software if the SPARC memory architecture for total store ordering was changed so that loads did not check the store buffer for hits (i.e., loads always go directly to memory)? What would the software have to do to compensate?

13.3   Consider the previous problem in terms of partial store ordering instead of total store ordering. Does this make a difference?

13.4   What would the software be required to do if the SPARC implementation of partial store ordering did not guarantee FIFO ordering of stores to the same address?

13.5   What would happen if SPARC did not stop issuing further memory operations once an atomic-swap instruction was issued?

13.6   Consider a modification to the total store ordering model where the store buffer monitors the bus for loads from other processors in the same way bus watching does with physical caches. If the addressed data is in the store buffer, it returns the data associated with the most recent store to that location. In this case, the other processor does not access main memory. Describe the effect this has from the software's point of view. Is it a good idea to implement this?

13.7   Repeat the previous problem with partial store ordering.

13.8   Is the presence of the store buffer a concern for an MP kernel when it is accessing a process's private data?

13.9   In Section 10.3, there is a discussion of cases which require no explicit locking on MP systems. Consider the last case examined in that section, where there is a single writer to a piece of shared kernel data. According to that discussion, no locking is needed since it does nothing to the inherent race condition. Is this still true when the hardware uses either total or partial store ordering? Explain.

13.9 Further Reading

[1]   *The SPARC Architecture Manual, Version 8*, SPARC International, 1991.

[2]   Adve, S., and Hill, M., "Implementing Sequential Consistency in Cache-Based Systems," *Proceedings of the 1990 International Conference on Parallel Processing*, August 1990, pp. I:47–50.

[3]   Adve, S., and Hill, M., "Weak Ordering—A New Definition," *Proceedings of the 17th Annual Internation Symposium on Computer Architecture*, May 1990, pp. 2–14.

[4]   Adve, S., Hill, M.D., Miller, B.P., and Netzer, R.H.B., "Detecting Data Races on Weak Memory Systems," *Proceedings of the 18th Annual International Symposium on Computer Architecture*, May 1991, pp. 234–43.

[5]   Catanzaro, B., *Multiprocessor System Architectures*, Sun Soft Press, 1994.

[6]   Dijkstra, E.W., "Solution of a Problem in Concurrent Programming Control," *Communications of the ACM*, Vol. 8, No. 5, September 1965, p. 569.

[7]   Dijkstra, E.W., "Cooperating Sequential Processes," in *Programming Languages*, F. Genuys (ed.), New York: Academic Press, 1968, pp. 43–112.

[8]   Dubois, M., Scheurich, C., and Briggs, F., "Memory Access Buffering in Multiprocessors," *Proceedings of the 13th Annual International Symposium on Computer Architecture*, June 1986, pp. 434–42.

[9]   Dubois, M., Scheurich, C., and Briggs, F., "Synchonization, Coherence, and Event Ordering in Multiprocessors," *IEEE Computer*, Vol. 21, No. 2, February 1988, pp. 9–21.

[10]   Dubois, M., and Scheurich, C., "Memory Access Dependencies in Shared-Memory Multiprocessors," *IEEE Transactions on Software Engineering*, Vol. 16, No. 6, June 1990, pp. 660–73.

[11]   Eisenber, M.A., and McGuire, M.R., "Further Comment on Dijkstra's Concurrent Programming Control Problem," *Communications of the ACM*, Vol. 15, No. 11, November 1972, p. 999.

[12]   Gharachorloo, K., Lenoski, D., Laudon, J., Gibbons, P., Gupta, A., and Hennessy, J., "Memory Consistency and Event Ordering in Scalable Shared-Memory Multiprocessors," *Proceedings of the 17th Annual International Symposium on Computer Architecture*, May 1990, pp. 15–26.

[13]   Gharachorloo, K., Gupta, A., and Hennessy, J., "Performance Evaluation of Memory Consistency Models for Shared-Memory Multiprocessors," *Proceedings of the Fourth International Conference on Architectural Support for Programming Languages and Operating Systems*, April 1991, pp. 245–57.

[14]   Knuth, D., "Additional Comments on a Problem in Concurrent Programming Control," *Communications of the ACM*, Vol. 9, No. 5, May 1966, pp. 321–2.

[15]   Mosberger, D., "Memory Consistency Models," *ACM SIGOPS Operating Systems Review*, Vol. 27, No. 1, January 1993, pp. 18–26.

[16]   Peterson, G.L., "Myths about the Mutual Exclusion Problem," *Information Processing Letters*, Vol. 12, No. 3, June 1981, pp. 115–6.

[17]   Scheurich, C., "Access Ordering and Coherence in Shared Memory Multiprocessors," Ph.D. thesis, University of Southern California, May 1989.

[18]   Torrellas, J., and Hennessy, J., "Estimating the Performance Advantages of Relaxing Consistency in a Shared Memory Multiprocessor," *Proceedings of the 1990 International Conference on Parallel Processing*, August 1990, pp. I:26–33.

[19]   Zucker, R.N., and Baer, J.-L., "A Performance Study of Memory Consistency Models," *Proceedings of the 19th Annual International Symposium on Computer Architecture*, May 1992, pp. 2–12.

Part III

Multiprocessor Systems with Caches

14

Introduction to MP Cache Consistency

This chapter introduces the use of caches in multiprocessor systems. The commonly used organization for SMP systems is presented, followed by a discussion of the problems MP caching presents to the operating system. We then show how these problems can be solved using software techniques. Hardware techniques to solve MP caching problems are presented in Chapter 15.

14.1 Introduction

As seen in Part I, caches provide a way to reduce the average memory access time on uni-processor systems by exploiting locality of reference. This benefit is, of course, highly desirable for multiprocessors as well, and provides the motivation for adding caches to these systems. A typical SMP system with caches is pictured in Figure 14–1.

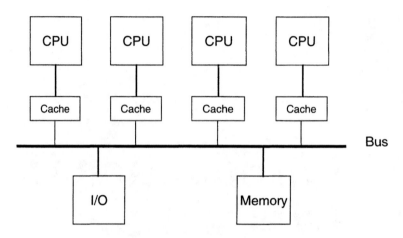

Figure 14–1: SMP system with caches.

In this organization, each CPU has a private cache, which is the most commonly used approach in SMP systems. While it is possible for the CPUs to use shared caches of some form, such as having two or more CPUs connected to a common cache or having a single cache between the bus and main memory, the use of private caches yields several advantages. First, having the cache connected directly to the CPU results in the lowest latency for accesses that hit in the cache. This eliminates the need for a bus operation that would be required if the cache were located next to the main memory unit. Since it is typical for 90 percent or more of a processor's references to hit in the cache, this can save up to an equivalent amount of bus transactions. (As will be seen, maintaining consistency requires some additional bus transactions, which slightly reduces the actual savings.) Reducing bus operations in turn reduces bus and memory bandwidth requirements, making it possible to support systems with larger number of processors than those without caches, or those that use a shared cache associated with main memory. Reducing bus operations also helps reduce contention for the bus, allowing ready access to main memory. Finally, any type of shared cache would cause some amount of contention between the CPUs that access it. There can be no such contention for access to a private cache. The result is that an MP system with caches can outperform one without caches.

The private cache organization has been embraced by the designers of modern microprocessors, as most of these systems contain on-chip, private caches. Examples include the MIPS R4000, the Intel 80486 and Pentium, and the TI SPARC processors. Since most commercial SMP systems are made using these microprocessors, the remainder of this book will focus on the private cache design. The private cache design has been used in systems from Silicon Graphics, Sequent Computer Systems, DEC, IBM, Pyramid Technology, Sun Microsystems, and others.

The caches themselves can follow any of the four main organizations presented in Part I, but, as will be seen in the next chapter, designers typically favor physical caches, or virtual caches that can also be indexed physically (such as the on-chip caches of the Intel i860 XP). It is also possible for each CPU to have separate instruction and data caches, or a hierarchy of caches, but it will be assumed that the caches connected to each CPU are identical. While one could design a system where each CPU had a cache that was organized differently, practical SMP systems are usually built using identical CPU/cache modules. Identical cache organizations also simplify the complexity of the operating system, as it only needs to be designed to handle one type of cache.

Note that the presence of caches does not change the main attributes of an SMP architecture as described in Section 8.2. Such a system is still tightly coupled, and uses a single globally accessible shared memory unit, and still exhibits symmetric access to that unit. However, as will be seen ahead, the addition of private caches can affect the memory model of the system. Hardware or software techniques (or a combination of both) can be used to restore a familiar memory model, such as the sequential memory model.

In Part II it was seen that the operating system for an MP must address the areas of system integrity, performance, and the external programming model. This is true for the kernel on MP systems with caches as well. Just as the operating system had to be modified to handle multiple processors, it must also be modified so that it executes correctly given the presence of multiple caches. Depending on the design of the cache hardware, this may require more work than the basic cache maintenance tasks described in Part I. This additional work may also affect the performance of the system. Finally, it is assumed that the external programming model will not be affected by the presence of caches. For the purposes of this book, any user program that executes correctly on the systems described in Part II will execute correctly on the systems described here without modification. As in Part I, the caches will be invisible to user programs.

The challenge of managing an MP system with caches, therefore, includes all the aspects of maintaining cache consistency from Part I, and all the areas of mutual exclusion and synchronization from Part II. These activities must now all be done so that they are synchronized across multiple caches.

14.2 The Cache Consistency Problem

In Part I a cache was said to be consistent with main memory if it was impossible for the software to access stale data. This could be achieved through software techniques by flushing the cache at appropriate times, or through hardware by utilizing a physical cache with bus watching, for example. With an MP system, multiple CPUs may be accessing shared data simultaneously. For MP systems that support the sequential memory model, the caches of such a system are said to be consistent if a read from any processor to any shared memory location always returns the most recently written value to that location. (Other memory models are discussed in Section 14.3.3.) As mentioned previously (in Part I), the terms "cache consistency" and "cache coherency" can be used interchangeably.

The problems of maintaining cache consistency on an MP system will be introduced with the following examples. Assume a two-CPU system uses write-back/write-allocate physical caches without bus watching or any special hardware to maintain cache consistency. Assume that both caches are initially empty (i.e., all lines are marked invalid). Consider a process that repeatedly sleeps for a second, increments a counter, and sleeps again. Assume this is the only activity occurring in the system, so there is nothing else to disturb the contents of the caches. If the counter is initially zero, the state of the caches and memory will be as shown in Figure 14–2 before the process runs the first time.

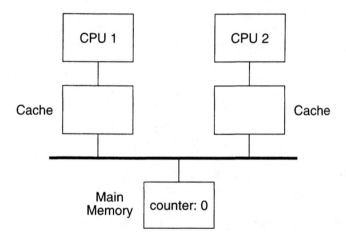

Figure 14–2: Initial state of memory and caches.

If the process runs on CPU 1, it will miss in the cache when it tries to increment the counter. This will cause it to fetch the value of zero from memory, which will be incremented and written back into the cache. Since the caches are physical, they are not flushed on context switch, so when the process returns to sleep, the memory state will be as shown in Figure 14–3.

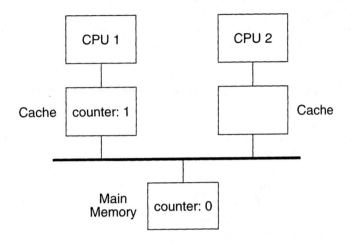

Figure 14–3: Memory state after first increment.

If the process runs on CPU 1 the next time it wakes up, it will get a cache hit on the counter variable and correctly update its value to 2. But if instead it runs on CPU 2, then it would miss in CPU 2's cache and read the stale value of the counter from main memory. This happens because nothing has been done to keep the two caches consistent. Inconsistencies like this must never be allowed to occur.

At first glance, it may seem that changing to write-through caching will solve the problem, since memory will then always be up to date. However, this is not sufficient to solve the consistency problem completely. If write-through had been used when CPU 1 initially incremented the counter to 1, then both main memory and the cache on CPU 1 would contain the value of 1 for the counter. If the process were then to run on CPU 2, it would indeed fetch the correct value from main memory when it missed in its cache. It would also write the updated value of 2 back to main memory, so the memory value would be correct. But if the process were now to run on CPU 1 again, it would generate a cache hit on the stale value of the counter. CPU 1 would still be caching a value of 1, since the write-through to memory from CPU 2 does nothing to CPU 1's cache.

As a second example, consider the case of two processors attempting to access and modify shared data simultaneously, as is done by Dekker's Algorithm from Section 13.2. Once again, assume that write-back caching is used and that the caches are initially empty. If both processors enter the lock function to acquire the same spin lock at the same time, then Dekker's algorithm fails to function properly. In this case, each CPU will set its lock status to the LOCKED state; however, the use of write-back caching means that the result of these store operations will not be immediately visible to the other CPU. They will both fetch the stale value of the other CPU's lock status from main memory and think that the spin lock is free. Both processors will then believe they have acquired the spin lock. Notice how the presence of a write-back cache is similar to that of the SPARC store buffer from the last chapter. The caches have altered the memory model of the MP system to be like partial store ordering. One difference though is that the contents of the store buffer are guaranteed to be written to main memory within a deterministic amount of time. With a write-back cache, data stored into the cache will remain there until it is explicitly flushed or replaced during a future cache miss. The contents of main memory will therefore remain stale for a nondeterministic amount of time.

As before, the use of write-through caching will not completely solve the consistency problems with Dekker's algorithm. If the second CPU tries to acquire a lock held by the first, then it will correctly read the other processor's lock status from memory, see that the lock is in use, and will spin on either the other CPU's lock status or the lock's turn field. When the lock is released, these fields will be updated in main memory if write-through caching is used. But the CPU attempting to acquire the lock will already have cached the previous values of these fields and will continue to spin on the stale values. Since that CPU's cache contents are unaffected by the write to main memory, it will spin until something causes the stale cache lines to be invalidated or replaced, such as might happen if an interrupt occurs and the interrupt handler references memory that indexes the same cache line. If nothing causes the stale lines to be invalidated, then the processor will spin forever.

Next, consider what happens when a processor tries to reacquire a lock that it has previously released. Assume that after the processor released the lock, the lock was acquired by the other CPU and is still being held. When `lock` is called to reacquire the lock, it will set the CPU's lock status field to the LOCKED state and check the other CPU's status. Since it had checked this status the previous time it acquired the lock, the other CPU's status could still be cached by the processor reacquiring the lock. If it is cached, then it is guaranteed to be stale since the other processor would have set its status to LOCKED when it acquired the lock. The processor reacquiring the lock will see the incorrect, stale data and think the lock is free. This violates the semantics of the locks and must be prevented.

Unlocking a spin lock can have cache consistency problems as well. If write-back caching is used, the stores that release a spin lock won't immediately be sent to main memory, causing other processors attempting to acquire the lock to use stale values. Again, even if write-through caching is used, another processor could have previously cached the values of these fields, which would now have been made stale by the write to main memory. That processor will then think the lock is still held after it has been released.

These basic consistency problems can manifest themselves in a variety of ways whenever data is accessed and modified by more than one CPU. Note that this includes both user and kernel data. To solve this problem, a technique is needed to keep the contents of the caches consistent. This can be done in software or in hardware. Software solutions involve flushing the cache(s) at appropriate times to prevent stale data from being accessed. For instance, the first example we've examined here can be fixed by writing back the cache (if write-back caching is used) and invalidating it each time the CPU performs a context switch. This causes the process to cache-miss each time it wakes up, allowing it to fetch the current value of the counter from main memory. Unfortunately, this defeats one of the main advantages of physical caches, namely the elimination of context switch time flushing. Because of this, hardware techniques have been invented to keep the caches and main memory consistent automatically. This is done by extending the concept of bus watching so that the caches not only monitor the bus for I/O DMA transactions, but for activity by other caches as well.

In order to understand fully the complexities of MP cache consistency, the following sections will cover software cache consistency techniques first. Because of their complexity and poor performance, pure software techniques are rarely used in practice, yet they clearly illustrate the problems that must be solved. The ensuing discussion applies to all types of caches, whether they be virtually or physically indexed or tagged. Hardware cache consistency is covered in the next chapter.

14.3 Software Cache Consistency

The first case to notice when maintaining cache consistency through software techniques is that no special treatment is needed for read-only data. Since this data never changes, any cached copies will match the copy in main memory and will thereby be consistent by default. In particular, normal program text (instructions) and kernel text fall into this category. (Self-modifying code, of course, is not included.) So in the example from the last section where the program was incrementing the counter, only the process's data need be flushed from the cache on context switch to maintain consistency. If the system uses separate instruction and data caches, then the instruction cache can be left alone.

Note, however, that the kernel is not relieved of the task of flushing the instructions when the process exits. In the case of a physical cache, all the management described in Chapter 6 must still be performed. But now it must be done to all caches in the system. For example, when the process in the previous example exits, the instructions left in the caches on both processors must be invalidated before the corresponding physical pages are reused. In systems that lack hardware to maintain cache consistency, a cache can be flushed only from the CPU to which it is connected. So if the process exits on CPU 1, that CPU will have to notify CPU 2 to flush its cache. This can be implemented in a variety of ways depending on the hardware. For instance, some systems support inter-CPU interrupts that allow one CPU to send an interrupt to another. Using this, a message can be written into main memory to indicate what type of action to take. Various optimizations are possible, too. For example, if the process never ran on CPU 2, then there is no need for that CPU to flush its cache when the process exits. Thus, the kernel could track which processors each process has run on to reduce the amount of cache flushing that needs to be done by other processors.

Another possibility is to use the delayed invalidation technique from Section 7.4. If physical caches are used, then the cache invalidation can be delayed until the contents of the dirty list are moved to the clean list. At this point, all CPUs can be notified to flush their caches, cleaning up all stale cached entries at once.

The main MP cache consistency problems occur when multiple processors can access and modify shared data. The next two sections present the additional management necessary to solve these problems. There are two main schemes for handling shared data: using uncached operation, and selectively flushing the shared data. These techniques apply equally to all four cache architectures presented in Part I.

14.3.1 Uncached Shared Data

In this approach, the MP consistency problem is eliminated by never allowing data that can be modified by more than one CPU to be cached in the first place. This technique was used on the ELXSI SYSTEM 6400 (a system available in the mid-1980s, see Reference [24]). To implement this, the cache must support an uncached mode. As mentioned in Part I, most architectures allow this to be specified on a per-page basis. Therefore, the data that is shared and modified between processors must be organized into separate pages from read-only data. If a hierarchy of caches is used, then all of them must treat this shared data as uncached.

In addition to read-only and shared data, there is a third class of data in an MP system: processor private data. This is data that is accessed and modified by only one CPU at a time. It can be cached if flushed at appropriate times as follows. One example of data that is private to a processor is the text, data, and stack associated with user processes. In traditional UNIX systems, there is only a single thread of control in the process, hence the process can be executing on only one processor at a time. Except during process debugging, none of the other processors in the system will access its address space, and so, its address space can be safely cached while it is running. (The case of process debugging is the same as for multithreaded processes and is covered ahead.) If a context switch is performed and the process runs on a different processor, then the cache of the processor it previously ran on must first be flushed (main memory validated, and the cache invalidated) to maintain consistency as pointed out in Section 14.2. The act of moving a process from one processor to another in this fashion is called *process migration*.

For a system that uses virtual caches, the cache is flushed during each context switch anyway, so no additional flushing is needed in the case of process migration. The other cache organizations, however, must be flushed as just described. Note that this eliminates one of the main advantages of these caches: the avoidance of context switch time flushing. This advantage can be partially regained by *binding* a process to a particular processor, which means that the process is not allowed to migrate on each context switch. Instead, only the processor that last ran the process can select it during a context switch. This then solves the consistency problem. (Binding processes in this way is also called *processor affinity*.) If all processes were permanently bound to individual processors, then the load across all processors in the system would most likely be unbalanced. Therefore, systems that bind processes to processors must also periodically unbind them and redistribute the load across the processors evenly. When load-balancing migration like this is done, the caches must be flushed, but this occurs less frequently than flushing them on each context switch. Note that with a master–slave kernel implementation, processor affinity is difficult to achieve for other than brief periods of time, since processes must migrate to the master in order to execute system calls. Processor affinity is therefore better suited to multithreaded kernels.

If the system allows multiple threads in an address space, then these cannot be allowed to execute simultaneously on multiple processors, because the shared address space would not be consistent. The case of process debugging is much like threads from a cache consistency point of view since another process is given access to the address space of another (usually via special system calls). There is no efficient solution in these cases when using software cache consistency techniques alone. One approach would be to make the entire process address space uncached. Any processor could then execute any thread at any time without consistency problems at the cost of the performance penalty for uncached operation. Likewise, a process's address space could be made uncached at the point where a debugger started accessing it. Another approach would be to bind all threads within a process to a single processor (and similarly force the debugger to execute on the same processor as the process being debugged). The address space could then be cached, but only one thread could run at a time. In this case, all threads are migrated together with the process.

Two processes using shared memory or mapped files must be handled similarly to threads. To maintain consistency, such processes must not be allowed to run simultaneously on different processors if shared memory is cached. As with threads, binding these processes to one processor solves the problem. Alternatively, the shared memory pages can be made uncached, allowing processes sharing them to execute anywhere and to migrate freely, but with reduced performance when accessing those pages.

Another type of processor private data is the kernel data structures associated with each process. These typically include the kernel stack and u-area. Since these are never accessed by other processes, they can be cached and need to be flushed only when the process is migrated.

While any processor private data can be cached, shared kernel data structures must be uncached. The particular structures that must be uncached depend on the kernel implementation. For example, if a master–slave MP kernel approach is used, then the only data structures shared between the processors are the run queues and the locks that protect them. For such a kernel, only these need be uncached. All the other kernel data structures are accessed only by the master processor, and so all these can be cached.

A multithreaded kernel is different. Here, any processor can execute any portion of kernel code and thus may access any shared data structure. In this situation, all such data structures must be uncached. For example, the process table entry of each process contains data that may be accessed by other processes. This is, therefore, a shared structure and cannot be cached. Note that all data structures used to implement MP primitives, such as spin locks and semaphores, must also be uncached, or the inconsistencies that happened with Dekker's algorithm will occur.

With the uncached approach, consistency is properly maintained, which preserves the integrity of the operating system and keeps the external programming model compatible with uniprocessor systems. This approach is also relatively simple to implement. The difficulty is that it is unable to take advantage of the caches on the processors in many instances, thereby reducing the performance benefit of the caches. Therefore, we must find a way to allow more data to be cached.

14.3.2 Selective Cache Flushing

Selective cache flushing is an approach that allows shared kernel data to be cached while a processor is using it. Consistency is maintained by having the kernel selectively flush the shared data from a processor's cache before inconsistencies can arise. Shared data can be cached by exploiting the fact that all shared data is protected by some lock. Once a processor acquires that lock, the associated kernel data can be cached, since mutual exclusion with other processors is guaranteed. In this way, the data structures temporarily become processor private data. When the lock is released, however, another processor could access the shared data; therefore, the processor releasing the lock must explicitly flush the data from its cache (validating main memory and invalidating the cache). This should be done just prior to releasing the lock. Main memory will therefore be up to date when the next processor acquires the lock. Since each processor invalidates the data from its cache upon releasing the lock, a cache miss is guaranteed to occur if it later reacquires the same lock and accesses the shared data. This assures that the processor will access the up-to-date copy of the data in main memory as opposed to using stale cached data corresponding to the previous access. As before, read-only data and program text can be cached without additional flushing. If the system uses a hierarchy of caches, the critical resource must be flushed from all caches on the processor before it releases the lock. Processor private data, including user program text, data, and stack, is handled as in the last section.

This approach relies on the mutual exclusion the locks provide in order to maintain consistency. Since there is no mutual exclusion between processors while attempting to acquire a spin lock, the spin lock data structure itself can never be cached. This prevents the inconsistencies shown in Section 14.2 from occurring. Next, the data structures used to implement higher level primitives, such as semaphores, sleep locks, eventcounts, and so on, are nothing more than shared kernel data structures themselves. This means that they may be cached, but they must be flushed from the cache before the processor releases the spin lock that protects them. Alternately, they can be left uncached.

Another requirement of the selective cache-flushing approach is that each critical resource must occupy a separate cache line. If two or more critical resources were to occupy the same cache line, then there would be the risk that the processor might access stale data. As an example, consider an array of counters in memory, where each counter is protected by a separate spin lock. Each counter, therefore, is a separate critical resource. Assume the counter is four bytes and that the cache line size is eight bytes, which means that a pair of counters will occupy each cache line. If CPU 1 acquires the lock for the first counter in the array and increments it, a cache miss will occur that causes the entire line containing both the first and second counters to be loaded into the CPU's cache. If the counters are initially zero, then the cache and main memory contents for the affected cache line after the increment is done can be pictured as shown in Figure 14–4. Note that the caches use write-back. (The first counter is shown on the left side of the cache line.)

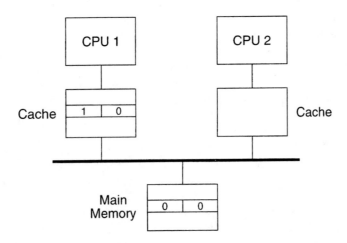

Figure 14–4: Critical resources sharing a cache line.

No inconsistencies have occurred yet, and none will occur as long as both CPUs never access both counters within a cache line at the same time. But if while CPU 1 is accessing the first counter, CPU 2 acquires the lock for the second one and increments that counter, then the result is as shown in Figure 14–5.

At this point, each CPU is caching stale data for the counter the other CPU is using. When the CPUs write back and invalidate the critical resource they are using, they will also write back the stale data associated with the other critical resource. Remember that there is only

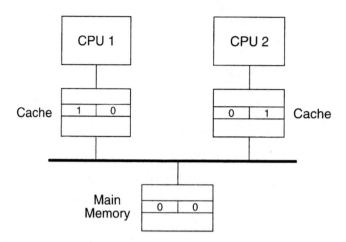

Figure 14–5: Both CPUs accessing critical resources in same cache line.

a single modified bit in each cache line (or subline), and so a write-back sends the entire line (or subline) back to main memory. Depending on the order in which the CPUs perform the write-back, one counter or the other will have the wrong value in main memory. Observe that this problem is similar to that described in Section 3.3.7, where DMA to a raw I/O buffer located in a shared memory region could cause inconsistencies if other data shares the same cache line. In both cases, an action by another unit on the bus causes memory to change without updating the processor's private cache, which causes an inconsistency.

Another type of inconsistency can occur if one processor tries to use both critical resources in a cache line at the same time. Starting with the cache and memory state as shown in Figure 14–5, while both CPUs are holding their respective locks, assume that CPU 1 tries to acquire the spin lock for the second element in the array (the one that CPU 2 is currently holding). When CPU 2 releases the lock, it will have updated main memory with the new counter value. CPU 1 can now acquire the lock, but since it has already cached the value for the second counter when it accessed the first, it will use the stale value in its cache instead of the up-to-date value in main memory. Because of these inconsistency problems, it must be guaranteed that each critical resource is in a separate cache line. In the case of caches that have separate valid and modify bits for each subline within a cache line, the critical resources need only occupy separate sublines.

Keep in mind that a process holding a long-term mutual exclusion lock may sleep while holding the lock. If the process is migrated to another processor while holding the lock, then any user or shared kernel data it accessed must be written back to main memory and invalidated from the cache on the old processor before the process can execute on the new processor. The reasons for this are as described in Section 14.2.

Note that this technique cannot be used to allow user shared memory regions to be cached and accessed simultaneously by processes on different processors. The external programming model for uniprocessors does not require any cache flushing operations to be explicitly coded into user programs, which this technique would mandate. Therefore, user shared memory should continue to be handled as described in the previous section, namely uncached.

Observe the similarities of this approach with that taken to support partial store ordering on the SPARC architecture (see Section 13.5). It too relied on the kernel's mutual exclusion locks to prevent other processors from accessing stale data in memory while a store to the critical resource was in one processor's store buffer. In that case, one had to ensure that these stores were sent to main memory before the store that released the lock. This was done by inserting a store-barrier instruction, which essentially flushed the store buffer before the lock was released. This was easy to implement since it was not necessary to know exactly which data structures were accessed in the critical region. For selective cache flushing, this is not so simple.

The complexity of implementing this technique varies according to the degree of multithreading in the kernel. For a master–slave implementation, the extra cache flushing is easy to add. For example, the `enqueue` function shown in Figure 9–9 needs only to write back and invalidate two pieces of data: the `p->p_next` field, and the `q->q_head` field. This must be done just prior to calling the `unlock` function. The `dispatch` function shown in Figure 9–10 is more complex since it traverses the entire linked list. In this case, it can write back and invalidate the entire contents of the cache just prior to releasing the spin lock. This eliminates the need to flush each queue element after it is examined.

Fine-grained multithreaded kernels are more complex to handle since each critical section must be modified to flush the associated critical resource from the cache before releasing the lock. Each critical resource must also be placed in memory so that it occupies a unique cache line. In many cases, this will require a careful analysis to determine which data was accessed while in the critical region so that it can be properly flushed. One could, of course, avoid this analysis by simply flushing the entire cache each time a lock was released, but the overhead of this, especially with large caches, would make the previous technique of using uncached access more attractive. Techniques where the compiler analyzes the data references made by the code and automatically inserts the required cache flushing have also been proposed. These have mainly been done to address multithreaded, shared memory user programs running on systems lacking hardware cache consistency, and have not generally been applied to operating systems (see References [6] and [8]).

While this approach allows kernel data to be temporarily cached, the benefit of this technique in terms of operating system performance is questionable, since constantly flushing shared data when locks are released reduces the hit ratio. User programs must still be flushed when migrated, so it offers no improvement for them over the previous technique. Due to the small performance gains it provides and to the complexity of implementing this technique, no commercial multithreaded systems are known that utilize it. (A detailed performance analysis can be found in reference Reference [2].)

14.3.3 Handling Other Memory Models

Architectures that contain store buffers, such as SPARC, can complicate matters when using software cache consistency. With the first technique of using uncached operation when accessing shared data, though, nothing more need be done over what is presented in Section 14.3.1 and Chapter 13. Since shared data and locks are not being cached, it is guaranteed that any stores to shared data that are in the store buffer will reach main memory before the store that releases the lock (either because the buffer is processed in FIFO order as with total store ordering, or because a store-barrier is inserted into the buffer prior to releasing the lock).

Selective cache flushing, however, requires additional attention in order to maintain consistency properly. When a store buffer is used in a system containing caches, data from the store buffer is sent to the cache, which may or may not send it to memory, depending on the cache architecture. In all cases, the contents of the store buffer are sent to the next level in the memory hierarchy. How the data is handled after that depends on the architecture of that level. With write-back caching that uses write-allocate, data from the store buffer is written into the cache, leaving main memory unaffected. Write-through caching will update both the cache and main memory as the store buffer empties.

So, if a system uses a store buffer and a single-level cache, for example, then the problem is that stores to the critical resource may still be in the store buffer when the selective cache flush operation is performed. If this were to happen when using a write-back cache, then main memory would be updated with stale data from the cache, not the current data in the store buffer. Also, the data from the store buffer would end up in the processor's cache after the cache had been invalidated. In order for selective invalidation to work, the data should have only been in main memory at this point. When the lock is released, other processors will access the stale data in main memory. Therefore, it must be guaranteed that the store buffer is flushed prior to flushing the caches.

In the case of the TI SuperSPARC processor, for example, the operation that flushes the on-chip data cache causes the entire contents of the store buffer to be sent out before proceeding with the flush. It also prevents further instructions from being issued until the flush completes. This conveniently ensures that the cache will be up to date before it is flushed, and that any stores done to release locks will occur after the cache has been flushed.

14.4 Summary

The addition of caches to an SMP system can improve performance by taking advantage of locality of reference. The private cache design is preferred as it offers the lowest latency from the CPU's point of view, and reduces bus contention and bandwidth requirements. Private caches, however, alter the memory model of the system as seen by the software. Unless special hardware or software techniques are used, stores by one processor are not immediately visible to others. This brings up the problem of maintaining cache consistency. The caches are consistent when a load by a CPU returns the value associated with the most recent store to that location by any CPU in the system.

Using software techniques alone, consistency can be maintained through one of two mechanisms. The first is simply not to cache data that may be accessed and modified by more than one CPU. Data that is private to any one processor, such as user program text, data, and stack, as well as process private kernel data structures like the kernel stack and u-area, can be cached while the process is running on a particular CPU. If the process is moved to another CPU during a context switch, then the caches on the CPU it previously ran on must be flushed to maintain consistency. The disadvantage of this approach is that it doesn't allow shared kernel data to be cached.

A second technique, selective flushing, allows shared kernel data to be temporarily cached while the processor using it is executing within the associated critical section. In this case, the mutual exclusion lock that protects the critical resource also prevents other processors from simultaneously accessing the shared data, thereby preventing inconsistency problems. Before the lock is released, however, the critical resource must be flushed from the processor's cache. It is also necessary to ensure that each critical resource occupies a separate cache line to prevent stale data from being written back to main memory.

Regardless of the cache organization, neither of these software techniques allows user shared memory to be cached, since this would require changes to the external programming model. Furthermore, process data must be flushed on migration, and spin locks can never be cached. This tends to diminish the advantages of using cache organizations that use physical tags. For these reasons, pure software cache consistency is rarely used. It is possible to move beyond these limitations by employing additional hardware to maintain cache consistency automatically. This is done by extending the concept of bus watching, which is explored in the next chapter.

14.5 Exercises

14.1   Consider a system where all processors are connected to a single, shared, physical cache. What flushing, if any, must be done to maintain consistency over that described in Chapter 6?

14.2   Can a virtual cache be used as a shared cache? What about a virtual cache with physical tags?

14.3   Consider the consistency problems of Dekker's algorithm as presented in Section 14.2. If the caches on a two-CPU system are initially empty, and one CPU acquires a lock before the other attempts to acquire the lock, then describe the consistency problems that occur when the second CPU tries to acquire the lock held by the first. Describe the problems for both write-through and write-back caching.

14.4   Modify the semaphore functions presented in Section 11.3 to work properly on a system using selective cache flushing. Each CPU has a write-back first-level cache and a write-through secondary cache. The first-level cache is flushed by calling the following function:

```
void flush_primary(char *addr, int len, int flag);
```

This function takes the starting address and length in bytes of the data to flush. The flag argument specifies whether a write-back, invalidation, or both should be performed. The values are WRITE_BACK and INVALIDATE, which can be OR'ed together to specify both. The secondary cache is flushed by calling:

```
void flush_secondary(char *addr, int len);
```

This invalidates the given range of addresses from the cache. A lock in uncached memory can be allocated by calling:

```
lock_t *alloc_lock();
```

14.5   Add selective cache flushing to the producer–consumer algorithm shown in Figure 12–5. Assume that the eventcount functions already contain proper flushing to manage their data structures.

14.6   Figures 14–4 and 14–5 show why each critical resource must occupy a separate cache line when using write-back caching. Explain what would happen in this example if write-through caching were used instead.

14.7 The Motorola MC68040 has a 16-byte line size, with a single valid bit per line, but with four separate dirty bits corresponding to each word within the line. Recall that write-back caches that have separate dirty bits for each subline (where a subline is a word on the 68040) write back only those words that have been modified when the line is replaced or flushed. Explain how the example pertaining to critical resources occupying separate cache lines in Section 14.3.2, where two CPUs accessed an array of counters, is affected by this cache architecture.

14.8 Repeat the previous exercise, assuming that the cache has a separate valid and modify bit for each word within the 16-byte cache line (i.e., each line has four valid bits and four dirty bits).

14.9 In Section 4.2.8, one approach to preventing user–kernel ambiguities was to use a separate key whenever executing in kernel mode. Does each processor have to use the same key when running in kernel mode if each processor has a private cache?

14.10 On a system with virtual caches with keys, does a user process have to continue using the same key when it is migrated to another processor?

14.11 When using selective cache flushing with a multilevel cache system where all caches are write-back, does it matter which order the caches are flushed in? Does the order matter when flushing the caches for process migration? Consider both write-back and invalidate flushing operations.

14.12 The selective cache-flushing technique relies on the mutual exclusion locks provide to ensure that only one processor can cache a critical resource at a time. Section 10.3 presented a case where locking could be avoided when accessing a process's IDs. This was possible due to the inherent race condition of accessing such data. Can the locking still be avoided when using selective cache flushing to maintain proper consistency?

14.13 When multireader locks are used, describe the selective cache flushing that must be done to maintain consistency of the critical resource that the lock protects.

14.6 Further Reading

[1] Adve, S., Adve, V., Hill, M., and Vernon, M., "Comparison of Hardware and Software Cache Coherence Schemes," *Proceedings of the 18th Annual International Symposium on Computer Architecture*, 1991, pp. 298–308.

[2]   Agarwal, A., and Owicki, S., "Evaluating the Performance of Software Cache Coherence," *Proceedings of the Third International Conference on Architectural Support for Programming Languages and Operating Systems*, April 1989, pp. 230–42.

[3]   Brantley, W.C., McAuliffe, K.P., and Weiss, J., "RP3 Processor-Memory Element," *Proceedings of the 1985 International Conference on Parallel Processing*, 1985, pp. 782–9.

[4]   Bolosky, W.J., "Software Coherence in Multiprocessor Memory Systems," Ph.D. thesis, TR 456, Computer Science Department, University of Rochester, May 1993.

[5]   Cheong, H., and Veidenbaum, A.V., "The Performance of Software-Managed Multiprocessor Caches on Parallel Numerical Programs," *International Conference on Supercomputing*, June 1987.

[6]   Cheong, H., and Veidenbaum, A.V., "A Cache Coherence Scheme with Fast Selective Invalidation," *Proceedings of the 15th Annual International Symposium on Computer Architecture*, June 1988, pp. 299–307.

[7]   Cheong, H., and Veidenbaum, A.V., "Stale Data Detection and Coherence Enforcement Using Flow Analysis," *Proceedings of the 1988 International Conference on Parallel Processing*, August 1988, pp. 138–45.

[8]   Cheong, H., "Compiler-Directed Cache Coherence Strategies for Large-Scale Shared-Memory Multiprocessor Systems," Ph.D. thesis, Department of Electrical Engineering, Univeristy of Illinios, Urbana-Champaign, 1990.

[9]   Cheriton, D.R., Slavenberg, G.A., and Boyle, P.D., "Software-Controlled Caches in the VMP Multiprocessor," *Proceedings of the 13th Annual International Symposium on Computer Architecture*, June 1986, pp. 367–74.

[10]   Cytron, R., Karlovsky, S., and McAuliffe, K.P., "Automatic Management of Programmed Caches," *Proceedings of the 1988 International Conference on Parallel Processing*, August 1988.

[11]   Dubois, M., and Scheurich, C., "Memory Access Dependencies in Shared-Memory Multiprocessors," *IEEE Transactions on Software Engineering*, Vol. 16, No. 6, June 1990, pp. 660–73.

[12]   Dubois, M., Skeppstedt, J., Ricciulli, L., Ramamurthy, K., and Strenstrom, P., "The Detection and Elimination of Useless Misses in MPs," *Proceedings of the 20th International Symposium on Computer Architecture*, May 1993, pp. 88–97.

[13]   Edler, J., Gottieb, A., Kruskal, C.P., McAuliffe, K., Rudolph, L., Snir, M., Teller, P., and Wilson, J., "Issues Related to MIND Shared-Memory Computers: The NYU Ultracomputer Approach," *Proceedings of the 12th International Symposium on Computer Architecture*, June 1985, pp. 126–35.

[14]   Edler, J., Gottleib, A., and Lipkins, J., "Considerations for Massively Parallel UNIX Systems on the NYU Supercomputer and IBM RP3," *Winter USENIX Conference Proceedings*, 1986.

[15]   Edler, J., Lipkins, J., and Schonber, E., "Memory Management in Symunix II: A Design for Large-Scale Shared Memory Multiprocessors," *Proceedings of the USENIX Supercomputer Workshop*, 1988, pp. 151–68.

[16]   Gharachorloo, K., Gupta, A., and Hennessy, J., "Performance Evaluation of Memory Consistency Models for Shared-Memory Multiprocessors," *Proceedings of the Fourth International Conference on Architectural Support for Programming Languages and Operating Systems*, April 1991, pp. 245–57.

[17]   Gupta, A., and Weber, W., "Cache Invalidation Patterns in Shared Memory Multiprocessors," *IEEE Transactions on Computers*, Vol. 41, No. 7, July 1992, pp. 794–810.

[18]   Lee, R.L., Yew, P.C., and Lawrie, D.H., "Multiprocessor Cache Design Considerations," *Proceedings of the 14th Annual International Symposium on Computer Architecture*, June 1987, pp. 253–62.

[19]   Lee, R.L., "The Effectiveness of Caches and Data Prefetch Buffers in Large-Scale Shared Memory Multiprocessors," Ph.D. thesis, Technical Report 670, Center of Supercomputing Research and Development, University of Illinois, Urbana-Champaign, August 1987.

[20]   Lopriore, L., "Software-Controlled Cache Coherence Protocol for Multicache Systems," *Information Processing Letters*, Vol. 33, No. 3, November 1989, pp. 125–30.

[21]   Louri, A., and Sung, H., "A Compiler Directed Cache Coherence Scheme with Fast and Parallel Explicit Invalidation," *Proceedings of the 1992 International Conference on Parallel Processing*, August 1992, pp. I:2–9.

[22]   McGrogan, S., Olson, R., and Toda, N., "Parallelizing Large Existing Programs—Methodology and Experiences," *Proceedings of the Spring COMPCON*, March 1986, pp. 458–66.

[23]   Min, S.L., and Baer, J.-L., "A Timestamp Based Cache Coherence Scheme," *Proceedings of the 1989 International Conference on Parallel Processing*, 1989, pp. 23–32.

[24]   Olson, R., Kumar, B., and Shar, L.E., "Messages and Multiprocessors in the ELXSI 6400," *Proceedings of the Spring COMPCON*, March 1983, pp. 21–4.

[25]   Olson, R., "Parallel Processing in a Message-Based Operating System," *IEEE Software*, June 1985.

[26]   Pfister, G.F., et al, "The IBM Research Parallel Processor Prototype (RP3): Introduction and Architecture," *Proceedings of the 1985 International Conference on Parallel Processing*, August 1985, pp. 764–71.

[27]   Scheurich, C., "Access Ordering and Coherence in Shared Memory Multiprocessors," Ph.D. thesis, University of Southern California, May 1989.

[28]   Smith, A.J., "CPU Cache Consistency with Software Support and Using One Time Identifiers," *Proceedings of the Pacific Computer Communications Symposium*, 1985, pp. 153–61.

[29]   Stenstrom, P., "A Survey of Cache Coherence Schemes for Multiprocessors," *IEEE Computer*, June 1990, pp. 12–24.

[30]   Tartalja, I., and Mulutinovic, V., "An Approach to Dynamic Software Cache Consistency Maintenance Based on Conditional Invalidation," *Proceedings of the 25th HICSS*, January 1992, pp. 457–66.

[31]   Thacker, C.P., "Cache Strategies for Shared-Memory Multiprocessors," *New Frontiers in Computer Architecture*, March 1986, pp. 51–62.

[32]   Veidenbaum, A.V., "A Compiler-Assisted Cache Coherence Solution for Multiprocessors," *Proceedings of the International Conference on Parallel Processing*, August 1986, pp. 1029–36.

[33]   Weber, W.-D., and Gupta, A., "Analysis of Cache Invalidation Patterns in Multiprocessors," *Proceedings of the Third International Conference on Architectural Support for Programming Languages and Operating Systems*, 1989.

15

Hardware Cache Consistency

This chapter shows how cache consistency on an MP system with private caches can be maintained automatically through the use of special-purpose hardware. A high-level description of the operation of the hardware is given, followed by the effects this has on the software. Examples using common microprocessors in bus-based MP systems are given. This chapter concentrates on bus-based systems as these are the most common type of memory interconnect. Consistency for other types of memory interconnects is discussed briefly.

15.1 Introduction

Hardware cache consistency mechanisms are used to maintain the consistency of data shared between processors without software intervention. This is done by extending the bus-watching concept presented in Section 6.2.6, which maintains consistency during DMA operations, to also monitor activities by other processors. Monitoring the bus and keeping the contents of the caches consistent are transparent to the software. While there is a variety of ways this can be implemented, all techniques enforce a set of rules that determine when shared data can be cached. First, data read by multiple processors may be cached by each, since no inconsistencies can arise as long as the data is treated as read-only. Second, when one processor modifies data shared among the processors, any cached copies in other processor's caches must be either invalidated or updated with the new value. Finally, if a processor misses on shared data whose associated main memory value is stale, due to the use of write-back caching, then the processor with the most recent version of the data must supply a copy of it to the processor that missed. Together, these rules ensure that any cached copies of shared data always reflect the most recent version. While the main memory value may be stale (if write-back caching is used), stale data is never allowed in any cache. This prevents all the inconsistency problems presented in the last chapter.

To enforce these rules, the caches communicate with one another over the system bus using a *cache consistency protocol* to track the location of shared data and prevent stale data from being cached. Shared data is tracked on a per-cache-line basis, which requires all caches in the system to be identical, since the cache line size is the unit for which consistency is maintained. Furthermore, most MP systems that use hardware cache consistency also use physical caches. With virtually tagged caches, the hardware has no means by which to resolve the ambiguities that occur between different processors using the same virtual addresses to refer to different data. Hardware cache consistency can, however, be used with virtual caches that can also be indexed physically, such as those of the Intel i860 XP. It is also possible to use virtually indexed caches with physical tags, although these are rarely found in commercial MP systems, since they require that the bus transmit both the virtual and physical addresses of the data in every transaction.

The protocols for bus-based systems are referred to as *snooping* protocols, since each cache monitors, or snoops, the bus for activity by other caches. Snooping protocols rely on the fact that all bus transactions are visible to all other units in the system (since buses are a broadcast-based communication medium) and can therefore be snooped by each processor's cache. Some protocols require additional state information to be stored in the cache tags so that the actions needed to maintain consistency can be determined. (Examples are given in the sections that follow.) Snooping for MP cache consistency and for I/O DMA consistency is combined into a single protocol, with DMA consistency simply being a subset of the general MP case. The particular cache consistency protocol employed dictates exactly what actions are taken and when.

Dozens of protocols have been proposed over the years, many of which are slight variations or improvements to others. Different protocols require different amounts of communication. Protocols that require too much communication waste bus bandwidth and increase bus contention, leaving less bandwidth available to satisfy ordinary cache misses. Therefore, designers have tried to minimize the bus traffic needed by the protocol to maintain consistency, or have tried to optimize certain frequent operations.

In general, the protocols fall into two main categories: *write-invalidate* and *write-update*. Write-invalidate protocols broadcast an invalidation to all other caches in the system when one processor modifies data that could have been cached by others. Write-update protocols broadcast the new value of the data when one processor modifies it so that all other caches in the system may update their values if they are caching the affected line. In either case, consistency is maintained by eliminating stale data at the point where one processor modifies data that is shared with other processors. Since the bus sequentializes all operations, two processors that try to store to the same line at the same time are sequentialized in a non-deterministic order (as explained in Section 8.3.2). This ensures that there is only one current version of the cache line at any point in time.

Using a hardware cache consistency protocol increases the complexity of the system, and therefore the cost. The advantage is that shared data can be transparently cached by all processors in the system without the overhead and complexity of the software cache consistency techniques described in Chapter 14. These advantages so overwhelm the hardware costs that hardware cache consistency is found in almost every modern MP system.

Hardware techniques can be used to maintain the consistency of instructions as well as data. Processors with a unified instruction and data cache, such as the on-chip cache of the Intel 80486, maintain consistency for both instructions and data simultaneously. No extra complexity is needed to ensure instruction consistency in this case since instructions just appear the same as data in the cache. Processors with separate instruction and data caches must check both during snoop operations if full consistency is to be maintained. Processors such as the Texas Instruments SuperSPARC, the MIPS R4000, and the Intel i860 XP operate in this manner, and it is now common practice to do so. (Early MP microprocessors with separate instruction and data caches would frequently forgo hardware instruction cache consistency, leaving that task to software, to reduce cost and complexity.) Not all processors with hardware consistency of the instruction cache monitor stores to the processor's own data cache (to cover the case of self-modifying code, for example). In systems such as these, the software must still explicitly invalidate the instruction cache to maintain consistency in these situations, just as it had to on uniprocessor systems (see Section 2.10). The Intel i860 XP operates in this manner. Its data cache uses write-back, so modified instructions must first be written back to main memory, and then the instruction cache can be invalidated. Cases of self-modifying code are rare enough that they do not impose an undue burden on the software.

The sections that follow describe several cache consistency protocols used by modern microprocessor systems. The purpose is to familiarize software engineers with the concepts so that other protocols can be readily understood when they are encountered. As such, the descriptions have been simplified by omitting hardware details that are not of concern to the software. The effects on the software are discussed in the sections after the hardware concepts have been presented.

15.2 Write-Invalidate Protocols

Write-invalidate protocols maintain consistency by ensuring that only a single cached copy of a line from main memory exists at the point where a store occurs to that line. To illustrate this, consider the case where a line has not been modified by any processor in the system. Here, copies of the line may be cached by multiple processors. When a store to the line occurs, all copies except the one on the processor performing the store are invalidated. The details of how this is accomplished depend on whether write-through or write-back caching is used, and on how the protocol operates. Three different write-invalidate protocols are described in the following sections.

15.2.1 The Write-Through Invalidate Protocol

The simplest write-invalidate protocol uses write-through caching and is used by the Motorola MC68040. The 68040 has separate instruction and data caches, each of which is a 4K physical cache with 16 bytes per line. Both caches snoop the bus and update their contents as appropriate to maintain consistency. The strategy it uses works as follows:

Shared data that may be modified by any processor in the system must be cached using the write-through policy. When a processor misses on shared data, it reads the data from main memory. The use of write-through caching ensures that the main memory copy is always up to date, regardless of which processor modified it last. So when multiple processors read the same data, each is allowed to cache a copy of that data. When a processor writes shared data, it is written to main memory. The bus transaction to do this write is snooped by the other caches in the system, and if the address written generates a hit in any of these caches, then they invalidate their copy of the cache line. This forces them to reread the new contents of the line from main memory on the next access from their associated CPU, ensuring that they always receive the most recently written value of the data. Notice that this is the same set of actions that maintained consistency in the I/O DMA example from Section 6.2.6. The 68040 uses it to maintain both MP and I/O cache consistency.

Since the bus can be used by only one processor at a time, all stores are sequentially ordered, and hence the system supports the sequential memory model even though shared data is cached. This means that Dekker's algorithm works correctly and that spin locks can be cached. There is no need to code selective cache flushing into the kernel, since the invalidation is now being done by the hardware. Therefore, all shared kernel data structures can be cached, as well as user shared memory. A full description of the software benefits of hardware cache consistency appears in Section 15.7.

The disadvantage of the write-through invalidate protocol is that it requires a bus transaction for every store to any piece of shared data. Bus traffic can be reduced by using write-back caching for processor private data (which the 68040 supports), but write-back cannot be used for shared data. If a store hits on an unmodified line when using write-back, the cache only updates its contents and does not send the modified data to memory. So there is no transaction for the other caches to snoop and invalidate their copies of the line if they have any. Therefore, a different protocol is needed to support write-back caching.

15.2.2 The Write-Once Protocol

A simple variation of write-back caching, called *write-once*, can be used to form a write-back invalidate protocol. Write-once was proposed by Goodman and, historically, is considered to be the first write-invalidate protocol (see Reference [23]). The Motorola MC88200 supports the write-once protocol. The main difference between write-once and normal write-back is that the first hit on an unmodified line during a store will update memory (i.e., write-through is used for the first modification to a line). This provides a bus transaction that the other caches can snoop and use to invalidate any cached copies of the line they may have. As with normal write-back caching, the use of write-allocate reduces bus traffic when one processor does multiple stores to the same line without doing an initial load.

The bus is used to sequentialize processors that attempt simultaneous stores to the same line. Assume several processors have a shared copy of a line cached and they all store to the line at the same time. The first to acquire the bus updates memory with its store, which causes all other cached copies of the line to be invalidated. Since the other processors no longer have a copy of the line, their stores generate a cache miss. The next to acquire the bus will read the updated copy of the line from main memory, insert the data from this processor's store (which may be to a different word in the line than the first processor modified), and write the line back to main memory (since write-once specifies write-through on the processor's first store to a line). All processors modifying the line proceed sequentially in this fashion, but in a nondeterministic order. Consistency is maintained since only the processor that is currently modifying the line is allowed to cache a copy of it.

A line enters the modified state when the processor stores to it a second time and no other processor has accessed the line since the first write-through to memory. Once in the modified state, subsequent stores by the same processor to the same line use normal write-back semantics. No bus transactions are generated for the modified line unless the line is replaced. Since memory is no longer up to date, the cache must also monitor the bus for memory reads from other processors. If the address another cache is reading hits on a modified line during a snoop, then the cache with the modified data must supply it to the cache that missed, since main memory is stale. The MC88200 implements this by aborting the bus transaction from the processor trying to read the line. The processor with the modified line then writes it back to main memory, marking its own copy as valid and unmodified. The processor attempting to read the line then retries the read, this time receiving the now up-to-date copy in main memory. Some implementations choose to have the processor read the line as the other is writing it back to main memory. This saves one bus transaction but is more complex to implement. Regardless of the implementation details, both caches then cache the line in the valid unmodified state.

If another processor stores to an address that misses in its cache but hits on a modified line in another cache, then a similar sequence occurs. The processor with the modified data writes it back to main memory but then invalidates its copy since the other processor will be modifying it. This ensures that there is only a single cached copy of the line at the point where it is modified.

When using normal write-back caching, each line can have one of three states: invalid, valid-unmodified, and valid-modified. For brevity, the valid-unmodified state is commonly referred to as valid and valid-modified is referred to as modified. To improve the performance of the write-once protocol, a new state is added to each line for a total of four states: invalid, valid, dirty, and reserved. (The terms "dirty" and "modified" are synonymous.) The first three are the normal states for a write-back cache. The *reserved* state is a new state to indicate that the line is valid and has been written by the CPU exactly once, and that main memory is up to date. It means that this is the sole cached copy of the line and that it can therefore move to the modified state the next time the CPU stores to it without having to broadcast an invalidate to the other caches. It also indicates that the line has been written only once by the CPU and does not have to be written back when the line is replaced, since the data has already been written through to main memory on the first store. The reserved state eliminates unnecessary bus transactions and improves performance.

It is typical for hardware cache consistency protocols to add new states to the cache lines. The states and the events that cause transitions from one to another are typically represented using a state diagram. The state diagram for the write-once protocol, shown in Figure 15–1, depicts the state transitions that occur to one line of one cache in response to the indicated events. Each line of each cache in the system executes an independent copy of this state machine.

The black arcs represent state transitions caused by events from the CPU connected to the cache. For example, if a line is in the valid state and the CPU performs a load that hits on that line, then the arc labeled "CPU load hit" shows that the cache line remains in the valid state at the conclusion of this operation. Likewise, if the CPU stores to an address that hits on a valid line, then the arc labeled "CPU store hit" shows that the cache line changes to the reserved state in response to this event. Note that the diagram shows the state transi-

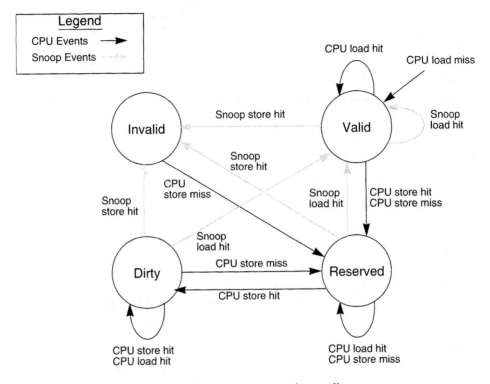

Figure 15–1: Write-once protocol state diagram.

tions alone, and not the actions associated with the transition. For example, in addition to causing a transition to the reserved state, a "CPU store miss" on a line in the dirty state causes the line to be written back to main memory and then replaced with the data associated with the address that missed. Since this is the first write to the data, the write-once protocol dictates that it be written through to main memory. After these actions are performed, the line enters the reserved state.

A "CPU load miss" that occurs while in any state causes the cache line to be replaced and then enter the valid state. To simplify the diagram, only a single "CPU load miss" arc is shown entering the valid state, as it does not matter what state the line was originally in.

The gray arcs show the transitions associated with events snooped off the bus. All caches snoop all bus transactions and update their contents as appropriate. For example, "Snoop load hit" means that another processor missed in its own cache during a load, has sent a bus transaction to read the cache line, and the address it was reading has hit in this processor's cache. Snoops that miss cause no state changes in the cache and so are not shown.

The state diagram makes it apparent that any stores done by other processors (causing the event "Snoop store hit" to occur) result in the line being invalidated from any other cache containing the line, since a "Snoop store hit" always changes the line to the invalid state. This enforces one of the rules of write-invalidate cache consistency protocols, where only a single modified copy of a line may exist. Similarly, a "Snoop load hit" occurring in any state (other than invalid) always causes the cache line to change to the valid state. If it hits on a dirty line, the line is written back to main memory. This is required since multiple caches will now be caching the line, so memory must be up to date. Multiple processors can cache the data only until one of them modifies it.

Finally, note that even though multiple events cause the same state transition to occur, it does not mean that they cause the same actions to occur in conjunction with the event. For example, both "CPU store hit" and "CPU store miss" cause a state change to the reserved state if the original state was valid. In the case of a store hit, the new data is inserted into the line and it is written through to main memory. For a store miss, the line must first be replaced by reading the line from memory (or from another cache, in the case of a snoop hit). Then the new data can be inserted into the line and written through to memory.

While the write-once protocol allows write-back caching to be used, which eliminates the need to write the data through to main memory on every store, it still requires an extra write to main memory over pure write-back caching when the reserved state is initially entered. This can be eliminated by a more sophisticated protocol, such as the one described in the next section.

15.2.3 MESI Protocols

MESI protocols add the concept of *ownership* to a cache line. Once a cache exclusively owns a cache line, it can modify it without the need to send an initial write-through bus transaction. This provides more efficient write-back caching. These protocols derive their name from the first letter of the four states of a cache line: modified, exclusive, shared, and invalid. This type of protocol is used by the Intel Pentium and the external cache controllers for the 80486. It is also one of several selectable protocols on the MIPS R4000. There are several variations of this type of protocol, one of which is described here.

The modified state is identical to the dirty state of the write-once protocol. It means that the line is modified relative to main memory, and it implies that no other cache has a copy of the line. Therefore, CPU stores that hit in the cache update the line without generating any bus transactions. The cache must also supply the data to other caches whose snoop operations hit on these lines.

The exclusive state is the same as the reserved state of the write-once protocol. It means that the line is consistent with main memory, and that no other cache has a copy of the line. As with the write-once reserved state, lines that are modified by the CPU while in the exclusive state change to the modified state without a bus transaction.

The shared state means the line is valid and can therefore be read by the CPU on load hits. It also means that the line may be cached by other processors as well, and so it cannot be modified without first sending a bus transaction to invalidate the other copies.

The difference between MESI protocols and write-once is in how transitions between the states are handled during a CPU load miss. When such a miss occurs, the CPU sends a bus transaction to read the line. When the data is returned, the MESI protocol supplies a special bus signal that indicates whether copies exist in other caches. (Each cache that finds a copy of the line during the snoop operation asserts the signal.) If no other copies are cached, then the line is loaded in the exclusive state. If other copies exist, then it is loaded in the shared state. By contrast, the write-once protocol always loads new data in the valid state and can only change to the reserved state after sending a bus transaction to invalidate other copies that may exist. The state diagram for the MESI protocol is similar to that shown in Figure 15–1, except that a CPU load miss can initially enter either the exclusive or shared state.

The advantage over write-once is that the CPU can modify data initially loaded in the exclusive state without the need for a bus transaction to invalidate copies in other caches, since it is known that none exist. As before, a cache that has a line in the modified state must supply the data to other caches during snoop operations. Likewise, consistency is maintained by allowing only one cache to have a modified copy of the line at a time, though multiple caches may share a read-only copy of a line.

15.3 Write-Update Protocols

Write-invalidate protocols maintain consistency by invalidating other cached copies of a line when one CPU modifies it. Write-update protocols maintain consistency by updating all cached copies of a line when one CPU modifies a shared line. The following examples illustrate this class of protocols.

15.3.1 The Firefly Protocol

The Firefly multiprocessor workstation from Digital Equipment Corporation used a write-update protocol. This protocol uses the same basic states as MESI, with some differences in the actions performed during state transitions. As with MESI, a cache line enters the exclusive or shared state after a CPU load miss depending on a bus signal from other caches in the system. Similarly, CPU stores that hit on exclusive or modified lines update only the local cache, since it is guaranteed that no other cache has the data.

The difference between this protocol and MESI is that stores to lines in the shared state cause a bus transaction to be generated that updates any copies cached elsewhere in the system, as well as updating main memory. (The MESI protocol would have invalidated the other copies, updated memory in this case, and moved to the exclusive state.) Note that when a line in the shared state is modified, other caches may have replaced their copies during misses, and hence the line may no longer be actually shared. The replacement of shared lines is not communicated on the bus, and so a CPU modifying a shared line must broadcast an update regardless. When it does so, the shared status of the line is returned to the cache that initiated the update just as in the case of a load miss. If it is found that other caches still have a copy of the data, then the line stays in the shared state. If not, then the line moves to the exclusive state. This saves sending future updates if other caches no longer have a copy of the line.

Write-update protocols assume that shared data will continue to be shared. Write-invalidate protocols can cause a "ping-pong" effect, where a line that is modified by multiple processors keeps moving back and forth between their caches as each invalidates the other copies. Since data is frequently read before it is written, the MESI protocol requires one bus transaction to read the line on the first miss, and a second transaction to invalidate other copies on the first write. With the Firefly protocol, however, once all processors obtain a copy of a line that they are sharing, only a single bus transaction is required to update the other copies each time any processor modifies the line. This has the potential to cut the bus traffic in half for heavily shared data.

The disadvantage, though, is that extra traffic over MESI may be incurred for data that tends to stay local to one CPU. For example, when a process migrates from one processor to another, the cache on the processor it previously ran on may still be caching some of its private data, such as the u-area and kernel stack, as well as the user program's text, data, and stack. When the new processor references this data, the lines will enter the shared state and remain there until they are replaced on the previous processor. This is undesirable since the new processor will send updates to the previous processor, wasting bus bandwidth, even though the previous processor won't be referencing the data further. For this type of data, it's best to invalidate old copies instead of updating them.

15.3.2 The MIPS R4000 Update Protocol

The MIPS R4000 allows the operating system to select one of five cache consistency policies on a per-page basis (by setting the appropriate bits in the page table entry). Among the five protocols is the *update* policy, which functions similarly to the Firefly protocol. The R4000 can be configured to use an additional fifth cache state, *modified-shared*, which affects when main memory is updated. The Firefly protocol updates main memory whenever an update is sent on shared data, or when a modified line is replaced. When using the modified-shared state on the R4000, updates are sent to other caches for data in the shared state, but main memory is not updated. The cache that modified the line enters the modified-shared state to indicate that a write-back to main memory will be needed when the line is replaced. Omitting the update of main memory can simplify the design of the memory subsystem and can improve the performance of update bus transactions. This idea is used in the Dragon protocol developed by Xerox PARC (Palo Alto Research Center) as well.

15.4   Consistency of Read-Modify-Write Operations

In Section 8.3.3, atomic read-modify-write operations were defined to read a value from main memory, modify it, and write it back, all as a single atomic operation. This is true for systems using write-through consistency protocols, such as the write-through invalidate protocol on the MC68040. These protocols always access main memory on writes, allowing other caches to snoop the transaction and invalidate any copies of the data they may have had. If the atomic read-modify-write operation begins and generates a cache hit on the read phase, then it can use this value as long as it has already acquired exclusive use of the bus to complete the operation. The value read from the cache is guaranteed to be consistent with main memory at that point (otherwise the protocol would have invalidated it). Acquiring the bus at the start prevents other processors from storing to the same memory location while the atomic operation is in progress. During the write phase to main memory, all other caches will snoop the transaction and invalidate copies of the data that they may have, causing them to miss and read the new value from memory on their next access. As on systems without a cache, a read miss at the start of an atomic operation causes the value to be read from main memory, modified, and written back atomically.

When using write-back protocols, it is not always necessary to access main memory. It is sufficient to ensure that the cache line containing the target of the read-modify-write operation is updated atomically. The cache consistency protocol will then ensure consistency and prevent two or more CPUs from simultaneously performing atomic operations on the same line.

To illustrate this, consider the atomic-swap operation as used by the TI SuperSPARC (defined in Section 8.3.3). Since the CPU will modify the line containing the word to be swapped, the CPU's cache must have the only copy of the line. Since the SuperSPARC uses the MESI protocol, if the line is already in the modified or exclusive state, then no bus transactions are necessary since this CPU is already the exclusive owner of the line. If there is a miss, then the cache must acquire an exclusive copy of the line. This is done with a special bus transaction that indicates the CPU's intent to modify the line. Other caches in the system therefore invalidate their copies after one supplies the data to the requesting CPU. If the line is initially in the shared state, then an invalidate is broadcast over the bus, and the line enters the exclusive state. At this point, the CPU doing the atomic read-modify-write operation is the exclusive owner of the line, and so it can proceed with the swap operation by merely exchanging the register value with the desired word in the line. In all cases, the line finishes in the modified state. If another CPU tries to access the line while the swap is in progress, the CPU owning the line will supply it to the other after the swap is complete. As always, when multiple CPUs simultaneously attempt to access the same line, the bus sequentializes the accesses in a nondeterministic order.

The load-linked, store-conditional operations used by the MIPS R4000 (also described in Section 8.3.3) rely on the hardware cache consistency protocol as well, but since the pair of instructions is not guaranteed to be executed atomically, it is possible for other processors to access the line between the load-linked/store-conditional pair. If this occurs, then the store-conditional operation is defined to fail. There are several ways to implement these instructions. One is by observing the state of the cache line before doing the store. When a load-linked operation is done, the CPU acquires the cache line in either the exclusive or modified states just as the atomic-swap operation does, and performs the load operation. It also sets a flag in the line to indicate that a load-linked/store-conditional pair is in progress. Any snoops that access the line cause the flag to be cleared. When the store-conditional is executed, it checks to see if the flag is still set. If so, then no other processor has accessed the line, and the store operation can complete successfully. Otherwise, another CPU has accessed the line between the load-linked/store-conditional pair, which causes the store-conditional to fail, since the line cannot be updated atomically.

Performing atomic operations in the cache as opposed to requiring an access to main memory has the advantage of reducing bus traffic, especially in the case where the data to be operated on is already cache-resident and so can help improve overall system performance. Note that when write-back caching is used, it is not necessary to update memory at all. The cache consistency protocol ensures the correctness of these operations in all cases.

15.5 Hardware Consistency for Multilevel Caches

Hardware techniques can also be used to maintain cache consistency in MP systems when each processor uses a hierarchy of caches. Both the MIPS R4000 and the TI SuperSPARC support multilevel consistency, with one minor difference between their on-chip caches. Both processors use on-chip instruction and data caches coupled with an off-chip secondary cache. The secondary caches of both use the write-back policy. For the on-chip data caches, the R4000 uses write-back while the SuperSPARC uses write-through. Both processors maintain consistency using the *inclusion property*. This means that the primary cache is always a subset of the secondary. To maintain inclusion, the secondary cache is loaded with a copy of the data whenever there is a miss in primary cache. Additionally, the corresponding primary cache line is written back and invalidated whenever a secondary cache line is replaced or invalidated. The use of inclusion means that snooping can be handled by interrogating the secondary cache alone and then only accessing the primary cache for snoop operations that hit in the secondary. Snoops that miss in the secondary are known not to affect the primary. This helps reduce contention for the primary cache, allowing more of the primary cache bandwidth to be used by the CPU.

To maintain consistency, the secondary cache snoops the bus for activity by other processors and proceeds according to the cache consistency protocol. For example, both the MIPS and SPARC processors support a write-invalidate protocol. So if the secondary cache detects a write to a line it has cached, it invalidates the line in the secondary. Since the primary cache could have a copy of the line, it too is checked whenever a snoop operation hits in the secondary. Since the primary cache on the R4000 is virtually indexed, the primary cache index stored in the secondary cache line is used to index the primary cache line where the data to be invalidated may be stored. (The operation of the caches on the MIPS R4000 is covered in detail in Section 6.3.2.) The TI SuperSPARC uses a physically indexed primary cache, so the physical address used by the snoop operation in the secondary is used to index the primary. In either case, if a hit occurs in the primary, then the line is invalidated.

When the caches are being snooped to satisfy a cache load miss on another processor, the secondary cache is checked first. Since the SuperSPARC uses write-through caching in its primary cache, the data requested by the snoop operation can be supplied directly without accessing the primary. This is not the case on the R4000, since its primary cache uses write-back. This requires that it too be checked for modified data under these conditions.

Stores from the CPU work as expected. On the SuperSPARC, a store that hits in the primary cache can immediately be written through to the secondary since inclusion guarantees the secondary will have a copy of the line. If it hits on a modified line in the secondary, then the write-invalidate protocol specifies that no bus transaction is necessary, since this processor is the only one caching the data. If the line in the secondary is instead unmodified, then an invalidate transaction must be sent out over the bus to eliminate any other cached copies that may exist. The secondary cache line then enters the modified state. Since the R4000 uses write-back caching in the primary cache, stores that hit on modified or exclusive lines need not access the secondary cache, nor generate any bus transactions when using the MESI write-invalidate protocol. Stores that miss in the primary on either processor cause the line to be allocated in the secondary cache if it is not already present, reading the data from main memory or another processor's cache.

15.6 Other Main Memory Architectures

Using a bus as the interconnect medium between the CPUs and main memory is a simple and cost-effective approach for systems with up to a few dozen processors. For example, Silicon Graphics produces the Challenge system, which can support up to 36 processors on a single main memory bus. But as the number of processors on the bus increases, contention increases and the bus becomes a bottleneck. In addition, electrical constraints limit the speed of the bus due to its length and the number of connections made to it. Ultimately, the bus becomes a limiting factor in the performance of large-scale MP systems, and so a different type of memory interconnect is needed. The type of interconnect used also impacts how hardware cache consistency is implemented.

15.6.1 The Cross-bar Interconnect

To get around the limitations of the single-bus approach, other types of interconnects have been proposed and used in large-scale MP systems. One such interconnect is the *cross-bar* and is shown in Figure 15–2.

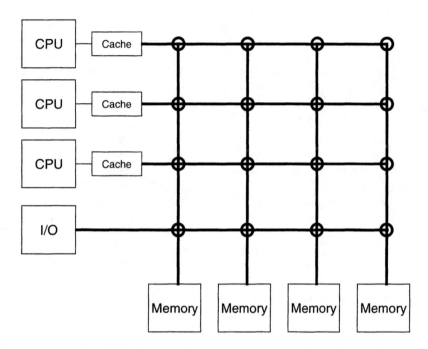

Figure 15–2: Example SMP system using a cross-bar memory interconnect.

Figure 15–2 shows an SMP system with three CPUs, each with a private cache, an I/O sub-system, and four main memory modules. (Designers are, of course, free to vary the number of processors, memory modules, and I/O devices. The cross-bar need not be square.) The idea of a cross-bar is to provide multiple buses that can be in use simultaneously in order to reduce contention, and to provide multiple memory modules that can operate in parallel, which increases overall memory bandwidth. The physical address space is divided among the memory modules such that the data associated with each address is stored in one and only one place. One way to do this is for each module to store a contiguous block of the physical address space. For example, if each module contained 256M, then the first module would store the data for physical addresses `0x0` through `0xfffffff`, the second would store `0x10000000` through `0x1fffffff`, and so on. While this approach is simple, the disadvantage is that accesses to adjacent addresses, which often happen within a short time due to spatial locality, will all go to the same memory module. To overlap the memory cycle times better, many designs will interleave the memory such that the physical address space is striped across the modules. In this case, the amount of contiguous memory stored in a module is usually equal to the cache line size. If the line size were 256 bytes, for example, then the data for physical addresses 0x0 through 0xff would be stored in the first module, addresses 0x100 through 0x1ff in the second, 0x200 to 0x2ff in the third, 0x300 to 0x3ff in the fourth, and then the addresses would wrap around to first module again for addresses 0x400 to 0x4ff, and so on. The exact way in which the physical address space is interleaved among the modules is invisible to the software and need not be considered further.

Each circle in the cross-bar array represents a switch that can be turned on and off by the hardware to connect the two intersecting buses temporarily. Normally, all switches are off until a CPU or I/O device needs to access memory. Based on the physical address being accessed, the cross-bar hardware throws the switch that connects the unit generating the request with the appropriate main memory module to form a path for the access. For example, if the uppermost CPU in Figure 15–2 needs to access the rightmost memory module, the cross-bar throws the switch in the upper-right corner for the duration of the access. When the access is complete, the switch is turned back off. If more than one CPU needs to access the same memory module at the same time, then the cross-bar hardware arbitrates these requests in much the same way as a standard bus, allowing one memory access to occur at a time to any one memory module. As such, only one switch in any column will be turned on at a time.

Despite the lack of a single common bus, this type of memory architecture still qualifies as an SMP system as described in Section 8.2. The CPUs, I/O, and memory are all tightly coupled within a short distance of one another. All memory in a cross-bar is shared and globally accessible. The access to that memory is symmetric from the processor's point of view. The cross-bar arbitrates simultaneous access to the modules and guarantees fairness.

Since the cross-bar allows only one CPU or I/O device to be connected to a given memory module at a time, it is clear that it can support all types of atomic memory operations in the same way that a single-bus system can. The vertical buses from each module sequentialize all memory accesses to that module in some nondeterministic order, just as a regular bus. Furthermore, the memory model the CPUs implement is unaffected by the presence of a cross-bar. Models such as partial store ordering only affect the order in which stores are sent to memory. How the interconnect routes the data to memory has no effect on the memory model or the software.

The advantage of a cross-bar architecture is that it provides multiple paths to memory, reducing contention. Additionally, parallelism is possible as well, since two or more CPUs can be accessing different memory modules simultaneously without interference. In the diagram in Figure 15–2, all four units on the left side could be simultaneously accessing memory as long as the physical addresses they use resolve to separate memory modules. Such parallelism is not possible in single-bus systems. A cross-bar also reduces the number of simultaneous connections to each bus, which alleviates some of the electrical constraints and allows faster bus speeds. In summary, it can reduce contention and allow for increased bandwidth to memory.

The disadvantage of a cross-bar is that multiple buses are more expensive than a single-bus system. The benefit is increased system performance. The second problem is that of maintaining cache consistency. Since each CPU has its own path to memory, and since other CPUs cannot be connected to a memory module while it is in use by another, snooping cache consistency schemes cannot be used. Snooping relies on the fact that all bus transactions are visible to all caches in the system. The lack of a single common bus negates this ability. Instead, hardware can maintain cache consistency automatically by use of a directory-based caching scheme.

15.6.2 Directory-based Hardware Cache Consistency

The snooping-based consistency schemes presented earlier all rely on using the state of the cache lines to determine what actions to take during snoop operations. In this regard, the information needed to maintain consistency is distributed among the caches. To determine if a line is shared, for example, all caches have to check for a hit and then the cache line states have to be examined. Distributing the information needed to maintain consistency is not appropriate for a cross-bar architecture since the lack of a broadcast capability means snooping cannot be done. Instead, this type of memory architecture stores the information needed to maintain cache consistency centrally in the main memory modules. This information is called a *directory*, and its purpose is to indicate which caches have copies of each line of memory and the cache line state.

Conceptually, the structure of main memory and the directory are best viewed by dividing the memory inside a module into cache-line–sized pieces. Associated with each piece is the directory information for that line, as shown in Figure 15–3. In this example, assume the line size is 256 bytes and that each memory module stores physically contiguous lines (i.e., memory is not interleaved between modules).

In the simplest case, the contents of the directory are a copy of the state bits from the cache tags of each cache in the system that is presently caching the corresponding physical memory line. This was the structure first proposed by Tang (see Reference [48]). The contents of the directory are not accessible to the software, and are used and updated automatically by the hardware to maintain consistency. By keeping a centralized copy of the cache tags, the hardware can determine what consistency actions to take without the need to broadcast the memory access to all processors. Communication needs to occur only to those caches that have copies of the referenced memory line.

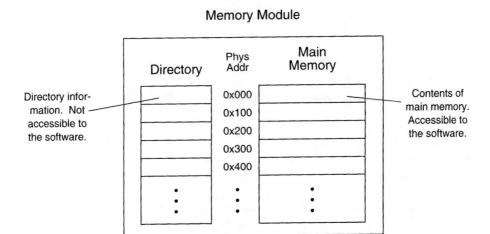

Figure 15–3: Memory module containing a directory.

As an example, consider the three-CPU system shown in Figure 15–2. For simplicity, assume the caches use write-through. This means that the only state information in the tags is the valid bit. (The address in the cache tags is not considered state information.) The directory information for each memory line therefore consists of three bits, which are copies of the valid bits from the three caches. Figure 15–4 shows what a line in the directory looks like.

CPU 1 valid bit	CPU 2 valid bit	CPU 3 valid bit

Figure 15–4: Contents of a directory line.

For each line in the memory module, the valid bit for a particular CPU in the corresponding directory line will be set if that CPU is caching a copy of the memory line. The bits in the directory are updated whenever the state of the cache line changes. So a cache miss occurring when a CPU does a load causes the appropriate bit to be set in the directory. This is done while the memory module is returning the requested data to the CPU. When a line is replaced in the cache, the memory module is notified so that the valid bit in the line's directory entry can be cleared. (Some implementations forgo this step to reduce communication. In this case, the state bits in the directory represent a superset of the caches with a copy of the line.) The data to replace the cache line is then accessed (possibly in a different memory module), and the valid bit in that line's directory entry is set for the CPU. The data is then returned to the cache.

Cache consistency is then maintained using the standard protocols. For this example, the write-through invalidate protocol is appropriate since write-through caching is used. As described in Section 15.2.1, multiple caches may cache copies of the same memory line while they are reading it. When one CPU writes the line, the others must be invalidated. The directory entry indicates which caches need to have invalidation commands sent to them. Consider the case where CPUs 1 and 2 are caching a copy of the line at physical address 0x100. CPU 1 now does a store to that location. The use of write-through means the new data will be sent to memory immediately. Once there, the directory entry for memory line 0x100 is checked and CPU 2 is found to have a copy of the line. The hardware then arbitrates and establishes a connection on the cross-bar between the memory module and CPU 2. The memory module then sends an invalidate to it for physical address 0x100. CPU 2 then invalidates that line from its cache. In the meantime, the memory module updates the contents of the memory line with the new data from CPU 1, and then updates the directory to show that now only CPU 1 has a copy of the line. The store operation is now complete. Observe that the cache connected to CPU 3 never had to be accessed since its valid bit for the line was off. Similarly, if the directory indicated that CPU 1 had the only copy of the line when it performed the store, then no other communication is necessary to ensure consistency. This is an advantage of directory-based consistency schemes over snooping schemes, as the directory helps reduce the amount of communication needed.

In summary, a directory allows consistency to be maintained without the need for broadcast operations. Any of the protocols previously described can be implemented on a cross-bar memory architecture using a directory, including the write-back protocols. The information in the directory can be organized in a number of different ways other than simply keeping an exact copy of the state bits from the cache tags. This is done to reduce the amount of information and to identify what consistency operations are needed more readily. The operation of the directory is transparent to the software regardless of its structure. The disadvantage of directories is, of course, that they require more memory parts than the distributed caches found in a bus-based system since the directory information is a redundant copy of the cache tags. Consult Section 15.12 for further reading on this subject.

15.7 Effects on the Software

The use of any of the preceding hardware cache consistency protocols, whether on a bus-based system or other memory architecture, allows all forms of shared data to be cached and relieves the operating system of the burden of flushing shared data to maintain consistency. First, consider the case of a user process's data. As described in Section 14.2, consistency problems arise when the process migrates from one processor to another and references stale data in the local cache or in main memory. Referring to the example and cache state shown in Figure 14–3, if the process runs on CPU 2 and reads the counter value prior to incrementing it, the hardware cache consistency protocol will snoop the current value from CPU 1's cache. When CPU 2 stores the incremented value, the old value cached on CPU 1 will be either invalidated or updated depending on the protocol used. Using hardware cache consistency, one ensures that the process will reference the correct copy of the data regardless of which processor it is presently executing on or where cached values may be located.

Similarly, the caching problems that occurred when using Dekker's algorithm are solved with hardware consistency. One of the problems was that stores from one processor are not immediately visible to others when write-back caching is used. A second problem was that one processor could access stale data in its own cache and think the lock was free when it was actually in use, or vice versa. Hardware cache consistency solves both these problems by providing each processor with the most up-to-date copy of the shared data, whether it be in a cache or in main memory. It also prevents caches from holding stale data. For this reason, all spin locks, whether they be implemented with Dekker's Algorithm or atomic read-modify-write operations, can be safely cached.

One of the additional constraints of the selective cache-flushing software consistency technique is that separate critical resources must occupy separate cache lines, otherwise different CPUs could simultaneously update different parts of the same cache line (see Section 14.3.2). This restriction is not required when using hardware cache consistency, since the hardware maintains consistency on a per-cache-line basis. If another CPU references a separate critical resource that shares a cache line with other resources, and that line is cached by another processor and in the modified state (as depicted in Figure 14–4), then the cache consistency protocol will cause a copy of the modified data to be given to the CPU referencing the line. For example, if a write-invalidate protocol had been used when CPU 2 read the cache line that had been modified by CPU 1 in Figure 14–4, then the line would have been written to main memory and both caches would have cached the line in the shared state. The state of the caches and memory would then be as appears in Figure 15–5.

If CPU 2 were now to increment and store the updated value of the counter in the right side of the cache line, the write-invalidate protocol will simultaneously invalidate any other cached copies of the line. This means that the situation shown in Figure 14–5 in the previous chapter can never occur, since all hardware protocols prevent two or more caches from caching different versions of the same line. Instead, the picture looks like that in Figure 15–6 after CPU 2 updates its critical resource (assume the protocol updates memory during invalidates).

If CPU 1 were to access its critical resource at this point, it would miss and read the current value from memory or CPU 2's cache depending on the protocol.

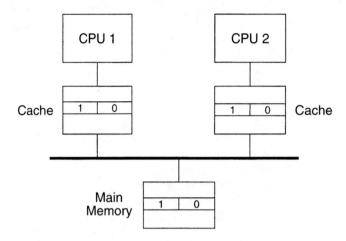

Figure 15–5: Both CPUs accessing critical resources in same cache line.

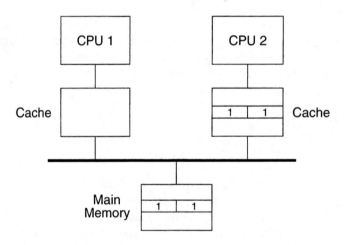

Figure 15–6: State after CPU 2 updates its critical resource.

In summary, the hardware cache consistency protocol handles all situations and so relieves the operating system of the need to manage shared data directly. As with DMA bus watching, the presence of the caches can largely be ignored as far as data consistency is concerned. This is true regardless of which MP kernel implementation technique from Part II is chosen.

15.8 Hardware Consistency for Nonsequential Memory Models

As described in Section 14.3.3, MP systems with caches whose CPUs support nonsequential memory models, such as total store ordering or partial store ordering, operate by sending the contents of the store buffer to the primary cache. How the data is handled at that point depends on the implementation of the caches and the consistency protocol. Since hardware cache consistency techniques effectively hide the presence of the caches from the software, the kernel need do nothing more to run on an MP system with caches and a nonsequential memory model other than the changes described in Sections 13.4 and 13.5. The use of locks and the special atomic operations to acquire the locks results in correct behavior for most algorithms when operating under total store ordering. The addition of store-barrier instructions when releasing locks solves the new problems presented by partial store ordering. As with MP systems lacking caches, algorithms that inherently rely on sequential ordering, such as Dekker's Algorithm, will fail on systems using hardware cache consistency.

The preceding illustrates an important fact: that the store buffer and hardware cache consistency should be viewed as two separate mechanisms that address different aspects of system performance. The store buffer transfers data from the CPU to main memory so that the CPU is not delayed. Hardware cache consistency presents a consistent view of memory to all processors. Even though the caches are faster than the main memory subsystem, store buffers are still useful, since they can hide some of the penalty of cache misses during store operations.

15.9 Performance Considerations for Software

As mentioned previously, different cache consistency protocols have been invented to reduce the amount of bus traffic needed to maintain consistency. By understanding how the protocol operates on a particular system, the programmer can take steps to further reduce bus traffic by avoiding operations that generate unnecessary snooping. Excessive snooping not only causes contention for the bus, but it can also cause contention for the caches on the processors responding to snoop requests, since there will be requests coming from the cache's own CPU and the bus simultaneously. Reducing the amount of snooping, therefore, helps improve overall system performance. The following sections describe several examples of situations to be considered.

15.9.1 Cache-Aligning Data Structures

The concept of aligning data structures on cache line boundaries was introduced in Section 7.5. The goal was to reduce the number of cache misses needed to load a data structure into a processor's cache, assuming there is a high degree of spatial locality within the data structure. By so aligning data structures in an MP system, not only are misses from the CPU's point of view reduced, but the number of snoop operations can be reduced as well. Data structures corresponding to critical resources can be well suited to this technique since it is known that only one processor will use the resource at a time.

As an example, consider a critical resource that is protected by a spin lock. Assume that its data structure, including the lock, can fit within one cache line, and that it is so aligned. Before a processor accesses the data structure, it will first acquire the lock. If spin locks are implemented with an atomic-swap operation, which operates as described in Section 15.4, then the atomic swap will acquire an exclusive copy of the cache to perform its operation. Assuming the lock is free, the processor will immediately acquire the lock, leaving the line in the modified state. At this point, the CPU can access the data structure without any further bus transactions (assuming the line doesn't get replaced during a miss). In the best case (when the lock is free), only a single transaction is required to obtain an exclusive copy of the line when using a MESI protocol. As different CPUs use the critical resource, it can migrate from one cache to another with a single transaction.

There is, however, a disadvantage to combining a data structure and its lock into the same cache line. If contention for the critical resource is high, other CPUs will be trying to acquire its lock, causing the cache line to move back and forth between them. This will cause the CPU using the resource to experience additional cache misses. One way to alleviate this is to allocate the lock such that it is in a separate cache line. This allows one processor to use the data structure without other processors causing contention as they spin for the lock. Unfortunately, if multiple processors are trying to acquire a lock that is already locked, the cache line containing the lock will ping-pong between the processors as they perform the atomic operation to acquire the lock. This results in unnecessary bus contention and wastes bus bandwidth, but can be solved using the technique described in the next section.

When cache-aligning data structures and critical resources, it is generally best to pad them so that each occupies its own line (as shown in Figure 7–10). Not only does this reduce misses that result when initially accessing the data structure, but it also prevents *false sharing*. False sharing occurs when two or more different critical resources occupy the same cache line, and they are in simultaneous use by multiple CPUs. This is shown in Section 14.3.2 (Figure 14–4). While the hardware will maintain proper consistency, either an invalidate or update will occur each time one of the processors writes to the line. This can cause the line to ping-pong between the processors and cause unnecessary bus traffic. Padding data structures so that they are aligned on and occupy individual lines eliminates false sharing and unnecessary bus traffic. The disadvantage is wasted memory and cache space.

15.9.2   Reducing Cache Line Contention When Acquiring a Spin Lock

The spin lock implementation as shown in Figure 9–2 repeatedly performs the atomic read-modify-write operation on the lock word until the lock is acquired. This is the correct approach for systems without a cache. However, it can cause the cache line containing the lock word to ping-pong between caches as described in the last section. This can be prevented by changing the implementation of the function that acquires the lock. Notice that the atomic read-modify-write operation cannot possibly acquire the lock while it is held by another processor. It is therefore unnecessary to use such an operation until the lock is freed. Instead, other processors trying to acquire a lock that is in use can simply read the current state of the lock and only use the atomic operation once the lock has been freed. Figure 15–7 gives an alternate implementation of the `lock` function using this technique.

```
void
lock(volatile lock_t *lock_status)
{
        while (test_and_set(lock_status) == 1)
                while (*lock_status == 1)
                        ;
}
```

Figure 15–7: Atomically locking a spin lock.

Here, one attempt is made to acquire the lock before entering the inner loop, which then waits until the lock is freed. The function could be written to read the lock status once before trying the atomic operation at all, but that would be beneficial only if a lock is typically already in use when another CPU wants it. This implies that there is too much lock contention, and the performance of the system would be improved by solving that problem before worrying about cache line contention.

To see how the code in Figure 15–7 affects the caches, assume a MESI protocol is used and that atomic operations are handled as described in Section 15.4. When a CPU attempts to acquire a lock that is already in use, the `test_and_set` function will cause an exclusive copy of the cache line containing the lock to be brought into that processor's cache. The processor will find the lock to be set and will execute in the inner loop until it is freed. If the data structure associated with the lock occupies a different cache line, the processor holding the lock will not be directly affected by this, since other processors won't reference the data structure until they acquire the lock. In the meantime, the processor trying to acquire the lock will perform continuous loads on the lock status word. Since it already has the corresponding line in its cache, no bus traffic will be generated. This is the ideal situation, as the spinning won't waste bus bandwidth or cause contention, and is a distinct advantage of using a hardware cache consistency protocol. If, while this is happening, a second CPU tries to acquire the lock, it will obtain an exclusive copy of the cache line once, then enter the inner loop as well. When the first CPU iterates on the inner loop, it will cache-miss (since the second CPU stole the cache line) and obtain a shared copy of the line since both CPUs are only reading the line. Now both CPUs will spin using the shared copy of the cache line without generating any further bus traffic.

When the lock is eventually freed, the `unlock` function updates the lock word, which causes the consistency protocol to obtain an exclusive copy of the line and invalidates all other copies that might exist. This causes the processors spinning for the lock to miss on their next iteration of the inner loop. The first one to obtain the bus will snoop the updated copy of the line from the processor that released the lock and will find the lock to be free. It will then attempt to acquire the lock for itself. Barring interrupts and other delays in obtaining an exclusive copy of the cache line, it will most likely be able to acquire the lock before the other processors. Any other processors waiting for the lock will see it still locked when they are eventually able to reobtain a copy of the cache line, and they will continue to spin on their cached copy of the line. The advantage of all this is that while trying to acquire a lock, bus transactions will typically be generated only at the points where the lock state changes, allowing processors to compete for the lock during the times when one of them can actually acquire it.

15.9.3 Matching Consistency Protocols to Data Usage

Some processors, such as the MIPS R4000, allow different cache consistency protocols to be used for different pages of memory. Matching the protocol to how the data in the pages will be accessed can reduce unnecessary bus traffic and improve system performance. The R4000 supports five different protocols: uncached, noncoherent, exclusive, shared, and update.

The uncached mode forces all loads and stores to pages so marked to bypass the cache and go to main memory. The processor's private cache is never checked for hits, and other caches in the system do not snoop the bus transactions these loads and stores generate. This mode is intended primarily for use when accessing I/O device control and status registers. As pointed out in Section 3.3.2, large block copy operations may benefit from uncached accesses as well. If it is known that no data from either the source or destination of the copy is cache-resident, then using uncached accesses for the copy operation prevents other useful data from being forced out of the local cache. Since no snooping occurs during such an operation, it must be ensured either that no cached copies of the data exist, or that they are explicitly invalidated to maintain cache consistency.

The noncoherent mode causes the processor to check its private cache for hits, but when misses occur, it reads the data directly from memory without snooping the other caches in the system. In this respect, the cache operates as if it is on a uniprocessor system (and is the appropriate mode to use when the R4000 is placed in that type of system). It is useful for accessing data that is private to the particular processor. It reduces bus traffic because invalidates do not need to be broadcast when a valid line is modified for the first time. Also, snooping can interfere with cache accesses by the CPU, so reducing the number of transactions that need to be snooped reduces cache contention. Examples of processor private data include such things as a separate stack that is used during exception and interrupt handling for that CPU (where each CPU has its own stack), per-CPU statistics, a local run queue, and any other private data structures. It is also useful for kernel text (assuming the kernel doesn't use self-modifying code). It could be used for ordinary user data (data, bss, and stack, but not shared memory), but then explicit flushing would have to be done if the process migrates to another processor. It can be used for user text as long as it is read-only.

The exclusive caching mode operates like a MESI protocol, but without the shared state. Here all data within exclusive pages is made cache consistent by the hardware, but only a single cache may have a copy of a line at any particular time. So if a CPU misses in its cache on a load, other caches snoop the bus transaction, and if a hit occurs in one, it returns the data to the cache that missed and invalidates its own copy. This mode can be useful for data that migrates with a process, such as its u-area and kernel stack. For example, when a process is migrated, it may have cached u-area data on the old CPU. When it resumes on the new CPU and reads this data, it can acquire the data in a state where it can be modified without further bus traffic. On the other hand, using MESI would require two transactions in this case: one to read a shared copy of the line on the first miss, and one to invalidate the old copy when the data is modified. Since the u-area and kernel stack are only referenced by the processor on which the process is currently executing (except possibly during debugging), the exclusive mode results in the fewest bus transactions. It is also a good match for nonshared user data (data, bss, and stack) and saves the explicit flushing that would be needed if noncoherent mode were used instead.

The shared mode implements a MESI protocol. It is suitable for most kernel data structures and user-level shared memory. Write-invalidate is used to maintain consistency. It works best for data structures that may be read by processes on different processors, since shared copies of the lines may be cached by each CPU.

Finally, the update mode implements a write-update protocol. Multiple caches may hold a shared copy of the given data. Whenever one CPU writes to the line, it broadcasts the update on the bus if others have copies. Because it can cause a bus transaction on every store, this mode should be used with care. It is best suited for data that is constantly read by multiple CPUs. In this case, it reduces the bus traffic compared to shared mode since only a single transaction is needed to update all copies. The shared mode would invalidate all copies but one on a store to the data, which then would require that each processor miss and do a bus transaction to read the new value. Examples of data suitable for use with the update mode might include the data that stores the time of day, and the run queue data structures (if the system uses a global run queue). Also, storing the locks in pages that use update mode may improve performance. If multiple processors are spinning on a lock in a shared cache line, such as in the inner loop of code in Figure 15–7, then when the store is issued to free the lock, all others are updated instead of invalidated. As described, this saves bus transactions over MESI. Once the lock is freed, the first processor to acquire the bus will send a second update to set the lock, which again saves bus traffic over write-invalidate protocols.

Matching the protocol to the needs of the data helps in systems that have less elaborate choices than the R4000 as well. Consider the MC68040 described in Section 15.2.1. The only hardware cache consistency protocol it supports is write-through invalidate. The disadvantage of write-through is that it generates a bus transaction on every write. The 68040 allows write-through or write-back to be selected on a per-page basis, with the use of write-back not guaranteeing cache consistency. However, write-back can be used in the cases where the noncoherent mode was used on the R4000. If used for nonshared user data, u-areas, and kernel stacks, it can reduce the amount of bus traffic over write-through. Explicitly flushing the caches on process migration will probably be less expensive in the long run, especially since the 68040 on-chip data cache is only 4K.

15.10 Summary

Hardware cache consistency maintains the consistency of data among the caches and main memory in an MP system without the need for explicit flushing by the software. In a bus-based system, this is accomplished by having each cache snoop the transactions on the bus and take appropriate actions based on the activities of other processors. Since physical addresses are used on the bus, only caches that can be physically indexed can be used with hardware consistency. Snooping and the actions associated with it are transparent to the software.

The cache consistency protocol specifies when the caches need to communicate and what actions they should take. There are two major classes of protocols: write-invalidate and write-update. Both allow multiple caches to hold shared read-only copies of the same data. They differ in the actions taken during writes. Write-invalidate protocols invalidate all other cached copies when one CPU writes to the data. This forces the other processors to miss on their next access and read the updated copy from the cache that modified the data or from main memory. Write-update protocols broadcast each write to shared data on the bus so that all other caches with a copy of that data can update their contents. In either case, stale cache data is eliminated at the point where one CPU modifies it. The same actions maintain consistency of atomic memory operations as well.

Systems that lack a common shared bus, such as those using cross-bar memory interconnects, can still maintain cache consistency in hardware by means of a directory. The directory is associated with main memory and records which CPUs are caching copies of its data, along with the state of the cache lines. This enables the memory module to determine what operations are necessary to maintain consistency. It is then responsible for communicating with the appropriate caches to obtain modified data (in the case of write-back caching), or to invalidate or update data being written by others.

Different cache consistency protocols generate varying amounts of bus traffic to maintain consistency. Each is best suited to certain situations. If the processor supports different cache consistency protocols, the operating system can match them with the expected access pattern of the data. This results in reduced bus communication, and hence less contention. Furthermore, by taking advantage of how the protocol works, the kernel developer can adapt the kernel's algorithms to reduce bus traffic. This is particularly useful in the case of acquiring spin locks, for example, since spinning can generate a rapid stream of memory operations. Likewise, data structures can be aligned on cache line boundaries and padded to eliminate extra misses and the ping-ponging effects of false sharing.

The end result is that the software overhead of maintaining cache consistency as presented in the last chapter is eliminated. For example, user data can be cached without the need to flush it on process migration. Spin locks can be cached, and the kernel does not explicitly have to write back and invalidate its data structures when releasing the locks that protect them. As such, the effect is as with physical caches on uniprocessor systems: they become transparent to the software.

15.11 Exercises

15.1　　Consider an MP system using the write-once protocol. When a cache miss occurs on a load, and the snoop operation hits on a modified line in another cache, it always writes the line back to main memory in addition to sending it to the cache that missed. Since the modified data isn't lost (both caches will now have a copy), why is it necessary to write the modified data to main memory?

15.2　　Does the write-once protocol work (i.e., properly maintain cache consistency) without the reserved state? Explain.

15.3　　Section 15.4 states that atomic read-modify-write instructions may not have to access main memory when using write-back protocols. How does this apply to the write-once protocol? Consider two cases: when the line is in the valid state as the atomic operation begins, and when the line is in the reserved state when it begins. Assume no other processor on the system is accessing the line when the atomic operation is in progress.

15.4　　Explain how the Firefly protocol ensures consistency in the case where two or more processors simultaneously perform an atomic read-modify-write operation to a shared line (i.e., all processors doing the atomic operation have a shared copy of the line).

15.5   Consider a simple protocol for use with write-back caching. Normal write-back semantics are used (i.e., it does not use write-once) in addition to snooping. If a load from one processor hits on a dirty line in another's cache, then that cache supplies the contents of the line (since memory is stale), simultaneously updating memory, and invalidates its own copy. If a store from one processor hits in another's cache (regardless of the line's state), then that cache invalidates its copy. Does this protocol properly maintain cache consistency?

15.6   Draw a state diagram for the protocol described in Exercise 15.5.

15.7   Section 15.9.2 showed that ping-ponging could result when spinning on a lock on a system using a MESI protocol. Would the solution of simply reading the lock status while busy-waiting instead of using the atomic operation be a good idea for systems using write-update protocols? Recall that write-update protocols do not invalidate lines when one CPU modifies them, which prevents ping-ponging from occurring.

15.8   Consider the master–slave MP kernel implementation described in Section 9.4. If the system uses the MIPS R4000, which of the cache protocols described in Section 15.9.3 would you use for each of the kernel data structures? Which protocol(s) would you use for user text, data, stack, bss, and shared memory? Explain your choices.

15.9   Given the semaphore implementation described in Section 11.3, how should the semaphore data structure be aligned and/or padded in the cache? Should the spin lock be stored in the same cache line? What if the semaphore protects a critical resource (as opposed to being used for synchronization purposes)? Should the semaphore be placed in the same line with its resource?

15.10   Draw a state diagram for the write-through invalidate protocol.

15.11   Imagine a system where the primary cache was a virtual cache with keys and the secondary cache was a physical cache. Is it possible to have the hardware maintain the consistency of both? If so, how would this work? Assume the system uses bus-based snooping.

15.12   Consider a system with a secondary cache that supports bus watching, but where the primary cache is not snooped and does not obey the inclusion property. What must the software do to maintain consistency?

15.12 Further Reading

[1]   Agarwal, O.P., and Pohm, A.V., "Cache Memory Systems for Multiprocessor Architectures," *Proceedings of the AFIPS National Computer Conference*, June 1977.

[2]   Agarwal, A., Simoni, R., Hennessy, J., and Horowitz, M., "An Evaluation of Directory Schemes for Cache Coherence," *Proceedings of the 15th Annual International Symposium on Computer Architecture*, June 1988, pp. 280–9.

[3]   Archibald, J., and Baer, J.-L., "An Economical Solution to the Cache Coherence Problem," *Proceedings of the 11th International Symposium on Computer Architecture*, June 1984, pp. 355–62.

[4]   Archibald, J., and Baer, J.-L., "Cache Coherence Protocols: Evaluation Using a Microprocessor Simulation Model," *ACM Transactions on Computer Systems*, Vol. 4, No. 4, November 1986, pp. 273–98.

[5]   Atkinson, R.R., and McCreight, E.M., "The Dragon Processor," *Proceedings of the Second International Conference on Architectural Support for Programming Languages and Operating Systems*, October 1987, pp. 65–71.

[6]   Baer, J.-L., and Wang, W.H., "Architectural Choices for Multi-Level Cache Hierarchies," Technical Report TR-87-01-04, Department of Computer Science, University of Washington, January 1987.

[7]   Baer, J.-L., and Wang, W.H., "On the Inclusion Property for Multi-Level Cache Hierarchies," Technical Report TR-87-11-08, Department of Computer Science, University of Washington, November 1987.

[8]   Barroso, L.A., and Dubois, M., "The Performance of Cache-Coherent Ring-based Multiprocessors," *Proceedings of the 20th Annual International Symposium on Computer Architecture*, May 1993, pp. 268–78.

[9]   Bitar, P., and Despain, A.M., "Multiprocessor Cache Synchronization Issues, Innovations, and Evolution," *Proceedings of the 13th Annual International Symposium on Computer Architecture*, June 1986, pp. 424–33.

[10]   Bolosky, W.J., and Scott, M.L., "False Sharing and its Effect on Shared Memory Performance," *Proceedings of the USENIX Symposium on Experiences with Distributed and Multiprocessor Systems*, September 1993, pp. 57–71.

[11]   Censier, L.M., and Feautrier, P., "A New Solution to Coherence Problems in Multicache Systems," *IEEE Transactions on Computers*, Vol. C-27, No. 12, December 1978, pp. 1112–8.

[12]   Chaiken, D., Fields, C., Kurihara, K., and Agarwal, A., "Directory-Based Cache Coherence in Large-Scale Multiprocessors," *IEEE Computer*, Vol. 23, No. 6, June 1990.

[13]   Colglazier, D.J., "A Performance Analysis of Multiprocessors Using Two-Level Caches," Technical Report CSG-36, Computer Systems Group, University of Illinois, Urbana-Champaign, August 1984.

[14]   Cox, A.L., and Fowler, R.J., "Adaptive Cache Coherency for Detecting Migratory Shared Data," *Proceedings of the 20th International Symposium on Computer Architecture*, May 1993, pp. 98–108.

[15]   Dewan, G., and Nair, V.S.S., "A Case for Uniform Memory Access Multiprocessors," *Computer Architecture News*, Vol. 21, No. 4, September 1993, pp. 20–6.

[16]   Dubois, M., and Briggs, F.A., "Effects of Cache Coherence in Multiprocessors," *Proceedings of the 9th International Symposium on Computer Architecture*, May 1982, pp. 299–308.

[17]   Dubois, M., and Wang, J.-C., "Shared Data Contention in a Cache Coherence Protocol," *Proceedings of the 1988 International Conference on Parallel Processing*, August 1988, pp. 146–55.

[18]   Dubois, M., and Scheurich, C., "Memory Access Dependencies in Shared-Memory Multiprocessors," *IEEE Transactions on Software Engineering*, Vol. 16, No. 6, June 1990, pp. 660–73.

[19]   Dubois, M., Skeppstedt, J., Ricciulli, L., Ramamurthy, K., and Strenstrom, P., "The Detection and Elimination of Useless Misses in MPs," *Proceedings of the 20th International Symposium on Computer Architecture*, May 1993, pp. 88–97.

[20]   Eggers, S., and Katz, R., "Characterization of Sharing in Parallel Programs and Its Application to Coherency Protocol Evaluation," *Proceedings of the 15th Annual International Symposium on Computer Architecture*, June 1988, pp. 373–83.

[21]   Eggers, S., and Katz, R., "Evaluating the Performance of Four Snooping Cache Coherency Protocols," *Proceedings of the 16th Annual International Symposium on Computer Architecture*, 1989, pp. 2–15.

[22]   Eggers, S.J., and Jeremiassen, T.E., "Eliminating False Sharing," *Proceedings of the 1991 International Conference on Parallel Processing*, August 1991, pp. A:377–81.

[23]   Gharachorloo, K., Gupta, A., and Hennessy, J., "Performance Evaluation of Memory Consistency Models for Shared-Memory Multiprocessors," *Proceedings of the Fourth International Conference on Architectural Support for Programming Languages and Operating Systems*, April 1991, pp. 245–57.

[24]   Goodman, J.R., "Using Cache Memory to Reduce Processor-Memory Traffic," *Proceedings of the 10th Annual International Symposium on Computer Architecture*, June 1983, pp. 124–31.

[25]   Goodman, J.R., "Coherency for Multiprocessor Virtual Address Caches," *Second International Conference on Architectural Support for Programming Languages and Operating Systems*, October 1987, pp. 72–81.

[26]   Goodman, J.R., Vernon, M.K., and Woest, P.J., "Efficient Synchronization Primitives for Large-Scale Cache-Coherent Multiprocessors," *Proceedings of the Third International Conference on Architectural Support for Programming Languages and Operating Systems*, April 1989, pp. 64–75.

[27]   Goodman, J.R., and Woest, P., "The Wisconsin Multicube: A New Large-Scale Cache-Coherent Multiprocessor," *Proceedings of the 15th Annual International Symposium on Computer Architecture*, 1988, pp. 422–31.

[28]   Greenberg, A.G., Mitrani, I., and Rudolph, L., "Analysis of Snooping Caches," *Proceedings of Performance 87, 12th International Symposium on Computer Performance*, December 1987.

[29]   Gupta, A., and Weber, W., "Cache Invalidation Patterns in Shared Memory Multiprocessors," *IEEE Transactions on Computers*, Vol. 41, No. 7, July 1992, pp. 794–810.

[30]   Handy, J., *The Cache Memory Book*, Boston, MA: Academic Press, 1993.

[31]   Katz, R.H., Eggers, S.J., Wood, D.A., Perkins, C.L., and Sheldon, R.G., "Implementing a Cache Consistency Protocol," *Proceedings of the 12th Annual International Symposium on Computer Architecture*, June 1985, pp. 276–83.

[32]   Lee., J., and Ramachandran, U., "Synchronization with Multiprocessor Caches," *Proceedings of the 17th International Symposium on Computer Architecture*, 1990, pp. 27–37.

[33]   Lorin, H., *Introduction to Computer Architecture and Organization, Second Edition*, New York: John Wiley & Sons, 1989.

[34]   Mano, M.M., *Computer System Architecture, Third Edition*, Englewood Cliffs, NJ: Prentice Hall, 1993.

[35]   Monier, L., and Shindu, P., "The Architecture of the Dragon," *Proceedings of the 13th IEEE International Conference*, February 1985, pp. 118–21.

[36]   Norton, R.L., and Abraham, J.L., "Using Write Back Cache to Improve Performance of Multiuser Multiprocessors," *Proceedings of the International Conference on Parallel Processing*, 1982.

[37]   Papamarcos, M.S., and Patel, J.H., "A Low Overhead Coherence Solution for Multiprocessors with Private Cache Memories," *Proceedings of the 12th International Symposium on Computer Architecture*, June 1985, pp. 348–54.

[38]   Prete, C.A., "A New Solution of Cache Coherence Protocol for Tightly Coupled Multiprocessor Systems," *Microprocessing and Microprogramming*, Vol. 30, 1990, pp. 207–14.

[39]   Ravishankar, C.V., and Goodman, J., "Cache Implementations for Multiple Processors," *IEEE Spring Compcon Conference*, February 1983.

[40]   Rudolph, L., and Segall, Z., "Dynamic Decentralized Cache Schemes for MIMD Parallel Architectures," *Proceedings of the 11th International Symposium on Computer Architecture*, 1984, pp. 340–7.

[41]   Sites, R.L., and Agarwal, A., "Multiprocessor Cache Analysis Using ATUM," *Proceedings of the 15th International Symposium on Computer Architecture*, June 1988.

[42]   Stenstrom, P., "Reducing Contention in Shared-Memory Multiprocessors," *IEEE Computer*, Vol. 21, No. 11, November 1988, pp. 26–37.

[43]   Stenstrom, P., "A Cache Consistency Protocol for Multiprocessors with Multistage Networks," *Proceedings of the 16th Annual International Symposium on Computer Architecture*, May 1989, pp. 407–15.

[44]   Stenstrom, P., "A Survey of Cache Coherence Schemes for Multiprocessors," *IEEE Computer*, June 1990, pp. 12–24.

[45]   Stenstrom, P., Brorsson, M., and Sandberg, L., "An Adaptive Cache Coherence Protocol Optimized for Migratory Sharing," *Proceedings of the 20th International Symposium on Computer Architecture*, May 1993, pp. 109–118.

[46]   Stone, H.S., *High Performance Computer Architecture, Third Edition*, Reading, MA: Addison-Wesley, 1993.

[47]   Sweazey, P., and Smith, A.J., "A Class of Compatible Cache Consistency Protocols and Their Support by the IEEE Futurebus," *Proceedings of the 13th International Symposium on Computer Architecture*, June 1986, pp. 414–23.

[48]   Tang, C.K., "Cache System Design in the Tightly Coupled Multiprocessor System," *Proceedings of the National Computer Conference (AFIPS)*, June 1976, pp. 749–53.

[49]   Thacker, C.P., "Cache Strategies for Shared-Memory Multiprocessors," *New Frontiers in Computer Architecture*, March 1986, pp. 51–62.

[50]   Thacker, C.P., and Stewart, L.C., "Firefly: A Multiprocessor Workstation," *Proceedings of the Second International Symposium on Architectural Support for Programming Languages and Operating Systems*, October 1987, pp. 164–72.

[51]   Tomasevic, M., and Milutinovic, V., *The Cache Coherence Problem in Shared-Memory Multiprocessors: Hardware Solutions*, Los Alamitos, CA: IEEE Computer Society Press, 1993.

[52]   Torrellas, H., Gupta, A., and Hennessy, J., "Characterizing the Caching and Synchronization Performance of an MP Operating System," *SIGPLAN Notices*, Vol. 27, No. 9, September 1992, pp. 162–74.

[53]   Vernon, M.K., Jog, R., and Sohi, G.S., "Performance Analysis of Hierarchical Cache-Consistent Multiprocessors," *Performance Evaluation*, August 1989, pp. 287–302.

[54]   Wilson, Jr., A.W., "Hierarchical Cache/Bus Architecture for Shared Memory Multiprocessors," *Proceedings of the 14th Annual International Symposium on Computer Architecture*, June 1987, pp. 244–52.

[55]   Yen, W.C., Yen, W.L., and Fu, K.-S., "Data Coherence Problem in a Multicache System," *IEEE Transactions on Computers*, Vol. C-34, No. 1, January 1985, pp. 56–65.

A

Architecture
Summary

This appendix provides a summary of the cache organization of the processors and systems used as examples throughout this book. It also includes relevant MP information regarding the MP cache consistency protocol and atomic instructions. All processors use the sequential memory model (strong ordering), except the TI SuperSPARC.

Apollo DN 4000

A uniprocessor system produced in the late 1980s that used the Motorola 68020, which lacked on-chip caches. The external cache was organized as:

cache type: virtual with keys, unified
cache size: 8K
set size: direct mapped
line size: 4 bytes
key size: 3 bits
write policy: write-through with write-allocate
replacement policy: direct mapped
notes: tags contain modified bit and user/kernel bit
reference: Frink, C.R., and Roy, P.J., "The Cache Architecture of the Apollo DN4000," *Proceedings of the Spring COMPCON*, March 1988, pp. 300–2.

Intel 80386

no on-chip caches

Intel 80486

cache type: physical, unified
cache size: 8K
set size: 4-way set associative
line size: 16 bytes
write policy: write-through, no write-allocate
replacement policy: pseudo-LRU
MP consistency protocol: write-through invalidate
atomic instruction: swap-atomic (mnemonic: **xchg**), can also lock the bus for an indivisible sequence of operations (mnemonics: **lock**, **unlock**)
reference: *Intel 486 Microprocessor Family Programmer's Reference Manual*, Intel order #240486, 1992.

Intel 82495DX

An external cache controller for use with the Intel 80486.

cache type:	physical, unified
cache size:	128K, 256K, or 512K
set size:	2-way set associative
line size:	16, 32, 64, or 128 bytes
write policy:	write-back with write-allocate
replacement policy:	LRU
MP consistency protocol:	MESI
reference:	*Introduction to the 50MHz Intel 486 DX CPU-Cache Subsystem Architectural Overview*, Intel order #241085.

Intel Pentium

cache type:	physical, separate instruction and data caches
cache size:	8K each
set size:	2-way set associative
line size:	32 bytes
write policy:	selectable write-back with write-allocate, or write-through
replacement policy:	LRU
MP consistency protocol:	MESI
atomic instruction:	swap-atomic (mnemonic: **xchg**), can also lock the bus for an indivisible sequence of operations (mnemonics: **lock, unlock**)
reference:	*Pentium Processor User's Manual Volume 3: Architecture and Programming Manual*, Intel order #241430, 1993.

Intel i860 XR

cache type:	virtual, separate instruction and data caches
cache size:	8K data cache, 4K instruction cache
set size:	2-way set associative
line size:	32 bytes
write policy:	write-back with write-allocate
replacement policy:	LRU
MP consistency protocol:	none
atomic instruction:	bus can be locked for an indivisible sequence of operations (mnemonics: **lock, unlock**)
reference:	*Intel i860 XR 64-Bit Microprocessor*, Intel order #240296, 1992.

Intel i860 XP

cache type:	virtual, separate instruction and data caches
cache size:	16K each
set size:	4-way set associative
line size:	32 bytes
write policy:	selectable write-back with write-allocate, write-through, or write-once
replacement policy:	random if all lines in set are valid
MP consistency protocol:	MESI
atomic instruction:	bus can be locked for an indivisible sequence of operations (mnemonics: **lock**, **unlock**)
notes:	caches contain physical tags for snooping and alias detection
reference:	*Intel i860 XP Microprocessor Data Book*, Intel order #240874, 1991.

MIPS R2000/R3000

No on-chip caches. An external cache is controlled instead.

cache type:	physical, separate instruction and data caches
cache size:	64K each
set size:	direct mapped
line size:	4 bytes
write policy:	write-back with write-allocate
replacement policy:	direct mapped
MP consistency protocol:	none
atomic instruction:	none
reference:	Kane, G., and Heinrich, J., *MIPS RISC Architecture*, Englewood Cliffs, NJ: Prentice Hall, 1992.

MIPS R4000

On-chip caches:

cache type:	virtual with physical tags, separate instruction and data caches
cache size:	8K each
set size:	direct mapped
line size:	16 or 32 bytes
write policy:	write-back with write-allocate
replacement policy:	direct mapped

External caches:

cache type:	physical, separate instruction and data caches or unified cache
cache size:	128K to 4M
set size:	direct mapped
line size:	16, 32, 64, or 128 bytes
write policy:	write-back with write-allocate
replacement policy:	direct mapped
notes:	tags contain primary cache index for snooping and alias detection

MP consistency protocol:	choice of MESI, write-update, or write-invalidate exclusive (same as MESI without the S state)
atomic instruction:	load-linked (mnemonic: **ll**), store-conditional (mnemonic: **sc**)
reference:	Heinrich, J., *MIPS R4000 Users Manual*, Englewood Cliffs, NJ: Prentice Hall, 1993.

Motorola 68040

cache type:	physical, separate instruction and data caches
cache size:	4K
set size:	4-way set associative
line size:	16 bytes
write policy:	selectable write-back with write-allocate, or write-through
replacement policy:	random if all lines in set are valid
MP consistency protocol:	write-through, invalidate
atomic instruction:	test and set (mnemonic: **tas**), compare and swap (mnemonics: **cas, cas2**)
reference:	*Motorola 68040 32-Bit Microprocessor User's Manual*, Phoenix, AZ: Motorola Literature Distribution, 1989.

Motorola 88000

The 88100 is the CPU chip, while the 88200 contains the MMU and on-chip cache. A complete system consists of one 88100 and two to eight 88200 chips. Minimally, one 88200 is needed for instructions, and one for data, giving the effect of separate caches. Each 88200 contains a single on-chip cache.

cache type:	physical
cache size:	16K
set size:	4-way set associative
line size:	16 bytes
write policy:	selectable write-once with write-allocate, or write-through
replacement policy:	pseudo-LRU
MP consistency protocol:	write-once
atomic instruction:	swap-atomic (mnemonic: **xmem**)
reference:	*Motorola MC88100 RISC Microprocessor User's Manual*, Englewood Cliffs, NJ: Prentice Hall, 1990.
	Motorola MC88200 Cache/Memory Management Unit User's Manual, Englewood Cliffs, NJ: Prentice Hall, 1990.

Sun 3/200

A Motorola 680X0-based uniprocessor system produced in the late 1980s that lacked on-chip caches. The external cache was organized as:

cache type:	virtual with keys, unified
cache size:	64K
set size:	direct mapped
line size:	16 bytes
key size:	3 bits
write policy:	write-back with write-allocate
replacement policy:	direct mapped
reference:	Cheng, R., "Virtual Address Cache in UNIX," *Proceedings of the Summer USENIX Conference*, June 1987, pp. 217–24.

Texas Instruments MicroSPARC

Data cache:

cache type:	physical
cache size:	2K
set size:	direct mapped
line size:	16 bytes
write policy:	write-through, no write-allocate
replacement policy:	direct mapped

Instruction cache:

cache type:	physical
cache size:	4K
set size:	direct mapped
line size:	32 bytes
write policy:	n/a
replacement policy:	direct mapped

MP consistency protocol:	none
atomic instructions:	swap-atomic (mnemonics: **swap**, **ldstub**)
reference:	*Texas Instruments TMS390S10 MicroSPARC Reference Guide*, 1992.

Texas Instruments SuperSPARC

On-chip data cache:

cache type:	physical
cache size:	16K
set size:	4-way set associative
line size:	32 bytes
write policy:	write-through, no write-allocate when using MCC secondary cache controller, otherwise write-back with write-allocate is used
replacement policy:	pseudo-LRU

On-chip instruction cache:

cache type:	physical
cache size:	20K
set size:	5-way set associative
line size:	64 bytes
write policy:	n/a
replacement policy:	pseudo-LRU

MCC (MultiCache Controller) external cache:

cache type:	physical, unified
cache size:	512K, 1M, or 2M
set size:	direct mapped
line size:	128 or 256 bytes
write policy:	write-back with write-allocate
replacement policy:	direct mapped

MP consistency protocol:	MESI
atomic instructions:	swap-atomic (mnemonics: **swap**, **ldstub**)
reference:	*Texas Instruments SuperSPARC User's Guide*, 1992.

B

Answers to Selected Exercises

Chapter 1

1.1   Text is shared read-only. Therefore, a store to the text segment would result in a protection fault occurring. Copy-on-write is never used for text during a fork operation. The only time it is allowed to be modified is during program debugging when the debugger inserts a breakpoint into the text. When this occurs, text sharing ends so that other processes executing the same program are not affected by the breakpoint.

1.2   It's possible to shrink a process's stack by deallocating the unused pages. By convention, the contents of memory beyond the current top of stack are undefined. On almost all architectures, the current top of stack pointer is kept in a well-defined register. Therefore, the kernel can read its contents and deallocate any unused pages as needed. The reason that this is not done is that little is gained by the effort. If it's the case that the user program will repeatedly call subroutines that need additional space for local variables (a very likely case), then much time will be wasted deallocating stack space in between calls and then reallocating it later on. If it's the case that the subroutine called is only used once during the life of the program and no other subroutine will ever be called that needs the stack space, then eventually the kernel will page out the unused portions of the space if it needs the memory for other purposes. In either case, the extra logic needed to recognize the case where a stack could be shrunk is unwarranted.

1.3   After process C forks, the mappings are as shown in Figure B-1 (all mappings are read-only). The child of C simply shares the same physical pages as the other two with copy-on-write. If C were to exit immediately after the fork of its child, then the mappings of process A and process C's child would be unaffected. Once a process has a copy-on-write mapping to a page, it only changes to read-write when the process itself attempts to modify the page. Activities by other processes have no effect.

1.4   If copy-on-write is used, then no physical pages are allocated, since the new child will share the parent's pages. If copy-on-write is not used, then the parent's entire address space must be copied to the child with the exception of the text region, since it is always shared read-only. Therefore, seven physical pages will be needed for the child's data, bss, and stack if copy-on-write is not used.

1.6   The last step of a buffered read operation is to copy the requested data from the kernel's buffer into the user's buffer. When the kernel does this, a protection fault will occur since the page(s) are being shared read-only. A new copy of the affected page(s) will be allocated for the child, and the copy operation associated with the `read` will complete. The main point is that it does not matter whether pages being shared with copy-on-write are modified by the user or the kernel. The same

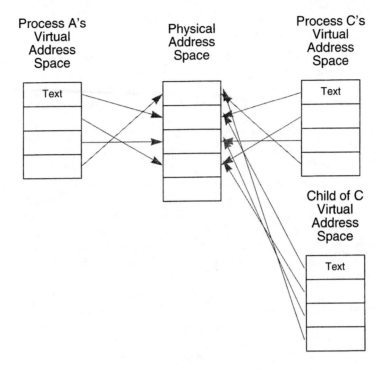

Figure B-1: Memory mappings after process C forks.

processing must occur in either case. Nothing need be done if a `write` system call is done instead, since this causes data to be copied from the user's buffer into the kernel's. No modifications to the user's data are made, so copy-on-write sharing continues unaffected.

1.10   When the child releases pages in its bss segment, copy-on-write sharing ends for those pages. When the child resets the break address back to its previous value, the kernel allocates new virtual memory for the child, which will have no relationship to the parent's. The child does not regain copy-on-write sharing of the parent's pages even though the virtual addresses are the same. When the child accesses or modifies these pages, new physical memory will be allocated.

Chapter 2

2.1   Any memory mapped hardware device should be accessed with uncached references. This includes I/O device control and status registers, as well as devices such as video and graphics frame buffers. Also, any type of volatile data in memory (data that can be simultaneously modified by the CPU and other hardware in the system) should be referenced with uncached accesses.

2.2   The memory devices used to construct the cache will power up with random contents, therefore the valid bits, address portion of the tags, and the data portion of the line will all contain meaningless, random values. If the CPU were to reference an address that happened to match the tag in a line where the valid bit was on, then a hit would occur and the cache would return the random data in the data portion of the line instead of going to main memory. This would be an extremely bad situation since the cache would power up with different contents each time, causing unpredictable and nondeterministic behavior. When the system is powered up, either the hardware or software must clear all the valid bits in the cache before it is used, so that the random contents of the lines will not affect the system.

2.3   Each line needs a tag to identify the main memory address of its contents. Many different addresses will all hash to generate the same index. The tag is therefore needed to uniquely identify the contents of the line. Likewise, each line within a set needs its own tag. It is important to understand that while consecutive bytes within a cache line are always from consecutive memory locations, and therefore do not need individual tags, there is no such relationship between the addresses in consecutive cache lines.

2.4   There are only 8 bits in <9..2>, meaning that the hashing algorithm would only be capable of indexing 2^8 or 256 cache lines. Since the cache instead has 512 lines and is direct mapped, half the lines could never be indexed and would be completely wasted. A 9-bit index is needed to address all 512 lines. If the cache were two-way set associative, then this would be a good hashing algorithm if the cache had four-byte lines, where bits <1..0> select the byte within the line.

2.6   No, it is not a good hashing algorithm, since only 64 cache lines would be used by the typical program. This is because the cache index is generated from the high-order two digits of the addresses from 0x1000 to 0x4fff. These addresses index lines 0x10 through 0x4f, 64 lines in total. This means that only 1024 bytes (64 lines * 16 bytes/per line) in the cache would be used for all references to the 16K region, causing 15K of the cache to be wasted. Increasing the set size to 16 eliminates this problem because this increases the number of lines that can be stored for each cache index by a factor of 16. Now the entire 16K memory region will map into a unique line within the 16K cache.

2.7   A two-way set associative cache with 4096 lines will have 2048 sets. The hashing algorithm must therefore generate an index in the range of 0 to 2047, requiring 11 bits. Since the line size is 16 bytes, the low-order four bits of the address (bits <3..0>) will select the byte within the line. For the best distribution of data in the cache, assuming good locality of reference, the next 11 bits above these should be used. So, bits <14..4> would be the best choice for the hashing algorithm. The tag portion of the line must hold all bits that have not yet been used. This would be bits <31..15>, so 17 bits are needed.

The percentage savings is calculated as follows. First the total cache size using the data just given is computed. Each line contains 16 bytes of data (16 × 8 bits/byte = 128 bits), 11 bits of address tag, 1 valid bit, and 1 modified bit (since it's a write-back cache), for a total of 141 bits per line. (An important point of this question is not to overlook the valid and modified bits.) There are 4096 lines, so 4096 × 141 = 577,536 bits. If the full address were saved in the tags, then each line would need 128 bits for the data, 32 bits for the address, 1 valid bit, and 1 modified bit, for a total of 162 bits per line and 663,552 bits for the entire cache. Therefore, storing on the minimum number of address bits saves about 13 percent.

2.9   For 4-byte lines:

$$\frac{2048 \text{ bytes}}{4 \text{ bytes/line}} = 512 \text{ lines} = 2^9 \Rightarrow 9\text{-bit line index}$$

Since 2 bits will index the byte within the line, then 9 + 2 = 11 address bits used for line indexing, leaving 32 − 11 = 21 address bits needed in the line tag. The total cache size is

$$
\begin{array}{rl}
21 & \text{address bits in tag} \\
1 & \text{valid bit} \\
+ \ 32 & \text{data bits/line} \\
\hline
54 & \text{bits/line} \\
\times \ 512 & \text{lines} \\
\hline
27{,}648 & \text{bits}
\end{array}
$$

For 32-byte lines:

$$\frac{2048 \text{ bytes}}{32 \text{ bytes/line}} = 64 \text{ lines} = 2^6 \Rightarrow 6\text{-bit line index}$$

Five bits are needed to select the byte within the line, so $6 + 5 = 11$ address bits have been used for indexing, leaving $32 - 11 = 21$ bits in the tags. The total cache size for this case is

$$
\begin{array}{rl}
21 & \text{address bits in tag} \\
1 & \text{valid bit} \\
+\ 256 & \text{data bits/line} \\
\hline
278 & \text{bits/line} \\
\times\ 64 & \text{lines} \\
\hline
17{,}792 & \text{bits}
\end{array}
$$

Thus, using 32-byte lines saves 36 percent in terms of the number of bits needed to construct the two different cache organizations, even though both store the same amount of data. This shows one of the benefits of longer line sizes: it reduces the number of cache lines, and therefore the number of bits used for control and tag information. Another advantage of longer line sizes is a better hit ratio for programs with good spatial locality. This is commonly the case for instruction references, since they tend to be sequential. The longer line size effectively prefetches more sequential instructions with each miss, reducing the overall number of misses over a cache with a smaller line size.

The advantage of smaller line sizes is a potentially better hit ratio for programs with good temporal locality, but poor spatial locality. This is because the cache contains more individually indexed and tagged lines, meaning data from more different addresses can be cached simultaneously. The 4-byte line size alternative has 8 times as many lines.

In general, the 32-byte line size would be the preferred choice, since it reduces hardware costs and can increase the hit ratio for programs with reasonable locality of reference.

2.13   The desired operation is an instruction that causes a cache line to be made valid and zero-filled without reading the contents of main memory. This is relatively easy to implement in hardware as it's similar to normal miss processing. The instruction takes the address of a memory location, and if that address misses in the cache, then normal miss processing occurs with respect to line replacement and write-back. But then, instead of reading the data at that address from main memory, the cache line is loaded with zeros, and the modified and valid bits are both set. No further action is needed to zero the memory on the part of the program. The result is that an entire cache line's worth of data can be zeroed with one single instruction and without referencing memory. The external cache controller on the TI SuperSPARC has support for such a facility.

Chapter 3

3.1   The full 32-bit address can be constructed using the portion stored in the tags and inferring the remaining bits by the line's position in the cache. The upper 14 bits from the tags are concatenated with the 14-bit cache index of the line being replaced. This reliably yields the upper 28 bits of the address since only those addresses where bits <17..4> indexed the line in question could be stored there. Since the lines hold 16 consecutive bytes from memory, the low-order four bits of the address can be generated according to which particular byte or word is being stored back to main memory.

3.2   a. Cache is consistent with main memory.

Line	Tag	Data
		⋮
0x200	0x2000	9876
		⋮
0x400	0x4000	9876
		⋮

b. Cache is not consistent with main memory.

Line	Tag	Data
		⋮
0x200	0x2000	9876
		⋮
0x400	0x4000	1234
		⋮

3.3   No, it doesn't matter whether write-through or write-back caching is used; it is guaranteed that the cache will always return the correct results. Since the cache is direct mapped and both aliases always index the same set of lines, the data will be consistent. Referencing one alias while the other is cached will cause a miss and will read the data from main memory. If write-through caching is used, memory will always be up to date and so the correct data will be read on a miss. If write-back caching is used, any modified data will be written to main memory when the miss occurs, which will subsequently reread the correct data to complete the miss.

3.8   Since the address space has been split between the user and the kernel, the high-order bit can be used to identify which portion of the address space is accessible. If a process running in user mode references an address where the high-order bit is set, then the hardware can immediately generate a trap before the cache is accessed. This prevents a process from accessing cached kernel data. Since user data stored in the cache has the high-order bit clear, then this data can never be mistaken for kernel data either.

3.10   None is needed since new virtual memory is allocated. This is conceptually the same as when sbrk allocates new memory. Since the newly allocated space was previously inaccessible to the process, it could have no cached data corresponding to that space.

3.11   In most UNIX kernel implementations, nothing need be done to a virtual cache when swapping pages out. Typically the kernel uses a separate process to handle swap outs. It chooses pages to be swapped based on reference history, and then performs the I/O to swap them out. Since these activities occur in a separate process, at least one context switch must occur before they are done. The cache flushing at context switch time ensures that main memory is up to date before the swap-out process can run; therefore, it is safe to do DMA from main memory out to the swap device. Before the swap-out process allows other processes to run again, it turns off the valid bits on the pages being swapped. This prevents a process whose pages are being swapped out from accessing them while DMA is in progress.

3.14   If a cachable page is changed to be uncached, then the cache must be flushed (validating main memory and invalidating the cache). Since the data from the page was previously cachable, some of it could be in the cache. Changing the page to be uncachable prevents the data associated with future misses from being cached, but does nothing for the data already in the cache. When the CPU does a load or store, most implementations access the cache before the MMU can check the cachability flag in the page tables. If a hit occurs, the data is returned to the CPU immediately. Therefore, the cached data from the page will remain cached until it is replaced, even though the page is marked as uncached.

Chapter 4

4.1   The key size is irrelevant when computing the bits needed for the address portion of the tags. The purpose of keys is to disambiguate identical virtual addresses from different processes. The cache still needs to identify fully the address stored in the line. So bits <3..0> will select the byte within the line, the next 9 bits (<12..4>) will select the set (1024 lines ÷ 2 lines per set = 512 sets = 2^9). That uses $4 + 9 = 13$ bits of the address, leaving 19 bits unused (bits <31..13>). Therefore, 19 bits are needed in the address portion of the tags. The number of bits is constant regardless of the key size.

4.2   A useful flush operation for a virtual cache with keys would be the ability to flush by key. With such an operation, one would specify a key and all lines tagged with that key would be written back to main memory (for a write-back cache) and/or invalidated from the cache. This would be very useful in cases such as `exec` or `exit`, where the entire address space is being deallocated and must be flushed. The Sun system described in this chapter provided this capability.

4.4   LRU would be an excellent algorithm for key reassignment in these circumstances. The least recently used key would have the fewest cache entries since all the processes that have run in the meantime would probably have forced all its entries out of the cache (except possibly for large caches). The process that owned the least recently used key would therefore have the least to lose in terms of cached data. This assumes that the cache has a flush-by-address or -key capability that only flushes the line if the address and key hit. The cache must still be flushed when reassigning the key to guarantee that no entries from the old process remain. If the cache only implements a flush-by-line capability that unconditionally flushes a line regardless of the key and address tag, no savings would be realized by using the LRU key.

4.6   It is possible for the parent and child to share the same key while they are sharing *all* pages in the address space with copy-on-write. The key sharing would have to end as soon as the first copy-on-write copy of a page was made. At that point different keys are needed since the virtual addresses in both processes no longer completely map to the same set of physical pages. Such a technique would make the fork system call appear to run faster since it wouldn't need to allocate a new key or flush the cache at that time. However, the overhead would be incurred on the first copy-on-write fault. It is highly unlikely that neither process will modify its address space before the child execs, so no net performance gain will be seen.

4.8   It is trivial for the kernel to handle the caching concerns for vfork properly. Since both the parent and child are completely sharing the same address space, they can both use the same cache key. This allows the child to reference any data the parent had cached directly, and causes any data the child brings into the cache to be tagged with the parent's key so that it will hit on the same data. Sharing the same key works for write-through and write-back, as well as for caches with any number of lines per set. A new key must be assigned to the child when it execs. If the child exits, the cache invalidation that is normally done must be skipped since the parent is still using the key.

4.11   Since the child process has its own address space (even if copy-on-write is used), the kernel must assign it a unique TLB key. If copy-on-write is used, the child will initially receive a copy of its parent's mappings. Giving the parent and child a unique key allows each process to modify its address space independently. Furthermore, when copy-on-write sharing is initiated, the parent's mappings are changed to read-only. Since the TLB could be caching mappings with write permission enabled, these must be flushed before the parent returns to user mode.

4.15   The simplest approach is to load both key registers with the same key at context switch time. The behavior of the caches is then the same as described throughout the chapter. Another possibility is to use different keys. Since the instruction cache contains read-only data, it is possible for all processes sharing the same text to use the same key for the instruction cache. In this way, one key would be assigned to each shared text segment. Each process would still use a unique key in the data cache. With this approach, instructions fetched from a shared text segment would be shared in the cache among all processes using that text key, possibly improving the hit ratio in the instruction cache. There are several disadvantages to this approach, however. First, if the cache is direct mapped and the shared text segments use the same virtual addresses, then they will likely replace each other in the cache and reduce, or eliminate, the potential improvements. Second, if processes use more than one shared text segment at a time, such as using one or more shared libraries in addition to the program's text, then the set of shared text segments that a program uses will have to be treated as a single unit for caching considerations. This is because there is only a single key for all instruction fetches a process makes. The effect of this will be that the shared library text will be replicated in the cache, since each different program that uses the same shared library will use a separate key when executing from it. Finally, this approach cannot be used if the program uses self-modifying code. If it fetches instructions from its data area, then those instructions will be cached in the instruction cache with the key of the shared text segment. If another process is executing the same program, then it could generate a hit on instructions that came from another process's address space.

Last, note that there is no advantage to assigning two unique keys to each process, where one is used for each cache. Using the same key in both caches accomplishes the same result.

Chapter 5

5.1   No, it does not. A virtual cache with physical tags is indexed with the virtual address and tagged with the physical address. A fully associative cache does not do any indexing, so an index derived from the virtual address is meaningless. With a fully associative cache, the only issue is how the lines are tagged.

5.2   With this cache organization, bits <3..0> will select the byte within the line. Bits <11..4> will select one of the 256 sets. Since all these bits are part of the page offset (bits <11..0>), and since the page offset is the same in the virtual and physical addresses, this cache should be considered a physical cache. No bits from the virtual page number are used to index the cache.

5.6   The problem that occurred with n-way set associative virtual caches with keys was due to aliasing. Even though the virtual addresses were the same, each process used a different key, which prevented one process from generating a hit when referencing data cached by the other when copy-on-write sharing was in effect. This meant that a different line within the set could be referenced. With a virtual cache with physical tags, two processes sharing data with copy-on-write are guaranteed to hit on each other's data in the cache, since they are both using the same virtual and physical address. No alias occurs and so the number of lines in the set is irrelevant.

5.8   Yes, the flushing can be safely postponed. When the shared memory region or mapped file is detached from the process's address space, the mappings will be changed so that these pages can no longer be accessed. Future references will cause a trap from the MMU before the cache access is complete.

5.9   Whenever a modified line is replaced in a write-back cache, it must be written back to main memory. When using a virtual cache with physical tags, the cache can construct the physical address to write the data back to without using the MMU. Therefore, no traps will occur because the cache stored data to a location that is not within a process's address space. Since the physical pages being written back to are not in use, there is no danger of corrupting another process's data. As stated in Section 5.2.5, the cache must be flushed before the pages are allocated to a new use.

Chapter 6

6.1   One acceptable drawing is shown in Figure B-2. The important aspects are as follows. No bits from the VPN may be used to index the cache. The address must first be translated so that bits <13..5> from the physical address can be used for the index. The index is formed by concatenating bits from the PPN and page offset (remember the page offset is the same in both the virtual and physical addresses). Also, it is unnecessary to store bits <13..11> in the tags as was needed for physically tagged virtual caches, since these bits have already been used during indexing and so would be redundant.

6.2   One could build a system that functioned in this manner, but it would not be desirable. The reason is that systems usually run different processes while transferring data for others. Loading all this data into the cache would force out the currently executing process's locality of reference, resulting in very poor cache performance. It is better to allow the process that read the data to establish a locality of reference within the data when it executes. This way the portions of the data that are not presently part of the locality of reference do not take up precious space in the cache.

        Secondly, this would be very difficult to implement for write-back caches. If the data from the read were to replace a modified line, then the modified data would have to be written back to main memory. The problem is that the bus is already in use by the DMA operation and so the data to be written back would need to be temporarily saved somewhere before being written back. This problem is compounded by the fact that many such replacements may occur during a single DMA read.

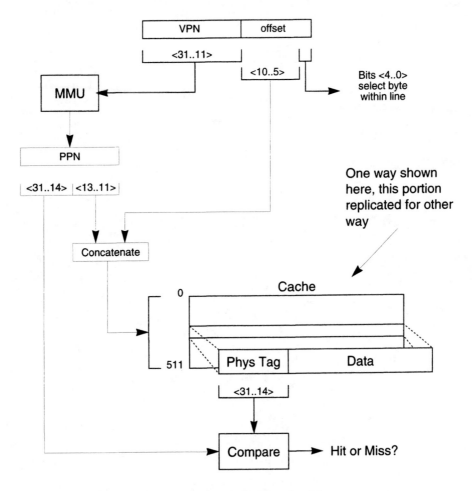

Figure B-2: Answer for Exercise 6.1.

6.4   One of the important aspects of this problem is to be sure all address bits get used. In particular, bits <11..10> need to be properly handled as shown, since they are neither translated by the MMU, nor used to index the set. Four-way set associative caches are generally built by running four direct mapped caches in parallel, one for each set. Therefore the cache and comparator shown in Figure B-3 are replicated four times (although only shown in the diagram once).

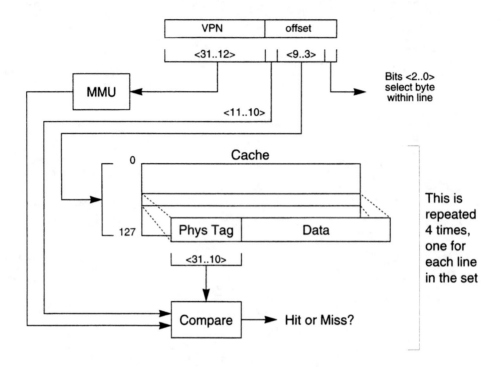

Figure B-3: Answer for Exercise 6.4.

6.5   Yes, it would work. If the cache were fully associative, it would simply mean that
        all lines are checked during each snoop operation. No indexing is done for a fully
        associative cache, so the need to derive an index from the page offset is
        eliminated.

6.7   It should be written into the secondary cache. It is neither necessary nor desirable
        to write the data to main memory. First, since the primary cache is always a subset
        of the secondary cache, it is guaranteed that the secondary cache already contains
        a copy of the primary cache line. So a miss in the secondary cache during a pri-
        mary cache line write-back is impossible. Second, writing it into the secondary
        cache is faster than accessing main memory. Third, the data being replaced may
        still be in the process's locality of reference, so it makes sense to continue to cache
        it in the secondary cache.

6.9   The secondary cache line that currently contains data from location 0x1000 must
        be replaced in order to complete the miss. Before doing so, however, the data as-
        sociated with this location must be written back (if necessary) and invalidated

from both the primary and secondary caches. The primary cache line must be written and invalidated even though it is not being replaced during this miss since it would otherwise contain data not present in the secondary cache. This is not allowed in the R4000 cache consistency model since bus watching and alias detection will no longer work reliably. The primary cache must always be a subset of the secondary, so whenever a secondary cache line is replaced, any primary cache lines associated with it must be removed. Once these lines are written back and invalidated, the new data may be loaded into both the primary and secondary caches. The index in the cache tags of the secondary cache line will be set to the new primary cache line index.

6.11   No, it would not work. The index in the secondary cache tags contains the index of the last primary line that held the data; however, that primary cache line may no longer contain data from the secondary cache line. Since the primary cache is smaller, lines in the primary will be replaced more frequently. The R4000 identifies this case by checking to see if the physical tag on the indexed primary line matches the physical tag of the secondary line. Since a virtual cache with keys does not contain the physical address, this test cannot be done.

6.13   No, it wouldn't be necessary. The index in the secondary cache tags is only needed when indexing a virtual primary cache. If the primary is physical, then the same physical address used to index in the secondary cache can be used to index the primary.

Chapter 7

7.1   If we assume that there is no self-modifying code in the application (i.e., instructions are never executed out of the data or stack region), then any virtual address may be chosen for the standard text region starting address, since none of the other regions will ever cause contention in the separate instruction cache.

Next, notice that it is impossible to prevent the data and stack regions from overlapping in the data cache, since the sum of their maximum sizes exceeds the cache size. In addition, since the address bits used to index the cache all fall within the page offset, it is impossible to choose page aligned region addresses that start anywhere other than on cache line zero. Because of this, any addresses can be chosen for the data and stack addresses without having any effect on cache line contention. The use of four-way set associative caching will help reduce the possibility of cache thrashing.

7.4   Pure virtual caches cannot maintain any process context across context switches. There is therefore nothing to be gained (as far as reducing cache line contention goes) in adding the overhead of dynamic address binding. There is simply no need to distribute the cache references from different processes when no more than one process context can be cached at a time.

      The technique does not apply to physical caches either, since the virtual address is irrelevant when computing a physical cache index. So even though a physical cache can cache multiple process contexts, distributing the virtual addresses would not reduce cache contention.

7.5   Since all cache index bits come from the page offset, the cache has one color.

7.9   Delayed cache invalidation techniques are only applicable to caches that are capable of storing multiple process contexts simultaneously. It is impossible to postpone any cache flushing with virtual caches since the tags do not contain the information needed to prevent stale data from being accessed. This is what causes them to be so prone to alias and ambiguity problems.

7.10 Delayed cache invalidation can be used with shared memory detaches and shrinking sbrks as long as the cache uses physical tags. Such caches always translate the virtual address while accessing the cache, and so the MMU page protections can be used to prevent access to portions of the virtual address that have been detached, but may still be cached. A virtual cache with keys does not use the MMU during the cache access, and so there is nothing to prevent a hit from occurring on cached data from the detached region. Therefore, delayed invalidation cannot be used in these cases.

7.12 Four bytes should be added to each entry in the array. This way each pair of entries in the array will evenly fit within one cache line. The goal is to prevent any one entry from occupying more than a single line. So padding each entry to be a full cache line is wasteful and incorrect for a uniprocessor. (There may be cases in multiprocessor systems with caches where padding each entry to a full cache line is appropriate. Cases where individual entries are typically only accessed by one processor at a time are examples.)

Chapter 8

8.1   Since I/O devices share the bus with the CPUs, their accesses are handled no differently from CPU accesses. The bus will sequentialize simultaneous accesses by CPUs and I/O devices. The exact ordering will be nondeterministic.

8.3   The value in location 0x100 will be 1 after CPU 1 finishes its store. The fact that CPU 2 is reading from that location will have no effect on the outcome of the store operation. There is no way to predict what value CPU 2 will read. As with all simultaneous accesses, the bus will sequentialize them in some nondeterministic order. If the bus chooses to service the read from CPU 2 before CPU 1's write, then it will read 10. Otherwise it will read the new value of 1.

8.4   For the purposes of the discussions in this book, only one transaction may be in progress on the bus at any given time. (High-performance SMP systems use techniques such as "split reads" that allow multiple read operations to different memory locations to be in progress simultaneously.)

8.5   The minimum time occurs in the ideal case when the bus is idle when the request is made. In this case, the transaction can start immediately, so the minimum time is zero. (Some system buses are clocked in such a way that each transaction must begin on a certain clock signal. So even if the bus is idle, then the requestor may still have to wait for up to one time unit before the beginning of the next cycle. Therefore, an answer of 1 is also acceptable given these assumptions.) The maximum time is simply the time needed to service one bus transaction from each CPU and I/O device. Since there are 15 total devices on the bus, an arbitrary one may have to wait for up to 14 time units before its request will be serviced. The maximum cannot be higher than this since round-robin scheduling is used and each device is allowed only one transaction at a time.

8.6
```
int test_and_set(int *addr)
{
    int state;

    do
        state = load_linked(addr);
    while (store_conditional(addr, 1) == 0);

    return (state != 0);
}
```

8.9   The technique to solving this problem is to temporarily store a flag in the word (−1 in this example, since the count never goes negative) to synchronize multiple processes trying to increment the same word. This requires the use of a special function to read the value.

```
void inc_atomic(int *addr)
{
    int value;

    while ((value = swap_atomic(addr, -1)) == -1)
        ;

    *addr = value + 1;
}

int read_counter(int *addr)
{
    int value;

    while ((value = *addr) == -1)
        ;

    return value;
}
```

8.10   Yes, it contains a race condition. If two (or more) processors execute the function simultaneously, then both will set the `next` pointer in their respective new list elements to the current value in `list`. They will then both try to store the address of their new elements into `list`. The bus will sequentialize these stores, causing the first one to be overwritten by the second. This will cause the new element being inserted by the processor that stored first to be lost.

8.13   Most uniprocessor UNIX kernel implementations do at least one of two things to guarantee that a process waiting for a lock is not starved forever. First, the sleep function is implemented as a FIFO linked list. When the code to unlock an object wakes up all processes sleeping for that lock, the processes are placed on the run queue in the order they slept, causing the one sleeping the longest to be run ahead of the others. This guarantees that the one that slept first has the first chance at getting the lock. Second, the scheduler can be implemented so that a process's priority increases over time if it wakes up only to find the lock already taken and goes immediately back to sleep. This will cause the oldest such process to have the highest priority and hence the first chance to acquire the lock over the other processes that came along after it.

Chapter 9

9.1
```
void lock(volatile lock_t *lock_status)
{
    do {
        while (load_linked(lock_status) == 1)
            ;
    } while (store_conditional(lock_status, 1) == 0);
}
```

The code for unlock is unchanged from that shown in Figure 9–3.

9.3
```
/* Data structure to implement a multireader,
 * single writer spin lock
 */

struct rw_lock {
    lock_t rd_cnt_lock;     /* protects rd_cnt field */
    int rd_cnt;             /* current number of readers */
    lock_t wr_lock;         /* writer lock */
};

typedef struct rw_lock rwlock_t;

struct list {
    elem_t *head;           /* first element on list */
    rwlock_t lock;          /* lock to protect list */
};

typedef struct list list_t;

void init_rwlock(rwlock_t *lock)
{
    lock->rd_cnt = 0;
    initlock(&lock->rd_cnt_lock);
    initlock(&lock->wr_lock);
}

void initlist(list_t *list)
{
    list->head = NULL;
    init_rwlock(&list->lock);
}
```

```
lock_reader(rwlock_t *lock)
{
    /* Wait for any writers to finish then increment count
     * of readers to block out new writers until we're done.
     */

    lock(lock->wr_lock);
    lock(lock->rd_cnt_lock);
    lock->rd_cnt++;
    unlock(lock->rd_cnt_lock);
    unlock(lock->wr_lock);
}

unlock_reader(rwlock_t *lock)
{
    lock(lock->rd_cnt_lock);
    lock->rd_cnt--;
    unlock(lock->rd_cnt_lock);
}

lock_writer(rwlock_t *lock)
{
    /* Wait for any other writers to finish, then wait for
     * readers to finish.  Hold the writer lock to block any
     * new readers or writers until we're done.
     */

    lock(lock->wr_lock);

    while (lock->rd_cnt)
        ;
}

unlock_writer(rwlock_t *lock)
{
    unlock(lock->wr_lock);
}
```

```
int search(list_t *list, int tag)
{
    elem_t *ep;
    int result;

    result = 0;

    lock_reader(&list->lock);

    for (ep = list->head; ep; ep = ep->next)
        if (ep->tag == tag) {
            result = ep->data;
            break;
        }

    unlock_reader(&list->lock);
    return result;
}

void add(list_t *list, elem_t *ep)
{
    lock_writer(&list->lock);
    ep->next = list->head;
    list->head = ep;
    unlock_writer(&list->lock);
}

elem_t *remove(list_t *list, int tag)
{
    elem_t *ep, *prev;

    lock_writer(&list->lock);

    for (ep = list->head; ep; ep = ep->next) {
        if (ep->tag == tag) {
            if (ep == list->head)
                list->head = ep->next;
            else
                prev->next = ep->next;

            break;
        }
        prev = ep;
    }

    unlock_writer(&list->lock);
    return ep;
}
```

9.5   No, deadlocks are not possible in these functions. The routines only have one lock in common and so AB–BA deadlocks cannot occur. If both functions begin execution at the same time on different processors, func2 will merely wait for func1 to complete. Func1 can complete without lock_c and is independent of func2.

9.6   Yes, the three functions can deadlock. This will happen only if all three routines begin execution on three different processors at the same time. If this happens, then each processor will acquire one of the three locks. Since all the locks are now taken, none of them will be able to lock the second in the function. This is a variation of the AB–BA deadlock problem to include three locks. func2 and func3 cause lock_a and lock_b to be locked in the opposite order from func1. Note that as long as the three routines do not begin execution simultaneously, then a deadlock will not occur.

9.9   Nothing special need be done by the master to notify the slave. It merely needs to post the signal to the process just as would happen in a uniprocessor kernel implementation. Recall from Section 9.4.4 that each slave processor checks for pending signals for the currently executing process on each clock interrupt. Therefore, at most one clock interrupt period will elapse before the slave notices the interrupt. Even if the process the slave is running is in an infinite loop, it will still be taking clock interrupts since these are never blocked while executing in user mode. When the slave notices the signal, it will place the process on the master processor run queue so that the signal can be handled. When it runs on the master, the signal will be handled and the process will terminate.

Chapter 10

10.1   When a clock interrupt occurs on a processor that is running a process executing in user mode, the only activities that need to be performed are to check if a context switch is required (when the time quantum has expired or there is a higher priority process to run), or if a signal has been posted to the process. Either of these can be checked without the need to acquire the kernel giant lock (assuming a separate run queue lock is used so that a context switch can be completed if necessary). This is the same situation as a master–slave kernel implementation.

It is not necessary for the processor holding the kernel giant lock to block clock interrupts the whole time it is holding the lock. The uniprocessor UNIX kernel was designed to allow clock interrupts to occur while executing in the kernel, except during brief code fragments where interrupts are explicitly blocked.

The periodic "housekeeping" tasks performed by the clock interrupt handler, such as keeping track of things like the time of day, alarm system call time-outs, adjusting process priorities, etc. (all of which are usually done once per second), must be done while the kernel giant lock is held. Race conditions could otherwise result, since the interrupt handler will be modifying data structures shared with other parts of the kernel. If the clock interrupt handler determines that it is time to perform these activities, it must check whether it interrupted a kernel-mode process. If it has, then that process must be holding the kernel giant lock (otherwise it couldn't be executing in kernel mode), and it must be at a point where clock interrupts are allowed (or else they wouldn't have been enabled). Therefore, the clock interrupt handler can proceed with its tasks without the threat of race conditions. If it instead interrupts a user-mode process and finds it's time to perform the housekeeping tasks, then it can make a conditional attempt to acquire the kernel giant lock. If if succeeds, then this means that no other processor is executing in the kernel, and so the clock interrupt handler now has exclusive access. If the attempt fails, then some other processor is running in the kernel. In this case, it is easiest to defer the housekeeping tasks until a clock interrupt occurs on the processor currently holding the giant lock. This way the processor that couldn't get the lock does not need to spin when it could be doing useful user-level work.

10.3   First, since the test-and-set instruction still works atomically, spin lock operations are not affected. Since spin locks provide mutual exclusion to data structures once the lock is acquired, it is guaranteed that no other processor will try to use the locked data structure simultaneously. This means that a simultaneous read and write to the same location cannot occur for any data structure protected by a spin lock. So no changes are needed to this code. The same is true for any data structure protected by a long-term lock. Access to process private data is not affected either. Problems can arise, however, in the situation of inherent race conditions were locking was omitted. On this type of MP system, it is not possible for a process to check its signal mask, for example, without holding the spin lock that protects the mask. It must acquire the lock first to prevent another processor from writing to the mask at the same time that it is reading the value. The same is true for other cases such as reading and changing a process's user and group IDs. These operations must now be done while holding a spin lock.

10.5   One simple way to implement this is to designate one processor as the master processor for running uniprocessor device driver code, and then force the process to context-switch to that processor before calling the device driver. Such a system represents a hybrid of the multithreading and master–slave techniques.

10.6   A simple method for enforcing deadlock-free lock ordering is to use the addresses of the locks themselves to define the order. By simply making the rule that the lock with the lowest address is acquired first, deadlocks can never occur. For ef-

ficiency, the following code makes an attempt to lock the new lock conditionally
when the locks are being acquired in the reverse order before going to the expense
of releasing and reacquiring the old lock.

```
void
lock_both(lock_t *old_lock, lock_t *new_lock)
{
        if (old_lock < new_lock) {
                lock(new_lock);
                return;
        }

        if (cond_lock(new_lock) == TRUE)
                return;

        unlock(old_lock);
        lock(new_lock);
        lock(old_lock);
        return;
}
```

Chapter 11

11.1   No, each semaphore does not require its own spin lock. As pointed out in Section
       10.5.4, different data structures may be protected by the same spin lock. Correct
       operation results is either case; the only difference is the level of contention for
       the spin lock. If all semaphores in the system are protected by a single spin lock,
       then excessive contention could result in fine-grained implementations on sys-
       tems with large numbers of processors. If each semaphore is given a separate spin
       lock instead, then contention becomes unlikely.

11.2   Yes, the original UNIX kernel could have used semaphores instead of sleep/-
       wakeup, since semaphores provide all the functionality of the uniprocessor mech-
       anism. In addition, semaphores work correctly for any number of processors in
       the system, including a uniprocessor. One trade-off to using semaphores on a uni-
       processor is space. If there are many semaphores in the system, then the sema-
       phore data structures will consume more space than those used by sleep/wake-
       up, since the latter uses a single set of shared queues for sleeping processes, while
       each semaphore has its own small structure. The time overhead for doing P and
       V operations versus sleep and wakeup is about equal. However, even uniproces-

sors can thrash when a `wakeup` operation causes many processes to awaken and compete for a mutual exclusion lock. This would not happen with semaphores since only a single process is awakened at a time.

11.3   The strategy is to use two semaphores per buffer, one to signal process B when it's full, and one to signal process A when it's empty.

One-time initialization code:

```
buf_t buffer[2];
sema_t buffer_full[2];
sema_t buffer_empty[2];
...
initsema(&buffer_full[0], 0);
initsema(&buffer_full[1], 0);
initsema(&buffer_empty[0], 1);
initsema(&buffer_empty[1], 1);
```

Code for process A:

```
current = 0;

while (1) {
    P(&buffer_empty[current]);
    fill buffer[current] with data
    V(&buffer_full[current]);

    current = !current;
}
```

Code for process B:

```
current = 0;

while (1) {
    P(&buffer_full[current]);
    use data in buffer[current]
    V(&buffer_empty[current]);

    current = !current;
}
```

11.5   This is a harmless race condition. Since the new reader has already incremented the m_rdwcnt field, the exiting writer will execute enough *V* operations so that once the new reader reaches the point of doing the *P* operation, it will not block.

11.6   There are two problems with using *broadcast-V*. First, it will alter the semantics of the implementation. The implementation is designed to block new readers once a writer arrives. If a writer and several other readers arrive just before the broadcast-V operation begins (which can happen once the spin lock is released), then the readers arriving behind the writer will be awakened by the broadcast when they should have slept in order to give the writer a chance at the critical section. Second, this will cause the m_rdcnt field to reflect an inaccurate count of readers, since it was set to the number of waiting readers before the others arrived. Since the count will be lower than the actual number of readers, this will cause writers to be able to acquire the lock before all the readers have exited the lock.

Chapter 12

12.2   This would mean that a new process entering the monitor could take the only element on the linked list before the signaled process had a chance to run. The signaled process could therefore not assume that an element is present on the list when it is awakened. The code would end up being very similar to the lock_-object code that uses spin locks and sleep/wakeup. There would have to be a while loop so that the list status could be retested when the process was awakened. If it finds an element on the list, it could then remove the element. If not, then another process has already taken it, and it would have to wait again. This would not be a desirable semantic for monitors since it complicates the algorithms that use them.

12.5   The eventcount itself has no accessible information regarding the processes that may be awaiting a particular value. Therefore, in order to implement a broadcast facility, processes must record the value they are awaiting in an external variable. This variable can simply represent the highest value that any process is awaiting (and should be updated while holding a spin lock). To awaken all such processes, one simply advances the eventcount value until it is equal to this value.

12.6   The simplest approach is to use the semaphore value to count the number of elements on the list. The semaphore is then used as with resource allocation. The list_count semaphore is initialized to zero.

```
void
add(elem_t *new)
{
    lock(&list_lock);
    add new elem to list
    unlock(&list_lock);
    v(&list_count);
}

elem_t *
remove(void)
{
    p(&list_count);
    lock(&list_lock);
    remove element from list
    unlock(&list_lock);
    return element;
}
```

Note that once the *P* operation in `remove` returns, it is guaranteed that there will be at least one element on the linked list. This differs slightly from the implementation using monitors where the list had to be explicitly tested to see if it is empty or not. Also, note that the implementation with monitors relies on the fact that a signaled process runs before new processes trying to enter the monitor. This guarantees that there will be an element on the list to remove when a waiting process is awakened. The implementation with semaphores does not guarantee that an awakened process will run before a new process entering the `remove` function for the first time. However, this can only happen when `add` is called twice, ensuring that both processes will find an element to remove.

12.8
```
typedef struct {
lock_t  *lock;   /* protects this structure */
char    state;   /* current sleep lock state */
proc_t  *head;   /* head of list of blocked processes */
proc_t  *tail;   /* tail of blocked process list */
} sleep_t;

#define LOCKED 1
#define UNLOCKED 0
```

```
sleep_t *
SLEEP_ALLOC()
{
    sleep_t *slp;

    slp = malloc(sizeof(sleep_t));
    slp->lock = LOCK_ALLOC(0, 0, NULL, 0);
    slp->head = NULL;
    slp->tail = NULL;
    slp->state = UNLOCKED;
    return slp;
}

void
SLEEP_DEALLOC(sleep_t *slp)
{
    LOCK_DEALLOC(slp->lock);
    free(slp);
}

void
SLEEP_LOCK(sleep_t *slp, int pri)
{
    pl_t old_pl;

    old_pl = LOCK(slp->lock, plhi);

    if (slp->state == LOCKED) {
            enqueue(slp, curproc);
            UNLOCK(slp->lock, old_pl);
            swtch();
            return;
    }

    slp->state = LOCKED;
    UNLOCK(slp->lock, old_pl);
}
```

```
bool_t
SLEEP_TRYLOCK(sleep_t *slp)
{
    pl_t old_pl;

    old_pl = LOCK(slp->lock, plhi);

    if (slp->state == LOCKED) {
            UNLOCK(slp->lock, old_pl);
            return FALSE;
    }

    slp->state = LOCKED;
    UNLOCK(slp->lock, old_pl);
    return TRUE;
}

void
SLEEP_UNLOCK(sleep_t *slp)
{
    proc_t *pp;
    pl_t old_pl;

    old_pl = LOCK(slp->lock, plhi);

    if (slp->head != NULL) {
            pp = dequeue(slp);
            UNLOCK(slp->lock, old_pl);
            enqueue(&runqueue, pp);
            return;
    }
    slp->state = UNLOCKED;
    UNLOCK(slp->lock, old_pl);
}
```

12.10   Since synchronization variables do not maintain state, separate variables, protect-
        ed by a spin lock, are needed.

One-time initialization code:

```
buf_t buffer[2];
int buffer_state[2];
lock_t *state_lock;
sv_t *buffer_full[2];
sv_t *buffer_empty[2];

#define EMPTY 0
#define FULL 1

state_lock = LOCK_ALLOC(...);
buffer_full[0] = SV_ALLOC(...);
buffer_full[1] = SV_ALLOC(...);
buffer_empty[0] = SV_ALLOC(...);
buffer_empty[1] = SV_ALLOC(...);
buffer_state[0] = EMPTY;
buffer_state[1] = EMPTY;
```

Code for process A:

```
pl_t old_pl;
current = 0;

while (1) {
    old_pl = LOCK(state_lock);

    if (buffer_state[current] == FULL)
        SV_WAIT(&buffer_empty[current], pri, state_lock);
    else
        UNLOCK(state_lock, old_pl);

    fill buffer[current] with data
    old_pl = LOCK(state_lock);
    buffer_state[current] = FULL;
    SV_SIGNAL(&buffer_full[current]);
    UNLOCK(state_lock, old_pl);

    current = !current;
}
```

Code for process B:

```
pl_t old_pl;
current = 0;

while (1) {
    old_pl = LOCK(state_lock);

    if (buffer_state[current] == EMPTY)
        SV_WAIT(&buffer_full[current], pri, &state_lock);
    else
        UNLOCK(state_lock, old_pl);

    use data in buffer[current]
    old_pl = LOCK(state_lock);
    buffer_state[current] = EMPTY;
    SV_SIGNAL(&buffer_empty[current]);
    UNLOCK(state_lock, old_pl);

    current = !current;
}
```

Chapter 13

13.2   The effect would be dramatic. It would mean that any load issued by the processor would return stale data from memory if a store to that location is present in the store buffer. Variables updated during one iteration of a loop, for example, could not be reliably read during the next iteration. Likewise, return values stored in memory by one function could not be reliably read by the caller. This is true for both UP and MP systems.

To make loads reliable, the software would have to issue an atomic-swap instruction to a dummy location in memory before issuing a load that may have been preceded by a store. The atomic swap prevents further instructions from being issued until the store buffer drains and the swap completes, ensuring that memory is up to date for subsequent loads. Note that this must be done whenever a subroutine returns and the caller wishes to use data the subroutine stored in memory. Such an approach would bring a substantial performance penalty, and so this type of architectural change should not be done.

13.4   The software would have to include store-barrier instructions between consecutive stores to the same address. Note that additional store-barrier instructions would be needed upon entry and exit to subroutines. This would ensure that stores issued before the routine was called were sent to memory before any stores the subroutine issues to the same address. The same is true for the return case. Since many additional store-barrier instructions would be needed in most cases, overall performance would suffer as the CPU fetches, decodes, and issues store-barrier instructions when it could be executing more useful instructions instead.

13.6   The change would have no effect on UP systems, since total store ordering already behaves the same as sequential ordering in this case. For MP systems, though, it makes the system behave as if it implemented sequential ordering. Dekker's algorithm will work as discussed in Section 13.2 without modification, since the store buffer of one processor is visible to loads done by another.

While this simplifies the software to some extent, it is not worth implementing. Since so few software changes are needed to support total store ordering, the additional hardware complexity, and possible performance penalty, needed to make the store buffer monitor the bus is not worthwhile.

13.8   No, it is not a concern at all. Since process private data is never accessed by more than one CPU at a time, there are no chances for another processor to access stale data in memory while a pending store is in the store buffer of the first. Even if a process is migrated while it is accessing private data, the techniques used to synchronize the store buffer with memory during context switch assures correct operation.

Chapter 14

14.2   No, a virtual cache cannot be used as a shared cache, since there would be no way to prevent ambiguities between the processors. A virtual cache with physical tags could be used, since the physical tags would prevent ambiguities caused by each processor using the same virtual addresses to reference different data.

14.4   Since the semaphore data structure is small, the easiest approach is simply to flush the entire structure from the cache. This saves the trouble of tracking which fields were modified on any given call. Since caches are flushed on a cache line basis, it is likely that the entire structure will fit within one or two cache lines anyway. Note that the primary cache must always be written back before flushing the secondary cache to avoid losing data. It is not necessary to flush after referencing u.u_proc since this is process private data. Finally, since the spin lock must be located in uncached memory, a pointer to the lock, instead of the lock itself, is stored in the semaphore structure.

```
struct semaphore {
        lock_t      *lock;      /* protects other fields   */
        int         count;      /* current semaphore value */
        proc_t      *head;      /* ptr to 1st blocked proc */
        proc_t      *tail;      /* ptr to last blocked proc*/
};

void
initsema(sema_t *sp, int initial_cnt)
{
        sp->lock = alloc_lock();
        initlock(sp->lock);
        sp->head = NULL;
        sp->tail = NULL;
        sp->count = initial_cnt;
        flush_primary(sp, sizeof(*sp), WRITE_BACK|INVALIDATE);
        flush_secondary(sp, sizeof(*sp));
}

void
p(sema_t *sp)
{
        lock(sp->lock);
        sp->count--;

        if (sp->count < 0) {
                if (sp->head == NULL)
                        sp->head = u.u_procp;

                if (sp->tail) {
                        sp->tail->p_next = u.u_procp;
                        flush_primary(&sp->tail->p_next,
                                sizeof(sp->tail->p_next),
                                WRITE_BACK | INVALIDATE);
                        flush_secondary(&sp->tail->p_next,
                                sizeof(sp->tail->p_next));
                }

                u.u_procp->p_next = NULL;

                flush_primary(&u.u_procp->p_next,
                        sizeof(u.u_procp->p_next),
                        WRITE_BACK | INVALIDATE);
                flush_secondary(&u.u_procp->p_next,
                        sizeof(u.u_procp->p_next));

                sp->tail = u.u_procp;
```

```
                        flush_primary(sp, sizeof(*sp),
                                WRITE_BACK | INVALIDATE);
                        flush_secondary(sp, sizeof(*sp));
                        unlock(sp->lock);
                        swtch();
                        return;
                }

                flush_primary(sp, sizeof(*sp), WRITE_BACK|INVALIDATE);
                flush_secondary(sp, sizeof(*sp));
                unlock(sp->lock);
        }


        void
        v(sema_t *sp)
        {
                proc_t *p;

                lock(sp->lock);
                sp->count++;

                if (sp->count <= 0) {
                        p = sp->head;
                        sp->head = p->p_next;
                        flush_primary(&p->p_next, sizeof(p->p_next),
                                INVALIDATE);
                        flush_secondary(&p->p_next, sizeof(p->p_next));

                        if (sp->head == NULL)
                                sp->tail = NULL;

                        flush_primary(sp, sizeof(*sp),
                                WRITE_BACK|INVALIDATE);
                        flush_secondary(sp, sizeof(*sp));
                        unlock(sp->lock);
                        enqueue(&runqueue, p);
                        return;
                }

                flush_primary(sp, sizeof(*sp), WRITE_BACK|INVALIDATE);
                flush_secondary(sp, sizeof(*sp));
                unlock(sp->lock);
        }
```

14.7   The fact that the cache writes back only those words that have been modified when the line is replaced or flushed solves part of the problem of keeping the counter array consistent, since each CPU will write-back only the counters it modified. This ensures that the memory copy stays consistent. The problem remains, however, that a processor will still be caching a possibly stale value of an adjacent counter in the same cache line. So the case where a processor acquires the locks for two adjacent counters at once would still lead to it using stale data. Therefore, the same types of flushing described in Section 14.3.2 must be done.

14.9   No, it is not necessary for each processor to use the same key. The keys are only needed to prevent ambiguities between user and kernel data on one particular processor. A key used by one processor has no effect on any other caches in the system. For convenience, the kernel probably will use the same key, but this is not required to maintain cache consistency.

14.11   Flushing order matters when using a multilevel cache architecture that contains at least one write-back cache. This is true whether the kernel is maintaining consistency with selective flushing or is migrating a process. When flushing to perform a write-back operation, the cache closest to the CPU must be written back first. If multiple write-back caches are present, then the caches must be written back in order from the cache closest to the CPU to the cache closest to the bus. This prevents modified data from being lost. When invalidating the caches, the order does not matter since the data is being discarded.

14.13   There are two possible approaches. The first is simply to flush the caches each time an unlock operation is performed. Readers only need to invalidate their caches, while writers must write back and invalidate the data. A second approach is to notice that no inconsistencies can occur while processors are using the lock in read mode. This is true of all read-only data. It is only when the lock is acquired for writing that cache flushing must take place. So, when the lock is acquired for writing, then the writer could broadcast an invalidation of the data associated with the critical resource to all processors. After that, the writer can continue, knowing that all other cached copies are gone. When the writer releases the lock, the caches on that processor must be written back and invalidated as usual.

Chapter 15

15.1   The data must be written back to main memory since a snoop load hit on a modified line causes both caches to store the line in the valid state. The data itself is not immediately lost (since both caches will have a copy of the line), but the fact that the line is modified relative to main memory is lost. With the lines now in the valid state, they could be replaced at any time and neither cache will write them back to main memory (assuming they never do a store to the line). This will cause the modified data in the line to be lost. Furthermore, it would be incorrect to leave the line in the modified state in the cache where the snoop hits. This would allow that CPU to modify the data without invalidating the copy given to the other cache. Writing modified data to main memory on snoop hits solves these problems.

15.3   Since the write-once protocol is a hybrid of write-through and write-back, main memory must be updated by the atomic operation in the case where the protocol specifies write-through operation. This occurs when a line in the valid state is modified. Here the atomic operation will update main memory. In the case where the line is initially reserved, then no bus or memory operation is necessary since it is known that no other cache has a copy of the line. The atomic operation can be performed completely in the processor's private cache.

15.5   No, it does not properly maintain consistency. One problem is that stores to valid cache lines do not generate bus transactions to invalidate copies of the line in other caches. So two processors could share a copy of the cache line, and each could modify it without invalidating the other. This causes two inconsistent copies of the line to be cached. Secondly, invalidating a modified line in response to a snoop store hit is incorrect. Even though the other processor intends to modify the line, it may be modifying a different portion of the line. This would cause the modified data written by the processor now caching it to be lost.

15.7   Yes, it is still a good idea to use the code shown in Figure 15–7 even though lines don't ping-pong when using write-update protocols. If the `lock` function busy-waits by doing the test-and-set operation, then it will generate a bus transaction each time through the loop to update the other cached copies in the case where multiple CPUs are contending for the same lock. This is a waste of bus bandwidth and can be eliminated by polling the lock status until it is freed.

15.9   Semaphores implement long-term locks and process synchronization. Therefore, one would not expect many CPUs to be accessing the semaphore data structure at the same time. This in turn means that the spin lock can be in the same cache line as the rest of the semaphore data structure without worrying about ping-ponging effects. Since every operation on a semaphore will access at least the lock and count fields of the structure, it would be best if the `semaphore` data structure were aligned such that it fit within a cache line and were padded if necessary so that unrelated data is not within the same line. If the semaphore protects a critical resource, then it may be advantageous to align and pad the semaphore and its critical resource together in the same cache line (assuming the line size is great enough).

15.11   It is possible, but requires additional space in the secondary cache tags. Mimicking the approach used by the MIPS R4000, the secondary cache would have to contain the information necessary to locate the line in the primary cache. In this case, the line index for the primary cache is kept in the secondary cache tags as the R4000 does. At this point, the R4000 was able to check for a hit in the primary cache since the lines were tagged with the physical address. This was easily done since the physical address was supplied from the bus transaction that caused the snoop. However, this is of no use when checking a virtual cache with keys. Instead, the portion of the virtual address stored in the primary cache tags and the key are needed. Like the primary cache line index, these could be saved in the secondary cache tags when the primary cache line was initially allocated (and hence allocated the secondary cache line as well using the inclusion property).

Index

68040, *see* Motorola 68040
80386, 80486, *see* Intel 80386, 80486
88000, 88100, 88200, *see* Motorola 88000,
    88100, 88200

A

AB–BA deadlock,   179–180, 221, 251
address space
    definition of,   5
    mapping,   7
address space id,   84
address space layout
    dynamic address binding,   136–137
    physically indexed caches,   137–139
    virtually indexed caches,   132–136
address translation cache,   94
advance, eventcount operation,   248
aliases,   64–67
aligning data structures on cache lines,
        142–144, 297–298, 327–328
ambiguities,   62–64
Apollo DN4000,   60–62, 70, 77, 85, 94,
        342
application job mix,   187
application program interface,   151
arbitration of the bus,   153, 155
associative memory,   43
asynchronous I/O,   75
atomic memory operations
    read-modify-write,   158–160
    reads and writes,   155–158
await, eventcount operation,   248

B

banker's algorithm,   222
base-level code, definition of,   163
big-endian, definition of,   xx
binary semaphores,   219
bit range, definition of,   xxi
block in a cache,   28
break address,   13
brk system call
    definition of,   13–14
    physical caches,   114
    virtual caches,   72
    virtual caches with keys,   90
    virtual caches with physical tags,   106
broadcast-V operation,   230
bss, definition of,   5
buffered I/O,   14
bus
    arbitration,   153, 155
    bandwidth,   153–154, 156
    definition of,   115
    for multiprocessors,   152, 155–158
    granting,   155
    transactions,   116
    transfer size,   156
    watching,   115, 308
busy-waiting for a lock,   177

C

cache
    accessing the cache,   26
    aliases,   64–67
    ambiguities,   62–64

block, 28
color, 35, 138
consistency, 31, 46
consistency, MP, 290–293
copy-back, 30
definition of, 24–26
direct mapped, 33–42
external, 26, 113
flushing, 46–47, 139–142, 296–300
fully associative, 45
fundamentals, 26–33
hardware consistency for MPs,
        308–333
hashing, 29, 34–37
hit ratio, 27
hit, definition of, 27
index, 29
invalidating, 46
key, 84
line, 28
line contention, 329–330
line size, 28
locality of reference, 24
LRU replacement policy, 43
miss processing, 40
miss, definition of, 27
modified bit, 28, 32
modulo hashing algorithm, 35
multiprocessor, overview, 288–289,
        308–310
one-way set associative, 33–42
performance, 49–51
physical cache, 112–127
        see also physical caches
private, definition of, 288
process key, 84
pseudo-LRU replacement, 45
replacement policy, 30, 40
searching, 29
separate instruction and data, 26,
        48–49
set, 42

software consistency for MPs,
        293–301
spatial locality, 25
stale data, 31
subline, 28
synonyms, see alias
tagging, 27
temporal locality, 25
two-way set associative, 42–44
typical sizes, 26
uncached operation, 47
valid bit, 28
validating main memory, 46
virtual cache, 60–78
        see also virtual caches
virtual cache with keys, 84–96
        see also virtual caches with keys
virtual cache with physical tags,
        100–107
        see also virtual caches with phys-
        ical tags
write policies, 30
write-allocate, 32–33
write-back, 31
write-once, 33
write-through, 30
cache consistency protocols
        definition of, 308
        see also hardware cache consistency
cache size bounded flushing, 139
cache utilization, 132–139
cache-aligning data structures, 142–144,
        297–298, 327–328
clock interrupt handling
        master–slave kernels, 186
coarse-grained locking, 200–202
        with semaphores, 226–227
coarse-grained MP kernel, definition of,
        196
color of cache lines, 35
cond_lock function, 198
conditional locking, 198, 201–202, 253,
        255

consistency of the cache, 46
consistent with respect to memory, 31
content-addressable memory, 43
context switch
    definition of, 8–9
    effects of partial store ordering, 279
    effects of software cache consistency, 294
    physical caches, 114
    virtual caches, 67–68
    virtual caches with keys, 85–86
    virtual caches with physical tags, 104
convoys, 231–233
copy-back caching, 30
copy-on-write
    definition of, 10–11
    virtual caches, 70–71
    virtual caches with keys, 87
    virtual caches with physical tags, 104
critical resource, definition of, 162
critical section, 162
    see also mutual exclusion
cross-bar memory interconnect, 320–322

D

deadlocks, 179–181, 221–222
DEC Firefly workstation, 315–316
Dekker's Algorithm, 160, 268–270, 277, 279, 291, 325
delayed cache invalidation, 139–142
Dijkstra semaphore, *see* semaphores
direct mapped cache, 33–42
direct memory access, *see* DMA
directory based cache consistency, 322–324
DMA
    definition of, 15
    effects of partial store ordering, 280
    physical caches, 115
    virtual caches, 73–77
Dragon protocol, 317
dynamic address binding, 136–137

E

efficient cache management, 132–145
ELXSI SYSTEM 6400, 294
enter, monitor operation, 246
enter_reader function, 235
enter_writer function, 237
event for sleep/wakeup functions, 164
eventcounts, 248–250, 259
exec system call
    definition of, 12–13
    physical caches, 114
    virtual caches, 71
    virtual caches with keys, 89
    virtual caches with physical tags, 105
exit system call
    definition of, 13
    implementation with semaphores, 229–230
    physical caches, 114
    virtual caches, 71
    virtual caches with keys, 90
    virtual caches with physical tags, 105
exit, monitor operation, 246
exit_reader function, 236
exit_writer function, 238
external cache, 26, 113
external programming model, 151

F

fine-grained locking, 203–209, 227–230
fine-grained MP kernel, definition of, 196
Firefly protocol, 315–316
first-level cache, definition of, 122
flushing bounded by cache size, 139
flushing of the cache, 46–47, 139–142, 296–300
fork system call
    definition of, 9–12
    physical caches, 114
    virtual caches, 68–71
    virtual caches with keys, 87–89

virtual caches with physical tags,
        104–105
four-way set associative cache,   44
fully associative caches,   45

G

giant locking,   196–198, 226–227
granting of the bus,   155
granularity of locks,   207–208
        definition of,   196

H

hardware cache consistency
        consistency of read-modify-write op-
                erations,   317–318
        directory based schemes,   322–324
        Dragon protocol,   317
        effects on software,   324–326
        Firefly protocol,   315–316
        MESI protocols,   314–315
        MIPS R4000 update protocol,
                316–317
        multilevel caches,   318–319
        non-sequential memory models,   327
        overview,   308–310
        separate instruction and data caches,
                309
        software performance consider-
                ations,   327–332
        write-once protocol,   311–314
        write-through invalidate protocol,
                310–311
hashing in a cache,   29, 34–37
hit ratio, definition of,   27

I

I/O
        effects of partial store ordering,   280
        on multiprocessors,   153
        physical caches,   115–121
        virtual caches,   73–77

virtual caches with keys,   94
virtual caches with physical tags,   107
i860, *see* Intel i860
IBM 370,   27, 158
IBM PC,   27, 112
inclusion property, definition of,   318
inconsistent with respect to memory,   31
index into a cache,   29
inherent race condition,   200
init_rdwrlock function,   235
initialized data segment, definition of,   5
initlock function,   177
initsema function,   223
Intel 80386,   26, 95, 112, 113, 155, 342
Intel 80486,   26, 32, 33, 44, 95, 112, 113,
        120, 155, 289, 342
Intel 82495DX,   30, 33, 343
Intel i860 XP,   44, 67, 70, 78, 103,
        120–121, 289, 309, 344
Intel i860 XR,   32, 42, 61, 70, 78,
        122–124, 343
Intel Pentium,   26, 32, 33, 34, 42, 95, 112,
        ·113, 120, 155, 289, 314–315, 343
interrupt handlers
        deadlocks with base level code,   181
        definition of,   4
        fine-grained kernels,   206
        giant locked kernels,   197
        mutual exclusion, uniprocessor,
                163–164, 167
        use of semaphores,   221
invalidating the cache,   46

K

kernel
        address space,   5
        level, definition of,   2
        nonpreemptability rule,   163, 167
        overview,   2–3
        preemption,   209
key sharing,   86
key, use in a cache,   84

L

least recently used replacement, 43
line of a cache, 28
line size, 28
little-endian, definition of, xx
load-linked/store-conditional, 160
locality of reference
    definition of, 24
    improving, 142–144
    spatial locality, 25
    temporal locality, 25
lock contention, 230–231
LOCK function, 252
lock function, 178, 269–270, 275–276
lock ordering, 179–180, 201–202, 221,
    251
LOCK_ALLOC function, 251
LOCK_DEALLOC function, 252
lock_object function
    for uniprocessors, 165–167
    using semaphores, 227–228
    using spin locks, 204–205
locking
    definition of, 165
    giant locking, 196–198
    granularity, 196, 207–208
    with partial store ordering, 278–279
    with total store ordering, 275–277
locking, see also eventcounts, monitors,
    semaphores, sleep locks, spin
    locks
long-term mutual exclusion
    semaphored kernels, 227–228
    spin locked kernels, 204–206
    uniprocessor, 164–167, 168
look-aside cache, 123
look-through cache, 123

M

mapped files
    definition of, 15
    see also shared memory

master–slave kernels
    clock interrupt handling, 186
    effects of software cache consistency,
        295, 299
    overview, 176–177
    performance considerations,
        187–189
    process selection for master, 186
    process selection for slaves, 184–186
    run queue implementation, 181–183
    running system calls on slaves,
        188–189
memory hierarchies, 24–26, 121–126,
    280–281
memory models
    definition of, 154
    hardware cache consistency, 327
    overview, 271–273
    partial store ordering, 278–280
    total store ordering, 273–277
MESI protocols, 314–315
micro-kernel, definition of, 3
MicroSPARC, see TI MicroSPARC
MIPS R2000, 26, 30, 33, 34, 45, 50, 95,
    113, 155, 344
MIPS R3000, 30, 33, 34, 45, 50, 95, 113,
    155, 344
MIPS R4000, 26, 32, 33, 34, 45, 95, 103,
    113, 120, 124–126, 155, 160, 271,
    289, 309, 314–315, 316–317,
    318, 318–319, 330–332, 345
MIPS R4000 update protocol, 316–317
miss processing, 40
modified bit, 32
    definition of, 28
modulo hashing algorithm, 35, 93, 106,
    138
monitors, 246–247, 260
Motorola 68040, 32, 33, 44, 45, 47, 95,
    120, 155, 158, 310–311, 317, 332,
    345
Motorola 88000, 95, 120, 155, 346
Motorola 88100, 159

Motorola 88200, 32, 33, 44, 45, 47,
        311–314
multilevel caches, 121–126
    hardware cache consistency,
        318–319
multiprocessors
    cache consistency, 290–293
    caching, overview, 288–289
    cases requiring no locks, 199–200
    coarse-grained locking, 200–202
    cross-bar interconnect, 320–322
    directory based cache consistency,
        322–324
    eventcounts, 248–250, 259
    external programming model, 151
    fine-grained locking, 203–209
    giant locking, 196–198
    hardware basics, 152–154
    hardware cache consistency,
        308–333
    I/O, 153
    lock granularity, 207–208
    long-term mutual exclusion, 204–206
    master–slave kernels, 176–190
    memory model overview, 154, 268
    monitors, 246–247, 260
    multireader locks, 234–236, 258
    non-bus memory architectures,
        319–324
    overview, 150
    partial store ordering, 278–280
    performance, 151, 187, 208–209
    problems with uniprocessor policies,
        167–168
    semaphored kernels, 218–239
    sequencers, 248–250
    sequential memory model overview,
        155
    sleep locks, 253–255
    sleep/wakeup effects, 209–211
    software cache consistency, 293–301
    spin locked kernels, 196–211
    SVR4.2 MP primitives, 251–261

    synchronization variables, 255–258,
        259–260
    system integrity, 151
    total store ordering, 273–277
multireader locks, 234–236
multireader locks, SVR4.2 MP interfaces,
        258
multithreaded kernel
    cases requiring no locks, 199–200
    definition of, 196
    effects of software cache consistency,
        296, 299–300
    performance, 208–209
mutual exclusion
    long-term, uniprocessor, 164–167,
        168
    overview, 160–162
    short-term, uniprocessor, 163
    uniprocessor approach, 162–168
    using eventcounts and sequencers,
        248–249
    using monitors, 246–247, 260
    using semaphores, 219
    using sleep locks, 253–255
    using spin locks, 177–179
    with interrupts, uniprocessor,
        163–164, 167
    with partial store ordering, 278–279
    with total store ordering, 275–277

N

nested locks, 180, 251
nonpreemptability rule, 163, 167, 209

O

one-way set associative cache, 33–42

P

P function, 224
P semaphore operation
    definition of, 218

see also semaphores
partial store ordering, 278–280, 300–301
Pentium, *see* Intel Pentium
physical address space
    definition of, 7–8
physical caches
    brk and sbrk, 114
    bus-watching, 115
    context switch, 114
    exec, 114
    exit, 114
    fork, 114
    I/O, 115–121
    overview, 112–114
    shared memory, 115
    user-kernel ambiguities, 115
position-independent code, 137
primary cache, definition of, 122
private cache, 288
process
    address space, 5
    definition of, 3
    scheduling, 4
    state, 3, 8
process key, 84
process migration, definition of, 294
process private data, 189, 199–200
    kernel stack, 199, 295
    u-area, 295
    user area, 199
process table entry
    definition of, 181
    locking, 199
processor affinity, definition of, 295
processor private data, 294
program
    definition of, 3
program order, definition of, 155, 268
program text, 5
pseudo-LRU replacement, 45

R

R2000, R3000, R4000, *see* MIPS R2000,
    R3000, R4000
race conditions, 158, 162
    see also mutual exclusion
raw I/O, 15
    see also DMA
read system call, definition of, 14
read, eventcount operation, 248
recursive locking, 181, 221
replacement policy
    definition of, 30
    least recently used, 43
    pseudo-LRU, 45
resource allocation with semaphores, 220,
    222
RW_ALLOC function, 258
RW_DEALLOC function, 258
RW_RDLOCK function, 258
RW_UNLOCK function, 258
RW_WRLOCK function, 258

S

sbrk system call, *see* brk
searching a cache, 29
secondary cache, definition of, 122
second-level cache, definition of, 122
selective cache flushing, 296–300
self-modifying code, 48, 124, 277
semaphored kernels
    coarse-grained locking, 226–227
    convoys, 231–233
    long-term mutual exclusion, 227–228
    overview, 218–219
    performance considerations,
        230–233
    short-term mutual exclusion, 228
    synchronization, 228–230
semaphores
    binary, 219
    comparison with other primitives,
        258–261

deadlocks, 221–222
definition of, 218
implementation, 223–226
in interrupt handlers, 221
mutual exclusion, 219
resource allocation, 220, 222
separate instruction and data caches, 26, 48–49
sequencers, 248–250
sequential memory model
atomic read-modify-write, 158–160
atomic reads and writes, 155–158
ordering between CPUs, 160–162, 268
overview, 155
set, definition of, 42
shared memory
definition of, 14
effects of total store ordering, 277
physical caches, 115
virtual caches, 72–73
virtual caches with keys, 90–94
virtual caches with physical tags, 106
shared memory multiprocessor, definition of, 153
short-term mutual exclusion
in semaphored kernels, 228
spin locked kernels, 203–204
uniprocessor, 163, 167
using spin locks, 177–179
signal, monitor operation, 246
slave processor, *see* master–slave kernels
sleep function, 164–167, 209–211
compared to semaphores, 218
sleep locks, SVR4.2 MP interfaces, 253–255
SLEEP_ALLOC function, 253
SLEEP_DEALLOC function, 253
SLEEP_LOCK function, 253
SLEEP_LOCK_SIG function, 254
SLEEP_TRYLOCK function, 255
SLEEP_UNLOCK function, 255
snooping, 116–121

snooping protocols
definition of, 308
see also cache consistency protocols
software cache consistency
handling other memory models, 300–301
overview, 293–294
selective cache flushing, 296–300
uncached shared data, 294–296
SPARC
partial store ordering, 278–280, 300–301
store buffer, 273
store-barrier, 278
swap-atomic, 159
total store ordering, 273–277, 300–301
SPARC, *see also* TI MicroSPARC and TI SuperSPARC
spatial locality, definition of, 25
spin locked kernels
coarse-grained locking, 200–202
fine-grained locking, 203–209
giant locking, 196–198
lock granularity, 207–208
long-term mutual exclusion, 204–206
mutual exclusion with interrupt handlers, 206
overview, 196
spin locks
cache line contention, 329–330
conditional, 198, 201–202
contention, 179
context switch deadlocks, 180
deadlocks, 179–181
definition of, 177
implementation, 177–179
recursive locking, 181
SVR4.2 interfaces, 251–253
spl function, 163, 167, 197
stale data, 31
stbar SPARC instruction, 278
store buffer, definition of, 273